DARK AND MIDDLE AGES READER

Putnam's

DARK AND MIDDLE AGES READER

Selections from the 5th to 15th Centuries

Edited by
HARRY E. WEDECK

Capricorn Books   New York

Acknowledgments

Grateful acknowledgment is made to the following sources for permission to reprint excerpts from the works cited:

Columbia University Press: V. G. Berry, Odo of Deuil's *De Profectione Ludovici VII in Orientem*; J. J. Parry, Andreas Capellanus' *The Art of Courtly Love*;

Victor Gollancz Ltd., London: *Adelard of Bath,* edited by H. Gollancz;

Routledge and Kegan Paul, Ltd., London: F. A. Wright, Liudprand's *Antapadosis*;

The Clarendon Press, Oxford: *Paston Letters,* edited by N. Davis (nos. 4, 5, 6);

The Royal Society of Literature, London: Adam of Usk's *Chronicon*;

Union of American Hebrew Congregations: J. R. Marcus, *The Jew in the Medieval World*;

University of California Press, Berkeley, Calif.: L. J. Paetow, John of Garland's *Morale Scholarium*.

Introduction

¶ THE DARK AND MIDDLE AGES present a rich, expansive, only partially explored field. But it is profitable to take samplings, significant and appealing in themselves, that would be representative of the multiple phases of medieval life. This anthology is intended to offer such samplings, presenting, in variety, interests, and trends, a conspectus of that culture.

Consciously or not, the present has been deeply affected by this medieval past. Sometimes the impact has been full and direct, as in the case of philological, linguistic, and literary assimilative and adaptive processes. But often the impingement has been less tangible, and the medieval view has seeped and flowed into theological speculations, metaphysical investigations, and cosmic, economic and political theories that have been rejected or only partly accepted, but which have stimulated theories and views still part of our culture. These partly accepted concepts have, in a sense, like impalpable gadflies or unpersonified Socratic goads, driven men of later ages to concepts and theories of major significance in our own time.

This expanse of some thousand years, from the fifth to the end of the fifteenth century, that we have called the Dark and Middle Ages, was not a homogeneous age: it was kinetic and adaptive, inquisitive and experimental. It was not a hieratically static era, accepting and retaining ideas without uncertainty or hesitation. Just as in the fields of travel and commerce and territorial expansion it spread and quested, particularly during the amazing ninth century of the Radanites, the merchant princes, so it was equally astir in less material but no less significant regions.

Both in scientific reasoning and in folklore, in the more furtive secret cults of sorcery and thaumaturgy, in the areas of alchemy and astrology, and the embedded beliefs in vampires, werewolves and inexplicable human transformations, the medieval mind flourished and produced, challenged and negated, and went off into cryptic tangents. The contributions to theory and exempla, the masses of matter in prose, verse, lyrics and drama, the philosophical dialogues and bawdy comedy, the devout and mystic meditations and earthy precepts, all provide a corpus so polyform, so dichotomous, so packed with historical truths and impossible hypotheses, such fantastic biology and unearthly science, that merely to dip into those centuries is a challenging and wholesome experience.

The Dark and Middle Ages dissected political theory and sketched educational policies, set up criteria for historical exposition and traveled the Seven Seas; and yet dealt with the workaday but intriguing immediacies of the time. With the vagantes, those rowdy, liberated scholars who, like Villon, combined ethical concepts with unethical practice, or, like Abelard, lived with the mystics and the world itself, the medieval spirit sang its way across academic Europe. Men corresponded on literature and God, on women and dress, on evil and the ideal state, on mythology and the minutiae of prosody, from Ireland to Italy, from England to Germany; for there was one intellectual cosmos, and it had no visible or spiritual frontiers.

The medieval world wove legends and told bizarre tales, created drama and produced literary criticism of remarkable permanence. It was vastly industrious, compiling encyclopedias that were wide in scope and learned in content. It overthrew dynasties and established new ones amid frenzy and bloodshed, and hailed the peaceful life and bucolic ways. It revolted and butchered, and upset hard and fast ideologies. It eulogized the courtly ways of chivalry, which were virtually elegant immoralities. It was hilarious and, on occasion, depressed; a world, as it were, gone manic. It swilled beer in boisterous inns, and meditated on the Ultimate Being in cloisters and nunneries. It relished things physical, but it was also assailed by the dread of Doomsday, the ominous Day of Wrath. And these conflicts and paradoxes at times appeared within the character of specific individuals, so that the cleric-poet Maximianus could produce the most shameless elegiacs, and Fortunatus, dedicated to the spiritual life, took an inordinate delight in the pleasures of the table.

Serfs and peasants contrasted with lavish prelates and princelings. Charity often began at home and remained there, although for the wandering pilgrim, the unsettled adventurer, the peripatetic cosmologist, there was formal hospitality in abbey or church or battlemented castle.

Predicating progress in terms of divine guidance, this era nevertheless foresaw human doom as motivated by human divergence, by man's very ambivalence and the conflict within himself. It groveled in sin, yet displayed a Promethean resilience, an unexpressed hope in humanity and final consummated perfection. In short, the Dark and Middle Ages were an amalgam—a not too closely knit synthesis of ignorance and prevision, of hardened adherence to accepted ways and speculative boldness, melancholic immersion and exalted mysticism—weaving together a sequence that, by its very variability, gave color to life and made that very color the basis of life.

Although the Dark and Middle Ages were permeated and directed by the religious spirit—as the multiple exempla, the "applications" in legend, the biographies of the saints, holy pilgrimages, crusading expeditions, and the architectonics of the medieval economy amply demonstrate—there were, at the same time and with increasing force, other activities that helped to shape the medieval world; commercial enterprise and travel, educational and experimental diversions, lusty tavern encounters and brigandage, satire on corruption in the ecclesiastical hierarchy, and the sullen, pervasive prevalence of sorcery and witchcraft. This anthology presents a cross section of these divergent aspects of medieval life, characteristics that virtually implied the emergence of a new world from a shell of formalism and dogmatic acceptance—a world of restless contemplation and action.

This book is not intended in any sense as an exclusively social, religious, historical or political survey of the medieval centuries. It is not directed to the scholar interested in one or more of these cultural phases. By means of a multiplicity of selections from varied sources, suggestive pieces not intended as examinations in depth, this book is designed primarily for the student and the literate reader as a panoramic conspectus of the variety and richness and complexity of the medieval world.

Contents

Part One

HISTORICAL EPISODES, PERSONALITIES, GEOGRAPHICAL DESCRIPTIONS

PAULUS OROSIUS

Asia in the Fifth Century   3
The Scythians   6
The Amazons   6

EUGIPPIUS

Famine Strikes!   8

GREGORY OF TOURS

Attila the Hun Invades Gaul   9

JORDANES

Death of Attila   10

ENNODIUS

Panegyric on King Theodoric   11

GREGORY OF TOURS

Chilperic the Tyrant   12
Escape from Captivity   13
Why History Is Written   17
Historical Survey   17
The Burning of Paris   18
Clovis, the Frankish King, Defeats the Alamanii and Becomes
    a Christian   20

FREDEGARIUS

The Saracens   22

GILDAS

Britain Invaded by Saxons   23

BEDE
    Caius Julius Caesar, the First Roman That Came to Britain   24

PAULUS DIACONUS
    The Lombards Settle in Italy   26

NENNIUS
    History of Britain   27

Annales Xantenses
    News Chronicle   38

EINHARD
    Charlemagne: His Habits and Studies   40

NOTKER
    Pirate Encounter   42

ASSER
    Portrait of a King   43

LIUDPRAND
    Palace Scene at Constantinople   44
    King Berengarius I Assassinated!   45
    Audience with Nicephorus Phocas, Emperor of
        Constantinople   47
    Liudprand Leaves Constantinople   51

RICHER
    Storming of Verdun   52

WIDUKIND OF CORVEY
    A Courageous Saxon   53

ADAM OF BREMEN
    Discovery of America   55

OSBERN OF CANTERBURY
    The Danes Sack Canterbury   56

OTTO OF FREISING
    Historical Cycles and Analogies   57

RAYMUND OF AGILES
    The Holy Spear Discovered in the First Crusade   59

ODO OF DEUIL
    Louis VII's March Eastward   64

FOUCHER
    Eyewitness Account of Crusaders at Jerusalem   65

GEOFFREY OF MONMOUTH
    The Origin of Wassail   70

SAXO GRAMMATICUS
    William Tell: Danish Style   71

Itinerarium Regis Ricardi
    Richard the Lion-Hearted   72

ORDERICUS VITALIS
    Wreck of the White Ship   73
    Ban on Women Causes Church Clamor!   74

WILLIAM OF TYRE
    Exhortation of Pope Urban II to the First Crusade   76

MATTHEW PARIS
    Disturbance at Oxford   77

GIRALDUS CAMBRENSIS
    Character of King Henry II, of England   79
    England Helps Ireland   82

ADAM OF USK
    Lamentation of King Richard II   84

THOMAS WALSINGHAM
    The Plague   84

GEOFFREY LE BAKER OF SWYNEBROOKE
    Prelude to Crécy   85

OLD BALLAD
    Bosworth Field   86

FROISSART
    Civil Conflict in Flanders   87
    Civil Revolt in Ghent   91
    Civil Revolt in England   94

Part Two

FANTASY, LEGEND AND FOLKLORE; MAGIC AND MIRACLES; POPULAR TALES

GREGORY OF TOURS
    The Boy and the Grapes   101

Historia Apollonii Regis Tyri
    A Shipwreck and a Rescue   102

PAULUS DIACONUS
    Legend of the Seven Sleepers   103

EKKEHARD IV
    Notker Meets the Devil   103

IOHANNES MONACHUS
    The Boy in the Burning Chimney   105

PETRUS ALPHONSUS
    True Friendship   107
    An Old Cure for Sleeplessness   108
    The Biter Bit   109

WILLIAM OF NEWBURGH
    A Scottish Vampire   111

ODO DE CERINTON
    How to Bell the Cat   112

WALTER MAP
    The Droll Tale of Sceva and Ollo, Merchants   112

JACQUES DE VITRY
    The Devil Marries a Quarrelsome Woman   117

CAESAR OF HEISTERBACH
    Diabolic Help   118

IOHANNES OF ALTA SILVA
    A Sinister Banquet   119

Gesta Romanorum
    The Speaking Statue   123
    Honor Among Thieves   125
    The Necromancer and the Knight   127
    The Hermit and the Devil   129
    The Three Talismans   132

Historia Septem Sapientum
    The Witch and the Spring   135

GIRALDUS CAMBRENSIS
    Welsh Soothsayers   137

Fabliaux
    The Norman Bachelor   138

ADOLPHUS
    The Blind Man and His Wife   140

Part Three

ALCHEMY, ASTROLOGY, COSMOLOGY, TECHNOLOGY AND SCIENCE

ISIDORE OF SEVILLE
    Etymological and Astrological Diversions   147
    The Origin of Glass   148
    Atoms   149
    Medicine   150

Anglo-Saxon Manual of Astronomy
    Astronomy in the Tenth Century   151

PHILIPPE DE THAUN
    Astronomical Lore   153

ADELARD OF BATH
    The Eye   156
    Science Problem   156

VINCENT OF BEAUVAIS
    The Branches of Knowledge   157

ROGER BACON
    Remarkable Inventions   158

ALEXANDER NEQUAM
    The Arts and the Planets   159

JACQUES DE VITRY
    Astrological Tale   160

ALBERTUS MAGNUS
    Astrological Lore   161
    Protection for Animals   162
    Scientific Difficulties   162
    The Properties of Things   162
    Science Notes   163
    Experiment   163

MICHAEL SCOT
    Auguries   164

JOHN BURIDAN
    Has the Earth Motion?   164

Part Four

THE SOCIAL SCENE: TRAVEL AND TRADE; SOCIAL MORES AND CHIVALRY

IBN KHORDADBEH
    The Routes of the Jewish Merchants Called Radanites   169

RICHER
    Journey of a Scholar from Rheims to Chartres   170

ABU MUHAMMAD ALI IBN HAZM
    Contentment in Love   172

ANDREAS CAPELLANUS
    What Love Signifies   179
    In What Manner Love May Be Acquired   179
    The Twelve Rules of Love   180

ÉTIENNE DE BOURBON
    Women's Ways   180

The Jew in the Medieval World
    Oath Taken by Jews, Frankfort on the Main: 14th Century   182
    Sumptuary Law   183

GIOVANNI BOCCACCIO
    Triangle Drama: Medieval Style   184

Paston Letters
    Country Life in England   194

Part Five

PHILOSOPHY, RELIGION AND THE RELIGIOUS LIFE

SULPICIUS SEVERUS
    Miraculous Power of St. Martin   201

FORTUNATUS
    A Royal Nun   202

CASSIODORUS
    Advice to Monks   203
    Monks as Doctors   204

BENEDICT OF NURSIA
    Duties of a Cellarer   205

ST. BENEDICT
    Monastic Labors   206

BOETHIUS
    The Conflict of Good and Evil   207

GREGORY THE GREAT
    Portrait of a Saint   209

IOHANNES SCOTUS ERIGENA
A Logical Explanation of the Universe   210

CHARLEMAGNE
Charlemagne as Educator   212

HRABANUS MAURUS
Heathen and Christian   213

NOTKER BALBULUS
St. Laurence's Martyrdom   214

REGINO OF PRÜM
Sketch of a Royal Monk   217

ST. ANSELM
The Existence of God   220

SUGER
Abbot Suger of Saint-Denis   221
Ecclesiastical Administration   222

THOMAS BECKET
Becket on Church and State   227

JOHN OF SALISBURY
King and State   228

BERNARD OF CLAIRVAUX
Gluttony in the Church   229

SALIMBENE
Fathers and Sons on Careers   231

JOCELYN OF BRAKELOND
Life in a Monastery   234

ODO OF ROUEN
Monastic Supervision   240

DANTE ALIGHIERI
The Universal Empire   242

ROGER BACON
The Degeneracy of the Age   249

IACOBUS DE VORAGINE
    Human Frailties   250

ALEXANDER OF HALES
    The Receptive Power Is of Divine Origin   253

JOHN OF GARLAND
    Morality and the Arts   254

ROGER BACON
    Obstacles to Truth   255

POPE BONIFACE VIII
    Papal Bull   256

WILLIAM OF OCCAM
    The Universals   257

Part Six

LITERARY, ACADEMIC AND EPISTOLARY WRITINGS

GREGORY THE GREAT
    Epistolary Advice   261

ALCUIN
    Scholastic Dialogue   261
    Alcuin as Teacher   266

ANONYMOUS
    Strasburg Oath   268

LUPUS OF FERRIÈRES
    Hazards of the Road   268
    Classical Texts   269

Hrotsvithae Opera
    A Nun Writes Comedies   270

GERBERT
    Plea to Emperor Otto II   272
    To a Friend   273

ABELARD
    Abelard to Héloïse   273

HÉLOÏSE
  Héloïse to Abelard   281
GUIBERT
  A Martinet Schoolmaster   282
JOHN OF SALISBURY
  The Value of Literature   283
Carmina Burana
  Scriptural Parody   284
ROGER BACON
  Educational Travesty   285
  On Translation   287
JOHN OF GARLAND
  Student Conduct   288
THOMAS SAMPSON
  Student's Letter to Father   288
FRANCESCO PETRARCA
  Letter to Posterity   289
RICHARD DE BURY
  That the Treasure of Wisdom Is Chiefly Contained in Books   298
ADAM OF USK
  Student Rivalries   301
Chartularium Universitatis Parisensis
  University Administration   301
Trierer Marienklage
  Judas Scene   304
SIR THOMAS CRAIG
  Feudal Law   304

Part Seven
POETRY

VENANTIUS HONORIUS CLEMENTIANUS FORTUNATUS
  A Sixth-Century Epicure   309

AVITUS

    Satan's Jealousy   310
    Paradise   311

FORTUNATUS

    Processional   312

BOETHIUS

    Lament on Life   313

HISPERICA FAMINA

    Love Rejected   314

Cantilena of St. Eulalie

    St. Eulalie   315

ANONYMOUS

    Lament for Charlemagne   316
    The Seafarer   318
    Watch-Song   320
    Song of the Pilgrims   321
    Invitation to Love   322

ST. ALEXIS

    The Good Old Days   323
    St. Alexis' Heavenly Love   324

ROBERT II, KING OF FRANCE

    Come, Thou Holy Spirit   324

PETRUS PICTOR

    Woman Is Evil   325

ANONYMOUS

    The Battle of Life   325

ABELARD

    Advice to a Son   326

BERNARD OF CLUNY

    Contempt of the World   327

ANONYMOUS

    Lament of Richard the Lion-Hearted   328
    A Song of Winter   329
    A Reluctant Farewell   331
    Rondel   331

GONZALO DE BERCEO

    Life of St. Millán   332

Carmina Burana

    A Wandering Student's Petition   332
    Drinking Joys   333
    Gretchen   334
    Cast Aside Study!   335
    Love's Plight   337
    Earthly Vanity   338
    Love's Lament   339
    Bacchic Frenzy   340
    Spring   341
    A Pastoral   342

ANONYMOUS

    A Sequence in Praise of Wine   343

WOLFRAM VON ESCHENBACH

    Parzival Meets a Heathen   344

ST. THOMAS AQUINAS

    Hymn   347

WALTHER VON DER VOGELWEIDE

    Song   348

Nibelungen Lied

    Knights on the March   349

CECCO ANGIOLIERI

    Sonnet of All He Would Do   351

GUIDO CAVALCANTI

    Ballata Concerning a Shepherd-Maid   352

NOTES ON THE VARIOUS AUTHORS   355

Part One

HISTORICAL EPISODES,
PERSONALITIES,
GEOGRAPHICAL DESCRIPTIONS

The selections in Part One are intended to illustrate the development of a progressive historical and critical faculty. Orosius, for instance, is naïve in manner and often legendary in content, while Odo of Deuil displays a ripe, mature awareness, a sense of social consciousness. In place of vast generalizations about migrations and racial origins, descriptions become localized, marked by circumstantial detail. Rhetoric plays a part in the presentation of matter; but just as frequently the writer is full of his subject, and gains his effects by the sheer significance of the content, rather than by contrived stylistic aids. Political machinations, royal intrigues, eyewitness accounts of siege and battle appear. Contrasts are noted between bodies of men, between ethnic outlooks. The individual grows in stature and notable personalities are sketched.

It should be noted that these readings are illustrative, not exhaustive. Many phases of the medieval scene are not touched upon in the selections chosen. In general, the emphasis is on the cultural history of the period. To clarify the context, in the case of particular passages, brief notes and comments are appended.

Asia in the Fifth Century

¶ OUR FOREFATHERS considered the entire world, bounded by the limit of the Ocean, as tripartite. They called its three parts Asia, Europe, and Africa: although some thought there were only two parts, that is, Asia and then Africa as included in Europe.

Asia is bounded on three sides by the Ocean, and extends over the entire region of the East. Toward the west, on its right, under the northern sky it touches the frontiers of Europe; on the left it breaks away from Africa; below Egypt and Syria it has the Mare Nostrum, which we generally call the Big Sea.

Europe begins, as I said, in the northern region, from the River Tanais[1] where the Riphaean Mountains,[2] opposite the Sarmatian waters,[3] pour forth the River Tanais: this, flowing past the altars and the *termini* of Alexander the Great, situated in the territory of the Roxolani, swells the Maeotic Marshes; the vast outflow of these marshes toward the city of Theodosia enters the Euxine Sea in a wide stream. Then long straits flow toward Constantinople, until the sea that we call Mare Nostrum receives them. The boundary of Europe in Spain is the western ocean,[4] especially where the Pillars of Hercules[5] appear near the Gades Islands, and the ocean tide enters the channels of the Tuscan Sea.[6]

Africa starts at the boundaries of Egypt and the city of Alexandria. Thence, extending across through the Ethiopian desert, it meets the southern ocean. The boundaries of Africa on the west are the same as those of Europe, that is, the inlet of the strait of Gades. Its farthest limit is Mount Atlas and the so-called Islands of the Blessed.[7] And since I have briefly given the general divisions of the tripartite world, I shall concern myself to mention the regions of those parts too, as I promised.

Asia has, toward the middle of the east, in the eastern ocean, the mouths of the River Ganges. On the left it has Cape Caligardamna,

1. The Don. 2. Caucasus. 3. Sea of Azov. 4. The Atlantic. 5. Strait of Gibraltar. 6. Tyrrhenian Sea.
7. Also known as the Fortunate Islands; reputedly identified with the Canary Islands or the Madeira Islands.

below which lies the island of Taprobane,[8] facing east; from this point the ocean begins to be called the Indian Ocean. On the right it has the Imaian Mountains, where the Caucasus ends, at Cape Samara. Below, to the north, lie the mouths of the River Octorogorra; hence the ocean is called the China Sea.

In these regions is India, which has on the west the River Indus that is received by the Red Sea; on the north the Caucasus Mountains; the rest is bounded by the Eastern and the Indian Oceans. India has forty-four nations, apart from the island of Taprobane which has ten cities, and apart from the very numerous remaining habitable islands. From the River Indus, which is in the east, to the River Tigris, which is in the west, the regions are these: Aracosia, Parthia, Assyria, Persia and Media; the land being mountainous and rough. They have on the north the Caucasus Mountains; on the south the Red Sea; in the center the notable rivers Hydaspes and Arbis. In these regions there are thirty-two nations. But the general name is Parthia.

From the River Tigris to the River Euphrates extends Mesopotamia, starting from the north between the Taurus Mountains and the Caucasus. Beyond are Babylonia, then Chaldea, lastly Arabia Felix, which extends between the Persian Gulf and the Arabian Gulf by a narrow strip of land facing the east. In these countries there are twenty-eight nations. From the River Euphrates, which is toward the east, to Mare Nostrum, then to the north, that is from the city of Dacusa, situated in the territory of Cappadocia and Armenia, to Egypt and the farthest point of the Arabian Gulf to the south, Syria extends, generally so called, and it has very large provinces: Commagena, Phoenicia, and Palestine, except the Saracens and the Nabataeans. At the summit of Syria is Cappadocia that has on the east Armenia, on the west Asia, on the north the Themiscyrian Plains, on the south the Taurus Mountains, below which lie Cilicia and Isauria. The region of Asia is everywhere surrounded by sea, except the eastern part; on the north by the Euxine Sea, on the west by the Propontis and the Hellespont, on the south by Mare Nostrum, where Mount Olympus is.

Lower Egypt has Palestine on the east, Libya on the west, Mare Nostrum on the north, on the south a mountain called Climax, and the River Nile that seems to rise from the shore where the Red Sea begins, in a place that is called Cinnamon Market. Then it flows for

8. Ceylon.

4

a long spell eastward, making an island called Meroë in the middle of the river. Lastly it turns north, swollen by seasonal floods, and waters the plains of Egypt. Some authorities declare that this river has a source not far from Atlas, and straightway loses itself in the sands; then, after a brief interval, it overflows in a vast lake and flows hence as far as the Ocean, toward the east through the Ethiopian desert, and flowing back to the left it descends into Egypt. The barbarians call it Dara near the source, the other inhabitants call it Nuchal.

Upper Egypt extends in length toward the east. On its north is the Arabian Gulf, on its south the Ocean. For it begins on the west in Lower Egypt, and is bounded on the east by the Red Sea, where there are twenty-four nations.

And since we have described the southern part of Asia, it remains to explain the other part, from the east to the north. The Caucasus Mountains come first, of which one ridge is visible as far as the uttermost east; and many incline to believe that this is a ridge of the Taurus Mountains because actually Parchoatras, a mountain of Armenia halfway between the Taurus and the Caucasus, is thought to join the Taurus with the Caucasus. But this is not so: the River Euphrates separates them, which, flowing from the base of Mt. Parchoatras and proceeding southward, cuts it off on the left, and the Taurus on the right. Therefore from Mt. Imaus and on the right side of the east up to the River Boreus, then up to the Scythian Sea, which is to the north, as far as the Caspian Sea and as far as the farthest ridge of the Caucasus, there are forty-two nations of Hyrcanians and Scythians, widely roaming nomads on account of the extensive barrenness of their lands. So from the Caspian Sea which is to the east, as far as the River Tanais and the Maeotic Marshes, there are thirty-four nations. But in general the nearest region, farther Albania, near the sea and the Caspian Mountains, is called the region of the Amazons.

As briefly as possible the territory of Asia has been described.

Historiae
Paulus Orosius: 5th century
Trans. by H. E. W.

The Scythians

¶ IN THE YEAR 480 before the Founding of the City, Vesores, king of Egypt, anxious either to stir up war in the south and north or to join them under one rule, declared a war of aggression on the Scythians. He first sent envoys to inform the enemy of the terms of submission. To this the Scythians replied that a very wealthy king had stupidly declared war on a helpless people, for he himself should be afraid rather than the other way around, because of the uncertainties of war.

Furthermore, they should not wait until the enemy came to them, but should actually go and confront their prey. There was no delay: no sooner said than done. First, they forced Vesores himself to take refuge in his realms. They attacked his abandoned army and would also have devastated all Egypt had they not been driven back, impeded by the marshes. They immediately retreated, subdued Asia, and made it a tributary. After a stay of fifteen years without an interval of peace they were finally recalled by the repeated demands of their wives who clamored that, unless they returned, they would have children by the neighboring tribes.

Paulus Orosius: 5th century
Historiae
Trans. by H. E. W.

The Amazons

¶ DURING THIS TIME there were among the Scythians two princes, Plynos and Scolopthus: exiled, they settled on the shores of Cappadocia and Pontus. For a long time they ravaged all the neighboring territories, and in a conspiracy of these neighbors they were slain by a stratagem. Their wives, affected by their exile and their widowhood, took up arms and killed the husbands who were left so that all, being in the same situation, would feel alike.

Aroused against the enemy by the massacre of their men, they executed vengeance for their slain husbands by destroying their neighbors. After peace was made by arms, they entered into foreign concubinage. Presently they killed off the adult males and made love to the women. They burned off the right breasts of the infants so that they would not be hampered in shooting arrows. Hence they were called Amazons.

They had two queens, Marpesia and Lampeto, who divided their forces in two, and in turn, by drawing lots, took charge of war and the protection of the home. When they had therefore subdued most of Europe, had captured a number of cities in Asia, founded Ephesus and other cities, they recalled home the principal force of their army, loaded with spoil.

The rest of the women, left with Queen Marpesia to protect her rule over Asia, were butchered by an assault of the enemy. Her place was taken by her daughter Sinope, who added to her remarkable courage her unassailable chastity.

Such wonder and fear had spread among the nations, alarmed by their reputation, that Hercules too, ordered by his master to show his weapons to the queen, as though doomed to certain danger, collected all the chosen youth of Greece and equipped nine warships. Not satisfied, however, with this strong force, he resolved rather to make a surprise attack and to encircle the Amazons unexpectedly. Two sisters then held the reins of power, Antiope and Orithya. Hercules crushed them in a surprise assault. Among the slain and captives were two sisters of Antiope.

After Orithya, Penthesilea took possession of the kingdom. We know of her most distinguished evidence of heroism among men, in the Trojan War. Alas! Human error is shameful. These women, refugees from their country, swarmed into Europe and Asia, the most flourishing areas of the world, roamed everywhere, destroyed, overthrew numberless cities for almost a hundred years, built others, and held them. The troubled times were not adapted to human misery.

Paulus Orosius: 5th century
Historiae
Trans. by H. E. W.

Famine Strikes!¹

¶ A TERRIBLE FAMINE had overtaken the city of Favianis, whose inhabitants believed that their sole remedy would be to invite and pray for the coming of a man of God from the city of Comagenis. Anticipating that messengers were coming to him, he was urged by the Lord to hasten with them. On his arrival he began to exhort the citizens with these words: "You can be delivered from the calamity of this great famine by the fruits of repentance."

When they prospered by these instructions, St. Severinus discovered by a divine revelation that a certain widow named Procula had hidden a great quantity of food. He had her brought forth and rebuked her vehemently. "Why," he said, "do you, nobly born, show yourself bound to desire and enslaved by greed, which is, as the apostle teaches, the slave of idols? Behold the Lord looks after his servants with compassion; but you will give nothing to help those who are ill-provided, unless perhaps you cast the grain, so wickedly hoarded, into the River Danube and show the fishes the humanity that you have denied your fellow men. Therefore help yourself rather than the poor from what you propose to keep, though Christ starve."

Hearing this, the woman, stricken with a great dread, gladly proceeded to distribute the hoarded food to the poor. And so shortly afterward, a large number of boats laden with goods from the Rhaetian regions appeared unexpectedly on the banks of the Danube. These boats had for many days been icebound. By the Lord's will the ice was soon melted, and they brought supplies of food to the starving people. Then all began with continued devotion to praise the Lord, who had brought them such unforeseen aid: for they had thought to perish of prolonged famine, and acknowledged that the boats, freed from the bonds of ice unseasonably early, had come to them through the prayers of the servant of the Lord.

Eugippius: 6th century
Vita Sancti Severini: Corpus Scriptorum Ecclesiasticorum, 13
Trans. by H. E. W.

1. Famine and plague were frequent occurrences throughout medieval Europe. These catastrophies are repeatedly mentioned in personal memoirs and monkish chronicles.

Attila the Hun Invades Gaul

¶ ATTILA, KING OF THE HUNS, came forth to crush many cities of Gaul. Advancing on Orleans, he attempted to storm it with a heavy assault of battering rams. Now there was at that time in the aforementioned city a bishop, St. Anianus, a man of infinite prudence and praiseworthy sanctity, whose virtuous deeds are faithfully remembered among us. When the beleaguered people called to their priest asking what they should do, the man of God warned them in an address that they should prostrate themselves and tearfully implore the instant aid of the Lord in this time of need. At length the holy man said to them: "Look down from the city wall and see whether God's mercy is now at hand." For he suspected that through God's mercy Aetius was advancing, having been away at Arles, unaware of the peril. Now gazing down from the wall, they observed no one. And he said: "Pray faithfully; for the Lord will free you this day." And when they had looked, they saw no one bringing aid. A third time he said to them: "If you ask with faith, the Lord will come speedily." But with weeping and great lamentation they implored the mercy of the Lord.

After his address was over, looking down from the wall for the third time at the elder's command, they saw at a distance a kind of cloud rising up from the ground. When they reported this the priest said: "It is the Lord's help." Then, as the walls were trembling from the attack by the battering rams and were on the point of collapsing, Aetius arrived; and Theodore, King of the Goths, and Thursemodus, his son, advanced to the city with their armies and threw back and repulsed the opposing enemy. And so the city was freed by the persistence of the holy man, and they routed Attila.

Attila went to the plain of Marne and made ready for battle. Hearing this, they manfully made preparations against him. So Aetius with the Goths and the Franks together joined battle with Attila. But seeing his army being wiped out in the carnage, Attila fled. Theodore, however, King of the Goths, continued the conflict. For no one suspected that the army of the Huns had been routed by the persistence of the holy man. However, Aetius with Thursemodus gained the victory and destroyed the enemy.

After the conclusion of the war, Aetius said to Thursemodus: "Hasten quickly and return to your country, lest you be deprived of your father's realm by your brother." Hearing this, Thursemodus speedily departed, as it were to forestall his brother and be the first to secure his father's throne. Likewise Aetius got rid of the King of the Franks by a stratagem. As they were retreating Aetius, despoiling the battlefield, returned victorious to his country with a great quantity of plunder. But Attila returned with little, and shortly afterward Aquileia was captured by the Huns, burned and sacked, and Italy was overrun and destroyed. Thursemodus, whom we mentioned previously, subdued the Alani in battle; then he himself after much strife and many wars was defeated by his brother and was strangled to death.

Gregory of Tours: 6th century
Historia Francorum, 2
Trans. by H. E. W.

Death of Attila

¶ THIS WAS HIS END, as Priscus the historian relates. He married a very beautiful girl named Ildico after having numberless wives, as was the custom among that race. Debilitated by excessive connubial indulgence and overcome by wine and sleep, he was resting on his back, unable to take his accustomed walk. A bloody flux—he usually suffered from nosebleed—passed into his throat and in its fatal course killed him. Thus drunkenness put a shameful end to a king glorious in war.

Toward the end of the following day royal attendants, suspecting something tragic, raised a great clamor, broke down the doors, and found Attila dead without a wound, through a blood flux, and the girl weeping beneath her veil, with downcast look. Then, as is the custom among that people, they cut some of their hair and gashed their faces with deep wounds so that the mighty warrior would be lamented not with the moans and tears of women but with manly blood. In this regard there occurred a remarkable incident. As Marcianus, Emperor of the East, lay asleep that same night, worried about such a ruthless foe, a divine form appeared to him in his dreams and presented Attila's broken bow, as though Attila's nation assumed great power in that weapon. This the historian Priscus declares that he confirms by an actual witness. For Attila was considered so terrible and so powerful that the gods showed that his death was a blessing.

Jordanes: 6th century
Getica
Trans. by H. E. W.

Panegyric on King Theodoric[1]

¶ LET ANTIQUITY now go and boast of Alexander in dramatic narratives that have eloquently enriched his fame, so that the sorry eulogy of his deeds seems to increase through the aid of gifted tongues. In the case of our own King Theodoric his merits do not require consolatory affirmation. They are smaller than his actual deeds, whereas the achievements of the ancients have been multiplied by falsehoods. You poets have invented mighty deeds, but you must confess that the present ruler has achieved even greater ones. Alexander, hero of Pella, wanted Chocrilius' praises of him to rest essentially on his beneficence, so that the populace would not detect his deceit and become a witness to the shamelessness that was used to heighten his victories. I detract in no sense from our forefathers, whom antiquity would have considered eminent, had not the exaltation of Roman fame given us yourself.

Ignorance, the mother of error, kept Alexander unaware of the true religion. In your case true instruction made you a worshipper of almighty God from the very threshold of birth. You never add to your tasks what a favorable issue offers. You know that concern for perfection rests with you, that the substance is with God. You act so that you may deserve to achieve prosperity, but, having secured it, you ascribe it to the Creator.

You reveal your kingship by your strength, your vigilance, your prosperity. Your priestly function you display by your clemency.

---

1. The panegyric, both in prose and verse, was a popular literary genre from antiquity on. A notable panegyric is Pliny the Younger's on the Emperor Trajan; a satirical panegyric in reverse is Seneca's on the Emperor Claudius.

Why did our forefathers uselessly call men godlike and priestly when they were given the scepter? It is a singular thing, to act like a saint and not to have a saintly reputation. Let my king rightly be Germanic, let him be called a foreigner, provided that the divine ruler leads a life in accordance with the fruits of his conscience and seeks not the meaningless expressions of overweening arrogance in whose ways the blandishments of the ancients serve truth.

Ennodius: 6th century
Corpus Scriptorum Ecclesiasticorum
Trans. by H. E. W.

Chilperic the Tyrant

¶ So, AS THEY HURRIED off with this plunder, Chilperic, the Nero and the Herod of our time, proceeded to the town of Calais, which is about 100 miles from the city of Paris. There he went hunting. One day, returning from the hunt as the night was growing dark, he was being helped down from his horse, keeping one hand on the groom's shoulder. A man approached and stabbed him under the arm with a dagger. He struck a second time and slit his belly. Instantly there was a copious stream of blood both through the mouth and the wound, and Chilperic sent forth his wicked spirit. The account given previously[1] explains what evil he wrought. He frequently laid waste many regions and destroyed them by fire, from which acts he derived a great deal of pleasure and no feeling of grief, just as Nero once did when he chanted his tragedies while the palace was burning. Often he punished men unjustly for their abilities. In his time few ecclesiastics attained bishoprics. He wallowed in gluttony, whose god was the belly. He attached to his person nobody more intelligent than himself. He wrote two books, in imitation of Sedulius, whose feeble little verses cannot stand on their own feet. Since he had no knowledge of meter, he put short syllables in place of long ones and long ones for short. Also he wrote other minor pieces, both hymns and masses, that are totally unacceptable. He had a hatred for the interests of the poor. Against the priests of the Lord he constantly blasphemed and on no other topic, when he was in his private

1. A reference to an earlier passage not included here.

quarters, did he express ridicule and make jokes than on the bishops of the Church. One man he considered changeable, another haughty, this one lavish, that one lascivious; this one he claimed was too exalted, another arrogant; holding nothing in greater hatred than the churches. He often declared: "Look, our treasury has remained impoverished. Look, our wealth has been transferred to the churches. There are absolutely no rulers but the bishops. Our honor has died away and been transferred to the bishops of the cities."

Acting thus repeatedly, he generally broke wills that had been drawn up in favor of the churches, and often trampled on his own father's injunctions, thinking that there would be no one to serve his wishes. Now in the matter of lust and luxury it is impossible to conceive in imagination what acts he did not perpetrate in actuality, and he was always in search of new, ingenious methods of injuring the people. For, during these latter times if he found anyone guilty, he ordered his eyes to be gouged out. And in the instructions that he gave the judges for his own advantage he added these words: "If anyone shows contempt for our instructions, he shall be punished by having his eyes torn out." He never loved anyone wholeheartedly, and by no one was he loved. Hence, when he breathed his last, all his friends left him. Bishop Mallulfus Silvanectensis, however, who for three days stayed in the tent and could not see the king, on learning that he was dead came and after washing him, clothed him in his best raiment. He spent the night singing hymns. Then he placed him on a ship and buried him in the church of St. Vincent, which is in Paris, leaving Queen Fredegund in the church.

Gregory of Tours: 6th century
Historia Francorum
Trans. by H. E. W.

Escape from Captivity

¶ THEUDERIC AND CHILDEBERT formed a pact, swearing not to make any move against one another. They exchanged hostages to make their pledges more binding, and by this act many senators' sons fell into hostage. But, after a dispute had again arisen between the kings,

13

these young men were reduced to public slavery, and anyone could take them into custody. Though many of them escaped in flight and returned to their own country, not a few were kept in slavery. Among these was Attalus, grandson of St. Gregory, bishop of Langres, who was reduced to slavery and assigned as guard of the horses of some barbarian in the vicinity of Treves. Eventually St. Gregory assigned some youths to search for him. When they found him they offered his master gifts, but he rejected them with these words: "This slave, of such noble birth, ought to be ransomed for ten pounds of gold."

When the messengers returned, a certain Leo, attached to St. Gregory's kitchen, said: "I wish you would permit me, and perhaps I could buy him back from captivity." His master was pleased, and Leo at once went to the place near Treves and tried to take away the boy secretly, but he could not. Then he made a bargain with a man and said: "Come with me and sell me in the house of that barbarian and let my price be profitable for you, so that I can have a better chance to do what I have decided."

And after the pledging of oaths, the man and the barbarian parted and Leo had been sold to the barbarian for twelve pieces of gold. When the buyer questioned the new slave, the latter told what work he knew. "In all kinds of food, at the table of my masters I am a skilled worker, and I do not think you can possibly find anyone equal to myself in this art. In fact, I declare to you that, even if you want to prepare a feast for a king, I am skilled in recipes for royalty, and there is no one better than myself."

The master said: "Look, the day of the sun is approaching (for so the barbarians are accustomed to call the day of the Lord). On this day my neighbors and relatives will be invited to my house. I ask you to make dinner for me that they will admire and say that in the king's palace we saw nothing better." To which the new slave said: "Let my master order a large number of roosters to be brought and I shall carry out your wishes."

When the preparations ordered by the boy were completed, Sunday dawned and the boy made a great feast crammed with delicacies. After dining and praising the meal, the relatives left satisfied. The master thanked the boy, who was given control over everything that his master had in the storehouse; and his master liked him very much and had him prepare food and meat for all his guests.

At the end of a year, when his master was now sure of him, Leo went into a meadow near the house with young Attalus, guard of the horses, and, lying down on the ground with him at a distance, back to back so that they would not be recognized together, he said to Attalus: "It is now time for us to think of our own country, and so I advise you, when you have taken in the horses to stall, not to fall asleep tonight, but to come as soon as I call you and we'll be off."

The barbarian master had invited many of his relatives to a feast, among them his son-in-law. At midnight, when the guests had risen and gone to sleep, Leo followed his master's son-in-law with a drink, and when he handed him the drink in hospitality the son-in-law said: "Tell me, trusted servant of my father-in-law, on your oath, when will you fulfill your wish to take his horses and go back to your country?" He said this as if he were delighted with the joke. The other likewise replied truthfully, as if jesting: "I intend to go tonight, if God wills." To which the son-in-law said: "I wish my servants would protect me so that you don't take anything of mine." And they went their ways, laughing.

When all were asleep, Leo called Attalus and, saddling the horses, asked whether he had a sword. Attalus replied: "The only thing I need is a little spear." Leo went into his master's house and took a shield and a spear. When someone asked him who he was and what he wanted, he answered: "I am Leo, your servant, and I am calling Attalus to get up faster and lead the horses to pasture. He is dead asleep like a drunk man."

Leo went outside, armed the boy, and by some divine luck found the courtyard gates unbolted, that at nightfall had been bolted with wedges of wood hammered in, as a protection for the horses. Giving thanks to God and taking the remaining horses with them, they went off, carrying a roll of bedding along with their clothes. When they came to the Moselle River they were stopped by some people and, in order to get across, they abandoned their horses and clothes, swam across the river lying on their shields, and emerged on the far bank. At night they entered the woods and lay in hiding. On the third night that they had marched without tasting any food, by God's will they came upon a tree laden with fruit commonly called plums. After eating and being somewhat refreshed, they proceeded toward Champagne. On their way they heard the sound of galloping horses and Leo said: "Let us crouch down on the ground so as not to be seen by the approaching men."

Unexpectedly there was a large bramblebush nearby, behind which they threw themselves on the ground, with drawn swords, so that if they were observed, they would instantly defend themselves from the attackers. When the men came to the spot, they halted behind the prickly bush, and one said, as the horses were urinating: "I'm ruined, for letting these rascals escape and not being able to bring them back. But I assure you, may I live so, if they are found, I'll order one to be condemned to the gallows and the other to be cut in pieces with the sword." The man who spoke was the barbarian, their master, who had come from the city of Rheims in search of them, and would have found them on the way if the darkness had not prevented him. At last, starting their horses, the men moved off.

That very night the fugitives reached the city and, entering, found a man whom they asked for the direction to Paulellus the priest's house. He told them, and while they were crossing the street the bell rang for matins (for it was Sunday). Knocking at the priest's door, they went in and Leo explained about his master. The priest said: "My dream is indeed come true. For last night I saw two doves flying and resting on my hand, one of them white, the other black."

To which the boy replied: "May the Lord forgive us for this holy day, but we ask you to give us some food. For this is the fourth day since we have tasted no bread or meat."

Hiding the boys, the priest offered them soup, with wine and bread, and went off to matins. The barbarian showed up again, asking about the boys. But the priest was there to misdirect him, and he turned back; for the priest had long been a friend of St. Gregory. When the boys had renewed their strength with food during a stay of two days in the priest's house, they departed and thus came to St. Gregory.

The pontiff rejoiced at sight of the boys, weeping on his nephew Attalus' neck. Releasing Leo from the yoke of bondage, with all his family, he gave him land for his own property, where he lived free all the days of his life with his wife and children.

Gregory of Tours: 6th century
Historia Francorum
Trans. by H. E. W.

Why History Is Written[1]

¶ THE CULTURE of the liberal arts was declining or rather actually dying in the cities of Gaul, good and evil contended, and savagery was rampant among the nations. The madness of kings grew more intense. Churches were attacked by heretics and protected by Catholics. Among many, faith in Christ flourished, but in others it was lukewarm. The churches themselves were either enriched by the devout or plundered by unbelievers, and no teacher skilled in dialectics could be found to depict this state of affairs either in prose or in metrical form. A great many people repeatedly bewailed this condition and exclaimed: "Woe to our times, for the study of literature has perished among us and no one has been found among our people capable of presenting current events in writing."

Accordingly, observing this and similar occurrences constantly, I have described events that recall the past so that they may be linked with accounts of later happenings. Although my style is uncouth, still it cannot obscure the conflicts between the wicked and the righteous; because, though it amazes me, I have often noticed that few people understand a philosophizing rhetorician while many understand a peasant's speech.

So I found it agreeable to start Book I with the very beginning of the world, to endure through the ages, and I have listed the several chapters below.

> Gregory of Tours: 6th century
> *Historia Francorum*
> Trans. by H. E. W.

Historical Survey

¶ I AM WEARY of describing the vicissitudes of the civil wars that lay low the nation and kingdom of the Franks. In this period we see the beginning of the troubled times that the Lord foretold: father rising against son, son against father, brother against brother, neighbor

---

1. The Greek historians Herodotus and Thucydides introduced their chronicles with a declaration of their motive in writing history; the practice was long continued.

17

against neighbor. The examples of earlier kings ought to have terrified them, for, once divided, they were instantly destroyed by their enemies. How often has that city of cities itself, the capital of the entire world, fallen to ruins when engaged in civil wars and, on their cessation, again risen, so to speak, from the ground. Would that you, kings, in those battles in which your fathers sweated, conducted yourselves so that the nations, terrified by your peace, would be crushed by your might. Remember what the source of your victories, Clodovic, did, when he killed rival kings, wiped out destructive nations, subjugated countries whose rule he left to you, entire and unimpaired. When he did this he had neither the gold nor the silver such as you now have in your treasuries. What are you doing? What are you seeking? What do you not abound in? In homes delicacies increase immeasurably; in the storehouses wine, wheat, and oil are in superabundance; in the treasuries gold and silver lie in heaps. You lack one thing: not having peace, you lack the grace of God. Why does one man take another man's possession? Why does a man covet what is not his? Beware of what the apostle says, I beg you: "If ye bite and devour one another, take heed that ye be not consumed one of another." Scrutinize carefully the writings of the ancients and you will see what civil wars produce. Examine what Orosius writes about the Carthaginians, when he adds, after saying that their state and territory were destroyed after 700 years: "What kept them safe so long? Harmony. What destroyed them after so many years? Discord." Beware of discord, beware of civil wars that ruin you and your people. What else have you to hope for except that, when your army has collapsed, you yourselves, deserted without comfort and crushed by hostile nations, immediately fall in ruins?

Gregory of Tours: 6th century
Historia Francorum
Trans. by H. E. W.

The Burning of Paris

¶ THERE WAS THEN in those days in the city of Paris a woman who said to the citizens: "Flee from the city, and you shall learn that it must be destroyed by fire." She was laughed at by many for saying that as a prophetic divination; or she had dreamed something like this; or she surely offered this information at the prompting of some demon. But she answered: "It is not at all as you say, for I speak the truth, because I saw in my dream a man coming to the Church of St. Vincent all aglow and holding in his hand a wax taper and setting fire to the homes of merchants one after the other."

Finally, on the third night after the woman uttered these words, as twilight fell, one of the citizens lit a lamp and entered his storehouse. He took some oil and other necessities and went out, leaving the lamp near a small barrel of oil. Now, this house was the first near the gate that gave exit to the south. The house caught fire from this lamp and was destroyed; other buildings too began to catch fire from it. Then as the fire spread destructively over the bounds of the prison, St. Germain appeared to the prisoners, and breaking the wooden beams and the fetters that bound them, he opened the gate of the prison and allowed them to escape from their confinement unharmed. They went out and proceeded to the Church of St. Vincent, where the tomb of the holy bishop is.

So the fire spread through the entire city, with the wind blowing in all directions, and when the conflagration was at its height it started to approach the other gate, where the oratory of St. Martin stood, built on the site where the Saint had cured a man of leprosy by kissing him. Now the man who had built the oratory, trusting in the Lord and not distrustful of the virtue of St. Martin, had his possessions below the walls and went about saying: "I believe, and it is my faith, that he averts the fire from this spot who often commanded fires and cleansed a leper in this spot with a healing kiss." For as the fire came nearer, great gusts of flame were swept forward; as they struck the walls of the oratory, they forthwith lost their fury.

Now the people cried to the man and the woman: "Flee, wretches, and escape. See, the weight of the fire has burst over you. See, the ashes of the fire along with the burning wood are spreading toward you like a mighty rain. Leave the oratory, otherwise the fire will burn you too." But despite the pleadings they could not in the least be moved by these words. The woman never went away from the window, through which the flames fitfully entered, for she was fortified with the firmest faith in the virtue of the holy saint. And so great was the virtue of the holy saint that he not only saved this oratory along with the house of his own disciple but in addition he did not allow the spreading flames to damage the other surrounding houses. And at that spot the fire, that had begun to destroy one part of the bridge, subsided.

19

In another area, however, the conflagration was so widespread that it stopped only when it had reached the river. At least the churches with their houses were not destroyed. For they said that this city had been as it were anciently consecrated so that fire would not get the upper hand nor would a snake or a dormouse appear there.

Gregory of Tours: 6th century
Historia Francorum
Trans. by H. E. W.

Clovis, the Frankish King, Defeats the Alamanni and Becomes a Christian

¶ QUEEN CLOTILDA however did not cease to pray that he [Clovis] would acknowledge the true God and abandon idols. But he could not be induced to this belief in any manner, until finally a war arose against the Alamanni, in which he was forced by necessity to confess what he had previously willfully denied.

Now it happened that in the bitter armed conflict the Alamanni were being slaughtered and Clovis' army began to rush toward the final carnage. Seeing this, he raised his hands to heaven and, heart-stricken, was moved to tears and said: "Jesus Christ, who, as Clotilda declares, are the son of the living God, who are worthy to give aid to those in distress and to grant victory to those who have faith in you, devoutly I beg your glorious aid, so that, if you concede me victory over those hosts, and I experience that virtue which she says the people have acclaimed about you, I shall believe and be baptized in your name. For I have called upon my own gods but, as I find, they are far from helping me; hence I believe that they are endowed with no power whatever, since they give no aid to those who obey them. I now invoke you, I long to believe in you, so that I may even be overwhelmed by my enemies."

When he said this, the Alamanni turned and began to retreat in flight. And when they saw their king struck down, they accepted the words of Clovis and said: "Let no more people perish, we beg you. Now we are yours." But he stopped the war and addressed the people; and after he returned, when peace was made, he told the queen that through the invocation of the name of Christ he deservedly gained the victory. This occurred in the fifteenth year of his reign.

Then the queen secretly bade Remy, the bishop of the city of Rheims, be summoned, saying that he should suggest a word of salvation to the king. The bishop summoned him and unobtrusively hinted to him that he should believe in the true God, the creator of heaven and earth, and abandon idols, that could protect neither himself nor others. But the king said: "I heard you gladly, holy father; but there is one thing: the people that serve me do not permit their gods to be abandoned. But I shall go and speak with them in accordance with your words."

Meeting with them, before he spoke and as the power of the Lord welled up in him, all the people cried together: "We shall deny our mortal gods, holy king, and we are prepared to follow the God that Remy declares immortal." They announced this to the priest, who was filled with great joy and bade them prepare the font. The streets were hung with embroidered awnings, the churches were adorned with white curtains, the baptistery was made ready, balsam was scattered, tapers burned and gleamed with the fragrance, and the entire baptistery was besprinkled with the divine fragrance, and the Lord gave such grace to those present that they thought they were amidst the fragrances of Paradise. Then the king asked to be baptized first by the priest. The new Constantine approached the font to wash away the disease of the old leprosy and to wash away in fresh water the former repulsive stains. As he intered into baptism, the holy man of God thus addressed him with eloquent tongue: "Gently bend your neck, Sigamber; adore what you have kindled, burn what you adored." Now the holy Bishop Remy was a man of great learning and deeply versed in the art of rhetoric, but in sanctity he was so renowned as to equal the virtues of St. Silvester. For there is now a Life of him which tells that he died and rose. The king then confessed Almighty God in the Trinity, and was baptized in the name of the Father, the Son, and the Holy Ghost, and was anointed with the consecrated oil with the sign of the cross of Christ. In the army more than 3,000 were baptized.

Gregory of Tours: 6th century
Historia Francorum
Trans. by H. E. W.

The Saracens[1]

¶ THE AGARENI, also called Saracens as Orosius' history testifies, are a race confined on one side of the Caucasus range, above the Caspian Sea, and long settled in a land called Ercolia. On account of an inordinate growth in population, they finally took up arms and made devastating inroads into the provinces of the Emperor Heraclius. Against them Heraclius directed his soldiers in a movement of resistance. When the conflict was joined, the Saracens defeated the soldiery and butchered them ruthlessly at the sword. It is said that in that battle 50,000 troops were slain by the Saracens. Their spoils the Saracens presented through envoys as a gift to Heraclius. Heraclius, in his eagerness for vengeance on the Saracens, resolved to accept nothing from them. He collected from all quarters of every province in his realm a vast military force, and sent an embassy to the Gates of the Caspian, that Alexander the Great of Macedon had commanded to be made of bronze and to be barred at the Caspian Sea, on account of the incursion of barbarous tribes that dwelt beyond the high Caucasus mountains. Heraclius ordered these same gates to be opened and let in 150,000 warriors and mercenaries hired for gold to do battle against the Saracens. The Saracens, under two commanders, equaled almost 200,000 men.

When each army had pitched camp not far from one another, so that on the following day they would enter battle in fighting form, that same night Heraclius' army was struck down by the sword of the Lord. In the camp 52,000 out of Heraclius' thousands lay slaughtered; and when on the following day it was necessary to go forth to battle, the soldiers, seeing most of their army slain by a divine judgment, dared not join against the Saracens. Heraclius' entire army retreated to its own quarters. The Saracens, as they had previously begun to do, proceeded ruthlessly to devastate the provinces of the Emperor Heraclius. When they were near Jerusalem, Heraclius, seeing that he could not withstand their force, filled with

1. Saracens: Latin, *Saraceni*. This term designates the nomads of the Middle East, particularly the Moslems who came in conflict with the Crusaders.

bitterness and grief as he was, and unhappily now an adherent of the heretical doctrine of Eutyches, abandoned Christian worship and, harassed by fever, ended his life violently. He had married the daughter of his sister. His successor to the imperial throne was his son Constantine.

Fredegarius: 7th century
Chronicon
Trans. by H. E. W.

Britain Invaded by Saxons

¶ So SOME OF THE wretched survivors, trapped in the hills, were butchered wholesale; while others, exhausted by hunger, were ready to surrender for good, provided they were not slain forthwith—which was a very great favor. Still others made for lands overseas amid loud lamentation, chanting thus, instead of the oarsmen's cries, as they hoisted sail: "Thou hast given us like sheep appointed for meat, and hast scattered us among the heathen." Others again preferred to live, always in fear of discovery, among the towering mountain ranges with their deep valleys and in the dense glades and the cliffs by the sea, and they remained in their country though with trepidation. After some time had passed, when the most ruthless of the pirates had departed, the survivors, the Lord giving them strength, were besieged by the poor citizens who swarmed around them from different directions, as eagerly as bees in their hive at the approach of a storm, and pleaded with Him, with all their heart and, as it is written, "charging the air with numberless prayers," not to be wiped out in total massacre. Their leader was Ambrosius Aurelianus, a man of modesty who alone of the great Roman nation had luckily survived when his royal parents had been slain in the same disastrous conflict. In his own days his progeny degenerated markedly from the ancestral good character. The victors seized power and offered a challenge to battle; with the Lord's approval victory fell to them.

From that time on the victory fluctuated between citizens and enemy, so that in that nation the Lord in His usual manner tried the new Israel to see whether He loved him or not: until the year of the siege of Mt. Badonicus and of the last and most frightful massacre of the robbers.

But not even now are the cities of my country inhabited as they were before. In ruined abandon they still lie waste, though foreign but not civil wars are ending. For the thought of aid for such a lamentable and unprovoked destruction of the island lingers in the memory of those who witnessed both events; and for this reason kings, state officials, private citizens, priests and the clergy each maintained their own station. But when they were gone and the succeeding era was ignorant of those times and used to the present tranquillity only, all controls over truth and justice were shattered and overthrown, with the result that not only no trace but not even the memory of them appears among the before-mentioned classes, except in the case of a few, and that a very few, who on account of the loss of such a vast number that is daily rushing to perdition, are considered such a small handful that in a way the venerable Mother Church does not see reclining on its bosom those whom alone it considered its true sons.

Gildas: 6th century (died 570)
De Excidio Britanniae: Monumenta Germaniae Historica, Auctores Antiquissimi xiii
Trans. by H. E. W.

Caius Julius Caesar, the First Roman That Came into Britain[1]

¶ BRITAIN had never been visited by the Romans, and was indeed entirely unknown to them before the time of Caius Julius Caesar, who, in the year 693 after the building of Rome, but the sixtieth year before the incarnation of our Lord, was consul with Lucius Bibulus, and afterwards, whilst he made war upon the Germans and the Gauls, which were divided only by the river Rhine, came into the province of the Morini, from whence is the nearest and shortest passage into

1. Compare with Julius Caesar's own account of his landing in Britain: *De Bello Gallico,* Book V.

Britain. Here, having provided about eighty ships of burden and vessels with oars, he sailed over into Britain; where, being first roughly handled in a battle and then meeting with a violent storm, he lost a considerable part of his fleet, no small number of soldiers, and almost all his horse. Returning into Gaul, he put his legions into winter quarters, and gave orders for building six hundred sail of both sorts. With these he again passed over early in spring into Britain, but whilst he was marching with a large army toward the enemy, the ships, riding at anchor, were by a tempest either dashed one against another or driven upon the sands and wrecked. Forty of them perished, the rest were with much difficulty repaired. Caesar's cavalry was at the first charge defeated by the Britons, and Labienus, the tribune, slain. In the second engagement he, with great hazard to his men, put the Britons to flight. Thence he proceeded to the river Thames, where an immense multitude of the enemy had posted themselves on the farthest side of the river, under the command of Cassibellaun, and fenced the bank of the river and almost all the ford under water with sharp stakes. The remains of these are to be seen to this day, apparently about the thickness of a man's thigh, and being cased with lead, remain fixed immovably in the bottom of the river. This being perceived and avoided by the Romans, the barbarians, not able to stand the shock of the legions, hid themselves in the woods, whence they grievously galled the Romans with repeated sallies. In the meantime the strong city of Trinovantum, with its commander Androgeus, surrendered to Caesar, giving him forty hostages. Many other cities, following their example, made a treaty with the Romans. By their assistance, Caesar at length, with much difficulty, took Cassibellaun's town, situated between two marshes, fortified by the adjacent woods, and plentifully furnished with all necessaries. After this Caesar returned into Gaul, but he had no sooner put his legions into winter quarters, than he was suddenly beset and distracted with wars and tumults raised against him on every side.

Bede: 8th century
The Ecclesiastical History of the English Nation, Vol. 2
Edited by Charles Plummer. Oxford, 1896

The Lombards Settle in Italy[1]

¶ AFTER THE ENTIRE NATION of the Goths was wiped out or conquered and those others of whom we spoke were similarly defeated,
Narses acquired great wealth in the shape of gold and silver and
other treasure. Thus he incurred great envy on the part of the
Romans, for whom he had labored mightily against their enemies. His
detractors made suggestions against him to the Emperor Justinian
and his wife Sophia in these terms. They said that it would have been
better for the Romans to be subject to the Goths rather than the
Greeks, where Narses the eunuch held sway and crushed them in
slavery. "And of these facts the most devoted Emperor is unaware.
Either free us from his hands or surely we hand over the Roman
state and our own selves to these people."

When Narses heard this, he replied briefly: "If I have done ill by
the Romans, it will go ill with me." Then the Emperor was so aroused
against Narses that he sent the prefect Longinus to Italy, to take
Narses' place. Narses, informed of this, became fearful; and he was so
terrified particularly by the Empress Sophia that he dared not return
to Constantinople. Among other things, since he was a eunuch, she
is said to have commissioned him to distribute the tasks of wool-
making among the girls in the women's quarters.

Narses' reply to this is said to have been that he would weave such
a web for her that she would not be able to lay it aside as long as
she lived. And so, goaded by hate and fear, he set off to the city of
Naples in Campania, and shortly thereafter he directed envoys to
approach the nation of the Lombards, ordering them to abandon the
miserable countryside of Pannonia and come to Italy to occupy it,
filled as it was with all kinds of wealth. At the same time he sent
them a great variety of fruit and other sorts of things to coax them
to come. The Lombards gratefully received the glad news and the

1. Lombards: Latin, *Langobardi*. The Lombards were a Teutonic people who
   settled in the sixth century in northern Italy. This region became known
   as Lombardy, with Pavia as the capital. The Lombards extended their con-
   quests over almost all Italy. Their kingdom lasted from late in the sixth
   century to the eighth century.

things that they so much wanted, and cheered themselves up with the thought of future advantages. All at once awesome portents were seen throughout Italy: fiery streamers appeared in the sky, gleaming over him who later on shed his blood.

Paulus Diaconus: 8th century
Historia Langobardorum
Trans. by H. E. W.

History of Britain[1]

¶ THE BRITAINS came to Britain in the third age of the world; and in the fourth, the Scots took possession of Ireland.

The Britains who, suspecting no hostilities, were unprovided with the means of defense, were unanimously and incessantly attacked, both by the Scots from the West and by the Picts from the North. A long interval after this, the Romans obtained the empire of the world. From the first arrival of the Saxons into Britain, to the fourth year of King Mermenus, are computed four hundred and twenty-eight years; from the Nativity of our Lord to the coming of St. Patrick among the Scots, four hundred and five years; from the death of St. Patrick to that of St. Bridget, forty years; and from the birth of Columcille to the death of St. Bridget, four years.

I have learned another account of this Brutus from the ancient books of our ancestors. After the deluge, the three sons of Noah severally occupied three different parts of the earth: Shem into Asia, Hem into Africa, and Japhet into Europe.

The first man that dwelt in Europe was Alanus, with his three sons, Hisicion, Armenon, and Neugio. Hisicion had four sons, Francus, Romanus, Alamanus, and Brutus. Armenon had five sons, Gothus, Valagothus, Cibidus, Burgundus, and Longobardus. Neugio had three sons, Vandalus, Saxo, and Boganus. From Hisicion arose four nations—the Franks, the Latins, the Germans, and Britains: from Armenon, the Gothi, Valagothi, Cibidi, Burgundi, and Longobardi;

---

1. A great deal of the "historical" matter in this account is of course legendary, intertwined and confused with historical facts, tradition and imaginative literature.

27

from Neugio, the Bogari, Vandali, Saxones, and Tarincgi. The whole of Europe was subdivided into these tribes.

Alanus is said to have been the son of Fethuir; Fethuir, the son of Ogomuin, who was the son of Thoi: Thoi was the son of Boibus; Boibus of Semion; Semion of Mair; Mair of Ecthactus; Ecthactus of Aurthack; Aurthack of Ethec; Ethec of Ooth; Ooth of Aber; Aber of Ra; Ra of Esraa; Esraa of Hisrau; Hisrau of Bath; Bath of Jobath; Jobath of Joham; Joham of Jafet; Jafet of Noah; Noah of Lamech; Lamech of Mathusalem; Mathusalem of Enoch; Enoch of Jared; Jared of Malalehel; Malalehel of Cainan; Cainan of Enos; Enos of Seth; Seth of Adam; and Adam was formed by the living God.

From ancient tradition, we have obtained this information respecting the original inhabitants of Britain. The Britains were thus called from Brutus; Brutus was the son of Hisicion; Hisicion was the son of Alanus; Alanus was the son of Rhea Silvia; Rhea Silvia was the daughter of Numa Pompilius; Numa was the son of Ascanius; Ascanius of Eneas; Eneas of Anchises; Anchises of Troius; Troius of Dardanus; Dardanus of Flisa; Flisa of Juuin; Juuin of Jafeth; but Jafeth had seven sons; from the first, named Gomer, descended the Galli; from the second, Magog, the Scythi and Gothi; from the third, Madian, the Medi; from the fourth, Juuan, the Greeks; from the fifth, Tubal, arose the Hebrei, Hispani, and Itali; from the sixth, Mosoch, sprung the Cappadoces; and from the seventh, named Tiras, descended the Traces: these are the sons of Jafeth, the son of Noah, the son of Lamech.

The Romans having obtained the dominion of the world, sent legates or deputies to the Britains to demand of them hostages and tribute, which they received from all other countries and islands; but they, fierce, disdainful, and haughty, treated the legation with contempt.

Then Julius Caesar, the first who had acquired universal empire, highly incensed against the Britains, sailed with sixty vessels to the mouth of the Thames, where they greatly suffered whilst he fought at Deal (the proconsul of the British king, who was called Belinus, and who was the son of Minocannus who governed all the islands of the Tyrrhene Sea), and thus Julius Caesar returned home without victory, having had his soldiers slain and his ships shattered. But after three years he again appeared with a large army and three hundred ships at the mouth of the Thames, where he renewed hostilities. In this attempt many of his soldiers and horses were killed; for the same consul had placed iron pikes in the shallow part of the river, and this having been effected with so much skill and secrecy as to escape the notice of the Roman soldiers, did them considerable injury; thus Caesar was once more compelled to return without peace or victory. The Romans were, therefore, a third time sent against the Britains; and, under the command of Julius, defeated them near a place called Trinovantum, forty-seven years before the birth of Christ, and five thousand, two hundred and twelve years from the Creation.

Julius was the first exercising supreme power over the Romans who invaded Britain: in honor of him the Romans decreed the fifth month to be called after his name. He was assassinated in the Curia in the Ides of March, and Octavus Augustus succeeded to the empire of the world. He was the only emperor who received tribute from the Britains, according to the following verse of Virgil,

"Purpurea intexti tollunt aulea Britanni."

The second after him who came into Britain was the Emperor Claudius, who reigned forty-seven years after the Birth of Christ. He carried with him war and devastation; and, though not without loss of men, he at length conquered Britain. He next sailed to the Orkneys, which he likewise conquered, and afterwards rendered tributary. No tribute was in his time received from the Britains. He reigned thirteen years and eight months. His monument is to be seen at Moguntia (among the Lombards) where he died on his way to Rome.

After the Birth of Christ, one hundred and sixty-seven years, King Lucius, with all the chiefs of the British people received Baptism, in consequence of a legation sent by the Roman Emperors and Pope Euaristus.

Severus was the third emperor who passed the sea to Britain, where, to protect the provinces recovered from barbaric incursions, he ordered a wall and a rampart to be made between the Britains, the Scots, and the Picts, extending across the island from sea to sea, in length one hundred and thirty-three miles: for the Scots from the west, and the Picts from the north, unanimously made war against the Britains.

The fourth was the Emperor Cartius, who, incensed at the murder of Severus, passed into Britain, and attended by the leaders of the Roman people, severely avenged upon the chiefs and rulers of the Britains the cause of Severus.

The fifth was Constantius, the son of Constantine the Great. He died in Britain; his sepulchre, as it appears by the inscription, is still seen near the city named Cair segeint. Upon the pavement of the above-mentioned city he sowed three seeds of gold, silver, and brass, that no poor person might ever be found in it.

Maximus was the sixth emperor that ruled in Britain. It was in his time that consuls began, and that the appellation of Caesar was discontinued: at this period also, St. Martin became celebrated for his virtues and miracles.

The seventh emperor was Maximianus. He withdrew from Britain with all its military force, slew Gratianus, the king of the Romans, and obtained the sovereignty of all Europe. Unwilling to send back his warlike companions to their wives, children, and possessions in Britain, he conferred upon them numerous districts from the Lake on the summit of Mons Iovis, to the city called Cant Guic, and to the western Tumulus, that is, to Cruc Occident. These are the Armoric Britains, and they remain there to the present day. In consequence of their absence, Britain being overcome by foreign nations, the lawful heirs were cast out, till God interposed with his assistance. We are informed by the tradition of our ancestors that *seven* Emperors went into Britain, though the Romans affirm *there were nine*.

The eighth was another Severus, who lived occasionally in Britain, and sometimes at Rome, where he died.

The ninth was Constantius who reigned sixteen years in Britain, and according to report, was treacherously murdered in the seventeenth year of his reign; and thus, agreeably to the account given by the Britains, the Romans governed them four hundred and nine years.

After this the Britains despised the authority of the Romans, equally refusing to pay them tribute or to receive their kings; nor durst the Romans any longer attempt the government of a country, the natives of which massacred their deputies.

We must now return to the tyrant Maximian; Gratian, with his brother Valentinian, reigned seven years. Ambrose, Bishop of Milan, was then eminent for his skill in the dogmata of the Catholics. Valentinus and Theodosius reigned eight years. At that time a synod was held at Constantinople, attended by three hundred and fifty of the fathers, and in which all heresies were condemned. Jerom the Presbyter of Bethlehem was then universally celebrated. Whilst Gratian exercised supreme dominion over the world, Maximus, in a sedition of the soldiers, was saluted Emperor in Britain, and soon after crossed the sea to Gaul. At Paris, by the treachery of Merobaudes, who flying to Lyons was taken and put to death, Maximus afterwards associated his son Victor in the government.

Martin, distinguished for his great virtues, was at this period Bishop of Tours. After a considerable space of time, Maximus was divested of royal power by the Consuls Valentinus and Theodosius, and sentenced to be beheaded: in the same year also his son Victor was killed in Gaul by Argobustes, five thousand six hundred and ninety years from the creation of the world.

Thrice were the Roman deputies put to death by the Britains, and yet these when harassed by the incursions of the barbarous nations, viz. of the Scots and Picts, earnestly solicited the aid of the Romans. To give effect to their entreaties, ambassadors were sent, who made their entrance with impressions of deep sorrow, having their heads covered with dust and carrying rich presents, to expiate the murder of the deputies. They were favourably received by the consuls, and swore submission to the Roman yoke, with whatever severity it might be imposed.

The Romans, therefore, came with a powerful army to the assistance of the Britains; and having appointed over them a ruler, and settled the government, returned to Rome: and this took place alternately, during the space of 150 years. The Britains, however, from the oppression of the empire, again massacred the Roman deputies, and again petitioned for succour. Once more the Romans undertook the government of the Britains, and assisted them in repelling their neighbours; and, after having exhausted the country of its gold, silver, brass, honey, and costly vestments, and having besides received rich gifts, they returned in great triumph to Rome. After the above-said war between the Britains and Romans, the assassination of their rulers, and the victory of Maximianus, who slew Gratian, the Roman power ended in Britain, which it had kept in awe during 400 years.

Vortigern then reigned in Britain. In his time, the natives had cause of dread, not only from the inroads of the Scots and Picts, but also from the Romans, and their apprehensions of Ambrosius.

In the mean time, three vessels, exiled from Germany, arrived in Britain. They were commanded by Hors and Henegest, brothers, and sons of Guictglis. Guictglis was the son of Guicta; Guicta of Guechta; Guechta of Vuoden; Vuoden of Frealof; Frealof of Fredulf; Fredulf of Finn; Finn of Folegualod; Foleguald of Geta, who, as they say, was the son of a god, not of the omnipotent God and our Lord Jesus

Christ (who, before the beginning of the world, was with the Father and the Holy Spirit, coeternal and of the same substance, and who, in compassion to human nature, disdained not to assume the form of a servant), but the offspring of one of their idols, and whom, blinded by some demon, they worshipped according to the custom of the heathen. Vortigern received them as friends, and delivered up to them the island which is in their language, called Tenet, and, by the Britains, Roihin. Gratianus Aequantius, at that time, reigned in Rome. The Saxons were received by Vortigern, four hundred and forty-seven years after the passion of Christ, and, "according to the tradition of our ancestors," from the period of their first arrival in Britain to the first year of the reign of king Edmund, five hundred and forty-two years; and to that in which we now write, which is the fifth of his reign, five hundred and forty-seven years.

At that time St. Germanus, distinguished for his numerous virtues, came to preach in Britain: by his ministry, many were saved; but many likewise died unconverted. Of the various miracles which God enabled him to perform, I shall here mention only a few: I shall first advert to that concerning an iniquitous and tyrannical king, named Belinus. The holy man, informed of his wicked conduct, hastened to visit him, for the purpose of remonstrating with him. When the man of God, with his attendants, arrived at the gate of the city, they were respectfully received by the keeper of it, who came out and saluted them. Him they commissioned to communicate their intention to the king, who returned a harsh answer, declaring, with an oath, that although they remained there for the space of a year, they should not find admission to the city. While waiting for an answer, the evening came on, and they knew not where to go. At length came one of the king's servants, who, bowing himself before the man of God, announced the words of the tyrant, inviting them, at the same time, to his own house, to which they went, and were kindly received. It happened, however, that he had no cattle, except one cow and a calf, the latter of which, urged by generous hospitality to his guests, he killed, dressed, and set before them. But holy St. Germanus ordered his companions not to break a bone of the calf; and, the next morning, it was found alive uninjured, and standing by its mother. Early the same day, they again went to the gate of the city, to solicit audience of the wicked king; and, whilst engaged in fervent prayer they were waiting for admission, a man, covered with sweat, came out, and prostrated himself before them. Then St. Germanus, addressing him, said, "Dost thou believe in the Holy Trinity?" To which having replied, "I do believe," he baptized, and kissed him, saying, "Go in peace; within this hour thou shalt die: the angels of God are waiting for thee in the air; with them thou shalt ascend to that God in whom thou hast believed." He, overjoyed, entered the city, and being met by the Prefect, was seized, bound, and conducted before the tyrant, who, having passed sentence upon him, he was immediately put to death; for it was a law of this wicked king, that whoever was not at his labour before sun-rising should be beheaded in the citadel. In the mean time, St. Germanus, with his attendants, waited the whole day before the gate, without obtaining admission to the tyrant. The above-mentioned, however, remained with them. "Take care," said St. Germanus to him, "that none of your friends remain this night within these walls." Upon this he hastily entered the city, brought out his nine sons, and with them retired to the house where he had exercised such generous hospitality. Here St. Germanus ordered them to continue, fasting; and when the gates were shut, "Watch," said he, "and whatever shall happen in the citadel, turn not thither your eyes; but pray without ceasing, and invoke the protection of the true God." And, behold, early in the night, fire fell from heaven and burnt the city, together with all those who were with the tyrant, so that not one escaped; and that citadel has never been rebuilt even to this day. The following day, the hospitable man who had been converted by the preaching of St. Germanus was baptized, with his sons and all the inhabitants of that part of the country; and St. Germanus blessed him, saying, "a king shall not be wanting of thy seed forever." The name of this person is Catel Drunluc: "from henceforward thou shalt be a king all the days of thy life." Thus was fulfilled the prophecy of the Psalmist— "He raiseth up the poor out of the dust, and lifteth up the needy out of the dunghill." And, agreeably to the prediction of St. Germanus, from a servant he became a king: all his sons were kings, and, from their offspring, the whole country of Powys has been governed to this day.

After the Saxons had continued some time in the island of Tenet, Vortigern promised to supply them with clothing and provision, on condition they would engage to fight against the enemies of his country. But the barbarians having greatly increased in number, the Britains became incapable of fulfilling their engagement; and when the Saxons, according to the promise they had received, claimed a supply of provisions and clothing, the Britains replied, "Your number is increased; your assistance is now unnecessary; you may, therefore, return home, for we can no longer support you": and hereupon they began to devise means of breaking the peace between them. But Hengist, in whom united craft and penetration, perceiving he had to act with an ignorant king and a fluctuating people incapable of opposing much resistance, replied to Vortigern, "We are, indeed, few in number; but, if you will give us leave, we will send to our country for an additional number of forces, with whom we will fight for you and your subjects." Vortigern assenting to this proposal, messengers were dispatched to Scythia, where, selecting a number of warlike troops, they returned with sixteen vessels, bringing with them the beautiful daughter of Hengist. And now the Saxon chief prepared an entertainment, to which he invited the king, his officers, and Ceretic, his interpreter, having previously enjoined his daughter to serve them so profusely with wine and ale that they might soon become intoxicated. This plan succeeded; and Vortigern, at the instigation of the Devil, and enamoured with the beauty of the damsel, demanded her, through the medium of his interpreter, of the father, promising to give for her whatever he should ask. Then Hengist, who had already consulted with the Elders who attended him of the Angle race, demanded for his daughter the province called in English Centland, in British, Ceint. This ponation was made without the knowledge of the regulus, who then reigned in Kent, and who experienced no inconsiderable share of grief from seeing his kingdom thus clandestinely, fraudulently, and imprudently resigned to foreigners. Thus the maid was delivered up to the king, who slept with her, and loved her exceedingly. Hengist, after this, said to Vortigern, "I will be to you both a father and an adviser; despise not my counsels, and you shall have no reason to fear being conquered by any man or any nation whatever; for the people of my country are strong, warlike, and robust: if you approve, I will send for my son and his brother, both valiant men, who, at my invitation will fight against the Scots, and the people who dwell in the North, near the wall called Guaul." The incautious sovereign having assented to this; and Ochta and Ebissa arrived with forty ships. In these they sailed round the country of the Picts, laid waste the Orkneys, and took possession of many regions, even to the Pictish confines.

But Hengist continued, by degrees, sending for ships from his own country; so that some islands whence they came were left without inhabitants; and whilst his people were increasing in power and number, they came to the province of Kent. In the mean time, Vortigern, as if desirous of adding to the evils he had already occasioned, married his own daughter, by whom he had a son. When this was made known to St. Germanus, he came, with all the British clergy, to reprove him; and whilst a numerous assembly of the ecclesiastics and laity were in consultation, the weak king ordered his daughter to appear before them, and in the presence of all, to present her son to St. Germanus, and declare that he was the father of the child. The immodest woman obeyed; and St. Germanus taking the child, said, "I will be a father to you, my son; nor will I dismiss you till a razor, scissors, and comb are given to me by your carnal father." The child obeyed St. Germanus, and going to his father, Vortigern, said to him, "Thou art my father, shave, and cut the hair of my head."

The king blushed, and was silent; and, without replying to the child, arose in great anger and fled from the presence of St. Germanus, execrated and condemned by the whole synod. But soon calling together his twelve wise men, to consult what was to be done, they said to him, "Retire to the remote boundaries of your kingdom; there build and fortify a city to defend yourself, for the people you have received are treacherous; they are seeking to subdue you by stratagem, and, even during your life, to seize upon all the countries subject to your power, how much more will they attempt after your death." The king, pleased with this advice, departed with his wise men, and travelled through many parts of his territories, in search of a place convenient for the purpose of building a citadel. Having, to no purpose, travelled far and wide, they came at length to a province called Guenet; and having surveyed the mountains of Heremus, they discovered, on the summit of one of them, a situation adapted to the construction of a citadel. Upon this, the wise men said to the king, "Build here a city; for, in this place, it will ever be secure against the barbarians." Then the king sent for artificers, carpenters, stone-masons, and collected all the materials requisite to building; but the whole of these disappeared in one night, so that nothing remained of what had been provided for the constructing of the citadel. Materials were, therefore, from all parts, procured a second and third time, and again vanished as before, leaving and rendering every effort ineffectual. Vortigern inquired of his wise men the cause of this opposition to his undertaking, and of so much useless expense of labour? They replied, "You must find a child born without a father, put him to death, and sprinkle with his blood the ground on which the citadel is to be built, or you will never accomplish your purpose." In consequence of this reply, the king sent messengers throughout Britain, in search of a child born without a father. After having inquired in all the provinces, they came to the field of Aelecti, in the district of Glevesing, where a party of boys were playing at ball. And two of them quarrelling, one said to the other, "O boy without a father, no good will ever happen to you." Upon this, the messengers diligently inquired of the mother and the other boys, whether he had had a father? Which his mother denied, saying, "In what manner he was conceived I know not, for I have never had intercourse with any man"; and then she solemnly affirmed that he had no mortal father. The boy was, therefore, conducted before Vortigern, his king; who, having heard what was said of him, a meeting took place the next day, for the purpose of putting him to death. Then the boy said to the king, "Why have your servants brought me hither?" "That you may be put to death," replied the king; "and that the ground on which my citadel is to stand may be sprinkled with your blood, without which I shall be unable to build it." "Who," said the boy, "instructed you to do this?" "My wise men," answered the king. "Order them hither," returned the boy; this being complied with, he thus questioned them: "By what means was it revealed to you that this citadel could not be built, unless the spot were previously sprinkled with my blood? Speak without disguise, and declare who discovered me to you": then turning to the king, "I will soon," said he, "unfold to you everything; but I desire to question your wise men, and wish them to disclose to you what is hidden under this pavement": they acknowledging their ignorance, "there is," said he, "a pool; come and dig." They did so, and found the pool. "Now," continued he, "tell me what is in it"; but they were ashamed, and made no reply. "I," said the boy, "can discover it to you: there are two vases in the pool." They examined, and found it so. Continuing his questions, "What is in the vases?" they were silent. "There is a tent in them," said the boy; "separate them, and you shall find it so." This being done by the king's command, there was found in them a folded tent. The boy, going on with his questions, asked the wise men what was in it? But they not knowing what to reply, "There are," said he, "two serpents, one white and the other red; unfold the tent." They obeyed, and two sleeping serpents were discovered. "Consider attentively," said the boy, "what they are doing." The serpents began to struggle with each other; and the white one, raising himself up, threw down the other into the middle of the tent, and sometimes drove him to the edge of it; and this was repeated thrice. At length the red one, apparently the weaker of the two, recovering his strength, expelled the white one from the tent; and the latter being pursued through the pool by the red one, disappeared. Then the boy, asking the wise men what was signified by this wonderful omen, and they expressing their ignorance, he said to the king, "I will now unfold to you the meaning of this mystery. The pool is the emblem of this world, and the tent that of your kingdom: the two serpents are two dragons; the red serpent is your dragon, but the white serpent is the dragon of the people who occupy several provinces and districts of Britain, even almost from sea to sea: at length, however, our people shall rise and drive away the Saxon race from beyond the sea, whence they originally came; but do you depart from this place, where you are not permitted to erect a citadel. I, to whom fate has allotted this mansion, shall remain here; whilst to you it is incumbent to seek other provinces, where you may build a fortress."—"What is your name?" asked the king. "I am called Ambros, in British Embresguletic," returned the boy. "A Roman consul was my father."

Then the king assigned him that city, with all the western provinces of Britain; and departing with his wise men to the sinistral district, he arrived in the region named Gueneri, where he built a city, which, according to his name, was called Cair Guorthegirn. At length Guorthemer, the son of Vortimer, valiantly fought against Hengist, Horsa, and his people; drove them to the isle of Tenet, and thrice enclosed them within it, and beset them on the western side.

The Saxons now dispatched deputies to Germany to solicit large re-inforcements, and an additional number of ships: having obtained these, they fought against the kings and princes of Britain, and sometimes extended their boundaries by victory, and sometimes were conquered and driven back.

Nennius: 9th century
Historia Brittonum
Trans. by Rev. W. Gunn

News Chronicle[1]

¶ THE YEAR 752.   Our holy father Boniface suffered martyrdom, an apostolic man, endowed with all wisdom, who traced his noble ancestry from the English nation and who was educated there most religiously in the holy life and nonetheless was noted for his learning and renowned for his miracles. Afterward, guided by divine piety, he went to the territory of Germany and excellently trained the Frankish nation, which was caught in the manifold snares of error, and relentlessly crushed the wicked errors of the heretics. Also he was so distinguished in evangelical doctrine that from his preaching you would have praised the age of the apostles. So, through his merits that shone in every direction, he was summoned by that most holy man, Gregory, the Pope of Rome. He was sent out for the enlightenment of all Germany, and ordained as bishop by the same Pope in the city called Mayence, and by his merit was raised to the honor of the Pontificate. There, established among men, he pursued a saintly life, won over to God the nation of the Franks and the Thuringian and Saxon peoples, and was glorious in all his sanctity. Lastly, after converting many of the Frisians to the Christian religion, he was slain by the sword by the surviving heathens. With the glory of martyrdom he passed on to the kingdom of heaven and his body was brought, amid great praises to God, accompanied by a vast throng of the faithful, to the monastery of Fulda, that he had built for himself in the Boconian solitude. He was buried with fitting honor and in the same spot became famous for many miracles. Along with him other holy men of his order suffered martyrdom—priests, deacons, and monks; but the noblest among them were Bishop Eoban and the priest Adalar, who previously received honorable burial in the monastery called Trech, but in the course of the

1. In the Middle Ages many abbeys and towns compiled their own chronicles, such as the Annals of Xanten and those of St. Vaast. In some instances they contain valuable historical source material, although they also lean toward fantastic views and interpretations of events and local minutiae.

years they too were transferred to Fulda, and rest nobly beside the body of their holy pastor Boniface.

The year 835. In the month of February there was an eclipse of the moon. The Emperor Ludovic with his son of the same name proceeded to Burgundy and there his son Pippin came to him. Meanwhile the heathens again invaded areas of Frisia and a considerable number were slain by them. And again they pillaged Dorsten.

The year 836. At the beginning of the month of February, strange streamers of light appeared at night, moving from east to west. Again, in the same year, the heathens invaded the Christians.

The year 837. A gigantic whirlwind broke out on several occasions and a comet appeared, emitting numerous trails of light in the east for a distance of some three cubits, before the amazed spectators. The pagans devastated Walicrum and abducted many women from there, taking also a huge sum of monies of various kinds.

The year 838. The winter was rainy and very windy and on January 21 thunder was heard and likewise on February 16 there were great claps of thunder and the intense heat of the sun scorched the earth, and in certain districts of the land an earthquake occurred, and the fiery shape of a dragon was seen in the air. In the same year a wicked heresy arose. In the same year on the fifth night before the birth of the Lord a great crash of thunder was heard and lightning was seen and in many ways the misery and misfortunes of men increased every day.

The year 839. On December 26 a huge whirlwind arose, so that the sea waves flooded all over the boundaries and the coast and pitifully wiped out a great number of people concentrated in the towns and villages, together with the dwellings. The ships sailing on the sea were damaged and flaming fires were seen over the entire sea. In the same year on March 25 strange streaks of light appeared in the sky in the evening, shaped like a round house, surrounding the entire area of the sky. In that year the bodies of Saints Felix and Agapitus and Felicitas came to the place called Fredenna.

The year 852. The steel of the pagans grew white hot: an excessive heat of the sun: famine followed: there was no fodder for the beasts, but the feeding of pigs flourished.

The year 853.   Great hunger in Saxony with the result that many ate horses.

The year 854.   The Normans, besides many other misfortunes that they inflicted on the Christians everywhere, set fire to the church of St. Martin, bishop of the city of Turo, where his tomb is.

The year 855.   In spring, Ludovic, king of the east, sent his son and his son of the same name to Aquitania, to receive in his behalf the kingdom of Pippin, his father-in-law.

The year 856.   The Normans again set up a king for themselves, a relative of the same name as his predecessor, and the Danes again, with renewed strength, attacked the Christians in a naval raid.

The year 857.   A great plague, with swelling of the bladder, raged among the people and destroyed them with horrible festering, so that their limbs dropped off and fell away before death.

The year 858.   Ludovic, king of the east, held an assembly of the people of his domain at Wangen.

The year 859.   On the first of January, after a service of matins was held, there was an earthquake at Worms, and at Mayence an earthquake occurred, thirteen times before dawn.

The year 860.   On February 5th thunder was heard; and the king returned from Gaul, his entire kingdom plundered and improved in no respect.

Annales Xantenses: 9th century
Trans. by H. E. W.

Charlemagne: His Habits and Studies

¶ IN FOOD AND DRINK he was temperate, but more so in the latter, inasmuch as he had the strongest abhorrence of drunkenness in any man, especially in his own case and that of his family. For in respect of food his control was not so great; he frequently complained that his hunger induced physical pain. He rarely had banquets, and that only during special festivities; then, however, he invited a large company.

His daily meal consisted of four courses only, except for a roast that the hunters usually brought in on spits. This he enjoyed eating more than any other food. During the meal there was some entertainment or a recital. History and accounts of ancient deeds were read to him. He liked too the works of St. Augustine, especially the *De Civitate Dei.*

He was so abstemious in wine and every kind of drink that at table he rarely had more than three drinks. In summer, after lunch he took some fruit and one drink. Then he disrobed, took off his shoes as he did at night, and rested for two or three hours. At night his sleep was broken four or five times not only by his waking up but also by his getting down from bed. When he was dressing he not only admitted friends, but even, if the Count Palatine said that there was some suit that could not be settled without Charlemagne's order, bade him bring in the litigants at once and, as if he were presiding in court, he declared his decision on hearing the case. This was the procedure not only on such an occasion, but whatever duty had to be performed on a particular day or whatever instructions his ministers had to be given he executed.

He had a readiness and richness of speech and a capacity for the most lucid exposition. Not satisfied with the vernacular, he even took pains to learn foreign languages; he mastered Latin so effectively that he was accustomed to pray in that language as well as in his native tongue. In Greek his understanding was better than his pronunciation. He was so eloquent in fact that he even appeared loquacious. He cultivated the liberal arts enthusiastically. Scholars he deeply respected and heaped great honors on them. In the study of grammar he heard the lectures of Peter Pisanus, an elderly deacon; in other subjects he had as teacher Albinus, surnamed Alcuin, also a deacon, a man of Saxon race from Britain, the most learned man of his time. Under him he devoted a great deal of time and effort to the study of rhetoric and dialectics and particularly astronomy. He learned the art of reckoning and with keen concentration he investigated in great detail the course of the stars.

He made attempts at writing, too, and was accustomed to surround his pillows on his bed with tablets and notebooks for this purpose, so that when he had any spare time he would train his hand to form letters. But he met with little success in these efforts because he had started too late in life.

Einhard: 9th century
Vita Karoli
Trans. by H. E. W.

Pirate Encounter[1]

¶ IT HAPPENED TOO that Charlemagne, while traveling, came unexpectedly to a certain city on the coast of Gallia Narbonensis. While he was dining there incognito, Norman pirates made a raid on the harbor. When their ships were observed, some said they were Jewish merchants; others, African; and others, British. The wise Charlemagne, deducing from the equipment of the boats that they were not traders but enemies, said to his attendants: "These ships are not loaded with merchandise but crammed with the most ruthless enemies." On learning this, in their eagerness to forestall each other they hurried quickly to the ships. But it was useless. For when the Normans found out that Charlemagne the Hammer, as they were accustomed to call him, was there too, to prevent all their weapons either from being battered there or broken into minute pieces and ruined, by a most remarkable flight from pursuit they escaped not only from sword attacks but from sight.

Now Charlemagne, pious, just, and devout, rose from table and stood at the east window, and for a long time wept copious tears, no one presuming to interrupt him. Finally he said to his belligerent nobles, justifying his action and his tears: "Do you know, my faithful warriors, why I wept so much? It is not that I am afraid these stupid nonentities may be able to harm me in any way, but I am certainly saddened that, during my lifetime, they have dared to approach this shore, and I am tortured with deep grief because I foresee the great evils they will bring upon my successors and their subjects."

Notker: 10th century
Gesta Karoli
Trans. by H. E. W.

1. Piracy, which was prevalent during the Dark and Middle Ages, was often conducted by the Northmen, who devasted the coastal towns of northern Europe and scoured the Mediterranean littoral.

Portrait of a King

¶ BUT, TO USE a marine metaphor, in order not to expose our ship to the waves and our sails to the winds and, sailing too far out from land, navigate too long amidst such great military disasters and chronological listings of events, I think we ought to return to what particularly induced us to undertake this work, that is, within the extent of my knowledge, and I believe some brief remarks should be included at this point on the childhood and boyhood of my revered master Alfred, King of the Anglo-Saxons.

Since he was fondly adored by the united love of his father and mother more than all his brothers, and indeed by all, and was always nurtured at the royal court, as he grew up from childhood and boyhood he seemed more comely in appearance than the rest of his brothers, and more handsome in look and talk and character. From the cradle onward, the nobility of his mind above all else, even his studies of life and the nobility of his birth, gained him the wisdom he desired. But alas! Through the shameful indifference of his parents and those who raised him he remained illiterate up to his twelfth year or even longer. But being a clever listener to Saxon poems day and night, and often hearing the tales of others, he learned them readily and retained them in his memory. In every hunting sport he was a regular hunter and constantly participated, not in vain. For he was incomparably better than everyone in skill and luck in that art, as he was in all the other God-given endowments, as is very often the case.

On a certain day his mother showed him and his brothers a book of Saxon poems that she held in her hand and said: "Whichever one of you can learn this book the quickest, I'll give it to him." Encouraged by these words, or rather by divine inspiration, and enticed by the beauty of the first letter of the book, Alfred thus replied to his mother and forestalling his brothers, older in years but not in grace, said: "Will you really give the book to one of us, to the one who can understand and read it to you first?"

With a smile she gladly repeated: "I shall give it to him." Then, immediately taking the book from her hand, he went to his master and read. When he had read it he brought it to his mother and recited.

After this he learned the daily service, that is, the celebration of the hours, and then certain psalms and many prayers. These, collected in one book, he carried around with him inseparably, in his pocket, everywhere, day and night, as we ourselves have seen, for the purpose of praying, amidst all the circumstances of the present life. But alas! What he desired most, namely the liberal arts, he did not achieve because, as he said, at that time there were no good teachers in the entire kingdom of the Western Saxons.

Asser: 10th century
Annales rerum gestarum Alfredi Magni
Trans. by H. E. W.

Palace Scene at Constantinople[1]

¶ NEXT TO THE PALACE in Constantinople there is a house of remarkable size and beauty that is called by the Greeks Magnaura, as if it were Magna Aula, the Great Court, the letter "r" being substituted for "l." On account not only of the Spanish envoys, who had recently arrived, but of myself and Liutefred, Constantine ordered that it be got ready in this manner.

Before the emperor's seat stood a tree of bronze, gilded over, whose branches were similarly filled with gilded bronze birds of various kinds. These birds uttered their respective notes according to their species. The emperor's chair was so ingeniously constructed that it seemed, in a second, now low, now higher, almost immediately very high up; gigantic lions, either of bronze or wood but certainly gilded, acted as guards. With their tails they lashed the ground, jaws open, and roared with quivering tongues.

In this chamber, then, leaning on the shoulders of two eunuchs, I was conducted into the emperor's presence. When the lions gave a roar at my entrance and the birds twittered according to their species, I was not in the least alarmed or amazed, since I had questioned those who were well informed about all these novelties. After bowing then three times in reverence to the emperor, I raised my

1. Constantinople, capital of the Byzantine Empire, was founded on the site of ancient Byzantium. A later variant name for the city was Neo-Roma.

head; and the man whom I previously saw sitting slightly raised above the floor I observed next moment, robed, sitting as high as the ceiling of the house. I could not imagine how it was done, unless he was lifted there by the hydraulic pressure that raises the beams of winepresses. He uttered no word himself now although he wished to do so, since the great distance between us made it unseemly, but he questioned me about Berengarius' life and health through a secretary. When I had replied suitably, at a sign from the interpreter I left and was soon taken to the lodging assigned to me.

Liudprand: 10th century
Antapodosis
Trans. by H. E. W.

King Berengarius I Assassinated![1]

¶ So, AFTER KING RODULF'S DEATH, the citizens of Verona devised an evil plan and contrived a plot against the life of Berengarius, of which Berengarius was well aware. The author and schemer of such a foul crime was a certain Flambert whom the king had favored by being godfather to his son at the boy's baptism. On the day before his death, Berengarius summoned this Flambert into his presence and said:

"If there were not many good reasons for our mutual affection, the things that are said about you could not be believed. They say you are plotting against my life; but I do not believe them. Now I want you to remember that, whatever accessions of fortune and prestige have been yours, you could not have attained them but for my favors. Hence your feeling toward me should be such that my prestige should rest in your love and loyalty. Never, I think, has anyone ever had such great concern for his well-being and fortune as I have had for your honor. To this matter I have devoted all my interests, effort, care, labors, and thought for the state. Know this one thing: If I find that you have kept faith with me, it will be more pleasant to show my gratitude for such loyalty than the consideration of my safety." The king ended, and extended to him a heavy gold

1. King Berengarius I was assassinated in 924.

45

goblet, adding: "For love of my welfare, drink the contents; take the container."

After the drink, actually and unquestionably, Satan entered into Flambert, as it is written of Judas the betrayer of our Lord Jesus Christ: after the sop Satan entered into him. Unmindful of past and present favors, he spent that night wakefully, instigating the people to murder the king. That night the king, as he was wont to do, stayed not in a house that could be guarded but in a pleasant little cottage near the church. But he had set no guards that night, since he suspected no harm.

> The rooster shakes itself and crows
> And rouses men from their repose.
> The brazen bell rings o'er the sward
> And chants the praises of the Lord,
> Calling righteously and well
> On men to throw off sleep's deep spell.
> For God who gives us life, commands
> We seek above the sacred lands.
> To church the king is on his way,
> The praises of the Lord to say,
> While Flambert hastens with a crowd
> Of men, to kill the king thus bowed.

> The king, suspecting nothing ill,
> An uproar hears. It is his will
> To find what brings to church such groups.
> And lo! He sees the armed troops.
> He calls out: "Flambert, tell me, sir,
> What means this crowd, this armed stir?"
> "Fear not. They come to quell the strife.
> Those others seek the king's own life."
> The king is caught deceitfully,
> As he advanced so trustfully.
> Struck by a wicked spear behind,
> Alas! he falls, that king so kind.
> His happy spirit take, O Lord,
> For righteously he claims reward.

Finally, how they shed innocent blood, and how much wickedness they wickedly committed, we shall not say, but a stone placed before

46

the door of the church shows to all passers-by the blood marks. No water can wipe out the stain of the spilt blood.

Liudprand: 10th century
Antapodosis
Trans. by H. E. W.

Audience with Nicephorus Phocas, Emperor of Constantinople

¶ TO THE OTTOS, unconquerable August Emperors of the Romans, and to the most glorious Empress Augusta Adelaide, Liudprand, bishop of the holy church of Cremona, craves for, desires, and wishes your continuous health, prosperity, and success.

The following explanation will make clear the reason why you did not receive previously a messenger or letters of mine. We arrived in Constantinople on June 4 and, to your shame, we were welcomed insultingly and treated discourteously and insultingly. We were confined in a building large and spacious enough, but it neither kept out the cold nor excluded the heat. Armed soldiers were stationed as guards to prevent my party from leaving or others from entering. We had the entire use of the house for ourselves, but we were confined in it, and it was so distant from the Palace that our breath was taken away not riding there, but walking. We had the additional worry that the Greek wine, being mixed with pitch, tar, and gypsum, was undrinkable. The house itself lacked water and we could not slake our thirst with the water that we secured on payment of money. To this great trouble another trouble was added: the man who supervised the houses, who disbursed the daily expenses, whose like you could not find if you looked for him on earth but perhaps in hell—for whatever misfortune, whatever robbery, whatever expense, whatever trouble, whatever misery he could imagine, he poured it all upon us like a torrent in spate. For in one hundred and twenty days not a single day passed that was free from lamentation and grief for us.

On June 4, as we have previously written, we came to Constantinople at the Carian Gate and until the eleventh hour we waited with our horses in a downpour of rain. At the eleventh hour Nicephorus, thinking that being so well dressed we ought not to ride at your expense, ordered us to come and we were conducted into the before-mentioned marble house, hateful, lacking water, sprawling. On June 6, the first Sabbath of the festival of Pentecost, I was brought into the presence of his brother Leo, the master of the Palace and the chancellor, and there I was worn out with a prolonged dispute about your prestige. For he called you, not Emperor, that is *empereur* in his tongue, but, in humiliation, *roi*, that is king in our language. Upon my informing him that the same thing was meant, although differently expressed, he declared that I had come to quarrel, not to make peace; and so, rising up in a fury he took your letter with deep indignation, not personally but through an interpreter; rather dignified in bearing, but falsely humble. If a man leans on him, he will pierce his hand.

On June 7, which was the holy day of Pentecost itself, in the house called Stephana, that is, the Crown Palace, I was taken before Nicephorus, a monstrosity of a man: a dwarf, swollen-headed, with small molelike eyes, a foul short beard, fan-shaped, thickly grown, half tinged with gray, with a neck the size of a finger, rather pig-faced with his long thick hair, his complexion that of an Ethiopian; a man you would not like to meet at midnight, with an enormous paunch, lean-buttocked, hips very long in proportion to his small size, short in the knee, his feet flat in their shoes, robed in a woolen but too old garment or foul and faded from long wear. He was shod in Sicyonian shoes: ready with his tongue, cunning as a fox, a very Ulysses in perjury or mendacity. You have always seemed to me, my august and imperial masters, handsome: how much more handsome by comparison with him? Always distinguished, how much more distinguished by comparison? Always powerful, how much more so by comparison? Always clement, how much more so by comparison? Always abounding in virtues, how much more so than he? On the left, not in the same row, but far lower down, sat the two young emperors, once his masters, now his subjects. He thus began his talk:

"We ought to have welcomed you, or rather we had wanted to, kindly and royally; but the wickedness of your master does not permit it. By a hostile assault he claimed Rome for himself. He took the life of Berengarius and Adelbert contrary to law and right. Some Romans he destroyed by the sword, others by hanging. He gouged out the eyes of some, banished others in exile and in addition he attempted to steal for himself by murder or fire certain cities within our empire. And because his evil disposition could not achieve this, now he has sent you, the prompter and instigator of his malice, under a pretense of peace, as an *espion,* that is, a spy."

My reply was: "My master invaded the city of Rome not by tyrannical force, but freed it from the yoke of a tyrant, or rather tyrants. Did it not have degenerate rulers? And, what was more serious or more disgraceful, were not prostitutes the rulers? Your power, I think, was dormant then, or rather that of your predecessors, who are called nominally, but not in actuality, Roman emperors. If they were powerful, if they were Roman emperors, why did they allow Rome to remain in the power of harlots? Were not the most holy popes banished, others persecuted by you, so that they could obtain neither their daily expenses nor charity? Did not Adelbert send the most insulting dispatches to Romanus and Constantine, your predecessors? Did he not plunder and rob the churches of the most holy apostles? Which one among all you emperors, inspired by the zeal of God, cared to avenge such a disgraceful deed and to re-establish such a great church to its proper condition? You were guilty of neglect, not my master. He, starting from the bounds of the earth and coming to Rome, drove away the wicked and delivered over to the vicars of the holy apostles all their power and honor. Afterward he killed, strangled, hanged, and sent into exile those who rose against him and the apostolic master as violators of oaths, sacrilegious, persecutors of his apostolic masters, robbers, according to the decrees of the Roman emperors Justinian, Valentinian, Theodosius, and others. If he did not act thus, he would be a wicked, unjust, ruthless tyrant. It is evident that Berengarius and Adelbert, soldiers who molded their own fortune, had received from his hands the gold scepter of the throne of Italy, and, in the presence of your servants who have survived to this day in this city, made a pledge of allegiance. And because, at the devil's instigation, they treacherously violated this pledge, he justly deprived them of the kingdom as deserters and rebels. You would act similarly in the case of those subject to you and later on rebellious."

"The second hour has now gone," said Nicephorus, "*la marche,* that is, the procession, must be celebrated. Let us now do what is urgent. When the moment is opportune, we shall reply to your arguments."

Let it not irk me to describe the procession itself and my masters to listen. A huge throng of merchants and of the common people collected for this celebration in welcome and praise to Nicephorus, and lined the sides of the road from the Palace to St. Sophia like a wall. Each one held a tiny little shield and a cheap little spear. He advanced barefooted, to increase the disgrace, because the majority of the people themselves had come barefooted to praise him. I believe that they thought they were thus rather honoring the holy procession itself. But his nobles, who had passed through the multitude of the barefooted rabble along with him, were dressed in wide tunics, torn and very old. They would have formed a more respectable procession if dressed in their everyday clothes.

There was no one whose forebears ever had new clothes. No one there wore gold ornaments or jewels, except Nicephorus himself, whom the imperial decorations, put on and designed for the person of his predecessors, had made more horrible. I swear by your life that is dearer to me than my own, one precious garment of yours is more precious than that of one hundred of these courtiers.

I was conducted to the procession itself, to a high seat near the *chanteurs*, that is, the singers, and there I remained stationed. And when that monstrous creature advanced like a reptile, the singers chanted in adulation: "Behold the Morning Star is coming, the Eastern Star arises, repelling the rays of the sun by confronting it, the pale death of the Saracens, Nicephorus *le prince*, that is, the prince!"

Then they chanted: "*Vive*, that is, long live Nicephorus, *le prince,* that is, the prince! People, adore him, worship him, submit your necks to such a great man!"

With how much greater truth should they have chanted: "Come, burnt-out coal, come, slow down, you old woman by your walk, you Pan-face, you boor, tramp, goat-footed, horned, two-limbed, boar, wild creature of the fields, savage, harsh, hairy, rebellious Cappadocian!"

Thus, swollen with those lying chants, he proceeds to St. Sophia, his imperial masters following him at a distance and genuflecting down to the ground in the kiss of peace. One of his knights, fashioning a pen out of an arrow, writes the date on the church when his reign began, and thus those who did not see it understand what the date signifies.

On the same day he ordered me to dine with him. Thinking that I was unworthy to have precedence over any of his courtiers, I sat fifteen from him and without a napkin. None of my companions not only did not sit down to table, but did not even see the house in

50

which I was a guest. At this banquet, that was rather prolonged and marked by the usual drunken obscenities, streaming with oil and soaking in some kind of foul fish sauce, he questioned me at great length about your power, your realms, and your soldiers.

When I answered him readily and truthfully, he exclaimed: "You are lying! Your master's troops can't ride, the infantry is inexperienced in battle, the size of your shields, your heavy breastplates, long swords, and the weight of the helmets prevent them from any effective fighting." Then, smiling, he added: "They are troubled by *la crapule,* that is, gluttony; their god is the belly; their daring, gorging themselves; their courage, drunkenness; their hunger, dissoluteness; their fear, sobriety. Nor has your master a fleet of ships on the sea. The bravery of seamen lies in me alone, who will attack him with my fleets, destroy his coastal cities in war, and reduce to ashes those that are near rivers. Who, tell me, will be able to withstand me, even on land, with a handful of troops? His son was present, he had his wife with him. The Saxons, Suevi, Bagoari, all the Italians were with him; and since they did not know how, or rather were unable, to capture one little city that offered resistance, how will they resist my coming, with so many troops accompanying me?

> "As many as the crops of Gargara,
> Or as the clusters of Methymnia,
> Or as the stars that stud the shining sky,
> Or as the waves in Ocean billow high."

Liudprand: 10th century
Relatio de Legatione Constantinopolitana
Trans. by H. E. W.

Liudprand Leaves Constantinople

¶ ON MY RECEIPT of this letter, saying good-bye, they sent me off with pleasant, friendly looks. As I left, they arranged for me an ambassadorial parting not appropriate for me, but worthy enough of themselves. For they gave horses to me and my escort only, nothing for the baggage. Accordingly, deeply disturbed by this situation, I gave my *conducteur,* that is, guide, a present of fifty pieces of gold. And since I had nothing then to give Nicephorus for his misdeeds,

on the wall of my hateful dwelling and on the wooden table I wrote
these few verses:

> Argolic faith is far to seek.
> Shun, you Romans, all things Greek.
> To Greek nor thought nor word reveal,
> Whate'er you say, whate'er you feel.
> In victory his colors true
> He shows. His wily oaths you'll rue.
> A house of marble: windows high,
> water? None. A prison nigh.
> Inviting heat and bitter cold,
> Where Bishop Liudprand was told
> To dwell, four summer months, alone.
> For Otto had attained the throne,
> And tried by slaughter and by flame
> To plunge all cities deep in shame.
> Let him return to Italy,
> I pray, with all his victory.
> False-speaking Greece had promised too
> A bride, no daughter, glad to woo. . . ,
> Lo! the day grim fates foresee
> Is nigh. May it averted be!
> Or war will rage in every place
> And peace will never show its face:
> Peace sought with such eagerness,
> Silenced by your wickedness.

Liudprand: 10th century
*Relatio de Legatione Constantinopoli-
tana*
Trans. by H. E. W.

Storming of Verdun

¶ THIS TOWN is so situated that to travelers the approach is over
a passable plain, but it is inaccessible from the rear. There, it extends
all around from its summit into the hinterland over a deep incline.

From its lower levels to the top it is enclosed by steep rocks. It not only abounds in springs and wells, to the advantage of the citizens, but it has also many groves, with the River Meuse washing it on the steep side. With the plain facing the city, the fighting forces set up various kinds of war engines. Also, those within the city prepared for resistance. Finally the fighting started, continuing for almost eight days without interruption. When, however, the citizens realized that no aid was being sent to them from the outside and that they could not withstand the weight of battle despite the rocky defenses, they made a decision and submitted to the enemy, unharmed and untouched. They opened the city and surrendered in defeat to Lothair.

After this, the king left Queen Emma there to guard the city. He returned to Laudun with the army, and also allowed his men to return to their homes. He enjoyed such favor among them on account of his benevolence that they promised to resume the march and advance farther if he so ordered; disregarding for the time being their homes and children, they would engage with the enemy at close quarters. Meanwhile Lothair deliberated with his men whether it was better to advance and to subdue all Belgium by force of arms, or to stay in Verdun and through the persuasive representations of envoys to mold the ways of the enemy to his own inclination. On the one hand, if he defeated them by the sword, at the cost of great bloodshed, he felt that in future little reliance could be placed in them. If, however, he acted with magnaminity and waited for them to come to him, he would have to be careful, for in the interval of such an armistice the enemy might become more insolent.

Richer: 10th century
Historiarum Libri Quattuor
Trans. by H. E. W.

A Courageous Saxon

¶ Now THERE WAS in the camp then a certain veteran soldier, rather advanced in years but still hale and hearty. His name was Hathagat, and he was called "father of fathers" on account of his good qualities. Seizing a standard that was considered sacred among them, displaying a lion and a dragon and over them an eagle in flight, he wanted to show the effectiveness of his courage and intelligence and such traits. Standing steadfast, in conformity with the fixity of his purpose, he declared: "I have lived thus far among the worthy Saxons, and my years have brought me almost to the last stage of old age, and never have I seen my fellow Saxons in flight; and how am I now compelled to do what I have never learned to do? I know how to fight, but I don't know how to flee, and I cannot. If fate does not let me live longer, let me at least fall with my friends—which is a very noble thing for me. Examples of my inherited courage are the bodies of those friends, lying prostrate about us, who preferred death to defeat, to give up their tireless souls rather than yield ground in face of the enemy. But what need have I to prolong this exhortation on contempt for death? Look, we'll go to those who are safe, to the massacre only, not to battle; for about the promised peace and our serious losses the enemy suspected nothing. They too, exhausted by today's battle, fearless as they are, wait without sentries and the usual guard. Then let us rush upon them unexpectedly, deep in sleep as they are. The task is slight. Follow me as your leader, and I pledge you this gray head of mine if it does not turn out as I say."

Cheered therefore by his encouraging words, they spent the remainder of the day in resting themselves. Then a signal was given at the first night watch, when deep sleep is wont to seize men. They caught up arms, the leader at their head, and assailed the walls. And finding the enemy without watch or guard, they entered the city with a mighty clamor. The enemy, aroused by the din, fled to safety: some staggering through the streets and along the city walls like drunken men; others falling among the Saxons in the belief that they were fellow citizens. The Saxons put to death all the elders, and kept the young people as captives. That night was filled with shouting, massacre, and plunder, until the red dawn rose and revealed the bloody victory. And when the final victory rested with the capture of the king, namely Irminfridus, he was found, after search, to have escaped with his wife and sons and a small escort.

Widukind of Corvey: early 11th century
Res Gestae Saxonicae: Migne, Patrologia Latina, Vol. 137
Trans. by H. E. W.

Discovery of America

¶ FURTHER, the King of the Danes related that there was an island in that ocean, discovered by many, and called Vineland, because the vine grows wild there, producing the best wine. For we learn not through unreliable rumor but from the convincing report of the Danes that grain is abundant there without seeding.

Likewise Adalbert, priest of holy memory, related to us that in the time of his predecessor certain nobles from Friesland had set sail to the north on a sea voyage because, according to the people of that land, from the mouth of the River Weser in a straight course northward there was no land beyond the boundless ocean. To investigate this strange phenomenon some companions made arrangements and set out from the Frisian shore with shouts of joy. Then, leaving Denmark behind, they next reached Britain and the Orkney Islands. Leaving them on their left, they had Norway on their right and in a long course they skirted along cold Iceland. Cleaving the seas next into the farthest point of the north, they again beheld all those islands that have been previously mentioned. Commending their daring venture to almighty God and the holy confessor Willehad, they suddenly plunged into that dark mist of the frozen sea that the eye could scarcely penetrate. And now the turbulent sea, in a narrow channel swirling back to the hidden source of its waters, with a tremendous force dragged the luckless seamen, now in despair or rather contemplating only death, to the deep abyss in which, it is said, all the swirling currents of the sea that appear to decrease are sucked in and finally belched out: this is commonly called a fluctuating swell. Then as they implored the mercy of God alone to save their souls, the swell swept away some of the men, while the ebb threw the others back and flung them far away. So, by the timely aid of God, they were saved from the immediate danger that their own eyes had beheld, and they rowed with all their might on the crest of the waves.

And now escaping the peril of the mist and the area of cold, they unexpectedly beached at a certain island girt with very high encircling cliffs, like a fortified town. Here they disembarked to view the place and found men skulking in underground caves in the middle of the day. In front of the entrances lay jars made of gold and metals of the kind that are considered rare and precious. And so the seamen took some of the treasure, as much as they could carry away, and joyfully and quickly returned to the ships. Suddenly they saw, coming after them, men of amazing stature, whom we call Cyclops. Preceding them came dogs, bigger than the usual size of these animals. The dogs rushed forward, caught one of the men, and in a moment he was torn to pieces in sight of the others. The rest reached the boats and escaped the danger, the giants, as they related, shouting and following them almost into the water. With such luck the Frisians reached Bremen. There they told the whole story in sequence to the priest Alebrand and to Christ and Willehad the confessor they made sacrifices for their safe return.

Adam of Bremen: 11th century
Gesta Hammaburgensis Ecclesiae Pontificum: Lappenberg, *Scriptores Rerum German.*, 1846
Trans. by H. E. W.

The Danes Sack Canterbury

¶ AFTER THE CITY was stormed the army entered, and a frightful din arose from the clamor of voices and the blaring of trumpets, to such a pitch that the entire foundations of the city seemed shattered. For some were butchered at the sword, others were burned in the flames, many more were thrown headlong from the wall, not a few expired, hanged by their genitals. The women were compelled to produce the treasures they did not possess: their hair disheveled, they were cast to the flames, every one of them, in each street of the city. The children, torn from their mothers' breasts, were speared or plowed under and crushed to pieces.

Now St. Elphege was unable to endure such a decimation of his people. When the throng of monks had been surrounded in the church, he suddenly escaped from the hands of his captors and dashed from the church. Running to a spot heaped with corpses, he made his way among the wedge formations of the enemy and cried out: "Spare them, spare them, and if you realize that you are men,

cease the persecution of innocent childhood. That is not victory for
you, when innocent babes are slain, and it is not accounted to your
glory, whatever is permissible in war against the meek and the mild.
Look at me, who have always frankly castigated your impious misdeeds, who shuddered at the captives punished by you, and clothed
them and ransomed them—let your fury be directed rather against
me."

And so presently he was captured; hands caught at his throat, pre-
venting him from speaking. He was handcuffed, his cheeks were
gashed by nails, and his sides were beaten with fists and feet. They
also set fire to the church and consumed the Lord's flock in the
jaws of the sword, and they kept the bishop for seven months in a
narrow cell. Meanwhile the Lord's wrath began to blaze against the
murderous nation so that in a short time 2,000 of theirs were laid low
by gastric agonies, and the remaining horde also, similarly affected,
awaited a like end.

Osbern of Canterbury: 11th century
Life of St. Alphage: Migne, *Patro-
logia Latina,* Vol. 149
Trans. by H. E. W.

Historical Cycles and Analogies

¶ EVEN AGAINST OUR WILL we are forced to consider the judgments
of God and the revolving universe. For, as I previously stated, we
observe that earthly matters and forces revolve in the course of time
like the heavens that turn from east to west. And, to prevent us from
thinking that mortal things find rest in some part of the universe,
there too they experience a decline like a sick person in a fever, as
you read in Job: "They turned the night into day and I hope for the
light again after the darkness."

Wherever they turn we see that things having no stability experience grief and agony. Does it not appear that the dignity of the
universe rolls back and forth like a sick man, as I said? For men in
a fever set their hope of rest in a change of position and so when
they are in pain they toss hither and thither in frequent turnings. So,
certainly, temporal power passed from Babylon to the Medes, then

to the Persians, afterward to the Greeks, lastly to the Romans and in the name of the Romans was transmitted to the Franks. While it seemed permanent as if it had established a fixed abode, it began to be exposed to so many misfortunes (as is clear in my earlier statements) that it could deservedly say with Job: "When I come to the day, wearied by night agonies, I wait for night, and while I have it, afflicted with greater sorrows, again I hope for the day to come."

Finally the Franks, long experienced in arms, after extending the boundaries of their kingdom over a very wide area, bringing Rome, the capital of the world, under their own rule, and becoming an object of terror to all nations and apparently invincible, were divided among themselves not only citizens against citizens, but brothers against each other, and had a presentiment that the kingdom that, turning from east to west in a kind of flight, was believed to have found rest and stability, would be destroyed according to the Gospel. From these instances then it is clear that no reliance should be placed in transitory things and that no one who wants to lean on himself can support another man falling. Hence the prophet aptly says:

"Cursed be the man that trusteth in man;
And maketh flesh his arm.
For how will he sustain you who cannot stand?
Or how shall he strengthen you who is himself weak?"

Since then the world passes and its lust, who can doubt that we must withdraw from it to the living God who remains motionless and unchangeable, and to his blessed and eternal City? Since therefore all the kingdoms of the world have been diminished, since the kingdom of the Franks, who deserved to be the last to possess Rome, appears diminished too, let us historians, in order to show how conditions change, turn, with this change of kingdom as sufficient proof, to the immutability of the heavenly kingdom and conclude this fifth book.

Otto of Freising: 12th century
Chronica
Trans. by H. E. W.

The Holy Spear Discovered
in the First Crusade

¶ AND SO, AS WE HAVE SAID, while our men were in confusion and on the point of despair, divine mercy came to them; and He who had corrected lascivious sons consoled those who were saddened in like manner. Therefore when the city of Antioch was taken, the Lord used His power and kindness and chose a certain poor countryman, of Provençal origin, through whom He comforted us all, and gave this message for the Count and for the Bishop of Le Puy. "Andrew, apostle of God and our own Lord Jesus Christ, once warned me four times, and ordered me to come to you after the city was taken, and bring you the spear that opened the Saviour's side. Now when I set out today to fight outside the city with the others, I was seized by two knights and was almost strangled as I returned. All but dead, I fell on a stone. As I was sadly staggering to my feet, overwhelmed with grief and fear, St. Andrew came to me with a certain companion and threatened me very sharply if I did not restore the spear quickly to you."

And when the Count and the Bishop asked him about the sequence of the revelation and the vision, he replied: "First there was an earthquake, that occurred in Antioch when the army of the Franks was besieging it; such a great fear seized me that I could say nothing but 'Lord help me!' For it was night, and I was abed. And there was no one in my hut to comfort me with talk. Now when, as I said, the quake had lasted rather long and my fear kept on growing, two men appeared before me in shining raiment. One was rather elderly, white-haired, with dark eyes in harmony with his face, a white beard, broad and full, and of medium height. The other was younger and taller in appearance for a man. And the older one said to me: 'What are you doing?' And I was greatly afraid, because I did not see anyone. And I answered: 'Who are you?' And he said: 'Arise, and fear not; and listen to what I shall tell you. I am Andrew the apostle. Bring the Bishop of Le Puy and Count St. Giles, and Peter Haimund of Altopullo, and you will say to them: 'Why does the Bishop neglect to preach and to warn them to bless the people with the cross? For it would benefit them greatly.' And he added: 'Come, and I shall show you the spear of our Father Jesus Christ, that you will give to the Count, for God granted it to him from whom he was born.'

"I rose up therefore and followed him into the city, dressed in nothing but my nightshirt. And he led me into the church of St. Peter through the southern gate that the Saracens had formerly called Bafumaria. Now in the church were two lamps that gave as much light as though it were bright noon. And he said to me: 'Wait here.' And he bade me stand at the pillar which was near the steps that they mounted at noon; and his companion stood off at a distance, before the altar steps. Now St. Andrew, going below, produced the spear and gave it to me with his own hands, and said: 'Look, here is the spear that pierced the side from which the salvation of the whole world came.' And while I held it in my hand, weeping for joy I said to him: 'Master, if you will, I shall take it, and bring it to the Count.' And he said: 'Without question; for it will come to pass that the city will be taken. And then you will come with twelve men, and you will search for it here where I took it and where I shall hide it.' And he hid it. After this, he led me over the city wall back into my house, and so they went away. Then I pondered over this, and considering the condition of my poverty and your magnificence, I was afraid to approach you.

"After the time when I had set forth to a certain castle near Roia to collect alms, on the first day of Lent, at cockcrow, there stood before me St. Andrew in the same habit, and with him his previous companion; and a great light filled the house. And St. Andrew said: 'Are you awake?' Thus aroused, I answered: 'I am not asleep, Master.' And he said to me: 'Did you say what I once bade you say?' And I answered: 'Master, did I not beseech you to send another man to them? For, fearful of my poverty, I hesitated to approach them.' And he said: 'Do you know why God has brought you here, and how much He loves you, and how He chose you especially? For contempt of Him and as a punishment He made you come here. He loves you so much that the saints, now reposing in peace and knowing the grace of the divine disposition, wanted to be in the flesh and to converse with you. God chose you from all the nations, as ears of wheat are gathered from a field of oats. For in merit and favor you surpass all those who came before you and will come after, just as gold surpasses silver in value.'

60

"After this they departed, and such a sickness came upon me that I lost the sight of my eyes, and made disposition of my meager poverty. Then I began to consider that, through disregard of the apostolic vision, these things happened to me justly. And so I was comforted, and returned to the siege. Again, reflecting on my terrible poverty, I began to be afraid, if I came to you, of being hungry and that you would say I was reporting such news to secure food. So instead I kept silent. And so as time went by, when I was at the port of St. Simeon, and was sleeping with my lord William Petri under the tent, there stood beside me St. Andrew with a companion, in the same habit as before, and he spoke to me thus: 'Why did you not tell the Count and the Bishop, and the others what I had bidden you?' And I replied: 'Did I not beg you, Master, to send someone to me who would be wiser and whom they would want to hear? Besides, the Turks are on the march; coming and going, they kill.' And St. Andrew said: 'Fear not, because they will do you no harm. This too you will tell the Count: When he comes to the River Jordan, let him not be baptized there, and let him sail across. Now when he has crossed, clothed in a shirt and linen trousers, let him be dipped in the river. And after his clothes are dry, he should put them on and save them along with the Lord's spear.'

"And my Lord William Petri heard this, although he did not see the apostle. So, being comforted, I returned to the army. When I wanted to say these things to you at the same time, I was unable to find you together. So I started out for Port Mamista. When I wanted to sail thence to the island of Cyprus for supplies, St. Andrew warned me to return quickly and report to you what I had been bidden. When I thought how I would return to camp, for the port was three days' march from the army, I began to weep most bitterly since I could discover no way to return. Finally, advised by companions and by my master, I embarked on a boat and started to sail for Cyprus. And as the oars and favorable winds sped us on our way all day long until sunset, suddenly a storm arose, and within an hour or two we were driven back to the port we had left. There a very grave lassitude overcame me. After the city was captured, I came to you. And now, if you please, test what I say." The Bishop thought these were merely words, but the Count forthwith believed, and handed over the man who had said this to be guarded by his chaplain Raymund.

The very next night our Lord Jesus Christ appeared to a certain priest named Stephen, who was lamenting his and his companions'

imminent death. For some men had terrified him when they came
down from the castle, saying that the Turks were now coming down
from the mountain into the city, and that our men were fleeing and
had been defeated. Besides, the priest, wanting to have God as a witness of his death, had gone into the church of the ever blessed Virgin
Mary, and had made confession and asked forgiveness. Then with
some companions he began to chant the psalms. While the others
were sleeping and he alone was awake, he said: "O Lord, who will
dwell in Your tabernacle, or who will rest on Your holy mount?"
Then there stood before him a stranger of the most extraordinary
beauty and he said to him: "Man, what is this nation that has entered the city?" And the priest said: "The Christians." And he said:
"What kind of Christians?" And the priest said: "They believe that
Christ was born of the Virgin and suffered crucifixion and was buried
and rose again on the third day and ascended into heaven." And the
other one said: "And if they are Christians, why do they fear the
multitude of the pagans?" And he added: "Do you recognize me?"
And the priest replied: "I do not recognize you, except that I see you
are the most handsome of all men." And the man said: "Look carefully at me." When the priest looked intently at him, he saw that from
his head came forth the shape of the cross far brighter than the sun.
And the priest replied to the man's question: "Master, we say that
there are likenesses of our Lord Jesus Christ that present an appearance like your own." And the Lord said: "You have spoken well,
for I am He. Is it not written of men that I am the 'Lord brave and
mighty, the Lord mighty in battle'? And who is the lord in the armed
ranks." And the priest answered: "Lord, there was never one master
alone, but they have more faith in the Bishop." And the Lord said:
"You will say this to the Bishop: 'Your people have estranged me
from them by their evil actions and for that reason you shall say to
them: "The Lord has spoken thus: 'Turn to me and I shall turn
to you.' " And when they go into battle, let them say: 'Our enemies
are gathered together, and they glory in their valor. Destroy their
courage, Lord, and scatter them, because there is no other that fights
for us, except our God.' And this too you will say to them: 'If you
do what I command for five days, I shall have pity on you.' " Now
as he was saying this, a certain woman of more than ruddy countenance approached. Looking at the Lord, she said: "Lord, what do
you say to this man?" The Lord replied: "Mistress, ask him what
this nation is that has entered the city." And the mistress said: "O my

Lord, they are those about whom I question you so much." When the priest struck his companion who was sleeping nearby, in order to have a witness to such a great vision, they vanished from his sight.

In the morning the priest ascended the mountain where our chiefs, except the commander, were opposite the castle of the Turks; he was guarding the castle on the southern hill. So, after calling a council the priest talked to our chiefs and, to prove the truth of his statements, he swore by the cross. Wishing to convince the unbelievers, he was ready to go through fire or to jump from the top of the tower. Then the chief swore that they would not flee from Antioch, nor would they leave it except by common consent; for the people at that time thought that the chiefs wanted to escape to the harbor. So, many were comforted. For the night before a few remained faithful, who had refused to flee. If the Bishop and Boymund had not opened the gates of the city, quite a few would have stayed. However, William of Granduna fled, along with his brother, and many others, laity and clergy. It happened however to many that, while they escaped from the city at the greatest risk, they incurred the greater risk of death at the hands of the Turks. At that time a great many revelations came to us through our brothers, and we saw a miraculous sign in heaven. For an enormous star stood over the city, through the night, and after a while it broke into three parts, and fell into the Turkish lines. So our men were somewhat comforted; and waited for the fifth day that the priest foretold.

Now on the next day, after making the necessary preparations and after sending out all others from the church of St. Peter, we began to dig, in company with the man who had spoken about the spear. Now among these twelve devout men were the Bishop of Aura, and Raymund the Count's chaplain, who wrote this, and the Count himself, and Pontius of Baladun, and Faraldus of Thouart. After digging from morning to night, in the evening some began to despair of finding the spear. For the Count had gone off to guard the castle; but in his place and that of the others who were tired of digging, we brought fresh men, who set to manfully.

A young man who had spoken about the spear, noting our weariness, went down in his nightshirt, stripped and barefooted into the pit; and he called upon us to beg God to give us His spear, for the comfort and the victory of His people. Finally the Lord, impressed by the grace of his devotion, revealed His spear to us. And I, who wrote this, kissed the point of it as it came into view above the ground. I cannot express the joy and exultation that filled the city then. The spear was found on the fourteenth of June.

Raymund of Agiles: 12th century
Historia Francorum qui ceperunt Jerusalem: Migne, *Patrologia Latina,* Vol. 155
Trans. by H. E. W.

Louis VII's March Eastward

¶ THUS FAR we were engaged in play, because we neither suffered injuries from men's ill will nor feared dangers arising from the cunning of crafty men. However, from the time when we entered Bulgaria, a land belonging to the Greeks, our valor was put to test and our emotions were aroused. When about to enter the uninhabited portion, we stocked ourselves in the poor town of Brandiz with provisions, the most of which Hungary supplied via the Danube. There the fleet which the Germans had brought and abandoned was so huge that for a long time it furnished the citizens with building material and firewood. Our men took the smaller types of these boats and, after crossing the stream, brought supplies from a certain Hungarian castle which was not far away. Here we first encountered the copper money *staminae,* and for one of these we unhappily gave five denarii, or rather we lost a mark on twelve solidi. Thus, at the entrance to their own land the Greeks stained themselves with perjury, for you should remember what has already been said, namely, that the messengers had sworn on behalf of their emperor to furnish us a suitable market and exchange. But we crossed the wasteland and entered the exceedingly beautiful and rich territory which stretches without interruption all the way to Constantinople. Here for the first time wrongs began to arise and to be noticed; for the other countries, which sold us supplies properly, found us entirely peaceful. The Greeks, however, closed their cities and fortresses and offered their wares by letting them down from the walls on ropes. But food furnished in such measure did not suffice our throng. Therefore, the pilgrims, unwilling to endure want in the midst of plenty, procured supplies for themselves by plunder and pillage.

Odo of Deuil: 12th century
De Profectione Ludovici VII in Orientem
Trans. by V. G. Barry. Columbia University Press, 1948

Eyewitness Account of Crusaders at Jerusalem

¶ THERE THEY STAYED for four days, during which they put the bishop in charge of the church of St. George and stationed men on the heights to guard the city. Then they continued their march to Jerusalem. On that very day they came to the fortress of Emmaus, as it is called. That night one hundred of our soldiers, inspired by cunning and prompted by honor, mounted their horses and in the early dawn passed near Jerusalem and rode on to Bethlehem.

One of these was Tancred, and another Baldwin of Burg. When the Christians who dwelt there, that is, the Greeks and Syrians, discovered that the Franks had arrived they were greatly overjoyed. However, unaware at first of the identity of these people, they thought they were either Turks or Arabs. But when they observed them more clearly at closer range and were sure they were Franks, they showed their joy instantly, taking their crosses and texts and going forward weeping and piously chanting and preceding them; weeping because they were afraid that such a small handful of people would very easily be slain by such a large host of pagans, who they knew were in the land, and singing because they rejoiced with those whose coming they had long been hoping for and who they felt would restore to its former prestige the Christianity that had for so long been ruined by these wicked people.

At once a thanksgiving service dedicated to God was held in the church of St. Mary. Then they visited Christ's birthplace, gave a warm kiss of peace to the Syrians, and rapidly returned to the holy city. Then our army followed and approached the city, leaving Gabaon

65

on the left. When the advance guard displayed their raised banner to the citizens, forthwith the enemy within came out. But those who had so hastily come out were presently driven back more hastily and retreated into the city.

The seventh of June dawned brightly when
The Franks besieged Jerusalem.

The city itself is situated on hilly ground, with no streams, forests or springs except the spring of Siloah, which produces sufficient water at times and at other times runs dry. This tiny spring lies in the depths of a valley under Mt. Sion, beneath the course of the River Cedron that flows in winter through the Valley of Josaphat. Many cisterns amply filled with water abound in the city. If they are properly supervised they offer at all times an unfailing supply to all the inhabitants, both man and beast, except for the winter storms. The city is of adequate size, built in a circular shape, giving the appearance neither of smallness nor of pretentious magnitude. On the west is the Tower of David and on either side a wall enclosing the city, which is hewn solidly from its base to the middle and built of blocks of quarrystone fastened together with molten lead. Fortified with provisions, with only fifteen or twenty men inside to defend it, it can never be stormed by force by any army whatever.

In this city too there is a circular temple of the Lord, situated in the same spot where Solomon in earlier times built his second wonder. Although it can in no sense be compared with that ancient plan, still it is a wonderfully constructed and very beautiful building. In the center there is a huge native rock, and where it is disfigured the temple itself is rather obstructed. I do not know why the Eternal allows the place to be occupied without destroying it utterly. They say, however, that is the spot where the angel who smote the people stood, on whom David gazed in great dread: "Lo, I have sinned: but these sheep, what have they done?"

They say, too, that on that rock stands the Ark of the Covenant, with the rod and the tablets of the Ten Commandments well fastened because Joshua King of Judea ordered it to be placed in the sanctuary of the temple, saying: "You shall in no wise carry it" from that place. For he foresaw the future Captivity. But there is an objection in what we read in Jeremiah's descriptions, that Jeremiah himself had hidden the rock in Arabia, saying that it must not be found until many nations gathered together. . . . For these and many other reasons the city is venerable and glorious At sight of it, when the Franks saw how difficult it was to storm, they were ordered by our leaders to make wooden ladders by means of which, when these were later on set against the wall, they mounted to the top in a powerful assault and, perhaps with the aid of God, attacked the city.

This done, on the following Sabbath at the command of the chiefs, with trumpets blaring in the clear morning light, in an amazing attack they assailed the city from all sides. When this had continued until the sixth hour of the day and still they were unable to enter over the ladders they had set up because they were too few, they dejectedly gave up the assault. Then a plan was devised and the engineers were ordered to build machines that could be moved up to the walls and, with God's help, thus achieve the result of their hopes. This was done. During this time there was no lack of bread or meat.

But as the location, as mentioned above, lacked water and rivers, our men and their beasts were greatly distressed for want of drinking water. Hence, under the compulsion of necessity, they searched for water far and wide and laboriously brought it for the siege in their leather skins, from a distance of four of five miles. Once the engines were ready, that is the battering rams and the mining devices, they prepared for the assault. Among other contrivances, they fastened together a tower made of small pieces of wood, because large timber was lacking. At night, at a given order, they carried it piece by piece to the most favorable point of the city. And so, in the morning, after preparing the catapults and the other contraptions, they very quickly set it up, fitted together, not far from the wall. This erection they tied fast and bound with leather thongs on the outside, slowly moving it nearer the wall. Then a few daring soldiers at the sound of the trumpet mounted it, and from that position they immediately began to launch stones and arrows. In retaliation against them the Saracens proceeded to defend themselves similarly and with their slings hurled flaring brands soaked in oil and fat and fitted with small torches on the previously mentioned tower and the soldiers on it. Many therefore fighting in this manner on either side met ever-present death.

In that spot where Count Raymund and his men stood, at Mt. Sion, they made a vigorous assault with their engines. Elsewhere, where Duke Godefrey was, and Robert Count of Normandy, and Robert of Flanders, the assault on the wall was more forceful. These were the tactics that day. On the following day, with trumpets resounding, they repeated their actions with greater vigor, breaching the wall in one place with battering rams. In front of the wall defenses two stakes hung, fastened with ropes, that the Saracens had prepared to stop the enemy rushing on them and showering stones. The tower was then moved up to the wall and the ropes that tied the bundles of wood were cut, and from the same wood the Franks fitted together a bridge that they cleverly extended and threw from the tower across the wall.

One stone citadel on the wall was now blazing away, over which our engineers had hurled burning firebrands. The fire was fed by the planks of timber, and the smoke and flame began to issue so that none of the citizen guards could stand there any longer. Presently therefore the Franks entered the city at midday, on the day dedicated to Venus, with bugles blowing and all in an uproar and manfully attacking and crying "Help us, God," and raised a standard on the top of the wall. The heathens, utterly disgraced, all changed their bold stand into a scurrying flight through the alleyways of the city. The more quickly they fled, the more quickly were they driven into flight. Count Raymund, attacking on another side, was unaware of this, and his men too, until they saw the Saracens leap over the top of the wall in front of them. At sight of this, they rushed joyfully as fast as possible to the city and with the rest began to rout and slay the wicked enemy.

Then some Saracens, both Arabs and Ethiopians, fled into the citadel of David, others shut themselves in the temples of the Lord and of Solomon. In the halls of these temples they were fiercely attacked; there was nowhere for them to escape from our warriors. On the top of the temple of Solomon that they had climbed in their flight, many were pierced to death by their arrows and wildly hurled down from the wall. In this temple too almost 10,000 were decapitated. If you had been there, you would have seen our feet bespattered to the soles with the blood of the slain. What is there to tell? Not a single life was spared. But they too spared neither women nor children. You would have seen an amazing sight when our squires and the poorest infantry troops, learning of the Saracens' cunning, slit the bellies even of the slain to extract from their bowels the bezants that they had swallowed while alive. After a few days they piled up the bodies in a great heap and burned them in order to find the coins more easily among the burnt ashes.

Tancred quickly entered the temple of the Lord and seized many gold and silver ornaments—a sinful theft—and precious stones. But atoning for this later on, he returned all of it to a holy place or bought it.

> Our soldiers now with swords drawn scour the city.
> They spare no one, they show no suppliant pity.
> Like rotting fruit that falls lie strewn the dead,
> Like acorns shaken from the oak, 'tis said.

After such a massacre they entered the homes and took whatever they found there so that whoever first entered a house, whether rich or poor, in no way prevented anyone else, to their own loss, from seizing and keeping as their own whatever they found in home or palace. This gave a sense of mutual right of possession. The result was that many who were poor became wealthy.

Then, going to the sepulcher of the Lord and His glorious temple, clerics and laity, chanting in a loud exulting voice the new hymn to the Lord, together joyously visited the sacred places so long yearned for, making offering and humble supplications. O what an hour craved by us all! What a moment to be remembered beyond all others! What an incident above all others desired! Truly craved, since it had always been an object of yearning by all worshippers of the Catholic faith in their innermost yearning heart, that the place in which the Creator of all creatures, God made man, by His manifold compassions for mankind, being born, dying, and being resurrected, conferred the gift of new-born salvation, a place at last cleansed from the contagion of the heathens dwelling therein, long defiled by their superstition, should be restored to its former prestige by the believers and the faithful. And truly memorable and rightly to be remembered, because whatever our Lord Jesus Christ, on earth a man dwelling with men, did and taught, was recalled and brought back to most glorious memory. . . .

> On July fifteenth, it was when
> The day was shining clear and bright
> Jerusalem was taken then
> By Gallic strength, by Frankish might.
> The year was centuries eleven
> Without the one to make it even
> Since Virgin Mary, at His birth,
> Gave us a king to rule the earth.

Meanwhile the Turks and Arabs and about 500 dark Ethiopians who had gone into the citadel of David begged Count Raymund, who was in lodgings near the tower, just to let them depart alive, their money being kept in the citadel itself. He granted this request and they went off to Ascalon.

Foucher: 12th century
Historia Hierosolymitana
Trans. by H. E. W.

The Origin of Wassail

¶ MEANWHILE the envoys returned from Germany, bringing eighteen ships filled with picked soldiers. They also brought Hengist's daughter, named Rowena, whose beauty seemed second to none. After they came Hengist invited King Vortigern to his home to see the new building and the new soldiers who had arrived. The king came immediately, privately, praised such a remarkable piece of work, and kept the invited soldiers. When he was refreshed at a royal banquet, a girl came out from her chamber bearing a gold goblet filled with wine; then, approaching nearer, she made obeisance to the king and said: "Lord King, wacht heil!" The king, gazing at the girl's face, greatly admired her beauty and became inflamed with desire. Then he asked his interpreter what the girl had said and what he should reply. The interpreter answered: "She called you Lord King and honored you with an expression of greeting. What you ought to reply now is: 'Drinc heil!' "

Then Vortigern replying "Drinc heil!" bade the girl drink; and he took the cup from her hand and kissed her and drank. From that day to this the custom prevailed in Britain for a person who drinks at a banquet to say to another: "Wacht heil!" The next man to drink responds: "Drinc heil!"

Now Vortigern, intoxicated with a different kind of drink as Satan entered into his heart, asked her father for her hand. Satan, I say, had entered into his heart because, although a Christian, he desired to have intercourse with a heathen. Hengist, like the wise man that he was, on discovering the king's fickleness, consulted his brother Horsa and the other elders who were present on what steps to take

70

regarding the king's request. But the unanimous opinion was that the girl should be given to the king, and they would ask in return the province of Kent. Immediately the girl was given to Vortigern, and the province of Kent to Hengist, without the knowledge of Count Goranganus who ruled in that province.

So the king married the heathen girl that very night, and she pleased him beyond measure. Hence he very soon fell foul of his nobles and his sons; for he had already sons whose names were Vortimer, Katigern, and Pascentius.

Geoffrey of Monmouth: 12th century
Historia Regum Britanniae
Trans. by H. E. W.

William Tell: Danish Style[1]

¶ TOKE, who had served some while with the king, had made many men foes to his virtues by the services wherein he overpassed the zeal of his comrades. Talking in his cups among the feasters, he chanced to boast that if an apple, however small, were set at a distance upon a stick, he would hit it with the first shaft he aimed. This speech, catching the ears of his detractors, reached the hearing of the king. But the unscrupulous monarch presently turned the father's confidence to the peril of the son, and commanded that this most sweet pledge of Toke's life should be put in the place of the stick with the apple on his head, and should suffer with his own head for that windy boast, unless he who made the promise should with the first arrow that he tried strike the apple off it. Thus the treacherous slanders of others took up his half-tipsy vaunt, and the soldier was forced by his king's behest to do better than his promises, so that his word bound him to more than their own consequences. . . .

So Toke brought the lad forth, and warned him straitly to await the singing of the arrow with steadfast ear and unswerving head, so as not to balk by any slight motion the successful trial of his skill. Also he considered a plan to remove the lad's fear and made him

1. Not only fantasy, but legend and folklore crept into the medieval histories; here is an example offering a familiar episode.

turn away his face, that he should not be scared by the sight of the missile. Then he put out three arrows from the quiver; the first that he fitted to the string struck the mark proposed. . . . But when the king asked Toke why he had taken three shafts from the quiver, when he was to try his fortunes but once with the bow, Toke answered: "That I might avenge on thyself the miss of the first with the point of the others, lest perchance my innocence might suffer and thy violence escape."

Saxo Grammaticus: 12th century
Historia Danica
Trans. by O. Elton. London: David Nutt, 1894

Richard the Lion-Hearted

¶ HE WAS TALL in stature, of handsome appearance, his hair between red and reddish yellow, straight-limbed, rather long in the arms, the better for drawing the sword or more effective for attack; none the less his legs were long, and his entire person was well-proportioned. He had a commanding look, to which his character and habits added a marked effect; capable of achieving the utmost praise not only through his ancestral prestige but from his own eminent qualities. But why strive to extol with boundless eulogies such a great person?

No stranger he needs to commend him, for merited glory
He has achieved in abundance; conjoined is his fame with his story.

Assuredly he surpassed all others both in his good character and in his great strength. Memorable in war and in his rule, his mighty deeds overshadow every manifestation of glory, however distinguished. He is certainly to be considered happy, in so far as a man may be, if he had not had rivals who envied his glorious deeds. This was their only source of hatred, that he was great, for one can never punish the envious more than by serving virtue.

Itinerarium Regis Ricardi: 12th century
Trans. by H. E. W.

72

Wreck of the White Ship

¶ THOMAS, THE SON OF STEPHAN, approached the king and offering him a gold mark, said: "Stephan the son of Airard was my father and all his life served your father on the sea. For he took him in his ship and sailed to England. In this kind of duty he pleased him, serving until his death, and was honored with many rewards and flourished exceedingly among his people. This privilege, your royal majesty, I ask of you and the vessel that is called the *White Ship* I have out-fitted well in the king's service." The king answered: "I thank you for your request. I have selected a suitable ship that I will not change; but my sons, William and Richard, whom I love like my own life, I now entrust to you, along with the nobility of my realm."

Hearing this, the sailors rejoiced and congratulated the king's son and asked him for a drink of wine. But he ordered three hogsheads of wine to be given to them. They took the wine and drank and toasted their companions repeatedly and indulging too much they became intoxicated. By the king's command a large number of vassals and their sons boarded the ship; about three hundred, I believe, were in the ill-fated vessel. Two monks of Tyre and Count Stephan with two knights and many others left the boat because they noticed a great crowd of wanton and insolent young people on board. There were fifty skilled oarsmen, rough marines who, seating themselves in the ship, became impudent and, forgetting themselves in their drunken state, addressed scarcely anyone with respect. Alas, how many of them had their vacant minds turned with righteous devotion toward God, who "tempers the wild fury of sea and air." Then they drove off the clerics who had come over to bless them, and the other assistants who brought holy water, mocking them and laughing disgracefully; but after a while they had their revenge for the derision they suffered.

Only passengers, with the king's treasure and the casks containing wine, were in Thomas' ship, and they advised him to follow closely the royal boat that was now far out at sea. Thomas, in his drunken stupor, was confident in his own courage and that of his men and boldly promised that he would outstrip all those who had gone ahead.

Finally he gave the signal to sail away. At once the seamen seized the oars eagerly, and joyfully, because they did not know what was before them, they made the ship speed through the water with a great impact. As the drunken oarsmen rowed with all their might and the luckless pilot was in no condition to steer a course through the sea, a huge reef that is hidden when the tide ebbs every day and is exposed as the sea flows in, violently dashed against the left side of the *White Ship*. Two planks were suddenly shattered, and the ship, alas, sank. In such a catastrophe they all raised a shout but the water soon filled their mouths, and they perished together. Only two men grasped the boom on which the sail hung, and clinging to it most of the night they waited for whatever help might come. One of them was the hangman of Rouen, named Beroldus, and the other was a boy of noble birth called Goisfredus, the son of Gislibert of Aquila.

The moon was then at its nineteenth in the sign of Taurus and for almost nine hours it lit up the world with its beams and made the sea visible to all upon it. Thomas the captain after the first plunge recovered his strength and warily raised his head above the waves and seeing the heads of those who clung, as best they could, to the spar, he asked: "What has become of the king's son?"

And when the shipwrecked men replied that he had perished along with all his companions, he said: "Henceforth my life is a misery." Saying this, in his despair he resolved to die right there rather than face the frenzy of the enraged king for the death of his son or endure the punishment of a long imprisonment.

Ordericus Vitalis: 12th century
Historia Ecclesiastica
Trans. by H. E. W.

Ban on Women Causes Church Clamor!

¶ GEOFFREY, THE ARCHBISHOP, having returned to Rouen from attending the Council of Reims, held a synod in the third week of November and, stirred up by the late papal decrees, dealt sharply and rigorously with the priests of his diocese. Among other canons of the council which he promulgated was that which interdicted them from commerce with females of any description, and against such transgressors he launched the terrible sentence of excommunication. As the priests shrank from submitting to this grievous burden and in loud mutterings vented their complaints of the struggle between the flesh and the spirit to which they were subjected, the archbishop ordered one Albert, a man free of speech who had used some offensive words, I know not what, to be arrested on the spot, and he was presently thrust into the common prison.

This prelate was a Breton and guilty of many indiscretions, warm and obstinate in temper, and severe in his aspect and manner, harsh in his censures and, withal, indiscreet and a great talker. The other priests, witnessing this extraordinary proceeding, were utterly confounded, and when they saw that, without being charged with any crime or undergoing any legal examination, a priest was dragged like a thief from a church to a dungeon, they became so exceedingly terrified that they knew not how to act, doubting whether they had best defend themselves or take to flight. Meanwhile, the archbishop rose from his seat in a violent rage, and hastily leaving the synod summoned his guards, whom he already posted outside with instructions what they were to do. The archbishop's retainers then rushed into the church with arms and staves and began to lay about them, without respect of persons, on the assembled clergy who were conversing together. Some of these ecclesiastics ran to their lodgings through the muddy streets of the city, though they were robed in their albs; others snatched up some rails and stones which they chanced to find, and stood on their defense; whereupon their cowardly assailants betook themselves to flight and sought refuge in the sacristy, followed closely by the indignant clergy. The archbishop's people, ashamed of having been discomfited by an unarmed tonsured band, in the extremity of their fury summoned to their aid all the cooks, bakers, and scullions they could muster in the neighborhood, and had the effrontery to renew the conflict within the sacred precincts. All whom they found in the church or cemetery, whether engaged in the broil or innocently looking on, they beat and cuffed, or inflicted on them some other bodily injury.

Then Hugh of Longueville and Ansquetil of Cropus, and some other ecclesiastics of advanced age and great piety happened to be in the church, conversing together on confession and other profitable subjects, or reciting, as was their duty, the service of the hours to the praise of God. The archbishop's domestics were mad enough to fall on these priests, treated them shamefully and so outrageously that they hardly restrained themselves from taking their lives, though they asked for mercy on their bended knees. These old priests, being at length dismissed, made their escape from the city as soon as they could, together with their friends who had before fled, without stopping to receive the bishop's license and benediction. They carried the sorrowful tidings to their parishioners and concubines, and, to prove the truth of their reports, exhibited the wounds and livid bruises on their persons. The archdeacons and canons and all quiet citizens were afflicted at this cruel onslaught, and compassionated with the servants of God who had suffered such unheard-of insults. Thus the blood of her priests was shed in the very bosom of Holy Mother Church, and the holy synod was converted into a scene of riot and mockery.

The archbishop, overwhelmed with consternation, retired to his private apartments, where he concealed himself during the uproar, but shortly afterwards when the ecclesiastics had betaken themselves to flight, as we have already related, his wrath subsided, and going to the church he put on his stole, and sprinkling holy water, reconciled the church which he had polluted and his sorrowing canons.

Ordericus Vitalis: 12th century
Historia Ecclesiastica
Trans. by T. Forester, 1856

Exhortation of Pope Urban II to the First Crusade

¶ YOU KNOW, my beloved brethren, and it is fitting that your charity should know, how the Creator of Mankind, assuming the flesh for the salvation of all of us, a man dwelling among men, had promised our fathers long ago the promised land, and illuminated it by His own presence, and by His works of dispensation and the numerous miracles He performed rendered it specially glorious. . . . The Prophet says: "The Lord loves the gates of Sion above all the tabernacles of Jacob." . . . The cradle of our salvation, then, the native land of the

Lord, the mother of religion, the people without a God and the son of the Egyptian maidservant possess in violence. . . . But what is written? "Cast out the maidservant and her son." For the unrighteous nation of the Saracens, followers of worldly traditions, has ruthlessly and tyrannically been oppressing for many long years now the holy places, where the steps of the Lord stood. The faithful have been subjugated and condemned to slavery. Dogs have entered the holy places, the sanctuary has been profaned; the people that worship God have been humiliated. The chosen race suffers unworthy servitude. . . . Virgins are forced to fornicate, or to perish by torture.

Woe is us, who have fallen into this calamity at this dangerous time, a calamity that David, the faithful king, the chosen of the Lord, foresaw in his heart when he lamented and said: "O God, the nations have come into your inheritance, they have defiled your holy temple."

You chosen men, therefore, arm yourselves with the zeal of God. Gird yourselves stoutly, each with his sword at his side. Gird yourselves and be the sons of the Omnipotent. For it is better to die in war than to see the tribulations of our nation and our saints. . . . Go forth, and the Lord will be with you. Turn the weapons that you stained unlawfully with mutual carnage against the enemies of the faith and the name of Christ.

William of Tyre: 12th century
Historia Rerum in Partibus Transmarinis Gestarum
Trans. by H. E. W.

Disturbance at Oxford

¶ AT THIS TIME the legate, having come to Oxford and been received with the highest honor, as was due to him, was entertained in the house of the canons, which was at Oseney Abbey, where the scholar-clerks before breakfast time sent him an honorable present, in the way of meat and drink, and after breakfast proceeded to his place of abode to pay their salutation to him and to visit him out of respect. On their approach, however, a transalpine porter, with unbecoming and improper raillery raising his voice after the manner of the Romans, and holding the door a little open, said: "What do you want?"

To which the clerks replied, "We want his lordship the legate, that we may pay our respects to him"; for they confidently believed that they would receive honor for honor. The doorkeeper, however, with taunting speeches saucily refused admittance to them all, with haughtiness and abuse; on seeing which the clerks rushed forward with impetuosity and forced their way in, whilst the Roman attendants, in their endeavors to keep them back, struck them with their fists and sticks. Whilst the contending parties were engaged in repeated blows and taunts, it happened that a poor Irish chaplain was standing at the door of the kitchen and had earnestly besought for something to be given to him, in God's name, after the custom of a poor and hungry man, when the master of the legate's cooks (who was also his brother whom he had placed at the head of that office, that no poison might be given to him, which he, the legate, greatly feared) heard him, but paid no heed to his request, and becoming angry with the poor man, threw in his face some boiling water drawn from the cauldron where fat meat was being cooked. At this injury to the poor man, one of the clerks, a native of the Welsh borders, cried out, "Shame on us to endure anything like this," and drew a bow which he carried (for as the tumult had increased, some of the clerks had seized on whatever arms came to hand) and by an arrow discharged from it himself pierced the body of the cook (whom the clerks satirically called "Nabuzardan," that means chief of the cooks), and on the fall of the dead man a cry was raised, at hearing which the legate was astounded and struck with fear, which can overtake the boldest man, and he betook himself to the tower of the church, clad in his canonical hood, and secured the doors behind him. When the darkness of the night had put an end to the tumult, he put off his canonical dress, quickly mounted his best horse and under the guidance of some persons who knew the most private fords, crossed the river at the nearest part to him, although with much danger, for the purpose of flying under the protection of the king's wings as soon as possible, for the clerks, carried away by rage, continued to seek for the legate in the most secret hiding places, crying out: "Where is that simoniacal usurer, that plunderer of revenues and thirster for money, who perverts the king, subverts the kingdom, and enriches foreigners with spoil taken from us?" The legate, in his flight, hearing the cries of his pursuers, said within himself—

> When madness at full speed doth run,
> A wise man seeks its path to shun;

and patiently enduring all these things, he became like a man who did not hear them, as if he had no power to refute them. Having crossed the river with much trouble (as above mentioned) and with only a few attendants, owing to the difficulty of the passage the rest remaining concealed in the convent, he came to the king breathless and in a state of alarm, and with tears and sighs interrupting his discourse, he explained to the king, as well as his attendants, the series of events which had happened, making a serious complaint in the matter. The king was astonished at his pitiable story and sympathized much with him, and sent the Earl of Warrenne with an armed troop to Oxford with all haste to rescue the Romans who were lying concealed there, and to arrest the scholars. Among the latter, one Master Odo, a lawyer, was roughly seized and, together with thirty others, was ignominiously consigned to close imprisonment in the castle of Wallingford, near Oxford; whilst the legate excommunicated all the abettors of this enormous offense.

Matthew Paris: 13th century
Chronica Maiora
Trans. by J. A. Giles, 1854

Character of King Henry II, of England[1]

¶ HENRY II, King of England, had a reddish complexion, rather dark, and a large round head. His eyes were gray, bloodshot, and flashed in anger. He had a fiery countenance, his voice was tremulous, and his neck a little bent forward; but his chest was broad and his arms were muscular. His body was fleshy and he had an enormous paunch, rather by the fault of nature than from gross feeding. For his diet was temperate, and indeed in all things, considering he was a

---

1. Henry II (1133–1189), founder of the Plantagenet line, is perhaps best remembered today for his dispute with Thomas à Becket. The Queen referred to is Eleanor of Aquitaine, and their children included Richard the Lion-hearted and John, among the more famous and infamous of England's kings.

prince, he was moderate, and even parsimonious. In order to reduce and cure, as far as possible, this natural tendency and defect, he waged a continual war, so to speak, with his own belly by taking immoderate exercise. For in time of war, in which he was almost always engaged, he took little rest, even during the intervals of business and action. Times of peace were no seasons of repose and indulgence to him, for he was immoderately fond of the chase and devoted himself to it with excessive ardor. At the first dawn of day he would mount a fleet horse and indefatigably spend the day in riding through the woods, penetrating the depths of forests and crossing the ridges of hills. On his return home in the evening he was seldom seen to sit down, either before he took his supper or after; for notwithstanding his own great fatigue, he would weary all his court by being constantly on his legs. But it is one of the most useful rules of life, not to have too much of any one thing, and even medicine is not in itself perfect and always to be used; even so it befell this king. For he had frequent swellings in his legs and feet, increased much by his violent exercise on horseback, which added to his other complaints, and if they did not bring on serious disorders, at least hastened that which is the source of all, old age. In stature he may be reckoned among men of moderate height, which was not the case with either of his sons; the two eldest being somewhat above the middle height, and the two youngest somewhat below.

When his mind was undisturbed and he was not in an angry mood, he spoke with great eloquence, and, what was remarkable in those days, he was well learned. He was also affable, flexible, and facetious, and, however he smothered his inward feelings, second to no one in courtesy. Withal, he was so clement a prince that when he had subdued his enemies, he was overcome himself by his pity for them. Resolute in war and provident in peace, he so much feared the doubtful fortune of the former that, as the comic poet writes, he tried all courses before he resorted to arms. Those whom he lost in battle he lamented with more than a prince's sorrow, having a more humane feeling for the soldiers who had fallen than for the survivors; and bewailing the dead more than he cared for the living. In troublesome times no man was more courteous, and when all things were safe, no man more harsh. Severe to the unruly, but clement to the humble; hard toward his own household, but liberal to strangers; profuse abroad, but sparing at home; those whom he once hated he would scarcely ever love, and from those he loved he seldom withdrew his regard. He was inordinately fond of hawking and hunting, whether his falcons stooped on their prey or his sagacious hounds, quick of scent and swift of foot, pursued the chase. Would to God he had been as zealous in his devotion as he was in his sports.

It is said that after the grievous dissensions between him and his sons, raised by their mother, he had no respect for the obligations of the most solemn treaties. True it is that from a certain natural inconstancy he often broke his word, preferring rather, when driven to straits, to forfeit his promise than depart from his purpose. In all his doings he was provident and circumspect, and on this account he was sometimes slack in the administration of justice, and, to his people's great cost, his decisions on all proceedings were dilatory. Both God and right demand that justice should be administered gratuitously, yet all things were set to sale and brought great wealth both to the clergy and laity; but their end was like Gehazi's gains.

He was a great maker of peace, and kept it himself; a liberal alms-giver, and an especial benefactor to the Holy Land. He loved the humble, curbed the nobility, and trod down the proud; filling the hungry with good things, and sending the rich empty away; exalting the meek, and putting down the mighty from their seat. He ventured on many detestable usurpations in things belonging to God, and through a zeal for justice (but not according to knowledge), he joined the rights of the Church to those of the crown, and therein confused them, in order to center all in himself. Although he was the son of the Church and received his crown from her hands, he either dissembled or forgot the sacramental unction. He could scarcely spare an hour to hear mass, and then he was more occupied in counsels and conversation about affairs of state than in his devotions. The revenues of the churches during their avoidance he drew into his own treasury, laying hands on that which belonged to Christ; and as he was always in fresh troubles and engaged in mighty wars, he expended all the money he could get, and lavished upon unrighteous soldiers what was due to the priests. In his great prudence he devised many plans which, however, did not all turn out according to his expectations; but no great mishap ever occurred which did not originate in some trifling circumstance.

He was the kindest of fathers to his legitimate children during their childhood and youth, but as they advanced in years looked on them with an evil eye, treating them worse than a stepfather; and although he had such distinguished and illustrious sons, whether it was that

81

he would not have them prosper too fast or whether they were ill-deserving, he could never bear to think of them as his successors. And as human prosperity can neither be permanent nor perfect, such was the exquisite malice of fortune against this king that where he should have received comfort, he met with opposition; where security, danger; where peace, turmoil; where support, ingratitude; where quiet and tranquillity, disquiet and disturbance. Whether it happened from unhappy marriages or for the punishment of the father's sins, there was never any good agreement either of the father with his sons, or of the sons with their parent, or between themselves.

At length, all pretenders to the government and disturbers of the peace being put down, and the brothers, his sons, and all others, both at home and abroad, being reconciled, all things succeeded according to his will. Would to God that he had, even late, acknowledged this crowning proof of the divine mercy by works worthy of repentance. I had almost forgotten to mention that his memory was so good that, notwithstanding the multitudes who continually surrounded him, he never failed of recognizing anyone he had ever seen before, nor did he forget anything important which he had ever heard. He was also master of nearly the whole course of history, and well versed in almost all matters of experience. To conclude in few words: if this king had been finally chosen of God and had turned himself to obey His commands, such were his natural endowments that he would have been, beyond all comparison, the noblest of all princes of the earth in his times.

Giraldus Cambrensis: 13th century
Expugnatio Hibernica
Trans. by T. Wright, 1881

England Helps Ireland

¶ So DERMOT MACMURROUGH, King of Leinster and ruler of a fifth of Ireland, governed in our time the eastern coast of the island next to Great Britain, except for the sea between them. From his early youth, and affected by his new kingdom, he oppressed the nobles and tyrannized monstrously and intolerably over the chiefs in his country.

There was another misfortune. For when O'Rourke, King of Meath, had set out on an expedition to distant regions, his wife, the daughter of O'McLaghlin, whom he had left on an island in Meath, was seized in her husband's absence by this Dermot, long burning with passion for her, and was ravished, because she wanted to be; and, since "Woman is ever fickle," she saw to it that she became the spoil of the despoiler. But since it is a fact, as both Mark Antony and Troy testify, that almost all great disasters have fallen upon the world through a woman, King O'Rourke, deeply disturbed on both accounts but far more grievously stricken by the disgrace than the loss, vented all his venom in revenge. Summoning therefore and gathering both his own forces and those of the neighboring nations, also the chief of Connaught and the monarch of all Ireland, he persuaded Roderick to the same purpose.

Now the people of Leinster, considering their king now placed in a dilemma and wedged in by the enemy on either side, recalling to their vengeful minds their wrongs long dissembled and stored deep in their hearts, feeling sympathetic with the enemy, abandoned Mac-Murrough to his fate. Dermot, seeing himself renounced on all sides by his forces and utterly deserted by fate and the favor of fortune, was now desperately troubled. After many sharp and unequal engagements with the enemy, finally, as though resorting to the last means of safety, he took ship and fled for protection. . . .

Thus, pursuing elusive fortune and very confident in the wheel of fate, MacMurrough, as his sailing ship plowed through the sea and the wind was favorable to his wishes, came to Henry II, King of England, with the intention of pleading for help. Although Henry was engaged, as a prince, in the remote regions of Aquitanian Gaul across the sea, he yet welcomed him in a kindly and affectionate manner, following his innate generosity and humanity. Hearing in sequence the reason for his exile and coming, after an oath of sub jection and a pledge of loyalty were given, he granted him letters patent to this effect: "Henry, King of England, Duke of Normandy and Aquitaine and Count of Anjou, to all his faithful English, Normans, Welsh, and Scottish and to all nations subject to his rule, greetings. When these present letters reach you, you shall know that Dermot, King of Leinster, has come under the protection of our grace and kindness. Wherefore everyone shall afford aid of restitution from our bountiful lands to this faithful subject of ours: and shall know that he has our favor and prerogative in this matter."

Giraldus Cambrensis: 13th century
Expugnatio Hibernica
Trans. by H. E. W.

Lamentation of King Richard II[1]

¶ ON SAINT MATTHEW'S DAY, just two years after the beheading of the Earl of Arundel, I, the writer of this history, was in the Tower, wherein King Richard was a prisoner, and I was present while he dined, and I marked his mood and bearing, having been taken thither for that very purpose by Sir William Beauchamp. And there and then the king discoursed in these words: "My God! a wonderful land is this, and a fickle; which hath exiled, slain, destroyed, or ruined so many kings, rulers, and great men, and is ever tainted and toileth with strife and variance and envy"; and then he recounted the histories and names of sufferers from the earliest habitations of the kingdom. Perceiving then the trouble of his mind, and how that none of his own men nor such as were wont to serve him, but strangers who were but spies upon him were appointed to his service, and musing on his ancient and wonted glory and on the fickle fortune of the world, I departed thence much moved at heart.

Adam of Usk: 14th century
Chronicon
Trans. by E. M. Thompson

The Plague

¶ IN THE YEAR OF GRACE 1349, which is the twenty-third of the reign of King Edward, the third since the Conquest, a great mortal plague spread through the world, starting from the southern and the northern areas, and ending with such devastating ruin that scarcely a handful of men survived. The towns, once densely populated, were emptied of their settlers and so rapidly did the intensity of the plague grow

1. For Shakespeare's handling of this see *Richard II*, Act III, Scene 2; the magnificent speech (lines 145 ff.) beginning "Let's talk of graves, of worms, and epitaphs . . ."

84

that the living could scarcely bury the dead. In certain monasteries, in fact, barely two out of twenty survived. Many estimated that hardly a tenth of the population remained alive. A disease among cattle followed closely on the pestilence; then the crops died; then the land remained untilled on account of the scarcity of farmers, who were wiped out. And such misery followed these disasters that the world never afterward had an opportunity of returning to its former state.

Thomas Walsingham: 14th century
Historia Anglicana
Trans. by H. E. W.

Prelude to Crécy[1]

¶ THE FRENCH ARMY was divided into nine battalions. The first battalion was in command of the King of Bohemia,[2] a man of marked discretion and military experience. On this day he asked the king[3] for the supreme command and predicted that he would die fighting against the noblest soldier in the world. For on saying that the King of England[4] would not retreat, he had been reproached for his foollish remark. Hence at his pressing insistence he had been placed in charge of the first battalion. So confident were the French leaders of this vast army that they individually singled out particular English warriors to surrender to their custody. The King of Majorca[5] asked that the King of England be assigned to him. Others asked for the Prince;[6] some for the Count of Northampton; and so on, according to their rank. But the cunning king, afraid that they would be too concerned about capturing the nobles for ransom and consequently too indifferent in achieving a common victory, ordered his standard, that is called an Oriflamme, to be unfurled. When it was raised, no one was permitted, on pain of death, to take a prisoner alive. It was called an Oriflamme, I repeat, because it signified that the profound

1. The Hundred Years' War between England and France extended from 1337 to 1453. One of its most famous battles was Crécy, fought in 1346. The English, under Edward III, decimated the French; it was here that the English longbow was first introduced on the Continent.
2. John of Luxemburg. 3. Philip VI of France. 4. Edward III. 5. James II. 6. Edward, the Black Prince.

pity of the French could not allow any man to live, just as burning oil cannot ignore anything inflammable. The space on the right of the royal standard of France displayed golden lilies with golden stems, beside the royal flag of the French, and floating, as it were, in empty space. In response, the King of England gave the order for his banner to be raised. Thereon was depicted an armed dragon, and hence it was called the Dragon, signifying that the leopard's ferocity and the lilies' gentleness had been transformed into the cruelty of dragons.

Geoffrey Le Baker of Swynebrooke
Chronicon, 1347
Trans. by H. E. W.

Bosworth Field[1]

Then to King Richard there came a Knight,
 And said, "I hold it time for to flee;
For yonder Stanley's dints they do so wight,
 Against them no man dree.

"Here is thy horse at thy hand ready,
 Another day thou may thy worship win,
And for to reign with royalty,
 To wear the Crown and be our King."

"Give me my battle-axe in my hand,
 Set the Crown of England on my head so high!
For by him that shaped both sea and land
 King of England this day will I die!

"One foot will I never flee
 Whilst the breath is my breast within!"
And as he said, so did it be;
 If he lost his life, he died a King.

Old Ballad

1. The thirty-year struggle for the throne of England between the Houses of Lancaster and York is remembered as the War of the Roses. The closing episode in this conflict was the Battle of Bosworth Field (1485), where Richard III was defeated by Henry Tudor, who became Henry VII.

Civil Conflict in Flanders[1]

¶ JACOB VON ARTAVELD, the citizen of Ghent that was so much attached to the King of England, still maintained the same despotic power over all Flanders. He had promised the King of England, that he would give him the inheritance of Flanders, invest his son the Prince of Wales with it, and make it a duchy instead of an earldom. Upon which account the king was, at this period, about St. John the Baptist's day, 1345, come to Sluys, with a numerous attendance of barons and knights. He had brought the Prince of Wales with him, in order that Jacob von Artaveld's promises might be realized. The king remained on board his fleet in the harbor of Sluys, where he kept his court. His friends in Flanders came thither to see and visit him; and there were many conferences between the king and Jacob von Artaveld on one side, and the councils from the different capital towns on the other, relative to the agreement before mentioned; as to which, those from the country did not unite in sentiment with the king nor with von Artaveld, who kept continually reminding him of their quarrel, and exhorting them to disinherit Earl Lewis, their natural lord, and his youngest son Lewis, in favor of the son of the King of England; but they declared they never would consent to such a thing. At the last conference, which was held in the harbor of Sluys, on board the king's ship, the *Catherine* (which was of such an enormous size that wonders might be told of it), they made this unanimous reply: "Dear sir, the request you have made has given us much uneasiness, and may in times to come be prejudicial to Flanders and our successors. True it is, that there is not in the world any prince whom we love so much, or for whose profit and advantage we would exert ourselves so greatly as for you; but we alone cannot agree to this proposition, unless all the commonalties of Flanders give their consent. Therefore each of us will return to our different towns, and will explain in a general way this business to the inhabitants; when, if the

---

1. Jacob von Artaveld (c. 1290–1345) was a Flemish statesman and Governor of Flanders from 1336 to the time of his death.

greater part of them shall consent, we also will agree to it. We will return to you again within a month, and bring such answers as we hope will be satisfactory." Neither the King of England nor Jacob von Artaveld could at that time obtain more or any other answer. They wished to have had a shorter day appointed, but in vain; so the king answered, he was satisfied that it should be as they determined. The conference broke up, and each returned to the town from whence he had been deputed.

Jacob von Artaveld remained some little time longer with the King of England, in order to be made acquainted with all his affairs. He, in return, promised and assured him that he would bring his countrymen over to his opinion; but he deceived himself, and did wrong in staying behind and not being at Ghent at the time when the citizens who had been deputed by the corporations of the town arrived there; for as soon as they were returned, taking advantage of the absence of von Artaveld, they collected a large meeting of high and low in the marketplace, and there explained to them the subject of the late conferences at Sluys, and what the King of England had required of them, through the advice and information of Jacob von Artaveld. The whole assembly began to murmur against him; and this request was received unfavorably by all. They said, "that if it pleased God, they never would be pointed out, or found so disloyal, as to disinherit their natural lord, in favor of a stranger." They then left the marketplace much discontented, and angry with Artaveld. Now, see how unfortunately it fell out; for if he had gone to Ghent, instead of Bruges and Ypres, and had remonstrated with them upon the quarrel of the King of England, they would all have consented to his wishes, as those of the two above-mentioned towns had done; but he trusted so much to his prosperity and greatness, that he thought he could recover every thing back in a little time.

When on his return he came to Ghent about midday, the townsmen, who were informed of the hour he was expected, had assembled in the street that he was to pass through; as soon as they saw him, they began to murmur, and put their heads close together, saying, "Here comes one who is too much the master, and wants to order in Flanders according to his will and pleasure, which must not be longer borne." With this they had also spread a rumor through the town, that Jacob von Artaveld had collected all the revenues of Flanders, for nine years and more; that he had usurped the government without rendering an account, for he did not allow any of the rents to pass to the

Earl of Flanders, but kept them securely to maintain his own state, and had, during the time above mentioned, received all fines and forfeitures; of this great treasure he had sent part into England. This information inflamed those of Ghent with rage; and, as he was riding up the streets, he perceived that there was something in agitation against him; for those who were wont to salute him very respectfully now turned their backs, and went into their houses. He began therefore to suspect all was not as usual; and as soon as he had dismounted and entered his hotel, he ordered the doors and windows to be shut and fastened.

Scarcely had his servants done this, when the street which he inhabited was filled from one end to the other with all sorts of people, but especially by the lowest of the mechanics. His mansion was surrounded on every side, attacked and broken into by force. Those within did all they could to defend it, and killed and wounded many; but at last they could not hold out against such vigorous attacks, for three parts of the town were there. When Jacob von Artaveld saw what efforts were making and how hardly he was pushed, he came to a window and, with his head uncovered, began to use humble and fine language, saying, "My good people, what aileth you? Why are you so enraged against me? By what means can I have incurred your displeasure? Tell me, and I will conform myself entirely to your wills." Those who had heard him made answer, as with one voice, "We want to have an account of the great treasures you have made away with, without any title of reason." Artaveld replied in a soft tone, "Gentlemen, be assured that I have never taken anything from the treasures of Flanders; and if you will return quietly to your homes, and come here tomorrow morning, I will be provided to give so good an account of them, that you must reasonably be satisfied." But they cried out, "No, no, we must have it directly, you shall not thus escape from us; for we know that you have emptied the treasury, and sent it into England, without our knowledge: you therefore shall suffer death." When he heard this, he clasped his hands together, began to weep bitterly, and said, "Gentlemen, such as I am, you yourselves have made me. You formerly swore you would protect me against all the world; and now, without any reason, you want to murder me. You are certainly masters to do it, if you please; for I am but one man against you all. Think better of it, for the love of God. Recollect former times, and consider how many favors and kindnesses I have conferred upon you. You wish to give me a sorry recompense for all the generous deeds you have experienced at my hands. You are not ignorant that, when commerce was dead in this country, it was I who restored it. I afterwards governed you in so peaceable a manner, that under my administration you had all things according to your wishes: corn, oats, riches, and all sorts of merchandise which have made you so wealthy." They began to bawl out, "Come down, and do not preach to us from such a height; for we will have an account and statement of the great treasures of Flanders, which you have governed too long without rendering any account; and it is not proper for an officer to receive the rents of a lord, or of a country, without accounting for them." When Jacob von Artaveld saw that he could not appease or calm them, he shut the window, and intended getting out of his house the back way, to take shelter in a church adjoining; but his hotel was already broke into on that side, and upwards of four hundred were there calling out for him. At last he was seized by them, and slain without mercy; his death-stroke was given him by a sadler, called Thomas Denys. In this manner did Jacob von Artaveld end his days, who in his time had been complete master of Flanders. Poor men first raised him, and wicked men slew him. News of this event was soon spread abroad; some pitied him, whilst others rejoiced at it. The Earl Lewis had remained all this time in Dendremonde, and with much pleasure heard of Jacob von Artaveld's death, as he had very much opposed him in all his undertakings. Nevertheless, he durst not yet place confidence in those of Flanders, nor return to Ghent.

When the King of England, who was waiting at Sluys, for the return of the deputies was informed in what manner the inhabitants of Ghent had slain his faithful friend and companion Artaveld, he was in a mighty passion, and sore displeased. He immediately departed, put to sea, and vowed vengeance against the Flemings and all Flanders, declaring that his death should be dearly paid for by them. The councils of the principal towns guessed that the King of England would not be much enraged against them; they therefore considered that their best method to soften his anger would be to go and excuse themselves from the murder of Jacob von Artaveld, especially those of Bruges, Ypres, Courtray, Oudenarde, and the franc of Bruges. They sent to the king and his council for a safe-conduct, that they might come over to make their excuses; and the king, whose anger was somewhat cooled, granted it to them.

The principal persons of all the chief towns in Flanders, except those of Ghent, came into England about Michaelmas. The king was at that time in Westminster, near London. They made very fair excuses, and swore most solemnly that "they were guiltless of the murder of von Artaveld, which, had they suspected, they would have guarded and defended him; that they were exceedingly vexed at his loss, and regretted it most sincerely; for they knew how kind he had been to them, how useful he was in all their affairs, and that he had reigned and governed Flanders most wisely; that since those of Ghent had slain him, they should make ample amends for it." They also explained to the king and his council, "that though Jacob von Artaveld was dead, he was not the less beloved, or less in the good graces of the Flemings, save and except in the investiture of Flanders, which he wished to be taken from the earl, their natural lord, however he may be attached to the French interest, and from his son, their lawful heir, to give it to the Prince of Wales; for the Flemings would not, on any account, listen to it. But, dear sir, you have a fine family of sons and daughters: the Prince of Wales, your eldest son, cannot fail being a great prince with an ample inheritance, without desiring that of Flanders, and you have also a young daughter; we have too a young lord, whom we are bringing up and taking care of, that will be lord of Flanders. It perhaps may be, that a marriage could be brought about between them, so that the county of Flanders will in the end be possessed by one of your children." These speeches softened very much the anger and ill-will of the King of England; and, in the end, both he and the Flemings were equally satisfied with each other. Thus, by degrees, was the death of Jacob von Artaveld forgotten.

Froissart
Chronicles
Trans. by Thomas Johnes, 1842

Civil Revolt in Ghent[1]

THE WHITE HOODS MURDER THE BAILIFF OF GHENT IN THE MIDST OF THE MARKET—THE HOUSES AND GOODS OF THE FAMILY OF THE MATTHEWS ARE DESTROYED—A GRAND CONFUSION IN GHENT

¶ NOT long afterwards, the bailiff of Ghent, Roger d'Auterme, came to town with full two hundred horse, in order to execute what had been planned between the earl, Gilbert Matthew, and his brothers.

1.   This episode occurred in 1345.

The bailiff, with his two hundred men, galloped up the streets, with the banner of the earl in his hand, unto the marketplace, where he halted and posted his banner before him. Gilbert Matthew, his brothers, and the deacon of the small craft immediately went thither. It had been determined that these men at arms should march instantly to the house of John Lyon, and arrest him as chief of the white hoods, with six or seven others, the most culpable, carry them to the castle of Ghent, and immediately cut their heads off.

John Lyon suspected some such thing; for he had received secret intelligence from his spies, scattered over different parts of the town. He knew of the arrival of the bailiff, and saw it was a thing determined upon. The other white hoods were informed that this day had been fixed on to arrest them, and were therefore ready prepared and assembled near the house of John Lyon, who was waiting for them. They came in bands of ten and twenty, and, as they marched up, they formed in the street; when they were all assembled, they were full four hundred. John Lyon marched off as fierce as a lion, saying, "Let us advance against these traitors, who wish to ruin the town of Ghent. I thought all those fine speeches which Gilbert Matthew brought back the other day were only meant for our destruction, and to lull us asleep; but we will make him pay dearly for them." He and his rout advanced hastily; they increased very much by the way, for there were those who joined him that had not as yet put on the white hoods, who cried out, "Treason! treason!"

They marched, by a roundabout way and a narrow street, to the corn market, where the bailiff, who represented the earl, had posted himself. Gilbert Matthew and his brethren, the moment they saw John Lyon and the white hoods enter the marketplace, left the bailiff and ran away as fast as they could; and neither order nor array was observed, except by the men at arms whom the bailiff had brought thither. Immediately on the arrival of John Lyon in the marketplace with the white hoods, a large body of them advanced toward the bailiff; and, without saying a word, he was seized, thrown on the ground and slain. The banner of the earl was then dragged through the dirt and torn to pieces; but not one man, except the bailiff, was touched. They then collected round John Lyon. When the earl's men at arms saw the bailiff dead and their banner torn to pieces, they were thunderstruck, and, like men defeated, took to flight, and left the town.

You may easily imagine that Gilbert Matthew and his brethren, who were known to be the enemies of John Lyon and the white hoods, did not think themselves very safe in their houses. They therefore set out as speedily as they could, and quitted the town through bye streets, leaving their wives, children, and goods behind them. They made what haste they could to the Earl of Flanders, to whom they related all that had happened, and the death of his bailiff. The earl was sorely afflicted at this intelligence, as well he might, for they had treated him with great contempt. He was much enraged, and swore that he would have ample revenge before he ever returned to Ghent, and before they should have peace from him, so that all other towns should take an example from it. Gilbert Matthew and his brothers remained with the earl.

John Lyon and the white hoods persevered in their outrages. After the death of the bailiff and the flight of the men at arms, as no one offered to revenge this murder, John, who wished to ruin the Matthews (for he bore them deadly hatred), said, "Come, let us go after those wicked traitors who this day intended to have destroyed the town of Ghent." They hastened down the streets to the residence of the Matthews, but found none, for they had all gone off. They were sought for in every room throughout the houses of the adjoining streets; and, when they were convinced they were gone, John Lyon was much vexed. He gave up to his companions all their goods, when the houses were completely pillaged and razed to the ground, so that no vestige remained, as if they had been traitors to the whole body of the town.

When they had done this deed, they retired to their homes; nor was there a sheriff, or any other officer belonging to the earl or to the town, who said they had acted wrong. Indeed, at that time all were afraid to say a word against them; for the white hoods were so numerous that none dared to provoke them, and they paraded the streets in large bodies without any opposition. It was said, both within and without the town, that they were connected with some of the sheriffs and rich men in Ghent, which was not unlikely; for such a ruffianly crew would never have dared to slay so noble a man as Roger d'Auterme, bailiff of Ghent, holding the banner of the earl in his hand at the time, if they had not depended on some good and able supporters in their wicked acts. They afterwards increased so much as to want no foreign aid, and became so powerful that none were bold enough to oppose any thing they thought proper to undertake. Roger d'Auterme was carried away by the Friar Minors to their church, where he was by them buried.

After this event, several of the wisest and richest citizens in Ghent began to murmur, and were much vexed. They said among themselves, that a great outrage had been committed when the earl's bailiff had thus been murdered in the execution of his office; and that their lord would be justly offended, and never grant them peace; that these wicked people had put the town to the hazard of being totally destroyed, if God did not speedily afford a remedy. Notwithstanding all these words, there was not one among them who had courage personally to correct or reprove the authors of these atrocities. John de Faucille, who at that time was a man much renowned for his wisdom in Ghent, on finding things carried to such lengths as the murdering of the earl's bailiff, thought it must end badly; that he might not be suspected by the earl, he left the town privately, and went to a handsome country house which he had near Ghent and there remained, having given orders to tell every one he was very unwell and melancholy, and could see none but his own people. Every day, however, he had news from Ghent; for he had left there the greater part of his family, his wife, his children and his friends; and thus he dissembled for a considerable time.

Froissart
Chronicles
Trans. by Thomas Johnes, 1842

Civil Revolt in England[1]

THE POPULACE OF ENGLAND REBEL AGAINST THE NOBILITY

¶ WHILE these conferences were going forward, there happened in England great commotions among the lower ranks of the people, by which England was near ruined without resource. Never was a country in such jeopardy as this was at that period, and all through the too great comfort of the commonalty. Rebellion was stirred up, as it was formerly done in France by the Jacques Bons-hommes, who did much evil, and sore troubled the kingdom of France. It is marvelous from what a trifle this pestilence raged in England. In order that it may

1. This episode occurred in 1381.

serve as an example to mankind, I will speak of all that was done, from the information I had at the time on the subject.

It is customary in England, as well as in several other countries, for the nobility to have great privileges over the commonalty, whom they keep in bondage; that is to say, they are bound by law and custom to plow the lands of gentlemen, to harvest the grain, to carry it home to the barn, to thrash and winnow it; they are also bound to harvest the hay and carry it home. All these services they are obliged to perform for their lords, and many more in England than in other countries. The prelates and gentlemen are thus served. In the counties of Kent, Essex, Sussex and Bedford, these services are more oppressive than in all the rest of the kingdom.

The evil-disposed in these districts began to rise, saying, they were too severely oppressed; that at the beginning of the world there were no slaves, and that no one ought to be treated as such, unless he had committed treason against his lord, as Lucifer had done against God; but they had done no such thing, for they were neither angels nor spirits, but men formed after the same likeness with their lords, who treated them as beasts. This they would not longer bear, but had determined to be free, and if they labored or did any other works for their lords, they would be paid for it.

A crazy priest in the county of Kent, called John Ball, who, for his absurd preaching, had been thrice confined in the prison of the Archbishop of Canterbury, was greatly instrumental in inflaming them with those ideas. He was accustomed, every Sunday after mass, as the people were coming out of the church, to preach to them in the marketplace and assemble a crowd around him, to whom he would say: "My good friends, things cannot go on well in England, nor ever will until every thing shall be in common; when there shall neither be vassal nor lord, and all distinctions leveled; when the lords shall be no more masters than ourselves. How ill have they used us! And for what reason do they thus hold us in bondage? Are we not all descended from the same parents, Adam and Eve? And what can they show, or what reasons give, why they should be more the masters than ourselves? except, perhaps, in making us labor and work, for them to spend. They are clothed in velvets and rich stuffs, ornamented with ermine and other furs, while we are forced to wear poor cloth. They have wines, spices, and fine bread, when we have only rye and the refuse of the straw; and, if we drink, it must be water. They have handsome seats and manors, when we must brave the wind and rain in our labors in the field; but it is from our labor they have wherewith to support their pomp. We are called slaves; and, if we do not perform our services, we are beaten, and we have not any sovereign to whom we can complain, or who wishes to hear us and do us justice. Let us go to the king, who is young, and remonstrate with him on our servitude, telling him we must have it otherwise, or that we shall find a remedy for it ourselves. If we wait on him in a body, all those who come under the appellation of slaves, or are held in bondage, will follow us, in the hopes of being free. When the king shall see us, we shall obtain a favorable answer, or we must then seek ourselves to amend our condition."

With such words as these did John Ball harangue the people at his village, every Sunday after mass, for which he was much beloved by them. Some who wished no good declared it was very true, and murmuring to each other, as they were going to the fields, on the road from one village to another, or at their different houses, said, "John Ball preaches such and such things, and he speaks the truth."

The Archbishop of Canterbury, on being informed of this, had John Ball arrested and imprisoned for two or three months by way of punishment; but it would have been better if he had been confined during his life or had been put to death, than to have been suffered thus to act. The archbishop set him at liberty, for he could not for conscience sake have put him to death. The moment John Ball was out of prison, he returned to his former errors. Numbers in the city of London having heard of his preaching, being envious of the rich men and nobility, began to say among themselves that the kingdom was too badly governed, and the nobility had seized on all the gold and silver coin. These wicked Londoners, therefore, began to assemble and to rebel. They sent to tell those in the adjoining counties, they might come boldly to London and bring their companions with them, for they would find the town open to them, and the commonalty in the same way of thinking; that they would press the king so much, there should no longer be a slave in England.

These promises stirred up those in the counties of Kent, Essex, Sussex, and Bedford, and the adjoining country, so that they marched toward London; and, when they arrived near, they were upwards of sixty thousand. They had a leader called Wat Tyler, and with him were Jack Straw and John Ball; these three were their commanders, but the principal was Wat Tyler. This Wat had been a tiler of houses, a bad man, and a great enemy to the nobility. When these wicked people first began to rise, all London, except their friends, were very much frightened. The mayor and rich citizens assembled in council, on hearing they were coming to London, and debated whether they should shut the gates and refuse to admit them; but, having well considered, they determined not to do so, as they should run a risk of having the suburbs burnt.

The gates were therefore thrown open, when they entered in troops of one or two hundred, by twenties or thirties, according to the populousness of the towns they came from; and as they came into London they lodged themselves. But it is a truth, that full two-thirds of these people knew not what they wanted, nor what they sought for; they followed one another like sheep, or like to the shepherds of old, who said they were going to conquer the Holy Land, and afterwards accomplished nothing. In such manner did these poor fellows and vassals come to London from distances of a hundred and sixty leagues, but the greater part from those counties I have mentioned, and on their arrival they demanded to see the king. The gentlemen of the country, the knights and squires, began to be alarmed when they saw the people thus rise; and, if they were frightened, they had sufficient reason, for less causes create fear. They began to collect together as well as they could.

The same day that these wicked men of Kent were on their road toward London, the Princess of Wales, mother to the king, was returning from a pilgrimage to Canterbury. She ran great risks from them; for these scoundrels attacked her car, and caused much confusion, which greatly frightened the good lady, lest they should do some violence to her or to her ladies. God, however, preserved her from this, and she came in one day from Canterbury to London, without venturing to make any stop by the way. Her son Richard was this day in the Tower of London: thither the princess came, and found the king attended by the Earl of Salisbury, the Archbishop of Canterbury, Sir Robert de Namur, the lord de Gommegines, and several more, who had kept near his person from suspicions of his subjects who were thus assembling, without knowing what they wanted. This rebellion was well known to be in agitation in the king's palace, before it broke out and the country people had left their homes; to which the king applied no remedy, to the great astonishment of everyone.

Froissart
Chronicles
Trans. by Thomas Johnes, 1842

Part Two

FANTASY, LEGEND AND FOLKLORE;

MAGIC AND MIRACLES;

POPULAR TALES

The people of medieval times were inordinately fond of the legends and mythologies of antiquity—Greek, Roman and Oriental. They absorbed these classic tales into their own literature, frequently distorting them, adding anachronistic details and intruding fantastic features, until there grew up a corpus of tales that were of antique origin only in their general framework. Lives of the saints included pagan elements; moral tales, called exempla, *adorned religious and homiletic expositions. Stories of fantasy and witchcraft, miraculous adventures in which historical characters mysteriously appeared, were highly popular. In the course of time, with the growth and development of the chivalric code, narratives acquired romantic elements, even sophistication and suggestiveness. And finally, as in "The Blind Man and his Wife," love became a subject of ribaldry.*

NOTE: Because many of the selections are taken from longer narratives or chronicles, or from collections of tales, they frequently begin with or include passing references to earlier passages not included here. These references have been retained in most cases so that the translation may conform more closely to the original.

The Boy and the Grapes

¶ SINCE WE are mentioning the great Florentius,[1] I think it is not right to pass over in silence what I learned from him.

Once he went to Galicia on an embassy and, coming into the presence of King Miro,[2] who was visiting there at the time, he explained the mission entrusted to him [while standing at a sanctuary to Saint Martin]. Before the portico of this sanctuary an arbor of vines extended over the vine-branches, with grapes hanging from them fresh as a painting. Beneath there was a path that led the wayfarer to the doors of a holy shrine. When the king passed beneath the arbor and approached the shrine for prayer, he said to his attendants: "Take care not to touch one of these clusters, or you may offend the holy bishop. For everything in this building is consecrated to him."

Hearing this, one of the boys said to himself: "I don't know whether these grapes are sacred to the holy man or not. But I know one thing; that it is my intention to eat them." At once he stretched out his hand and began to pull at the end of the cluster; and forthwith his right hand, clinging to the arbor, grew stiff and his arm rigid. The king's jester was there, who could provoke laughter with jokes. But no laughter or tricks of his skill could help the boy. And as the pain increased, the boy began to speak and say: "Help a poor fellow, aid me in my misery, relieve my dejection, pray for me to the virtuous Saint Martin; for I am tortured by this accident, I am afflicted by this assault, I am torn apart by this cutting pain."

The king came out and, learning what had happened, was so incensed against the boy that he would have cut off his hands if he had not been prevented by his courtiers. These attendants said: "Do not, O King, add your revenge to the judgment of God, or perhaps the injury you threaten the boy with may fall back upon you."

Then compunction seized him, and he went into the church and prostrated himself before the holy altar, and wept and prayed to the

---

1. Gregory of Tours, whose name was Georgius Florentius.
2. King of the Suevi, in Spain (Galicia is a region in Spain). King Miro died c. 583.

Lord. And he did not arise from the floor until the flood of tears cleansed the boy of the crime. The boy was released from his bondage and entered the church. The king then rose up, and welcoming the unharmed boy, returned to the palace.

The great Florentius testified that he had learned of this incident from the king himself, just as we have related it.

Gregory of Tours: 6th century
De Miraculis S. Martini
Trans. by H. E. W.

A Shipwreck and a Rescue[1]

¶ IN THAT MIST AND STORM all perished, but Apollonius was cast on the shore of Pentapolitae. Meanwhile standing naked on the beach, gazing at the calm sea, he said: "O Neptune, ruler of the sea, deceiver of innocent men, for this you have saved me, needy and poor, so that the cruel King Antiochus may pursue me more readily! Where shall I go? What region shall I seek? Or who will save an unknown man?"

As he reproached himself, all at once he noticed an old man, wrapped in a filthy cloak. Prostrating himself at his feet, he exclaimed, bursting into tears: "Take pity on me, whoever you are; help a poor castaway, born with no mean birthright. If you want to know whom you are pitying, I am Apollonius of Tyre, king of my country. Listen now to the tragedy of my misfortune; for, prostrate at your feet, I beg for my life. Help me so that I live!"

So the fisherman, seeing the young man's appearance, was moved to pity and raised him up and holding his hand led him within the walls of his home, and set a meal before him as well as he could. When his compassion was satisfied, he took off his cloak, tore it in two equally, and gave one part to the young man, with these words: "Take what I have and go to the city. Perhaps you will find someone to take pity on you. If you don't find anyone, come back here and work and fish with me. Whatever my poverty is, it will be enough for

1. The story of Apollonius of Tyre, very popular in the Middle Ages, was originally a Greek romance (now lost), but its most familiar form is this Latin version, which served as the source for Shakespeare's *Pericles*.

us. But I warn you, if by God's favor you are restored to your birth-right, remember my pitiful poverty."

To this Apollonius answered: "If I don't remember you, may I be shipwrecked again and not find another like yourself!"

Historia Apollonii Regis Tyri: 5th–6th
centuries
Trans. by H. E. W.

Legend of the Seven Sleepers

¶ I DO NOT think it irrelevant to defer for a little the sequence of my history and—since my subject is still Germany—to relate briefly a miracle that is held in general esteem there, and even to describe a few others. In the farthest northwest regions of Germany, on the very shore of the Ocean, there is a cave under a beetling cliff where seven men lie, plunged in deep sleep. It is not known how long they have been sleeping. Not only their bodies but their clothes as well are so free from decay that on account of this very fact that they have en-dured through so many ageless cycles without any corruption, among these unlettered and barbarous people they are held in veneration.

The sleepers, as far as their appearance indicates, are seen to be Romans. A certain man was urged in his eagerness to exhume one of them, but presently his arms grew stiff. His punishment terrified the others so that no one dared to touch them any more. It can be seen to what end divine providence preserves these sleepers through so many ages. Perhaps some day those nations are to be saved by the prayers of those men, because they are thought to be none other than Christians.

Paulus Diaconus: 8th century
Historia Langobardorum
Trans. by H. E. W.

Notker Meets the Devil

¶ NOW NOTKER WAS, as we have said, brave in spirit, as courageous against demons as Tuotilo was against men; but physically he was different, fasting, wakeful, wiry, as we have said, and lean. Now it happened that coming to a church early one night and walking round the altar, as he usually did, he said his prayers. Then entering the crypt of the twelve apostles and St. Columbanus, his eyes keener after coming from the altar and filled with tears, he thought he heard a dog growling. Meanwhile, becoming aware of the sound of a grunting pig, he realized it was the Tempter.

"Are you," he said, "again there? How fares it with you, wretch, growling and grunting after those glorious voices that you heard in heaven?"

He lit a lamp and looked to see in what corner he was hiding. As he approached the left corner, the Devil tore at his clothes like a mad dog.

"Here," cried Notker, "I must complete your subjection outside the crypt; for those punishments that they say you suffer are of no avail. I am going to prepare something harsher for you. I order you, in the name of these saints and of my God, to wait for me in the same body of a dog as you are in now."

And the other said: "I shall do so, if I wish."

And Notker, as he quickly went away, said: "I trust in the Lord because, willy-nilly, you will wait for me." Then he swiftly advanced toward the altar of St. Gall and took his staff that had performed many miracles, along with the famous globe of the holy cross, and at the right of the entrance of the crypt he put down the globe, with the staff on the left side, and approached the Satanic dog. Now when he began to beat the Devil with the holy staff, the Devil uttered his cries as before, more loudly, with snarling and grunting. Finally, when he had reached the holy globe, fleeing from the blows of the staff and powerless to advance any farther, he now stood still, and unable to bear the repeated blows with which he had been struck, he shrieked in his barbarous tongue: "O woe! Alas for me!"

In the meantime when the sacristan entered the church and heard the horrible sounds, he quickly seized a light and hurried to the crypt. But when Notker had administered to the Devil his last blow with the staff, he broke the holy rood into pieces. And had it not been for the sacristan who, at sight of the globe, had taken it up and thus permitted the dog to escape, Notker would still have been striking him. The sacristan, looking at the staff, cried in astonishment: "Did you, master, defile the holy staff on that dog?" As Notker kept silent, he added: "Who was it who cried 'Woe is me!'" Thinking that Notker in his piety was concealing some thief or other, he marched through the entire church, eager to arrest the thief. But finding neither thief nor dog, he thought it over with himself; wondering, because on entering he had closed the church after him, what could have happened. After that, he never dared to address the monk, who kept his silence. But, as he was humble and wise, he called the sacristan outside and took him into his confidence and after giving him his blessing, said: "Since I broke the staff, my son, unless you help me, my secret must be known. But since it is not for me to walk with great miracles beyond my comprehension, I entrust what happened to the silence of your faith." Thus he revealed the incident as it happened.

The sacristan, secretly getting a smith to repair the staff, for some time kept the incident hidden. But in the course of time the story became known.

Ekkehard IV: 11th century
Casus Sancti Galli, edited by G. M. von Knonau, 1877
Trans. by H. E. W.

The Boy in the Burning Chimney

¶ THERE WAS a certain Jew who lived in Constantinople, a glass-blower by trade, who had a chaste and charitable wife and a young son who learned his letters near the church of St. Sophia.

Now it happened that there were fragments of the body of the Lord in the sacristy, as is usually the case. When the guardian of the holy vessels observed this, he went to the master who taught the boys and said: "Please, master, dismiss the boys and let them come into the church and take the remaining fragments before they perish." For that was his habit. The master gave orders to the boys as follows: "If there is anyone hungry, let him go and take." Together with the Christian boys the Jewish boy entered the sacristy and took some of the holy wafers, as they did.

At the regular hour the master dismissed the boys, to go home. Likewise the Jewish boy too was dismissed and he went into the workshop where his father shaped the glass. A very bright furnace was burning and he was working at something he liked. His father said: "Did something delay you today, son, more than usually?"

105

"Certainly, Father," the boy replied, "I ate today with the boys in a very fine church."

And the father said: "What did you eat?" The boy replied: "The priest gave us some very white bread, and we all ate it."

Enraged, the father said: "Did you dare to take communion with Christians?" And, seizing the boy, he threw him into the fiery chimney; then, closing the chimney, he went away. Now the apprentice who worked with him, observing the incident, ran off and told the boy's mother what had occurred. Hearing such a story, her very heart was moved for what had happened to her boy, and she ran moaning and lamenting along with the apprentice and the neighbors and a large crowd of people who had heard what had happened to the boy. And breaking in the doors, they entered the house. They opened the chimney and found the boy uninjured, by the gracious favor of Christ.

The mother said to the boy: "My dearest child, what are you doing here?"

To which the boy replied: "Father put me here, Mother, because I went with the boys into the church of the Christians and took communion with them."

As the boy came out of the chimney unhurt, he was questioned by the people and by his own mother how he had not been burnt. He answered: "A lady shining bright poured water over me and said: 'Do not fear.' "

The mother took her boy and running to the venerable Menna, who was in those days ruler of the see of Constantinople, with all the people following her, she told all that had happened to the boy. When the patriarch heard the miracle that had been performed, he was eager to tell the Emperor Justinian. Summoning the Jewish woman, along with her son, he came and reported the miracle, begging that holy baptism be deservedly granted to him. She accepted, with her son, by the grace of Christ.

Calling the Jew, they urged him to ask forgiveness for his crime and to accept baptism. But the unbeliever had no wish whatever to consent. Then, though repeatedly admonished by the patriarch to believe, he still did not agree.

This was told to the emperor, who ordered him to be thrown into the same chimney into which he had thrust his own son. When this was done, the wretch was burnt at once and reduced to nothing and lost both his present and his eternal life. All those who had seen and heard of the miracle gave praise to God, who performs miracles for our salvation, to whom is due praise and glory forever. Amen.

Iohannes Monachus: 11th century
Liber de Miraculis
Trans. by H. E. W.

True Friendship

¶ AN ARAB, on his deathbed, called his son to him and said: "Tell me, my son, how many friends have you made during your lifetime?" The son replied: "I have made a hundred friends, I think."

FATHER: A philosopher says: "Do not praise your friend until you have tested him." I was born before you and I have scarcely acquired half a friend. Now since you have made one hundred, son, come now and test them all, to find out whether any one of them all is a real friend to you.

SON: How do you advise me to test them?

FATHER: Take a calf and kill it and cut it in pieces and put it in a sack, so that on the outside the sack is stained with blood; and when you come to a friend, say to him: "My dear friend, I accidentally killed a man and my house is sure to be searched. So he has to be buried and hidden. I ask you to bury him secretly; for no one will suspect you, and so you will be able to save me."

The son did as the father ordered. The first friend that he approached said: "Carry the dead man yourself on your shoulders, as you committed the crime. Suffer the penalty; you shall not enter my house."

When he had thus solicited his friends individually, they all replied to the same effect.

Returning then to his father, he reported what he had done. The father said: "What the philosopher said happened to you. 'While there are many numbered as friends, there are few in an emergency.' Go to the half friend that I have and see what he says."

He went and told the man what he had told the others. The man answered: "Come inside, this is not a secret that ought to be revealed

107

to neighbors." He therefore sent away his wife and all his family and dug a grave. When he saw that everything was ready, the son explained the situation as it really was and thanked the friend. Then he related to his father what he had done. His father said: "With such a friend, the philosopher says, 'He is a true friend who helps you when the world fails you.' "

Petrus Alphonsus: 12th century
Disciplina Clericalis
Trans. by H. E. W.

An Old Cure for Sleeplessness

¶ A KING had a storyteller who was accustomed to tell him five stories every night. At last it happened that the king, perturbed by certain cares, could not fall asleep at all, and asked to hear more than the usual number of stories. The storyteller then told five more, but short ones. Still the king asked for more. But the other did not at all want to, for he had already told many tales as he had been bidden.

To this the king said: "You have told me a great many, but they were very short. I should like you to tell me a story that can be drawn out in many words and then I should allow you to go to sleep." The man consented, and began thus:

"There was a countryman who had a thousand solidi. When he went to trade, he bought two thousand sheep, each costing six denarii. It happened that as he was returning a great flood arose. Since he could cross neither the ford nor the bridge, he went away in perplexity, looking for a way to cross with his sheep. At length he found a tiny skiff and in the emergency he put two sheep in it and crossed the water."

After saying this, the storyteller fell asleep. The king accordingly roused him and reminded him to finish the tale he had begun. The storyteller said in reply:

"The waves were high, the boat was tiny, and the flock of sheep was without number. Let the previously mentioned countryman take his sheep across, and I shall continue to the end the story that I began."

Petrus Alphonsus: 12th century
Disciplina Clericalis
Trans. by H. E. W.

The Biter Bit

¶ I WAS TOLD that a certain Spaniard proceeded to Mecca and on his way arrived in Egypt. Wishing to enter and cross the desert, he thought that he would leave his money in Egypt; and before he resolved to give it into safekeeping, he asked if there was any reliable man in that region to whom he could intrust his money. They referred him to an aged man, known for his honesty and trustworthiness, to whom he assigned one thousand talents out of his wealth. Then he went on.

When his journey was completed, he returned to the man to whom he intrusted his money and asked him for what he had intrusted to him. But the other, full of wickedness, declared that he had never seen him before. Thus tricked, he hastened to the honest men of that district and reported to them how the man to whom he had intrusted his money had treated him. The neighbors, hearing such a tale, refused to credit it and said there was nothing to the story. The man who had lost his money went every day to the home of the man who illegally kept his money and with coaxing entreaties begged him to return the money. The trickster listened, and then rebuked him, telling him not to say such things about him any more and not to come to him; if he did, he would suffer deserved punishment.

On hearing the threats of the gamester, he sadly started to leave and on his way back met an old woman clothed in hermit's rags. She supported her feeble limbs on a staff and on her way, giving praise to God, she picked up stones to prevent the feet of travelers from getting hurt. Seeing the man in tears, she recognized that he was a foreigner. Moved by pity, she called him into an alley and asked what had happened. He told her the story from the very beginning. On hearing it, the woman said: "Friend, if your story is true, I'll help you."

HE: How can you help me, servant of God?

SHE: Bring me a man from your country whose words and actions you can trust.

He brought such a man. Then she ordered this friend of the victimized man to bring ten boxes painted on the outside in fine colors

109

and fastened with silver-plated iron, with good locks, and to bring them to his host's house, and to fill them with broken stones. He did so. Now the woman, on seeing everything ready as she had ordered, said:

"Now seek out ten men to go to the house of the man who tricked you and bring the boxes, one after the other, along with me and your friend, going in a long line. As soon as the first one comes to the swindler's house and rests there, you too come and ask for your money, and I promise you in the Lord's name that your money will be restored to you."

He did as the old woman bade him. She, mindful of the plan she had proposed, started on her way. She came with the friend of the outwitted fellow to the cheat's house, and said: "A man from Spain has been a guest of mine and wishes to go to Mecca and asks me for a trustworthy man to whom he can hand over his money, that is in ten boxes, to be kept until his return. I ask you therefore for my sake to keep it in your house, and since I have heard and know that you are a good and reliable man, I do not want anyone else to be responsible for this money except your own self."

While she was talking the first man came carrying the box, the others appearing to view in the distance.

Meanwhile the victim, remembering the old woman's injunctions, came after the first box, as he had been told. The man who had hidden the money, full of wickedness and evil cunning, at the sight of the man whose money he had concealed, was afraid that if he asked for his money, the other man who was bringing his would not trust it to him. Without hesitation he advanced toward him and said: "Friend, where have you been so long? And where did you stay? Come and get your money that you intrusted to my reliability long since, for I found it and I am tired of keeping it any longer."

The other gladly took his money and thanked him. When the old crone saw that the man had his money, she rose and said: "I and my friend will now go for our boxes. Tell them to hurry. You wait until we return, and take good care of what we have already brought."

The rogue joyfully kept an eye on what he had received, and waited and waited for the arrival of the rest of the boxes. Thus the sum of money was restored to the victim through the old beldame's cleverness.

Petrus Alphonsus: 12th century
Disciplina Clericalis
Trans. by H. E. W.

A Scottish Vampire

¶ IN THE NORTHERN REGIONS of England, we learn that another incident occurred at the same time, not dissimilar and equally strange. There is a village at the mouth of the River Tweed that is called, according to royal Scottish prerogative, the royal burgh. There a poor man, but a very evil one as was later made evident, was buried at his death through the agency of Satan, as the belief ran. At night he would leave the grave and, accompanied by a pack of loudly barking dogs, roam hither and yon, throwing all the inhabitants into a state of great terror. Before dawn he returned to the grave. This went on for many days, and no one dared to be found out of doors after sunset. Everyone dreaded meeting the deadly monster.

The elders and the younger people discussed among themselves what had better be done. They were afraid that the more simple-minded among them, if any careless action were taken, would have their blood sucked by the undead creature. The shrewder ones pondered carefully. If they took measures slowly, the air, fouled and polluted by the frequent movements of the plague-ridden corpse, would cause disease and death to many. This had to be prevented: there were many similar occurrences to be guided by. So they hired ten young men, noted for their daring, to exhume the horrible corpse and cut it to pieces, limb from limb, reducing it to fire and fuel for fire. This was done, and the plague ceased. For the monster itself, while it was dragged around by Satan, as they said, declared to some men that it chanced to meet that as long as it remained unburned, the people would have no rest. So, once it was burned, the people appeared to enjoy peace, but a plague that came as a result carried off the majority of the folk. For nowhere else did it rage so fatally, although it was widespread in all the territory of England at that very time, as will be revealed more fully in its proper place.

William of Newburgh: 12th century
Historia Rerum Anglicarum
R. A. Browne, *British Latin Selections: A.D. 500–1400*. Oxford: Blackwell, 1954
Trans. by H. E. W.

How to Bell the Cat

¶ THE MICE made a plan to protect themselves from the cat, and one of them, wiser than the others, said: "Let a bell be tied to the cat's neck. Then we shall be able to beware of him and to hear how he goes and thus avoid his snares."

All were delighted with the plan, and one mouse said: "Who among us has such staunch courage as to tie the bell on the cat's neck?"

One mouse answered: "Certainly not I."

Another declared: "I certainly wouldn't dare approach the cat for anything in the whole world."

Metaphorically. So it generally happens that clerics, monks, and subjects rise against their prelate, saying: "I wish so and so were removed and we had another prelate." This plan appeals to all. Finally they ask each other: "Who will set himself against him? Who will accuse him?" Then one and all, afraid for their own safety, say: "Certainly not I," "Nor I," and so the subjects let the prelates go on living.

Odo de Cerinton: 12th century
Narrationes
Trans. by H. E. W.

The Droll Tale of Sceva and Ollo, Merchants

¶ SCEVA AND OLLO, sons of the common people, of the same age but unlike in character, acquired a modest competence. In our time they became traders first in a small way, then on a large scale as their success grew. From packmen they rose to two-horse carters and eventually became owners of many wagons, always remaining faithful partners. And, as their merchandise increased, their love of money grew with their profits. Now the bond of their companionship and their joint union of goods became a source of discontent, and they decided on separate ownership. They divided all their belongings and drew lots, each taking what was by lot placed before him, and they agreed to break their partnership. Sceva, being gracious and naturally polite, tearfully begged Ollo that they should not fail to communicate with each other by an interchange of messengers, in whatever towns or cities they lived, and maintain their association, although they might be separated, by frequent messages of affection.

Sceva chose to stay in Ravenna, remained a bachelor for a long time, and devoted himself to the barter of goods. Ollo married a handsome wife of Pavia. At first many messengers went back and forth between them but finally they dropped off. Then Sceva went to Pavia to visit Ollo with a large retinue of servants. By chance, he met Ollo on the way, hurrying off to distant markets with a loaded two-horse wagon. They embraced each other and Ollo asked Sceva where he was coming from and where he was going; although their old affection ought to have made him turn back and entertain such a friend. Moreover, hearing that he himself was the only reason for Sceva's coming, he excused his return on account of the markets, and added that Sceva could not be welcomed at all in his home for many good reasons; then he went off to his wagon. Sceva felt aggrieved. Near Pavia, he chanced to meet Ollo's shepherd. He addressed him and learning who he was, asked him about Ollo's position in regard to stock and real estate. Informed of all the intimate details of Ollo's family, he used this information to ensure a hospitable welcome from Ollo's wife. This he received; but he announced that what was available in the house was not good enough for either himself or Ollo's family, and, since there was much procurable outside, he gave an order to purchase, as he boasted, his usual delicacies. Then he prepared at his own expense such a splendid and lavish banquet that it evoked the admiration of even the neighbors.

He invited the folk standing in the square to come in, even passers-by, and lavished such a generous supply of food and drink that both Ollo's wife and all the others hoped for Ollo's continued absence and Sceva's presence. This went on for many days, the festivities becoming more and more expansive. He welcomed all that came; he eagerly and joyfully honored unbidden guests, loading them with gifts. The entire province rushed to see what they heard about. Through the

113

towns and cities the wonder spread and caught up with Ollo in his flight. He was amazed, and resolved not to return until the other had gone. Worried and jealous about his wife, he became frantic and wasted away, poisoned by jealousy. He was no longer, as he used to be, enthusiastic about promoting his merchandise. He did not lament his losses. He did not crow over profits. He did not plan to increase or save his money. He was lavish in some things but sparing with his wife; and now, while trying to guess what was going on between his wife and Sceva and what he should do about it, he chanced to hit on what was actually happening. For Sceva was fully occupied in doing just what Ollo feared. With his utmost skill Sceva enticed Ollo's wife to his wishes and when he had had his way with her he was not content with this illicit intercourse, but added:

"My dearest only darling, whom I love more than my own life, if you liked, you could soothe my troubled mind that is utterly inflamed with passion for you, so that we could live together securely, in every way. Don't admit Ollo when he returns but, as though you admired all men equally, disavow him, and rebuke him and deny that you know the fellow. I shall see to it that this is done by all the neighbors and well-known people. I shall win over to this plan the Viscount and his attendants, provided you give me your favors. Whoever tries to make the judges or any other authority believe that he was either your husband or the owner of your wealth will become silent immediately he hears me; and, if it becomes necessary, they will swear to the contrary so that Ollo will discredit himself and think that he is out of his mind."

She gave her consent, although she did not expect that it could be done. Then Sceva lavished gifts on all hands, together with promises of more, and so bought all Ollo's well-known friends; for friendship is weak where character is depraved. He won over the chief magistrate and the judges and suborned them, just as they are wont to be fooled. All thought it was a good trick and a humorous deception; moreover they thought it useful to cut down the sterile fig and plant the ripe olive.

Sceva stayed with the wife as her lawful husband in her home, and giving instructions with inventive treachery he never stopped telling everyone how to answer Ollo. Ollo, as it seemed best to him, remained circumspectly absent, watching until the other went away, in order to avenge his wrongs on his wife and to punish her without any outside help, and to avoid seeing the immense expenditure of his possessions that he had heard about. For when a miser does not see his possessions disappearing, it is less painful than when he has to watch them dwindle.

Finally, realizing he was delaying too long and afraid of even worse calamity, he returned home. He knocked at the door and fell into a rage when the door was not opened at once. He rushed in noisily and became furious and indignant, shouting threats. Nicholaus, whom Ollo had appointed doorkeeper, haughtily called: "Who is it?" And, standing before his erstwhile master, continued in an arrogant tone: "Who are you? What are you mad about? What demon has got into you? Why inflict on us the torture of your mad mind? Why do you disturb the peace of my master? Are you insane, or similarly afflicted? If you are an idiot, we'll make you wise, in a moment. If you don't keep quiet, a cudgel will do it."

Then Ollo said: "Servant, am I not myself?"

NICHOLAUS: I know that you are you, but you don't know it yourself.

OLLO: Don't you know that you are my servant?

NICHOLAUS: I know a servant who is mad about possessions.

OLLO: Open my door at once.

NICHOLAUS: Yours! Wasn't it just proved that you are mad? You'll keep quiet or this club will silence you for good.

OLLO: You worthless fellow, am I not Ollo, that made you keeper of this house?

NICHOLAUS: You, you miserable fool? Ollo is inside, lying in bed with my mistress.

OLLO: With what mistress, you devil?

NICHOLAUS: It's you who are a devil. With my beautiful mistress, Biblis.

Ollo, hearing Biblis' name, fell into a fit. For some time he remained there in a trance; then he said: "Come outside, Nicholaus, so that you can take a better look at me and get wise and see that I am your master and Biblis' husband."

Then Nicholaus broke into a burst of laughter. "I see you clearly enough through my peephole, and you may be Ollo, but not the Ollo who is married to Biblis."

OLLO: On the contrary, I am the Ollo that in your own presence took her as a bride from her father Mela and her mother Bella.

NICHOLAUS: I never saw a drunkard or a madman with such a good memory. You remember names; however they may have been

115

taught to you—Mela and Bella and Nicholaus. Did you ever hear of our maid Christina?

OLLO: I don't need to *hear* of her, for I brought her up and you and all of you, and I built this house and everything in it is mine.

NICHOLAUS: Christina, Christina, hello there, Christina! Come and look at a fellow who is in the last stages of madness. He knows everything, he brought up everybody, he owns everything; but this madness of his is funny, because it makes him a king. Look, isn't he the one that was recently going to be hanged for murder and escaped to sanctuary? And now he says he raised us. What do you think?

CHRISTINA: I wanted to tell you, that's the man and we must be gentle with him; whatever he does, he's under the melancholic influence and such men are entitled to do anything.

OLLO (*musing*): How bold and stubborn is the arrogance of servants: bribed by Sceva they disavow me, and when he leaves, filled with my delicacies, falling at my feet they will beg my pardon, saying that they made a mistake through their ignorance. May Ollo drop dead if he does not show them his snarling teeth.

NICHOLAUS: Mumble to yourself, you miserable lunatic. If you don't want to be beaten, get out of here fast.

CHRISTINA: Here you, that call yourself Ollo, you say we are mad, and we say you are. Call your neighbors, and when they tell you what we did, consider yourself possessed.

Ollo summoned the neighbors, and explained about the wrongs done to him. Denying having seen or heard of the fellow, they laughed at him, and urged each other to tie him up and set him straight and drive him out with stones if he persisted. Shortly after, he was similarly repulsed by the judges as well. When he found the same expression on everyone and everyone talking the same way, he began to accept from these people their version of his identity, where he came from, and how the situation arose, completely in contradiction to his own feeling. In short, he began to believe less in himself than in what the others said.

Everyone to whom he talked had been bribed by Sceva. At last one of them, named Baratus, said: "Master, we know the truth of the matter, but you are so grim and snarling and disdainful that what we know as the truth we have to hide for fear of you. Your house and Biblis, whom you seek here, are at Ravenna. If you will, let us all go there and you will find what you think you have seen here."

116

So they started out and on the first night of their journey he was deserted by his companions. He went almost out of his mind for shame. He saw his great possessions destroyed, except what he was then dealing with. He approached his shepherds and drove them from the enclosures and carried off whatever goods he could. Hearing of this, Sceva followed and overtook him and led him away bound like a thief. Ollo was afraid of the judges and, ashamed of the derision he would provoke, actually agreed to Sceva's entire calumny. Believe me, giving is a clever thing.

Walter Map: 12th century
De Nugis Curialium
Trans. by H. E. W.

The Devil Marries a Quarrelsome Woman

¶ I HAVE HEARD that a certain demon in human guise served a rich man, and since his service and diligence pleased the man very much, he gave him his daughter as a wife and also great wealth. Every day and night, however, she quarreled with her husband, and gave him no rest. At the end of the year he said to his father-in-law: "I want to leave and return to my country."

The father answered: "Haven't I given you many things so that you want for nothing? Why do you want to go away?"

THE DEVIL: I want to go back to my country in the strongest way.

FATHER-IN-LAW: Where is your country?

THE DEVIL: I shall tell you without concealing the truth. My country is Hell: where I have never endured such discord and annoyance as I experienced this year from my quarrelsome wife. I prefer to be in Hell rather than stay with her any longer.

Saying this, he vanished from their sight.

Jacques de Vitry: 13th century
Sermones
Trans. by H. E. W.

117

Diabolic Help

¶ IN THE CHURCH of St. Simeon, in the diocese of Trèves, there was a young schoolboy. One day he was given a subject by his master, but, unable to compose any verses on it, he was sitting sadly when the devil in human form appeared before him.

THE DEVIL: Why are you grieving, boy? Why are you sitting so sadly?

THE BOY: I am afraid of my master, because I cannot compose any verses on the theme he gave me.

THE DEVIL: Do you want to do homage to me, and I shall compose verses for you?

The boy, not understanding what the devil, the enemy of all men, meant by his evil trick, replied: "Yes, master. I am prepared to do whatever you command, provided I have the verses and am not whipped." He did not know, of course, who he was. He extended his hand, doing homage to him. Forthwith he received the verses dictated on the tablets, and did not see the man who dictated any more.

When he gave the verses to his master at the appointed time, the latter regarded their excellence in amazement and dread, estimating that they contained divine, not human, knowledge. He said: "Tell me, who dictated these verses to you?"

The boy replied: "Myself, master."

When the other, incredulous, kept on persistently repeating the question, the boy confessed in detail everything that he had done. Then the master said: "My son, that evil versifier was of course the devil," and he added: "My dear boy, are you sorry for having done homage to that seducer?"

THE BOY: Yes, sir.

MASTER: Just renounce the devil and his homage and all his ceremonies and all his works.

And the boy did so.

Then the master, cutting off the sleeves of his garment, threw them to the devil, with these words: "These sleeves are yours, seducer of men. You shall possess nothing else of this creature of God."

118

At once the sleeves were whisked away in the presence of all and were struck by lightning; the boy's body, however, remained unharmed. This tale was told to me by a certain prior of the church of Trèves.

Caesar of Heisterbach: 13th century
Dialogus Miraculorum
Trans. by H. E. W.

A Sinister Banquet[1]

¶ THERE FLOURISHED in Rome during the same time the most famous poet Virgil, who came from Mantua, a city in Sicily,[2] and was well known to the king because he had often been honored by him with gifts. On account of his renown and because at that time he was considered eminent among philosophers, a father sent his son to him with great gifts, begging him by his gods to instruct the boy in his learning and to guard him very carefully from the wiles of evil men. For the father was afraid that he would suffer some evil through envy, for having received this knowledge from soothsayers and astrologers. But Virgil, receiving the boy through respect and friendship for the king, first instructed him in the alphabet, and then, by coaxing and endearments, as is the custom of teachers, taught him within a short time to form syllables from letters and sentences from syllables and discourses from sentences. So, as the boy gradually became proficient, he began to read on his own account and to speak both languages, that is, Greek and Latin.

Virgil was pleased and admired the talented speed shown by the boy and, conceiving greater hope for him, devoted more care to him. The boy adapted his mind to his master's instruction. Being naturally of exceptional ability, he immediately committed, with his subtle talent, whatever he once heard and understood to his vivid memory; and there was no need to ask his master about it a second time. Hence it happened that within the space of one year he outshone his fellow

---

1. A tale that typically mingles fact and fantasy; Virgil is presented here, as in many other medieval tales, as a legendary figure not unlike Alexander the Great, an ageless, powerful miracle worker. 2. Virgil came from Mantua, but Mantua is not in Sicily.

pupils who were older than he and had already been in training under masters for five or seven years; and he asked Virgil to consider him worthy of more profound studies. Observing that the boy's crudeness had disappeared and that he was now clever enough to appreciate a knowledge of the arts, he willingly acceded to his wish. By reason therefore of his love of the liberal arts, Virgil condensed their vast prolixity into the brief compass of a small manual; and anyone could easily learn to perfection in three years the subjects that he had scarcely been able to absorb even with great effort. This booklet he was never willing to intrust to anyone even for an hour, neither to master nor pupil, and not even to Augustus, the ruler of the world himself, except to Lucinius, to whose proficiency he devoted himself. To him, for whose use he had produced it, he handed over the manual, discussing the arts amicably with him in his room and apart from the others.

To begin with, he expounded grammar to him, the first and the mother of the arts. This he absorbed with such rapidity that even Virgil himself marveled. Next, they advanced to dialectics, in which it is remarkable how much acuteness the boy displayed. For no one there even among the experienced teachers was more skillful in propounding questions, no one readier in solving them. Then he passed on to the flowery fields of rhetoric whereby he fully acquired the charms of eloquence. Having then completely mastered these three subjects, he proceeded to the remaining four, that we call the *quadrivium,* and these he learned without much effort and declared that the last one, that is astronomy, was more valuable than the others. To this he put his mind so intently that by means of certain rules furnished him by Virgil, he discovered from the movements of the planets and the other stars and the appearance of the atmosphere whatever happened throughout the entire universe. This knowledge was of great benefit to him, as will be shown in what follows.

After Lucinius attained complete knowledge of all the arts, he did not neglect Virgil's lectures on the books of the poets and the philosophers. Then and thereafter directing his mental vision to the higher philosophy, he gained the reputation and prestige of the great philosophers—not, however, without incurring the envy of many men. For he was envied in the highest possible degree by those who could not reach the lofty comprehension of his knowledge and resented that respect shown to a boy which was denied them in their old age. Hence they planned to rid themselves of him by poison or some other means, but their fear of Virgil and the authority of the royal family checked them to some extent. But since envy always possesses and torments its possessor, nor gives him even a moment's peace, the hatred of these men for Lucinius, engendered and stimulated by envy, at last brought them to the point of plotting to mix poison in the wine at a banquet to which he was insidiously invited. Lucinius was, however, quite aware of the situation, because long before that he had discovered, through the previously mentioned rules, this very scheme and their ill-will toward him. However, shrewdly feigning ignorance of this, he told his hosts that it was neither respectful nor right that such an important banquet of such important personalities should be held without Virgil and the Roman nobles. If he came, he would gratefully accept their hospitality, prepared, should the opportunity arise, to repay them for their generosity. But since he had been intrusted to Virgil's protection and feared beyond measure the master's ferrule, he declared that without him he not only could not but did not even dare to make the slightest move. Hearing these and similar excuses, blinded by their wickedness, they invited Virgil and also asked some Roman citizens, thinking it of little account if they died from the poisoned drink, provided Lucinius did not escape from their murderous clutches.

When the banqueters were seated, each guest reclined according to difference in age and rank. Virgil, however, as being the most distinguished, whom Caesar had commanded all to honor, occupied the first place at the banquet. The man who had sent out the invitations and who was the organizer of the plot attended to the arrangements along with certain others. The guests were served with innumerable dishes, various kinds of wines were drunk and amid great joy and lavishness the banquet proceeded. Meanwhile, Lucinius, mentally pondering over his rules, waited for the drink that they had concocted for him to be brought on.

While the banquet went on and the guests were regaled with everything that human skill could devise for eating, the pestiferous tortuous snake whom I called the head of the conspiracy brought a huge gold goblet, filled with death, and set it down in front of Virgil. Immediately the nostrils of the guests dilated with a kind of sweet aroma, and everyone was provoked to drink. Now one by one they called for the deadly potion, and it was just being handed to Virgil when Lucinius snatched the goblet and with his hand motioning all to silence, said:

121

"I am afraid that the pleasant flavor has something bitter in it, because the bee carries a sting with his honey and the fisherman throws a hook in his bait to catch fish."

The conspirators were stricken by their seared conscience, and as the poet has it:

> "They confessed their guilty crime
> by the pallor of their face."

In an attempt, however, to dissemble and to make some reply, they said the king's son was giving unparalleled thanks to those who were making obeisance to him, and he had made the remark jestingly. But Lucinius retorted: "By this act will it be proved that you are guiltless in regard to this remark that I have uttered not jokingly but in anger, and that your fellow guests were invited in honest and simple faith, if you are the first to drink from this potion. Otherwise, by my father and Caesar's life, you plotted against our life."

What should they do? Where should they turn? What should they reply to the accusations? On all sides, a tight situation; among all of them, a breathless panting feeling: complete despair of being saved. For they saw two courses open to them, one of which they could not escape: to die, or to drink. But they did not know which of the two courses to choose, for they knew that, though they drank, they would have to die; if not, they would be handed over to Caesar as criminals, to be punished by various kinds of torture. However, they thought it was better to fall by their own hand than to subject themselves to the sport of others. "By this token," they said, "you will know, Lucinius, that we plotted no evil against you or your fellow guests, if after taking this wine we survive three days."

The one who had proffered the cup took it and drank and then gave it to his accomplices in the crime to drink. They did so, and, according to the philosopher's statement, instantly falling into the pit that they had dug for others, in full view they expired, their eyes starting from their head. Thus the eminent youth freed himself and cleverly punished his rivals and acquired for himself a famous reputation among the nobles and the rabble; and not only did no one after that dare to contrive any evil against him, but no one even thought of it, as everyone believed there was something divine in him by means of which he had a foreknowledge of future events. Though he was so great and was considered so great by men and though

Virgil declared him equal to himself in every faculty, he never however wanted to sit down with Virgil or to be considered an equal, but always remained under his sway and training, as though he were first learning the alphabet. Hence his humility was particularly praised on this account, that, though he was tall of stature and Virgil was small, walking or standing with his master he contracted his body and bent forward so that he would not seem taller or more distinguished.

Iohannes of Alta Silva: 13th century
Dolopathos
Trans. by H. E. W.

The Speaking Statue

¶ WHEN TITUS was emperor of Rome, he made a decree that the natal day of his first-born son should be held sacred; and that whosoever violated it by any kind of labor should be put to death. This edict being promulgated, he called Virgil, the learned man, to him and said, "Good friend, I have established a certain law, but as offenses may frequently be committed without being discovered by the ministers of justice, I desire you to frame some curious piece of art which may reveal to me every transgressor of the law." Virgil replied, "Sire, your will shall be accomplished." He straightway constructed a magic statue, and caused it to be erected in the midst of the city. By virtue of the secret powers with which it was invested, it communicated to the emperor whatever offenses were committed in secret on that day. And thus, by the accusation of the statue, an infinite number of persons were convicted. Now, there was a certain carpenter, called Focus, who pursued his occupation every day alike. Once, as he lay in bed, his thought turned upon the accusations of the statue, and the multitudes which it had caused to perish. In the morning he clothed himself and proceeded to the statue, which he addressed in the following manner: "O statue! Statue! Because of thy informations, many of our citizens have been apprehended and slain. I vow to my God that, if thou accusest me, I will break thy head." Having so said, he returned home. About the first hour, the emperor, as he was wont, dispatched sundry messengers to the statue, to inquire

123

if the edict had been strictly complied with. After they had arrived and delivered the emperor's pleasure, the statue exclaimed, "Friends, look up; what see ye written upon my forehead?" They looked, and beheld three sentences which ran thus: "Times are altered. Men grow worse. He who speaks truth will have his head broken." "Go," said the statue, "declare to his majesty what you have seen and read." The messengers obeyed, and detailed the circumstances as they had happened.

The emperor, therefore, commanded his guard to arm and march to the place on which the statue was erected; and he further ordered that, if any one presumed to molest it, they should bind him hand and foot, and drag him into his presence. The soldiers approached the statue and said, "Our emperor wills you to declare who have broken the law, and who they were that threatened you." The statue made answer, "Seize Focus the carpenter! Every day he violates the law and, moreover, menaces me." Immediately Focus was apprehended and conducted to the emperor, who said, "Friend, what do I hear of thee? Why dost thou break my law?" "My Lord," answered Focus, "I cannot keep it! For I am obliged to obtain every day eight pennies, which, without incessant labor, I have not the means of acquiring." "And why eight pennies?" said the emperor. "Every day through the year," returned the carpenter, "I am bound to repay two pennies which I borrowed in my youth; two I lend; two I lose; and two I spend." "You must make this more clear," said the emperor. "My lord," he replied, "listen to me. I am bound, each day, to repay two pennies to my father; for, when I was a boy, my father expended upon me daily the like sum. Now he is poor and needs my assistance, and therefore I return what I borrowed formerly. Two other pennies I lend to my son, who is pursuing his studies; in order that if, by any chance, I should fall into poverty, he may restore the loan, just as I have done to his grandfather. Again, I lose two pennies every day on my wife; for she is contradictious, willful, and passionate. Now, because of this disposition, I account whatsoever is given to her entirely lost. Lastly, two other pennies I expend upon myself in meat and drink. I cannot do with less; nor can I obtain them without unremitting labor. You now know the truth; and, I pray you, give a righteous judgment." "Friend," said the emperor, "thou hast answered well. Go, and labor earnestly in thy calling." Soon after this the emperor died, and Focus the carpenter, on account of his singular wisdom, was elected in his stead, by the unanimous choice

of the whole nation. He governed as wisely as he had lived; and at
his death his picture, bearing on the head eight pennies, was deposited
among the effigies of the deceased emperors.

Gesta Romanorum: 13th–14th centuries
Trans. by C. Swan

Honor Among Thieves

¶ IN THE REIGN of a certain emperor, there were two thieves who
bound themselves by an oath never to quit one another on any
emergency, even though death were the alternative. They afterwards
committed many depredations, and were, on some occasions, guilty
of murder. It happened that one of them, being caught in some theft,
was imprisoned and placed in fetters. His companion, understanding
what had chanced, hastened to him and said, "My friend, by the
engagement which we have formed, I adjure you to tell me what
I can do to serve you." "It appears," answered the other, "that I must
die, having been taken in the fact for which I am sentenced. But
I will show you how to oblige me. Obtain permission to remain in my
place, while I hasten to arrange my affairs and provide for my wife
and children. Having done this, I will return in due time and liberate
you." "My friend," answered the first, "I will readily comply with
your wishes."

He went therefore to the judge, and spoke thus: "My lord, my
friend has been thrown into prison and condemned to death. It seems
that there is no chance for him; let it please you, then, to permit him
to return home to arrange the affairs of his family, and I, in the mean
time, will become his surety and remain in prison." "On such a day,"
replied the judge, "he, with some others, will be executed. If, upon
that day, he return not before a certain hour, look you to it; your
death is inevitable." "My lord," answered the man, "I am prepared
for the worst." "Let him go, then. I consent to your wishes."

The judge ordered the substitute to be manacled and placed in
prison in the room of his friend, who immediately set out to his
family. So long, however, did he postpone his return that the day of

125

execution arrived and his pledge was unredeemed. The latter, therefore, was brought, with many others, to the seat of judgment. "Where is your friend?" asked the judge. "He has not arrived to make good his word." "I hope the best, my lord," replied the other. "I do not think he will fail me."

Some time passed over, and still he came not; and the prisoner was at length conducted to the cross. "You must attribute your death to yourself," said the judge; "do not charge it upon me. You have rashly trusted to your friend, and he has deceived you." "My lord," replied he, "defer the crucifixion but for a moment, and suffer me to play upon an instrument three times before my death." "Play!" exclaimed the judge. "Of what nature is that playing?" "I will shout, my lord." "As you please."

According he began to vociferate. He shouted loudly once, twice, and at the third shout he distinguished, at some distance, a man running toward them with surprising velocity. "My lord! My lord! There is a man coming; stay the execution—perhaps it is my friend, and I shall yet be liberated!" The judge waited, and the person they looked for made his appearance. "I am the man you expect," he exclaimed. "I have arranged my affairs, and meanwhile my friend had been in peril of death for me; let him now freely depart, for I am ready to suffer death for my crimes."

The judge regarded him for a few moments with attention, and then said, "My friend, tell me whence it comes that you are so faithful to one another?" "My lord," he replied, "from our youth up we have been friends, and ever pledged ourselves to be faithful. For this reason he put himself in my place till I had settled my affairs." "Well," said the judge, "because of this remarkable instance of fidelity, I pardon you. Remain with me, and I will provide all things necessary for your well-being." They returned thanks to the judge, and promised equal fidelity to him. He then received them to favor; and all praised the judge who showed them this mercy.

Gesta Romanorum: 13th–14th centuries
Trans. by C. Swan

The Necromancer and the Knight

¶ IN THE REIGN of Titus there lived a certain noble and devout knight who had a beautiful wife; but she dishonored herself, and persisted in her dishonor. The knight, therefore, was very sorrowful, and resolved to visit the Holy Land. In this determination he said to his wife, "My beloved, I go to the Holy Land, and leave you to the guidance of your own discretion." No sooner had he embarked than the lady sent for a certain skillful necromancer whom she loved; and he dwelt with her. It happened that, as they lay in bed, the lady observed, "If you would do one thing for me, I might become your wife."

"What is it," replied he, "that will please you, and which I can perform for you?"

"My husband is gone to the Holy Land, and loves me little; now, if by your art you could destroy him, all that I possess is yours."

"I acquiesce," said the clerk, "but on condition that you marry me." To this the lady bound herself, and the necromancer fashioned an image under the similitude and name of the knight, and fixed it before him on the wall.

In the meantime, while the knight was passing through the main street of Rome, a wise master met him in the way, and observing him narrowly, said, "My friend, I have a secret to communicate."

"Well, master, what would you please to say?"

"This day you are one of death's children, unless you follow my advice; your wife is a harlot, and contrives your death."

The knight, hearing what was said of his spouse, put confidence in the speaker and said, "Good master, save my life, and I will amply recompense you."

"Willingly," answered the other, "if you will do as I shall tell you."

The knight promised, and the master took him to a bath, undressed him, and desired him to bathe. Then putting into his hand a polished mirror, he said, "Look attentively upon this, and you will see wonders." He did so, and the meanwhile the master read to him from a book. "What see you?" he asked.

"I see," said the knight, "a certain clerk in my house, with an image of wax which resembles me, and which he has fastened in the wall."

"Look again," continued the master; "what do you perceive now?"

"He takes a bow, and places in it a sharp arrow; and now he aims at the effigy."

"As you love your life, the moment you discern the arrow flying to its mark, place yourself in the bath, and remain there until I tell you to come out."

As soon, therefore, as the arrow quitted the string, he plunged his body into the water. This done, the master said, "Raise your head and look into the mirror. What do you perceive now?"

"The effigy is not struck, and the arrow is sticking by its side. The clerk appears much concerned."

"Look in the mirror once more," said the master, "and observe what he does."

"He now goes nearer to the image, and refixes the arrow in the string in order to strike it."

"As you value your life, do as before."

Again the knight plunged his body into the water as soon as he saw by the mirror that the clerk was bending the bow; and then, at the command of the master, resuming his inspection of the mirror, said, "The clerk makes great lamentation, and says to my wife, 'If the third time I do not strike the effigy, I shall lose my life.' Now he approaches so near that I think he cannot miss it."

"Take care," said the master." As soon as you see him bend the bow, immerse your body as I before told you." The knight watched attentively, and as soon as he saw the clerk draw back the bow to shoot, plunged below the water.

"Rise quickly, and look into the mirror."

When he had done so, he began to laugh. "My friend," said the master, "why do you laugh?"

"I observe," answered he, "very distinctly that the clerk has missed the effigy, and that the arrow, rebounding, has entered his bowels and destroyed him. My wife makes a hole under my bed, and there he is buried."

"Rise, then, dress yourself, and pray to God."

The knight returned sincere thanks for his life and, having performed his pilgrimage, journeyed toward his own home. His wife met and received him with much apparent pleasure. He dissembled for a few days, and then sending for her parents, said to them, "My dear friends, hear why I have desired your presence. This woman, your daughter and my wife, has committed adultery; and, what is worse, designed to murder me." The lady denied the accusation with an oath. The knight then began to relate the whole story of the clerk's actions and end. "And," he continued, "if you do not credit this, come and see where the clerk is buried." He then led them into the bed-chamber, and dragged the body from its hiding place. The judge was called, and sentenced her to be burnt, and her ashes to be scattered in the air. The knight soon afterwards espoused a beautiful virgin, by whom he had many children; and with whom he finished his days in peace.

Gesta Romanorum: 13th–14th centuries
Trans. by C. Swan

The Hermit and the Devil

¶ THERE FORMERLY LIVED a hermit, who in a remote cave passed night and day in the service of God. At no great distance from his cell a shepherd tended his flock. It happened that this person one day fell into a deep sleep, and in the meantime a robber, perceiving his carelessness, carried off his sheep. When the keeper awoke and dis-covered the theft, he began to swear in good set terms that he had lost his sheep; and where they were conveyed was totally beyond his knowledge. Now, the lord of the flock, when he heard this, was filled with rage, and commanded him to be put to death. This gave great umbrage to the hermit before mentioned. "O Heaven," said he to himself, "seest thou this deed? The innocent suffers for the guilty; why permittest thou such things? If thus injustice triumph, why do I remain here? I will again enter the world, and do as other men do."

With these feelings he quitted his hermitage and returned into the world; but God willed not that he should be lost: an angel in the form of a man was commissioned to join him. Accordingly, crossing the hermit's path, he thus accosted him: "My friend, where are you going?" "I go," said the other, "to the city before us." "I will accom-pany you," replied the angel. "I am a messenger from heaven, and come to be the associate of your way." They walked on together toward the city. When they had entered, they entreated for the love of God harborage during the night at the house of a certain knight, who received them with cheerfulness and entertained them with much magnificence. The knight had an only son lying in the cradle, whom he exceedingly loved. After supper, their bedchamber was sumptuously decorated; and the angel retired with the hermit to rest. But about the middle of the night the angel got up and strangled the sleeping infant. The hermit, horror-struck at what he witnessed, said within himself, "Never can this be an angel of God. The good knight gave him everything that was necessary; he had but this poor innocent, and this strange companion of mine has strangled him." Yet he was afraid to reprove him.

In the morning both arose and went forward to another city, in which they were honorably entertained at the house of one of the inhabitants. This person possessed a superb golden cup which he highly valued; and which, during the night, the angel purloined. The hermit thought, "Verily, this is one of the lost angels; our host has treated us well, and yet he has robbed him." But still he held his peace, for his apprehension was extreme.

On the morrow they continued their journey; and as they walked they came to a certain river, over which a bridge was thrown; they ascended the bridge, and about midway a poor man met them. "My friend," said the angel to him, "show us the way to yonder city." The pilgrim turned and pointed with his finger to the road they were to take; but as he turned, the angel seized him by the shoulders and precipitated him into the stream below. At this the terrors of the hermit were again aroused—"It is the devil," exclaimed he internally, "it is the devil, and no good angel! What evil had the poor man done that he should be drowned?" He would now have departed alone; but was afraid to give utterance to the thoughts of his heart.

About the hour of vespers they reached a city in which they again sought shelter for the night; but the master of the house to whom they applied sharply refused it. "For the love of Heaven," said the angel, "afford us a shelter, lest we fall a prey to the wolves and other wild beasts." The man pointed to a sty—"That," said he, "is inhabited by pigs; if it please you to lie there, you may—but to no other place will I admit you." "If we can do no better," returned the angel, "we must accept your ungracious offer." They did so; and in the morning the angel, calling their host, said, "My friend, I give you this cup," and he presented to him the stolen goblet.

The hermit, more and more astonished at what he saw, said to himself, "Now I am certain this is the devil. The good man who received us with all kindness he despoiled, and gives the plunder to this fellow who refused us a lodging." Turning to the angel, he exclaimed, "I will travel with you no longer. I commend you to God."

"Dear friend," answered the angel, "first hear me, and then go thy way. When thou wert in thy hermitage, the owner of the flock unjustly put to death his servant. True it is he died innocently, but he had formerly done deeds for which he deserved to die. God allowed him to be slain, to enable him to escape the future consequences of those former sins of which he had not repented. But the guilty man who stole the sheep will suffer eternally, while the owner of the flock will repair, by alms and good works, that which he ignorantly committed. As for the son of the hospitable knight, whom I strangled in the cradle, know that before the boy was born he performed numerous works of charity and mercy, but afterwards grew parsimonious and covetous in order to enrich the child, of which he was inordinately fond. This was the cause of its death; and now its distressed parent again is become a devout Christian. Then, for the cup which I purloined from him who received us so kindly, know that before the cup was made, there was not a more abstemious person in the world; but afterwards he took such pleasure in it, and drank from it so often, that he was intoxicated twice or thrice during the day. I took away the cup, and he has turned to his former sobriety. Again, I cast the pilgrim into the river; and know that he whom I drowned was a good Christian but had he proceeded much farther, he would have fallen into a mortal sin. Now he is saved, and reigns in celestial glory. Then, that I bestowed the cup upon the inhospitable citizen, know nothing is done without reason. He suffered us to occupy the swine-house, and I gave him a valuable consideration. But he will hereafter reign in hell. Put a guard, therefore, on thy lips, and detract not from the Almighty. For He knoweth all things." The hermit, hearing this, fell at the feet of the angel and entreated pardon. He returned to his hermitage, and became a good and pious Christian.

Gesta Romanorum: 13th–14th centuries
Trans. by C. Swan

The Three Talismans

¶ KING DARIUS was a circumspect prince, and had three sons, whom he much loved. On his deathbed he bequeathed the kingdom to his first-born; to the second, all his own personal acquisitions; and to the third a golden ring, a necklace, and a piece of valuable cloth. The ring had the power to render anyone who bore it on his finger beloved, and, moreover, obtained for him whatsoever he sought. The necklace enabled the person who wore it upon his breast to accomplish his heart's desire; and the cloth had such virtue that whosoever sat upon it and thought where he would be carried, there he immediately found himself. These three gifts the king conferred upon the younger son, for the purpose of aiding his studies; but the mother retained them until he was of a proper age. Soon after the bequests, the old monarch gave up the ghost, and was magnificently buried. The two elder sons then took possession of their legacies, and the mother of the younger delivered to him the ring, with the caution that he should beware of the artifices of women, or he would otherwise lose the ring. Jonathan (for that was his name) took the ring, and went zealously to his studies, in which he made himself proficient. But walking on a certain day through the street, he observed a very beautiful woman with whom he was so much struck that he took her to him. He continued, however, to use the ring, and found favor with everyone, insomuch that whatever he desired he had.

Now, the lady was greatly surprised that he lived so splendidly, having no possessions; and once, when he was particularly exhilarated, tenderly embraced him and protested that there was not a creature under the sun whom she loved so much as she did him. He ought therefore, she thought, to tell her by what means he supported his magnificence. He, suspecting nothing, explained the virtues of the ring; and she begged that he would be careful of so invaluable a treasure. "But," added she, "in your daily intercourse with men you may lose it; place it in my custody, I beseech you." Overcome by her entreaties, he gave up the ring; and when his necessities came upon him, she asserted loudly that thieves had carried it off. He lamented bitterly that now he had not any means of subsistence; and, hastening to his mother, stated how he had lost his ring. "My son," said she, "I forewarned you of what would happen, but you have paid no attention to my advice. Here is the necklace; preserve it more carefully. If it be lost, you will forever want a thing of the greatest honor and profit."

Jonathan took the necklace, and returned to his studies. At the gate of the city his mistress met him, and received him with the appearance of great joy. He remained with her, wearing the necklace upon his breast; and whatever he thought, he possessed. As before, he lived so gloriously that the lady wondered, well knowing that he had neither gold nor silver. She guessed, therefore, that he carried another talisman; and cunningly drew from him the history of the wonder-working necklace. "Why," said the lady, "do you always take it with you? You may think in one moment more than can be made use of in a year. Let me keep it." "No," replied he, "you will lose the necklace, as you lost the ring; and thus I shall receive the greatest possible injury." "O my lord," replied she, "I have learned, by having had the custody of the ring, how to secure the necklace; and I assure you no one can possibly get it from me." The silly youth confided in her words, and delivered the necklace.

Now, when all he possessed was expended, he sought his talisman; and she, as before, solemnly protested that it had been stolen. This threw Jonathan into the greatest distress. "Am I mad," cried he, "that after the loss of my ring I should give up the necklace?" Immediately hastening to his mother, he related to her the whole circumstance. Not a little afflicted, she said, "Oh, my dear child, why didst thou place confidence in the woman? People will believe thee a fool; but be wise, for I have nothing more for you than the valuable cloth which your father left; and if you lose that, it will be quite useless to return to me." Jonathan received the cloth, and again went to his studies. The harlot seemed very joyful; and he, spreading out the cloth, said, "My dear girl, my father bequeathed me this beautiful cloth; sit down upon it by my side." She complied, and Jonathan secretly wished that they were in a desert place, out of the reach of man. The talisman took effect; they were carried into a forest on the utmost boundary of the world where there was not a trace of humanity. The lady wept bitterly, but Jonathan paid no regard to her tears. He solemnly vowed to Heaven that he would leave her a prey to the wild beasts unless she restored his ring and necklace; and this she promised to do.

Presently, yielding to her request, the foolish Jonathan revealed the power of the cloth; and, in a little time being weary, placed his head in her lap and slept. In the interim, she contrived to draw away that part of the cloth upon which he reposed, and sitting upon it alone, wished herself where she had been in the morning. The cloth immediately executed her wishes, and left Jonathan slumbering in the forest. When he awoke and found his cloth and his mistress departed, he burst into an agony of tears. Where to bend his steps he knew not; but arising and fortifying himself with the sign of the cross, he walked along a certain path until he reached a deep river, over which he must pass. But he found it so bitter and hot that it even separated the flesh from the bones. Full of grief, he conveyed away a small quantity of that water, and when he had proceeded a little farther, felt hungry. A tree upon which hung the most tempting fruit invited him to partake; he did so, and immediately became a leper. He gathered also a little of the fruit, and conveyed it with him. After traveling for some time, he arrived at another stream, of which the virtue was such that it restored the flesh to his feet; and, eating of a second tree, he was cleansed from his leprosy. Some of that fruit he likewise took along with him.

Walking in this manner day after day, he came at length to a castle, where he was met by two men, who inquired what he was. "I am a physician," answered he. "This is lucky," said the other; "the king of this country is a leper, and if you are able to cure him of his leprosy, vast rewards will be assigned you." He promised to try his skill, and they led him forward to the king. The result was fortunate; he supplied him with the fruit of the second tree, and the leprosy left him; and washing the flesh with the water, it was completely restored. Being rewarded most bountifully, he embarked on board a vessel for his native city. There he circulated a report that a great physician was arrived; and the lady who had cheated him of the talismans, being sick unto death, immediately sent for him. Jonathan was so much disguised that she retained no recollection of him, but he very well remembered her. As soon as he arrived, he declared that medicine would avail nothing, unless she first confessed her sins; and if she had defrauded anyone, it must be restored. The lady, reduced to the very verge of the grave, in a low voice acknowledged that she had cheated Jonathan of the ring, necklace, and cloth; and had left him in a desert place to be devoured by wild beasts. When she had said this, the pretending physician exclaimed: "Tell me, lady, where these talismans are?" "In that chest," answered she; and delivered up the keys, by which he obtained possession of his treasures. Jonathan then gave her of the fruit which produced leprosy; and, after she had eaten, of the water which separated the flesh from the bones. The consequence was that she was excruciated with agony, and shortly died. Jonathan hastened to his mother, and the whole kingdom rejoiced at his return. He told by what means God had freed him from such various dangers; and, having lived many years, ended his days in peace.

Gesta Romanorum: 13th–14th centuries
Trans. by C. Swan

The Witch and the Spring

¶ KING BOCRE had one son, whom he loved like his own life, and he did not send him away outside his domain, for fear that some trouble would chance to befall him. The boy begged a certain wise man, a counselor to the king, to request his father to let him go riding and hunting. Then the counselor spoke to the king, as the boy wished. And the king said to the counselor: "Go with him." And the counselor said: "Gladly."

Then the king's son went forth with the counselor, and seeing a stag in a field, they pursued it. The counselor said to the attendants: "Leave the prince alone to follow the stag, so that he may learn wisdom."

The king's son followed the stag and outdistanced his companions and could not return to them, since he had lost his way in the glade. But they searched for him and not finding him, returned to the king and said: "A lion became angry and devoured your son."

Then the king rent his garment and was overwhelmed on account of his son.

But the boy was in the forest and beheld a very beautiful maiden and cried out to her and said: "Who are you?"

"I am the king's daughter," she answered. "Sleep overtook me as I rode on an elephant that led me out of my way, and I fell down and stayed here. Take me on your horse and free me."

The boy replied: "I am a king's son too, and this is what happened to me."

The girl said: "I know the way."

He took her on his horse behind him and they rode fast and came to a desert, and the maiden said: "I am going to wash my feet."

She dismounted and came to a spot where she stayed.

Now the boy, noticing that she was lingering, dismounted and watched from a crack in a wall. The girl was a witch and was standing around with others and saying: "I brought the king's son here."

The other witches said: "Lead him to such and such a spot, and we shall have our will of him."

The young man, hearing this, was struck with fear and remounted his horse. The witch turned back into a girl and went out and mounted the horse. The prince trembled with a great dread and his face changed color. The woman realized that he was terrified and said: "What are you afraid of, boy?"

He answered: "I have a false evil friend, and I am afraid of him."

But she retorted: "Didn't you say that your father is a king?"

And he said: "My father has no power over him."

She said: "Deceive him with silver and gold."

To which the boy answered: "I cannot make him a friend with silver or gold."

Then she said: "Call upon God above Himself."

The boy extended his hands heavenward and declared: "O God, free me from the hands of this witch, so that I may not be in her power."

When she saw that she was known to the boy, she fell from the horse and broke her hips.

He fled through the desert and suffered great thirst. He came to a spring, from which whoever drank, if a man, turned into a woman, and if a woman, into a man. He did not know this, but he drank, and was changed into a woman and began to weep and was afraid to drink any more water. That night he stood there, sadly, and suddenly a troupe of girls came playing and singing near the spring. He too rose up to play with them, because he thought he had turned into a witch. The girls questioned him and said: "Who are you and where do you come from?"

He told them everything that had happened to him. One of them said: "Swear to marry me and I shall free and bring you back to your father."

And he swore. Then she said: "Drink from the water of that spring."

He drank, and was changed into a man. Then she took him and brought him to his father, to whom he related all that he had seen. Then the father commanded the counselor to be punished.

Historia Septem Sapientum: 13th century. Hilka: *Sammlung mittellateinischer Texte*
Trans. by H. E. W.

Welsh Soothsayers

¶ THERE ARE, too, among this Welsh people what you will not find elsewhere, many men called Awennithion, that is, inspired. When consulted regarding some ambiguity, in an ecstasy they are immediately seized with a frenzied exaltation, and finally become possessed. But they do not forthwith prophesy what is required of them; rather, through devious obscurities and varied talk poured forth in spate, trifling and light rather than coherent but still well expressed. The person who skillfully notes the response in some last minute verbal turn, will receive a clear answer. So finally they are aroused by the others from this state of ecstasy as if from a deep sleep, and are almost forcibly compelled to come to. Then you will discover two remarkable features: because after giving a response, unless they are violently aroused and recalled to themselves, they usually do not recover from such a frenzy; and, when they have recovered, they will recall none of all those things that were uttered by them in the interval. Hence, if they happen to be consulted on this point again or on another and have to speak, they will give utterance in altogether other and different terms. Perhaps on occasion they speak, as it were, through ecstatic and possessed, though unaware, spirits. These gifts usually come to them on sleep, through visions. For some of them seem to have sweet milk or honey flowing from their lips. In the case of others it seems that a paper with writing on it is placed on their mouth. Once wakened from their sleep, and soothed by a melody, they declare that they offered this favor for the public benefit.

Giraldus Cambrensis: 13th century
Descriptio Cambriae
Trans. by H. E. W.

The Norman Bachelor

When Acre yielded to the hostile host
('Twas but a year or two ago at most),
A pleasant chance in Normandy befell,
Which, as my memory serves, I mean to tell.

A needy bachelor had dwelling there,
Of worldly means in sooth so passing bare,
He once was fain his dinner meal to make
On the poor pittance of a farthing cake.

To help this miserable morsel down
He hied him to a tavern in the town,
And bade the vintner, as he meant to dine,
To draw him straight a farthing's worth of wine.

The vintner, one it seems of churlish kind,
Who car'd but little how his neighbor din'd,
From the next vessel fill'd his measure up,
And, as he pour'd it thence into a cup,
Slubber'd with such ill grace the business o'er,
That half the draught was spilt upon the floor.

To crown the deed, with supercilious pride,
"You'll soon grow rich, sir Bachelor!" he cried.
"Wine spilt, they say (be't true or falsely spoken),
For sequent good doth evermore betoken."

The Norman deem'd it were but labor lost
To chafe or wrangle with his boorish host;
His wit to artifice he wisely bent,
And thus devis'd the caitiff's punishment.

In his poor purse remain'd one farthing still;
This, with frank guise, as one who thought no ill,
He tender'd to his host, so would he please
To furnish him a farthing slice of cheese.

Up to the loft where all the cheeses lay,
The vintner hied, but muttering all the way:
That selfsame instant turn'd the knight about,
And from the wine-cask pluck'd the spigot out;

Forth gush'd the guggling liquor, bright and good
And the wide floor was delug'd with the flood.
Back sped the host, and, furious at the sight,
First pegg'd his cask, and next assail'd the knight;

But the strong Norman sternly shook the thrall,
Hurl'd back, and crush'd his wine-pots with his fall;
And, but that entering neighbors quell'd the fray,
The vintner then had seen his dying day.

The matter soon was to the king made known
(Count Henry of Champagne possess'd the throne);
And first the plaintive vintner stoutly spoke,
And claim'd redress; wine lost, and vessels broke.

The prince doom'd not the knight to recompense,
But will'd him first to argue his defense.
He the plain truth from end to end expos'd,
Then with these words his frank recital clos'd:

"Great sire!" he said, "this worthy host of mine
Foretold much good would spring from spilling wine;
That I, forsooth, whose cup was half thrown down,
Should soon become the wealthiest wight in town!

"My gratitude, I own, o'ercame me here,
And, weening wealth might ne'er be bought too dear,
I strove to make him richer than myself,
And shed full half a cask to purchase pelf."

He ceased, loud plaudits rang through all the court.
No tale was ever told so full of sport.
All rang'd them seemly by the Norman's side;
While good King Henry laugh'd until he cried;
Then thus dismiss'd the parties and their suit,
"What's spilt, is spilt—betide or bale or boot."

Fabliaux: 12th–13th centuries
Trans. by G. L. Way, 1815

The Blind Man and His Wife

¶ THERE WAS A BLIND MAN who had a very beautiful wife and watched over her chastity in mental agony, for he was very jealous. Now it happened on a certain day that they were sitting pleasantly in a garden near a pear tree. When the wife wanted to climb the tree to gather pears, the blind man consented but, to prevent any other man from approaching her, he encircled the trunk of the tree with his arms. The tree had many branches, and before the wife climbed up, a young man hid there, waiting for the woman to mount. So they met joyfully and embraced and kissed, and with Venus' plow the tufted sward and shady grove was furrowed. While the young man was engaged in the work, as powerfully as he could, and the wife responded with equal vigor to the furious thrusts upon her, the blind man heard the sounds they both made and in his agony he cried out: "O you most wicked woman! Though I lack sight, my hearing is very keen, making me aware that a lover is with you. I lay my complaint therefore about this most unspeakable crime before the mighty god Jupiter, who can bring joy to sad hearts and restore the sight of the blind."

At these words his sight was at once restored and as he looked up at the tree he saw the lover and suddenly exclaimed: "O you most deceitful woman! Why do you invent such tricks against me, when I believed that you were chaste and good? Woe is me! for I shall never again have a happy day with you!"

The wife, on hearing her husband reproaching her, was at first somewhat frightened, but assuming a cheerful look she quickly thought of a lie and answered her husband, exclaiming: "I thank all the gods and goddesses who have listened to my prayer and restored his sight to my dearest husband! For, my beloved, you must know that your sight is due to my effort and my prayers. For after spending up to now a great deal of money on medicine in vain, I resolved to pray to the gods to heal you and restore your sight. At last the god Mercury, at the command of almighty Jupiter, appeared to me in a dream, and said: 'If you climb the pear tree, and play the game of love with a young man, his former sight will be restored to

140

your husband.' Which I have now done in order to cure you. So you owe me gifts for such a service, since I have now restored your sight."

The blind man gave credence to the fraudulent trick of his wife and forgave her for her wickedness, and by giving her presents won her over as having been unjustly debauched against her will.

Adolphus: 14th century
Fabulae: Latin prose version in Wright's *Latin Stories*, 1854. Source of Chaucer's *Merchant's Tale*.
Trans. by H. E. W.

Part Three

ALCHEMY, ASTROLOGY, COSMOLOGY, TECHNOLOGY AND SCIENCE

The heritage of antiquity, both Greek and Roman, was largely transmitted to later ages. In the area relating to factual or scientific matter, treatises on medicine, anatomy, botany, architecture, mathematics, astrology, meteorology and physics were absorbed into the context of medieval knowledge. Greek texts were translated into Latin, the lingua franca *of European scholarship.*

In the medieval world the Arabs were particularly notable as possessors and disseminators of scientific knowledge, and also as original researchers. They absorbed the knowledge of classical (especially Greek) antiquity, and then transmitted it, with modifications, exegetical commentaries and corrective additions, to the Western world. The Arabs were pioneers in mathematics, astronomy, and medicine. Al-Kindi wrote on physics. In the tenth century Jabir ibn Hayyam expounded chemical theory. Al-Khwarizmi was a mathematician. Rhazes treated chemistry. Al-farabi tried to reconcile Greek philosophy with Islamic dogma. Haly Abbas produced works ˮon medicine. Averroës dealt with physics and cosmography.

The ancient heritage, as well as the contemporary Arabic studies, became matter for translation. Among such translators were Adelard of Bath, Robert of Chester, Gerard of Cremona, Moses Farachi, John of Seville, Michael Scot, Hennicus Aristippus, William of Moerbeke, Burgundio of Pisa, Robert Grosseteste.

Works of an encyclopedic nature were particularly in vogue. They gathered up into a vast, comprehensive treasury the totality of all available knowledge. Among the compilers of such works were:
Martianus Capella (fifth century): De Nuptiis Philologiae et Mercurii.
Isidore of Seville (560?–636): Etymologies.
Thomas of Cantimpré (thirteenth century): De Naturis Rerum.
Vincent of Beauvais (died c. 1264): Speculum Maius.
Roger Bacon (1214?–1294): Opus Maius.

Alchemy was the testing ground for what later became chemical truths. Alchemical experimentations began with mystical, philosophical postulates and hypothetical concepts, and culminated in the scientific spirit of Roger Bacon. Other branches of science developed in similar fashion; medicine, for example, based for centuries on traditional authorities, culminated in the anatomical truths of Vesalius. In some measure, the parallel can be followed through in the relationship of astronomy to astrology.

Though the Arabs made many significant contributions to medieval culture, in philosophy, literature and the physical and mathematical sciences, the original sources are only meagerly available in English renderings. For the interested student, there are French and German translations, commentaries and studies. Muhammed ibn Zakariya Razi's treatise on anatomy is available in Koning's edition, published in 1903. For technical matter from Arab and non-Arab sources, George Sarton's Introduction to the History of Science *(5 vols.; Baltimore, 1927–1947) may be profitably consulted, as well as the monumental* History of Technology, *edited by Charles Singer, et al. (5 vols.; 1954—). A. C. Crombie's* Medieval and Early Modern Science *(2 vols.; Anchor, 1959), is an excellent survey.*

Etymological and Astrological Diversions

¶ DAY: Day is the presence of the sun, or the sun above the earth, as night is the sun beneath the earth. For according as it is day or night, that is the reason why the sun is above the earth or under the earth. The day properly consists of twenty-four hours, until the day and the night, by the revolution of the heavens, complete the span of their course from the east to another sun in the east. Incorrectly, one day is the interval from the rising sun to the setting sun. There are two intervals in the day, daytime and nighttime: and the day is the length of twenty-four hours; the interval is twelve hours. Day is so called from the better half. Hence the term is used so that, without mention of the night, we talk of the number of days, as it is written in Holy Scripture: "And the evening and the morning were the first day."

According to the Egyptians, the day begins with sunset; according to the Persians, with sunrise; according to the Athenians, with the sixth hour of the day; according to the Romans, at midnight. . . . Day stems from the word *gods*[1], whose names the Romans consecrated to certain stars. For they called the first day after the Sun, that is the chief of all the stars, just as that same day is the principal one of the others. They called the second day after the Moon, that in splendor and magnitude is next to the Sun and derives its light from it. They called the third day after Mars, named Vesper. The fourth day they called after Mercury, that they said was a white disc. The fifth day they called after Jupiter, named Phacthon: the sixth, from Venus, that they call Lucifer, that gives most light of all the stars. The seventh day is called after Saturn whose position is in the sixth heaven and that is said to complete its course in thirty years. Accordingly the pagans took the names of the days from these seven stars because they believed that these days were somehow propitious for

---

1. Latin: *dii*. This derivation, as with so much medieval etymology, is not based on what modern scholars would consider scientific principles.

them. From the Sun, they declared, came the spirit; from the Moon, body; from Mercury, talent and language; from Venus, pleasure; from Mars, blood; from Jupiter, temperance; from Saturn, fluids.

Such was the stupidity of the pagans, who concocted such absurd inventions. Among the Hebrews the first day is called the Sabbath: among us, Sunday. The pagans dedicated it to the Sun. The day after the Sabbath is the second day of the week, that the pagans call Monday. The third day after the Sabbath is the third day of the week, that they called the day of Mars. The fourth day after the Sabbath is the fourth day of the week, that the pagans call the day of Mercury. The fifth day after the Sabbath is the fifth day of the week, that is, the fifth from Sunday, called by the pagans Jupiter's day. The sixth day after the Sabbath is the sixth day of the week, called by these same pagans the day of Venus. The seventh day is the day of the Lord, that the pagans dedicated to Saturn and called Saturn's day. The Sabbath, a Hebrew expression, is translated as *rest* in Latin, because God rested on that day from all his labors.

Isidore of Seville: 7th century
Etymologies
Trans. by H. E. W.

The Origin of Glass

¶ GLASS is so called because by its transparency it is translucent to sight. In the case of other materials, whatever is contained within is hidden, but in glass whatever fluid or substance is within is revealed identically from without; as though, closed, it is as it were exposed. This was the origin of glass: In that area of Syria called Phoenicia, next to Judea, around the base of Mt. Carmel there is a swamp whence rises the River Belus, flowing for a distance of five miles into the sea near Ptolemais, whose sands are washed clean of rubble by the river. The story goes that a ship carrying natron[1] traders was wrecked there. When they were preparing a meal at various points along the beach, and had no stones for placing under the utensils,

1. Hydrated sodium carbonate, a mineral found in salt lakes.

they put down lumps of natron from the ship. When these lumps burned, mixed with sand on the beach, a new liquid flowed in translucent streams; this was the origin of glass. Presently, as cleverness is ingenious, they were not satisfied with natron alone, but were eager to develop this art with other mixtures. A fire is made with light, dry wood. Copper and natron are added in steadily heated furnaces to melt the metal, and lumps are formed. Afterward in the workshop the lumps are poured back and shapes are formed by blowing, or smoothed on a lathe, or chased like silver. . . .

There is a legend that in the reign of Tiberius Caesar a certain artisan discovered at what temperature glass is malleable and ductile. Admitted into Caesar's presence, he handed him a phial which the latter indignantly dashed to the ground. The artisan picked up from the ground the phial that had become indented like a bronze vase. Then taking out a hammer he repaired the phial. When he had done this, Caesar said to him: "Is there anyone else who knows this characteristic of glass?" After he had sworn that no one else knew, Caesar ordered him to be decapitated; otherwise, if the truth were known, gold would have the value of mud and the value of all metals would be gone. And this was true, because if glass vases did not break, they would be better than gold or silver.

Isidore of Seville: 7th century
Etymologies
Trans. by H. E. W.

Atoms

¶ WHAT PHILOSOPHERS call atoms are certain parts of bodies in the universe so minutely small that they are invisible and incapable of *tomein,* that is, cutting: hence they are called atoms. These atoms are believed to sweep through the void of the universe with restless motions and to be driven in all directions, like very tiny particles of dust that appear to stream through windows with the sun's rays. From these atoms some ancient philosophers considered that trees and grass and all crops originate, and that fire and water and all universal things spring thence and are composed of these atoms.

There are atoms in bodies, in time, or in number. In a body, as for instance a stone. You break the stone into parts and divide the parts themselves into grains like sand. And again divide these same grains of sand in the most minute dust until, if possible, you reach a minuteness that cannot be divided or cut any further. That is the atom in bodies. The meaning of atoms in time is as follows: Say you divide the year into months, the months into days, the days into hours. The parts of the hours still admit of division, until you reach a point of time and an infinitesimal second that cannot be stretched into the smallest interval; hence it cannot be divided further. This is the atom of time. In numbers, assume the division of eight into four parts, the four parts into two, then the two into one. It is an atom when it is indivisible. So with words. Divide a speech into words, words into syllables, syllables into letters, The letter, the smallest part, is an atom, and is indivisible. An atom therefore is that which is indivisible, as a point in geometry. In Greek *tomos* means division; *atomos*, indivisibility.

Isidore of Seville: 7th century
Etymologies
Trans. by H. E. W.

Medicine

¶ MEDICINE IS THAT which preserves or restores the health of the body. Its sphere is diseases and wounds. With it are associated not only matters involving the practice of those who are properly called physicians, but also food and drink, clothing and shelter; in short, every protective defense that serves to ensure the body against external impacts and hazards.

The founder and inventor of medicine is called among the Greeks Apollo. His son Aesculapius glorified and enlarged the art. But after Aesculapius was struck by lightning and perished, the art of healing is said to have been prohibited. The practice lapsed with its founder, and for almost five hundred years it was in abeyance until the time of Artaxerxes, King of the Persians. Then Hippocrates, son of Asclepius, brought it back into use on the island of Cos.

The three individuals mentioned originated the three schools. The first, the Methodical school, began with Apollo. It adheres to remedies and incantations. The second, the Empirical school, that is the most experimental school, springs from Aesculapius. It is founded not on diagnostic symptoms but solely on experience. The third, the Logical school, that is the rational school, was due to Hippocrates. The Empiricists adhere to experience alone. The Logicians add reasoning to experience. The Methodics observe neither the rationale of the elements, nor time, age or cause, but merely the incidence of the disease.

> Isidore of Seville: 7th century
> *Etymologies*
> Trans. by H. E. W.

Astronomy in the Tenth Century

¶ ALL THAT IS WITHIN the firmament is called the world. The firmament is the ethereal heaven, adorned with many stars; the heaven, the sea, and earth, are called the world. The firmament is always turning round about us, under this earth and above, and there is an incalculable space between it and the earth. Four and twenty hours have passed, that is one day and one night, before it is once turned around, and all the stars which are fixed in it turn around with it. The earth stands in the center, by God's power so fixed that it never swerves either higher or lower than the Almighty Creator, who holds all things without labor, established it. Every sea, although it be deep, has its bottom on the earth, and the earth supports all seas, and the ocean, and all fountains and rivers run through it; as the veins lie in a man's body, so lie the veins of water throughout the earth. Neither sea nor river has any position but on earth. . . .

As the sun's slackness begets a day and a night always in four years, so also the moon's swiftness throws out one day and one night of the number of his course in nineteen years, and this day is called *saltus lunae,* that is, the moon's leap, because he overleaps one day,

151

and the nearer the nineteenth year, the larger does the new moon appear. The moon was at the beginning made in the evening, and ever since in the evening changes his age. If before evening he be renewed from the sun, he is then reckoned new immediately after sunset. But if he be changed after sunset, or at midnight, or at cock-crowing, he is never reckoned new, although he have three and twenty hours before he comes to the evening on which he was made. Of this there is often such discourse, when the unlearned will have the moon according as they see him, and the learned estimate him by this aforesaid reason. Sometimes the moon is lighted of the sun by day, sometimes by night, sometimes in the evening, sometimes at early morning, and so variously; but still he is not new before he sees the evening. No Christian shall divine anything by the moon; if he doth so his belief is naught. The longer is the day that the new moon appears above, and the shorter is the day that the new moon appears beneath. If the sun lights him from above, then he will stoop; if she lights him athwart, then is he equally horned. If the sun lights him from below, then he inclines up. Because he turns always his back toward the sun, he is so turned as the sun lights him. Now say some men, who do not know this reason, that the moon turns him according as the weather shall be in the month; but neither weather nor un-weather turns him from that which is his nature. Nevertheless men say, those who are curious observe by his hue, and by the sun's or the sky's what kind of weather is coming. It is natural that all earthly bodies are fuller at the increasing moon than at the waning. Also the trees that are cut down at full moon are harder against worm-eating and more durable than those which are cut down at new moon. The sea and the moon agree between them, ever they are companions in increase and in waning; and as the moon daily rises four points later than he did the day before, so also the sea flows always four points later.

Some men say that stars fall from heaven. But it is not stars that fall, but it is fire from the sky, which flies from the heavenly bodies as sparks do from fire. Certainly there are still as many stars in the heavens as there were at the beginning, when God made them. They are almost all fixed in the firmament, and will not fall thence while this world endures. The sun, and the moon, and the evening star, and the day star, and three other stars, are not fast in the firmament, but they have their own course severally. These seven are called *septem planetae*. And I know that it will seem very incredible to unlearned men if we speak scientifically concerning the stars, and concerning their course. Arcton is the name of a constellation in the north part, which has seven stars, and on that account is called by another name, *septemtrio,* which untaught men call carle's-wain. It never goes down under this earth as the other constellations do, but it turns down and sometimes up during the day and the night. There is another constellation on the south part like this, which we can never see. Two stars stand also still, one on the south part, the other on the north part, which are called in Latin *axis;* the southern star we never see; we see the northern, which men call the ship star. These are called axis, that is, axletree, because the firmament turns on the two stars, as a wheel turns on the axletree, and therefore they stand always still. Pleiades is the name given to the seven stars which rise in autumn and shine through all the winter, going from the east to the west. Through all the summer they go at nighttime under this earth, and by day above. In the wintertime they are up by night and down by day. The stars are called comets which appear suddenly and unusually, and which are rayed so that the ray goes from them like a sunbeam. They are not seen for any long time, and as oft as they appear, they forebode something new toward the people over whom they shine. Though we should speak more of the heavenly constellations, still the unlearned may not learn their luminous course.

Anglo-Saxon Manual of Astronomy:
tenth century
Trans. from Anglo-Saxon by Thomas
Wright, 1841

Astronomical Lore

¶ MASTERS, NOW ATTEND, aid me in this need, remember what the peasant said by reflection—the friend is found and proved in need; there was never a friend who failed in our need, as long as he could aid or advise in anything. Therefore I say, delay not, but listen to my reason. I pray you to hear it, and then to amend it. For now I will begin that of which I intend to treat, and state the chapters, if you will amend them. You will do it, I know well; so here I state them.

Of the hours, and of the day, of nights and their length; of weeks, the reasons of the names of days and of months; of calends, of ides, of nones and of signs; of the year, and who found it, and where it begins; how to keep the *bissextile*, and place it in February; of the bissextile of the moon, of the leap and of the embolismus; of the moon which we see when it is new; of the rules of the day, of the value of the concurrent; of the regular lunal; to find the epacts; of the *termini* and the *claves*; to find the inductions; of the equinoxes and of the fasts; of the table of Philip de Thaun; of the table of the resurrection; of the table of Dionysius the old; of the table of Gerlant, the wise and meritorious clerk. Now ends the list of chapters, and the book begins.

In a divine book, which is called Genesis, there reading, we find that God made by reason the sun and the moon, and every star. On this account it pleases me to speak, of this is my matter, which I will show both to clerks and laics, who have great need of it, and will perish without it. For science hidden was never praised; therefore it please me to speak, now may the true Lord be with it!

When God made creatures of divers kinds, he gave them all names according to their quality; but he found unity, which he called time, of which the wise man knows not how to speak, or to recount the end, nor was there ever mortal man who was without that. So St. Augustine, who was a very good theologian, says in one of his sermons, where he explains why he knows not how to tell anything to satisfy anybody, nor how much by stations, which we call hours, is the division of them by such reason. For one they call prime, tierce, midday, and noon; the fifth *remontée*, and the sixth vespers. Still they leave one between each, which is to keep an account and remembrance of it. But he who will number right may find twelve of them. And when they are past, they are all renewed, they all hold their course in their turns. And you ought to know that, and believe it for truth, that the night contains twelve of them, and similarly the day which comes after, when the night and the day have equal length. Let nobody wonder, or be astonished, because I thus name the night, and place the day after it. Night was before day, when our Creator placed it before, and overthrew the night by His resurrection and by very great right. And that signifies that He found us in sin, and that from great darkness He drew His own people to light, who will be no more troubled or obscured by night. According to the theologians, and according to the Latins, night is named from hurting (*nox a nocere*), and it makes the people sleep, repose in the evening lest they keep awake to work, because they have not daylight they cease from their labor; otherwise they would perish, and die of their labors. Nevertheless it is no disparagement to the people; but still night benefits everything. For by night the moon shines, and every star; that is good for the navigator who sails on the sea, for the calculators of the Compotus, for the astronomers; and that we shall say in the book, if God gives us life, how precious the moon is for everything alive. But now we will show by demonstration what is night. Night is completely whole when being without light; and would last always, were there no sun; but he, by his light, drives away the darkness, as the theologians say, and God in the book of Genesis, that this light is called day— light is called day, and darkness night. They are divided in the following manner: the one is popular and the other natural; the popular day contains twelve hours, and the natural day twenty-four in his course. Thus Moses says for truth in his writing, "The evening is done, and all the morning, the evening he called night, and the morn day"; that he held for a day, truly and without error. And for this reason, and by his design, four and twenty hours are included in the day. But now we ought to look, inquire, and prove, by divers reasons, what regulates the length of the day. The Greeks and the theologians, and the clerks in Latin, the calculators of Compotus, and the astronomers have discovered in the heaven a visible way, by which the sun goes and always makes his course; the Greeks call it by the name of *Zodiacus*; in the Latin truly we call it *Signiferum*; in French it has the name of "Sign-bearer." And the signs which it holds, and how it maintains them, we will name them all very briefly.

Aries, taurus, gemini, cancer, leo, virgo, libra, scorpio, and sagittarius, after it capricornus, pisces, aquarius. The sun rightly each year goes through them and makes his complete course. And when he goes from capricornus to cancer, the days lengthen and the nights diminish; thus he goes diagonally, when he goes along, the days are not long; but when he goes across, then they lengthen. Thus is its nature, as you see its figure; the zones are placed within, side by side, as we find in Ovid the great. In May is rightly the equinox, and that is the zodiac which goes up diagonally; cancer is above at the head, and capricorn at the bottom; the burning zone surrounds the earth, which makes the sparklings which we see there. That heat signifies this mortal life. I will not say more of it, but will begin another subject.

Philippe de Thaun: 12th century
Livre des Créatures
Trans. by Thomas Wright, 1841

The Eye

NEPHEW: Since thou knowest all, having gained it by diligent lore, and thou hast none nearer to thee than myself to profit, do thou invest me with but one portion of thy knowledge, and instruct me on the point: What is the nature of eyesight, and why does the eye see?

UNCLE: Ask of me, and I will give thee thine inheritance, and will answer thy question whilst breath be yet within me. Understand that light is, as it were, a rapid and rare form of atmosphere of the nature of fire, and is known to have been created from that kind that goes to make up the two nerves that run from the brain to the eye-cavities, called delicate organisms, and their endings are not found in all the forehead and round about, which is all hard, with the exception of these two very delicate cavities; and it is from them that sight proceeds. Even sight is material, since the air proceeding from the brain is said to be matter, compounded indeed of the four elements, but the element of fire preponderates to a very great extent.

> Adelard of Bath: 12th century
> *Quaestiones Naturales*
> Trans. by H. Gollancz

Science Problem

NEPHEW: Now, tell me, why is sea-water salt?

UNCLE: By reason of the salt which is in the Great Sea, it being wide and long, and receiving the power of the sun's heat as it rushes on. Being so extensive, it is always exposed to the full power of the sun, and catches its rays; the heat stirs the water as it flows to a certain density, and through this heat and density the waters acquire the taste of salt. If you do not believe it, you need only ask the people who live near the sea, and they will tell you that, without any effort on man's part, salt is found as the residue of the waters on the dry places of the rock which are exposed to the sun and stars; while if you inquire of those removed from such places exposed to the heat of the sun, they will tell you they have not seen any salt, and they can only produce it by the agency of fire and by piles of wood. You can judge for yourself that the heat of fire will produce salt in water. If you do not believe me, inquire, and you will find that sea-water in summer is salt, as water may be in winter in the kettle. Hence it shows that the salt taste depends upon heat.

Adelard of Bath: 12th century
Quaestiones Naturales
Trans. by H. Gollancz

The Branches of Knowledge

¶ IF ANYONE should wish to accuse me of presumption (inadequately trained as I am, I shall not say in every subject or art, but even in any single one) for having dared so industriously to include in this work the branches of all knowledge and arts and the matter and arrangement of each subject, he would hear that I am at all times writing not as an author but as an excerptor, and that my purpose has not been to elucidate the problems in any of the arts, but to set down certain slight and simple matters about individual subjects, useful to remember, in a kind of compendious form.

Although there are perhaps some subjects that it is not very necessary to know, still on occasion it is a disgrace not to understand them. Since too they will easily vanish from the memory of those who come after us, it seemed best to produce a sort of compendious digest of these matters among other subjects in this work, in a logical sequence, to which the industrious reader may return at a suitable place and time. I have been encouraged in this intention by the studies of our writers, namely Isidore of Seville and Hugo of St. Victor and Richard of Paris. The first of these, in his book entitled *Etymologiae*, among other subjects discussed touches briefly on every field of knowl-

157

edge. The second, in his book called *Didascalicon*, makes a general division of knowledge and briefly describes the content of each subject, and the third—who is so called—does likewise in his *Excerpts*.

But since all these writers treat each subject very briefly and cursorily, for this reason too I have turned to the books of the philosophers who discuss these matters at greater length and more comprehensively; and from this source I have briefly excerpted a few noteworthy items that I have suitably and within my power added to the sayings of the above-mentioned Catholics.

Furthermore, all the arts serve the Divine Knowledge as a Queen; hence those liberal arts, as they are called, usually are considered as a declaration of ecclesiastical dogma.[1]

Vincent of Beauvais: 13th century
Speculum Maius
Trans. by H. E. W.

Remarkable Inventions

¶ I SHALL THEREFORE now describe first of all works of skill and marvels of nature, in order to designate afterward their causes and characteristics. There is no magic in them, so that all the power of magic seems inferior to these mechanisms and unworthy of them. And first, through the shaping and planning of skill alone. Instruments for navigation can be made without rowers, so that the largest ships, both on river and on sea, are steered by one man only in control at a greater speed than if they were filled with men. Similarly, carts can be made to move without animals at an incalculable velocity, as we think the chariots with scythe blades attached must have been in which the ancients fought. Similarly, flying machines can be made so that a man sits inside the machine rotating some ingenious contraption by means of which the wings, artfully arranged, beat the air like a bird flying. So, a machine, small in size, can be made, for raising and lowering weights almost infinitely, a most useful device in an emergency. For with an instrument three fingers high and the same in width and less in size, a man could escape with his companions

1. The usual attitude of the medieval Church was that all knowledge, even the knowledge of pagan antiquity, served to confirm ecclesiastical truth.

from every danger of imprisonment and raise and lower himself. Also an instrument could easily be devised whereby a single man could draw a thousand men forcibly toward him against their own will, and so with attracting other objects. Also instruments can be made for walking in the sea or rivers right down to the bottom without any physical risk. Alexander the Great used such instruments to probe the secrets of the ocean, according to the stories of Ethicus the astronomer. These things were done in antiquity and in our own day as well, and this is unquestionable; except a flying machine, that I have not seen or known anyone who did. But I know quite well the adept who thought out this device. And an infinite number of such objects is possible: such as bridges over rivers, without columns or any support; and machines, and unheard-of ingenuities.

> Roger Bacon: 13th century
> *De Secretis Operibus*
> Trans. by H. E. W.

The Arts and the Planets

¶ THE STUDY of the liberal arts, although of the greatest use itself, breeds much vanity too through superfluous investigations. Yet the arts are commendable in themselves, but those who abuse them deserve censure.

Now there is a difference between the capacity of the faculties and discipline. Capacity is the ability to discourse for or against, as if one held a double-edged sword, as grammar, dialectics, rhetoric. Discipline is directed toward one phase only, unless the instructor uses the syllogism *ad impossibile,* as arithmetic, music, geometry, astronomy. Just as therefore the seven planets illuminate the universe, so the liberal arts grace and reinforce all knowledge. The moon, with which grammar is compared, is nearest to the earth, and postulates the first frontiers. The sun, to which the studious reader will find dialectics very similar in many respects, holds the second place, according to the attribution of certain philosophers. Mercury, in the third position, is compared with rhetoric. Venus is gracious in aspect, with which arithmetic is compared, on account of the great charm of this discipline. Theology knows its usefulness as it diligently investigates the mystery of numbers. Music looks to Mars, as it is not human, not earthly, but instrumental. For the varied harmony of trumpets and clangorous shawms calls armed men to battle. To Jupiter geometry acknowledges itself beholden, because it treats of an immovable magnitude. Astronomy, closer to the stars than the other planets, serves Saturn, because it treats of a movable magnitude.

Alexander Nequam: 13th century
De Naturis Rerum
Trans. by H. E. W.

Astrological Tale

¶ AGAINST THOSE who assert that the heavenly luminaries are in the nature of signs of the future and who put their faith in augury and divination, I heard that when a certain astrologer was foretelling the truth, just as certain demons forsee the future, the king, in whose household he was, began to display great belief in him and to rely on his divinations.

Now on a particular day he stood, very sad, before the king. When the latter asked him why he was sad and dejected, he refused to tell. Finally, with much coaxing, moaning and lamenting he told the king secretly: "Master, I have looked at my astrolabe and I have deduced with certainty from the position of the stars that you cannot live more than six months." On hearing this, the king believed it and every day began to be alarmed, tormented, and extremely downcast, so that his knights wondered greatly and grieved. For the king did not want to see or speak with them in his usual cheerful manner. At length after many entreaties and at the insistence of one who was very intimate with him, he admitted that his cleric, who was an excellent astrologer, had predicted his imminent death. Then the knight, afraid that the king would be overwhelmed with grief and, incurring serious sickness, would die (for many people die through fear of dying), called the astronomer into the presence of everyone and said: "How are you certain about the king's death?"

The other replied: "I am sure of his death that I deduced from my art, which is infallible."

To which the knight retorted: "You must have better knowledge of yourself than of anyone else. Do you know how long you will live?"

THE ASTROLOGER: I know and I am certain that I shall not die for twenty years.

THE KNIGHT: By your life, you have lied.

And, drawing out a dagger, he slew him in the presence of all. Then the king, waiting for the astrologer's prediction to be proved false, with renewed vigor was comforted and lived for a long time afterward.

Jacques de Vitry: 13th century
Exempla
Trans. by H. E. W.

Astrological Lore

¶ OF THE STARS AND THE PLANETS we ought to know that Sunday has its star under the Sun.

Monday has its star under the Moon.

Tuesday has its star under Mars.

Wednesday has its star under Mercury.

Thursday has its star under Jupiter.

Friday has its star under Venus.

Saturday has its star under Saturn.

Note that every act must occur under its own planet. And it is better if it occurs in the special day of that planet and in its particular hour; for instance:

under Saturn: life, building, learning, change.

under Jupiter: honor, desires, wealth, clothing.

under Mars: war, imprisonment, marriage, hostility.

under the Sun: hope, riches, fortune, inheritance.

under Venus: friendship, alliance, travel, relations, pilgrimage.

under Mercury: sickness, loss, debt, fear.

under Luna: palace, sleep, trade, theft.

Albertus Magnus: 13th century
De Virtutibus Animalium
Trans. by H. E. W.

Protection for Animals

¶ IF YOU want to render dogs or hunters helpless to harm any animal they pursue:

Place in their presence the stone called Iuperius, and at once the animal will run toward the stone. This stone is found in Libya, and all wild beasts run to it as though to their defender; for it prevents dogs or huntsmen from injuring them.

Albertus Magnus: 13th century
De Virtutibus Lapidum
Trans. by H. E. W.

Scientific Difficulties

¶ MANY PHILOSOPHERS AND PHYSICIANS have believed that the entire miracle of experiments and wonders derived from natural sources when they are brought into the light through heat and cold, dryness and moisture; and they have determined these four qualities and have established the very roots of all miracles and have predicated this in their works and have required their experiments to fail or be accepted, to maintain themselves and be verified by this means. And when they find many experiments of philosophers, they are not able to verify them by heat and cold, and generally reject what they see.

Albertus Magnus: 13th century
De Mirabilibus Mundi
Trans. by H. E. W.

The Properties of Things

¶ IF THEN you wish to experiment, it is first of all proper for you to know whether objects are hot or cold. Once this is known, you next learn the disposition and the natural property of an object: whether it is bold or timid, beautiful or sterile; for whatever nature every single thing that exists has, that nature it assimilates in those

162

objects with which it is associated: as a lion is a fearless animal, endowed with natural fearlessness, especially in the forehead and the heart; and hence anyone who acquires for himself the eye of a lion, or its heart, or the skin between its two eyes, becomes daring and unafraid and inspires all animals with fear. And in general there is in the lion the virtue of granting fearlessness and magnanimity. Similarly in a prostitute there is a boundless courage. Hence the philosophers say that if anyone puts on a public prostitute's camisole, or looks into her mirror, or has a mirror into which she herself has looked, he becomes daring and fearless.

Albertus Magnus: 13th century
De Mirabilibus Mundi
Trans. by H. E. W.

Science Notes

¶ THE PHILOSOPHERS say that when a tortoise is poisoned it eats marjoram and is cured; and hence knows that marjoram is effective for poison.

And the philosophers have found out that if a woman is sterile, and the object producing the sterility is placed next to her, she loses her sterility.

And it is said that if you make a ring from the twig of a freshly cut myrtle and put your ring finger through it, any abscess subsides.

And Aristotle declares that when mares smell smoke from an extinguished lamp, they are abortive; and likewise this happens to certain women when they are pregnant.

Albertus Magnus: 13th century
De Mirabilibus Mundi
Trans. by H. E. W.

Experiment

¶ A REMARKABLE EXPERIMENT that makes a man go through fire without harm or carry in his hand fire or a hot iron without injury:

Take the juice of a double marrow and the white of an egg and the seed of fleawort and a stone, and pulverize and pour into the white

163

of the egg the juice of radish. Mix together. With this concoction smear your body or hand and let it dry and afterward smear it again, and after this you will be able to endure fire with impunity, without ill effect.

Albertus Magnus: 13th century
De Mirabilibus Mundi
Trans. by H. E. W.

Auguries

¶ AUGURIES ARE FOUND in the canons of the Church, although we say that certain auguries are received through an encounter with a man or some animal or heard through a voice; or this and that is augury, if a man, through such knowledge, predicts the future and hence, by means of the signs of this knowledge, knows and has discovered how to judge everything according to its category. Hence we should realize that certain kinds of auguries signify an auspicious event; others, an unfavorable event; still others, a balance between the two extremes. For there are certain notable factors that are properly matters for consideration in augury: as a sneeze during sleep, meeting a flight of birds, hearing the songs of birds, a passionate voice, a proleptic dream about a business decision. . . . Auguries are twelve in number, like the twelve signs of the Zodiac.

Michael Scot: 13th century
De Secretis Naturae
Trans. by H. E. W.

Has the Earth Motion?

¶ *Twenty-second problem*. The next problem is whether the earth is always static in the center of the universe.

The negative argument is that any natural body has or may have some natural motion; hence the earth either has natural motion or at least may have natural motion. And if it has natural motion, then it must move sometime, because it would be inconsistent to declare that a natural force is restrained throughout all eternity from ever moving into action.

Again, the earth is spherical in shape, and a spherical shape has a certain tendency to spherical or circular motion. Now as was said about force, I likewise assert that a natural tendency must not be inactive throughout all eternity.

Again, Aristotle declares that for every simple body there must naturally be some simple motion, and that simple gravity means a simple downward motion. Now, it is absurd to declare that some natural motion acts on the earth and yet that it itself never moves by that motion.

Again, the speculations of the ancient philosophers declare that a nobler position is due to a nobler element, and that fire is a nobler element than the earth; hence fire ought to have a nobler position. But the nobler position, and one in which what is in it can be preserved with greater care, is the middle position; hence, for this reason, it was the custom for the king to install himself in the center of his realm—for he was better protected there, because his enemies did not come in contact with him so quickly.

Aristotle posits the contrary; he even posited this conclusion: the heavens always revolve in a circular sense; therefore the earth is always static in the center.

That is a difficult problem. For, to begin with, there is great doubt whether the earth is directly in the center of the universe so that its center is the center of the universe. Then there is a strong doubt whether the earth sometimes moves completely by a direct motion; because there is no doubt that many parts of it do frequently move, as is apparent to our senses.

John Buridan: 14th century
Quaestiones super libris quattuor de caelo et mundo, edited by E. A. Moody. The Mediaeval Academy of America, 1942
Trans. by H. E. W.

Part Four

THE SOCIAL SCENE: TRAVEL AND TRADE; SOCIAL MORES AND CHIVALRY

The Routes of the Jewish Merchants Called Radanites

¶ THESE MERCHANTS speak Arabic, Persian, Roman, the language of the Franks, Andalusians and Slavs. They journey west to east, from east to west, partly on land, partly by sea. They transport from the West eunuchs, female and male slaves, silk, castor, marten and other furs, and swords. They take ship in the land of the Franks, on the Western Sea, and steer for Farama. There they load their goods on the backs of camels and so by land to Kolzum in five days' journey, over a distance of twenty-five parasangs. They embark in the East Sea and sail from Kolzum to el-Jar and Jeddah; then they go to Sind, India, and China. On their return they carry back musk, aloes, camphor, cinnamon, and other products of the Eastern countries to Kolzum, and bring them to Farama, where they again embark on the Western Sea. Some make sail for Constantinople to sell their goods to the Romans; others go to the palace of the King of the Franks to place their goods.

Sometimes these Jewish merchants prefer to carry their goods from the land of the Franks in the Western Sea, making for Antioch (at the mouth of the Orontes); thence they go by land to al-Jabia, where they arrive after three days' march. There they embark on the Euphrates for Baghdad, and then sail down the Tigris to al-Obolla. From al-Obolla they sail for Oman, Sind, Hind, and China. All this is connected with one another. These different journeys can also be made by land. The merchants that start from Spain to France go to Sous al-Akza, and then to Tangiers, whence they march to Kairouan and the capital of Egypt. Thence they go to al-Ramla, visit Damascus, al-Kufa, Baghdad, and Basrah, cross Ahwaz, Fars, Kirman, Sind, Hind, and arrive at China. Sometimes they likewise take the route behind Rome, and, passing through the country of the Slavs, arrive at Khamlif, the capital of the Khazars. They embark on the Jorjan Sea, arrive at Balkh, betake themselves from there across the Oxus, and continue their journey toward the Yourts of the Toghozghor, and from there to China.

Ibn Khordadbeh: 9th century
The Book of the Roads and the Kingdoms
Trans. by J. Jacobs

Journey of a Scholar
from Rheims to Chartres

¶ IN MY EAGERNESS to study the logic of Hippocrates of Chios, I frequently and deeply thought about the liberal arts. One day, in Rheims, I met a citizen of Chartres. When I asked him who he was and of what family, why and whence he had come, he replied that he was a legate of Heribrand the cleric of Dourdan and wished to speak with Richer, monk of St. Rémy. On learning the name of this new-found friend and the reason for his mission, I said that I was the man he was looking for, and after embracing we turned aside. After a while he produced a letter that encouraged me in my desire to study the Aphorisms. Quite pleased with this, I picked up a boy with a horseman of Chartres, and I arranged to make a speedy trip to Chartres. Making a detour, I accepted from my abbot the comfort of an extra saddle horse. Without money, without change of clothes and other necessities, I reached Orbais, known for its great expensiveness. Refreshed by a talk with Dom D., the Abbot, and at the same time sustained by his hospitality, on the next day I rode fast as far as Meaux. When I entered the winding groves with my two companions, unfortunate incidents occurred. In the confusion of the roads we went six leagues out of our way. After passing the castle of Theodoric, my saddle horse that had before seemed a veritable Bucephalus slowly turned into a donkey. The sun had disappeared at midday, and all the air had dissolved into rain; then, as the sun began sinking in the west, the gallant Bucephalus, exhausted by a supreme effort, fell, collapsing on the mounted boy's thighs, and, as if struck by lightning, expired six miles from the city.

What great confusion and anxiety ensued, those may judge who have at any time experienced similar accidents, and they may make their own corresponding conclusions. The boy, unaccustomed to the difficulty of such a long journey, was completely exhausted and, unreining his horse, he lay down. Without a mount there were obstacles ahead. A storm brought a heavy rain. The sky was overcast with clouds. Now the setting sun threatened darkness. As I hesitated in all this, God put a plan into my head. I left the boy there with all the trappings, and telling him what to say to wayfarers if he were questioned and to fight against an attack of sleep, accompanied by the horseman of Chartres only, I reached Meaux. Barely seeing the bridge for the scanty light, I started upon it. While I was looking about me carefully, another mishap again overtook me. For the bridge was broken in so many places that scarcely any citizens but those forced to do so crossed it at that time. The man of Chartres, possessed of sufficient forethought in making the journey, anxiously looked around everywhere for a skiff. Finding none, he returned to the hazards of the bridge, beseeching heaven to let the horses cross safely. In the spaces that gaped open, he occasionally put his shield under the horses' feet; at other times he fitted together cast-away planks; now bent over, now erect, now advancing then running back, he managed to take the horses across as I rode along with him.

The night had grown threatening and had covered the heavens with a foul mist when I entered the church of St. Pharo, while the brethren were still preparing their loving cup.[1]

On that day they had dined ceremoniously. The chapter had been read by the steward of the monastery, this being the reason for the late potation. Welcomed by them as a brother, I was refreshed by their pleasant conversation and the sufficiency of food. I sent back the Chartres horseman with his horses to fetch the boy, so he had to attempt once more the perils over the bridge. In the manner already described, he made the crossing; and at the second night watch, wandering about, he just barely found the boy, although he called him again and again. He took him up and when he came near the city, mistrusting the risks over the bridge that he had discovered by sad experiment, he put up at a certain hut along with the boy and the horses. Without food for an entire day, they remained there that night, not to dine but to rest. I spent that night sleepless and my agony

1. A drinking vessel that was filled with wine and passed among guests at a banquet or monks in a refrectory; each drank from the cup and handed it to his neighbor. Thus the loving cup was a symbol of hospitality.

can be imagined by those who at some time have been forced to lie awake concerned over dear ones.

When dawn came at last, worn out by extreme hunger, they got to the monastery very quickly. Food was placed before them. The horses too were given grain and straw bedding. Leaving the boy in the good hands of the Abbot Augustine and accompanied only by the man from Chartres, I hurriedly reached Chartres. The horses were shortly after sent back, and I recalled the boy from Meaux. When he was brought back, and all anxiety had been removed, I gave myself energetically to the study of the Aphorisms of Hippocrates, under Master Herbrand, a man of great graciousness and knowledge. When I had learned there the prognosis of diseases and the simple recognition of sickness, which did not satisfy my desires, I asked him to read with me also the book entitled *On the Harmony of Hippocrates, Galen, and Suranus*. I learned much in this way for he is so skilled as to be quite familiar with the medicaments of pharmacy, botany, and surgery.

Richer: 10th century
Historiarum Libri Quattuor
Trans. by H. E. W.

Contentment in Love

¶ A LOVER WHO IS prevented from union must seek contentment in what he finds, and verily in this there is a pleasant illusion for the soul, a diversion toward expectation, and a renewal of wishes, and some appeasement; and there are various degrees of it, according to what may be done and possibly attained.

The first is the visit, which indeed is a kind of hope and the most sublime that good fortune may offer, despite what it causes in the way of shyness and bashfulness, on account of what each one of the two lovers knows to exist in each other's soul. There are two kinds of visit:

One, when the lover visits his beloved, and this aspect is a vast (subject); and the second, when the beloved visits her lover, but there is no way of doing anything except look at each other and talk to each other publicly; and on this subject I say:

And if you are distant from me when we get together,
I shall be contented with a glance of the eye, if (other) union is
    impossible;
And I shall be satisfied with meeting you once a day,
Though I was not contented with twice what I had from you be-
    fore:
Thus the ambition of a governor is very high,
Yet he is content barely to save his soul when dismissal comes!

And as regards the returning of greeting and speaking to (the beloved) it is (also) a kind of hope, though I had said in one of my
poems:

(*Ṭawīl*)

Here I am dissimulating and am contented gladly
With returning the greeting when it is feasible at times!

But this is only in case one is transferred from a grade to one which
is below—for creatures are trying to differentiate themselves in merit
in all qualities, according to their taking on a relation to what is
above them or below them. And I know a person who was saying to
his beloved: "Make me a promise and lie," seeking contentment in
that he would console himself by his promise (of invitation), even
though it not be truthful; and I said on that subject:

(*Kāmil*)

If my union with you is not to be desired,
And to be near you is forbidden, (then) promise me and lie!
And perchance the pleasant illusion of meeting you will retain
    (preserve)
Life in the heart, grievously punished by the long separation:
Often those who suffer from drought console themselves when they
    see,
Flashing on the horizon, the lightning not followed by rain!

What also belongs to this chapter is something I saw and others
have seen with me, namely: a man, one of my friends, had been
wounded by the person he loved by a knife, and I saw him kissing

173

the spot of the wound, and scratching it over time and again; and on that subject I say:

(Mutaqārib)

They say: "He whom you love desperately wounded you!"
And I said: "By my life, he did not wound me,
But my blood perceived him to be near, and flew toward him and
   did not turn aside;
Oh you, who kill me at the same time unjustly and justly,
May I be your ransom for the beneficent tyrant!"

Contentment is also when a person is glad or satisfied with some belongings of his beloved, and it surely produces a great effect on the soul, even if there were nothing to cite except what God, Most High, has shown to us in Jacob's recovering his sight when he smelled the tunic of Joseph, peace be upon them both, and on that subject I say:

(Sarī^c)

When I was prevented from being near to my lady
And she insisted on avoiding me, and did not treat me justly;
I began to content my eyes with her dress,
Or was contented with something she had touched:
Thus Jacob, the prophet of true guidance,
When the grief for Joseph caused him suffering,
Smelled the tunic which came from him,
And he was blind and from it he got well!

And I never saw two (persons) passionately in love with each other but they were giving to each other locks of hair, perfumed with ambergris, sprinkled with rose water, which have been put together at their roots with mastic or pure white wax, and wrapped up in pieces of colored silk cloth or pongee silk and such like, so they may serve as souvenir during absence; and as regards mutual gifts of toothpicks after they had been bitten, and mastic after it had been used (chewed), it is frequent among all lovers when meeting has been made impossible for them; and on that subject I say:

(Ṭawīl)

I see in her saliva the water of life with positive certainty,
Though she did not leave to me, because of love, any heart!

174

Story. One of my friends informed me as from Suleimān b. Aḥmad the poet, that he had seen Ibn Sahl, the *ḥā gib* in the island of Sicily, and mentioned that he was extremely handsome; and he saw him one day in a promenade place walking; and there was a woman behind him looking at him, and when he walked away some distance she came to the place where his steps had left traces, and began to kiss and caress the earth in which there was the trace of his feet; and on that subject I composed a poem, beginning thus:

(*Ṭawīl*)

They blame me wrongly on account of the traces of his feet:
If they knew, the one who blamed me would become envious of
 me!
Oh people of the land where clouds are not liberal with water,
Take my advice: and you will become free, and you will be thank-
 ful:
Take some of the dust on which his footprints are impressed,
And I guarantee that drought will be far removed from you,
For every bit of dust upon which his foot has tread
Is good soil, it cannot be denied!
Thus did the Sāmirī when there appeared
To his eyes the glorious footprint of Gabriel,
And he put some of that earth inside the calf,
And there came for him out of it a prolonged bleating!

and I say:

Blessed is the land in which you are dwelling,
And blessed are those who dwell in it, and happiness has descended
 upon it!
Hence its stones are pearls, and its thistles are roses,
And its waters are honey, and its dust ambergris!

Contentment is also the visit in a dream vision, and the greeting of (its) image; and this happens only because of a remembrance which does not separate itself (from the mind), and a fidelity which does not pass away, and a thought which does not cease: and when eyes are asleep and motions (of the body) quiet down, the vision makes its nightly journey, and on that subject I say:

175

The dream vision visited the young man who had been long in
   deep love,
Despite the guarding of watchers and guardians:
And I passed my night joyful and rejoicing,
And the delight of the dream vision makes one forget the delight of
   waking!

and I say:

(*Ṭawīl*)

The dream vision Nuᶜm came to my couch after a brief slumber;
And night was ruling and her shadows were spread all over;
And my last recollection of her was that she was lying under the
   dust:
Yet she came just as I used to know her before!
And we became as we used to be, and our time came back to us,
Just as we used to know each other before, and the return is
   sweeter!

Poets have made some astonishingly rare statements concerning the
cause of the visit of dream vision, of vast scope, wherein they tried
to outstrip each other in ingenious invention to arrive at some deep
meaning: so Abū Isḥāq b. Sayyār b. an-Naẓẓām, chief of the Muᶜta-
zilites, postulated as the cause of the visit of dream vision the fear of
the spirits of the watcher watching over the mutual understanding
made between the bodies; and Abū Tammām Ḥabīb Ibn Aus aṭ-
Ṭā'iyi postulated as its cause that coit in dream does not pollute love
and coit in reality does; and Al-Buḥturī postulated as the cause of its
coming the lover's being illuminated by the fire of his amorous rap-
ture and the cause of its disappearance the fear of being drowned
in his tears; and I say—without likening my poetry to theirs, because
they have the virtue of precedence and priority, and we are mere
gleaners while they have been the harvesters—but imitating their
models, and running on their course, and following their method
which they have traced and made clear—verses in which I have, in
a very short detached poem, explained the vision in dream:

I am jealous, because of you, of the glance of my eye;
And I fear lest the touch of my hand make you melt;
Hence I refrain from (personal) meeting for fear of this,
And am planning a meeting when I am asleep;
Thus my spirit, if I dream of you, is separated from the body, con-
cealed and hidden:
And the union of the spirit is more beautiful to happen with you,
Than the union of the body a thousand times!

And the condition of the one visited is divided into four categories:

1.—The lover who has been avoided and has long been bearing his grief, sees in his light sleep before midnight that his beloved has come to him, and is filled with joy on account of it, and gladdened; then he wakes up and grieves and sighs afflicted, when he learns that what he experienced was only the soul's desire and something evoked by itself, and on that subject I say:

(*Khafīf*)

You are stingy (with your love) at the dawn of the day,
And when night is covering (the world) you are generous;
You consider the sun as taking your place for me:
Impossible! this deed is not well done on your part!
Your vision visited me from afar and comes
Uniting with me as a sick man's visitor, and a boon companion;
Except that you have forbidden me perfect existence,
But have permitted me only to obtain a smell of it;
So that I am like people on the Aᶜrāf:
My dwelling is not the Paradise, and I do not fear Hell!

2.—The lover who is in friendly relations (with his beloved) fears the change which will happen. He had seen in his deep sleep that his beloved would avoid him, and becomes greatly worried over it; then he wakes up from his sleep and finds out that it is all vain and (only) some false promptings of fear.

3.—The lover who is near the house (of his beloved) sees that the going away to a faraway place smote him, and is worried and frightened over it; then he wakes up and all this fades away and turns into joy; and on that subject I composed a poem from which I quote:

(Ṭawīl)

I saw you in my sleep as if you were traveling away,
And we began to take leave of each other and tears were flowing:
And my sleep departed from me, and you were embracing me;
And my grief, when I saw that, ceased:
So I renewed my embrace and hug, as if
I were coming back after a long separating absence!

4.—The lover who is far away sees that the place of visit has been brought near, and the dwellings were brought next to each other, and he is relieved, and becomes calmed at the absence of sorrow; then he awakens from his sleep and sees that it is not true, and becomes more aggrieved than he was before.

In one of my poems I put down as the cause of sleep the desire of a vision in dream, and I said:

The vision appeared in dream to him who is tormented by desire
and infatuation;
Were he not looking out for the visit in dream, he would not fall
asleep;
Do not wonder that it could travel at night, though the night is
very dark:
For its light frightens the darkness away from the earth!

Contentment is also when the lover is content with looking at the walls, and contemplating walls which enclose the one whom he loves, and we have seen cases of this quality of his. And I was told by Abū-l-Walīd Ahmad b. Muhammad b. Isḥāq Al-Khāzin, may God have mercy upon him, about a man of high rank, that he had told about himself something like this.

Contentment is also when the lover rejoices when he sees someone who had seen his beloved and seeks relief in his companionship, and also when he sees someone who came from the beloved's country— this is very frequent—and on that subject I say:

(Ṭawīl)

It had been abandoned by its dwellers, yet it seemed
As if they were dwellings of ᶜĀd, whom Temūd has succeeded!

Abu Muhammad Ali ibn Hazm:11th
century
Risala: The Dove's Neck-Ring
Trans. by A. R. Nykl

What Love Signifies

¶ LOVE GETS ITS NAME (amor) from the word for hook (amus), which means "to capture" or "to be captured," for he who is in love is captured in the claws of desire and wishes to capture someone else with his hook. Just as a skillful fisherman tries to attract fishes by his bait and to capture them on his crooked hook, so the man who is a captive of love tries to attract another person by his allurements and exerts all his efforts to unite two different hearts with an intangible bond, or if they are already united he tries to keep them so forever.

Andreas Capellanus: 12th century
The Art of Courtly Love
Trans. by J. J. Parry

In What Manner Love
May Be Acquired

¶ IT REMAINS next to be seen in what ways love may be acquired. The teaching of some people is said to be that there are five means by which it may be acquired: a beautiful figure, excellence of character, extreme readiness of speech, great wealth, and the readiness with which one grants that which is sought. But we hold that love may be acquired only by the first three, and we think that the last two ought to be banished completely from Love's court, as I shall show when I come to the proper place in my system.

Andreas Capellanus: 12th century
The Art of Courtly Love
Trans. by J. J. Parry

The Twelve Rules of Love

1. Thou shalt avoid avarice like the deadly pestilence, and shalt embrace the opposite.
2. Thou shalt keep thyself chaste for the sake of her whom thou lovest.
3. Thou shalt not knowingly strive to break up a correct love affair that someone else is engaged in.
4. Thou shalt not choose for thy love anyone whom a natural sense of shame forbids thee to marry.
5. Be mindful completely to avoid falsehood.
6. Thou shalt not have many who know of thy love affair.
7. Being obedient in all things to the command of ladies, thou shalt ever strive to ally thyself to the service of Love.
8. In giving and receiving love's solaces let modesty be ever present.
9. Thou shalt speak no evil.
10. Thou shalt not be a revealer of love affairs.
11. Thou shalt be in all things polite and courteous.
12. In practicing the solaces of love thou shalt not exceed the desires of thy lover.

Andreas Capallanus: 12th century
The Art of Courtly Love
Trans. by J. J. Parry

Women's Ways

¶ AGAINST THOSE WOMEN WHO, in spite of their age, paint and adorn themselves as if they were images so that they seem to be masked, like those jesters who wear painted masks that are called in French *artifices,* with which they make fun and delude men.

It is a great and singular glory for humans that they bear the image and the likeness of God, in which they have been created. But some women appear to inflict an injury on God and to declare, as it were, to their Creator: "You made me badly, I shall make a good job. You made me pale, I shall make myself red. You made me dark, I shall make myself white. You made me old, I shall make myself a young girl."

I have heard that a certain actor at the court of a noble, observing an old woman entering thus painted over, filled his mouth with water; and when she was among the women, the actor approached and suddenly, as tanners do who prepare skins, sprinkled the water in his mouth into her face. The water spread and made her visage look leprous.

Similarly, when a woman of the same type came to converse with a great and powerful noble, on seeing her appearance as he reclined on his cushion, he wanted to disconcert her. He made a little hole in the cushion and gradually, as it was pressed down, the feathers came out and he gently blew them into her face. They stuck to her painted and rouged cheeks. When she left the dark room, her face, covered with feathers, appeared to public view, to her own confusion. As she wanted to wipe them away and remove them by rubbing them off, they stuck all the more and the paint revealed her old age, making her more unsightly than ever, like a repaired image.

So with the trains that the ladies trail behind them, more than a cubit long. They commit a heinous sin, for they purchase them at a high price and rob Christ's poor. The trains collect fleas, sweep the ground, keep men praying in church from their orisons, stir up dust and darken the churches. They pollute and defile the altars and the sacred places as if with incense and dust; and on these trains they carry along the devil as though in a chariot Master Jacob says that a holy man, seeing the devil laugh, adjured him to say why he was laughing. A certain lady, on her way to church, took along a companion in her train. When she had to cross over a muddy spot she raised her dress and the companion fell into the mud. Observing this defilement, the devil had been provoked to laughter.

They choose to resemble the devil more than God and the angels. Of Christ we read that he had one head, while the serpent, that is the devil, had seven. Likewise, sometimes one woman has many heads, that is many ornaments on her head. For she has one head for the night, another for the day, another for a festive day. According to the change of day and festival, she changes her head, that is the ornaments on her head. At home she has one head; out of doors, another; a different one among strangers. For her inner head she pays her husband; for when she is with him alone, she is satisfied to wear the worst ornament that she has, though she apologizes for her vain and unnecessary ornament when she is censured, saying that she adorns herself for her husband. I sometimes rebuked a certain woman for her vanity and the superfluous decorations on her head. She would reply that she did it for her husband, who had up till then bought her seven very expensive adornments for her head. She kept them in her chest, but put on none of them when she went into her husband's bedroom. She was content to have on her head a coarse-woven coif or a thread network cap, and laid aside all her other ornaments. But when she went to meetings or other places where other men congregated, then she put on other head adornments. Hence I charged her with adorning herself not for her own husband but for the covetous eyes of other libertines.

Étienne de Bourbon: 13th century
*Tractatus de diversis materiis praedi-
cabilibus*
Trans. by H. E. W.

Oath Taken by Jews,
Frankfort on the Main:
14th Century[1]

¶ THIS IS INDEED an oath for Jews. How they shall take an oath.

The Jew shall stand on a sow's skin, and the five books of Master Moses shall be before him, and his right hand up to the wrist shall lie on the book and he shall repeat after him who administers the oath of the Jew.

Regarding such property of which the man accuses you, you know

1. Hostility toward the Jews increased in force and extent over the centuries and reached its height in the period after the Crusades. Religious wars, social and political upheavals, and blind and intense fanaticism continuously added to this situation. This enmity was fostered by the Church, by the rulers and princelings of Europe, and by economic conditions.

nothing of it nor do you have it. You never had it in your possession, you do not have it in any of your chests, you have not buried
it in the earth nor locked it with locks, so help you God who created
heaven and earth, valley and hill, woods, trees, and grass, and so help
you the law which God himself created and wrote with His own hand
and gave Moses on Sinai's mount. And so help you the five books
of Moses that you may nevermore enjoy a bite without soiling yourself all over as did the King of Babylon.

And may that sulphur and pitch flow down upon your neck that
flowed over Sodom and Gomorrah, and the same pitch that flowed
over Babylon flow over you, but two hundred times more, and may
the earth envelop and swallow you up as it did Dathan and Abiram.
And may your dust never join any other dust, and your earth never
join other earth in the bosom of Master Abraham if what you say
is not true and right. And so help you Adonai you have sworn the
truth.

If not, may you become as leprous as Naaman and Gehazi, and
may the calamity strike you that the Israelite people escaped as they
journeyed forth from Egypt's land. And may a bleeding and a flowing
come forth from you and never cease, as your people wished upon
themselves when they condemned God, Jesus Christ, among themselves, and tortured Him and said: "His blood be upon us and our
children." It is true, so help you God who appeared to Moses in a
burning bush which yet remained unconsumed. It is true by the oath
that you have sworn, by the soul which you bring on the Day of
Judgment before the Court, Abraham, Issac, and Jacob. It is true,
so help you God and the oath you have sworn.

The Jew in the Medieval World,
J. R. Marcus

Sumptuary Law

Forli, Italy. May 18, 1418

¶ IN ORDER TO HUMBLE our hearts, and to walk modestly before our
God, and not to show off in the presence of the Gentiles, we have
agreed that from today, until the termination of the time already
mentioned [1426] no Jew or Jewess of the above recorded Jewish

communities, towns or villages shall be so arrogant as to wear a fur-lined jacket, unless, of course, it is black. Also the sleeves must not be open, nor be lined with silk, for that would be arrogant. These fur-lined jackets, however, other than black, may still be worn, provided that the sleeves and the garments themselves are closed at the sides and at the back. Likewise no woman shall openly wear any girdle or belt if its silver weighs more than ten ounces.

The Jew in the Medieval World,
J. R. Marcus

Triangle Drama:
Medieval Style

¶ THE GENTLEWOMAN by her countenance, seemed content, when Menedon, sitting next to her side, said: "Most high and noble queen, now it is come unto my turn to propound my question here in your presence. Wherefore by your license if in my talk I shall be very long, yet during the same I shall first of all of you, and next of the standers-about, pray pardon. Because ye cannot be made fully to understand that which I intend to propound unless a tale that peradventure shall not be short, do precede the same." And after these words thus he began to say:

In the country where I was born I remember there was a noble knight, surpassing rich, the which loved in most loyal love, a noble gentlewoman, born likewise there, whom he took to wife. Of whom being as she was exceeding fair, another knight, called Tarolfo, was after enamored and with so great good will loved her as he saw nothing he more desired than her. And in sundry sorts, now with passing before her house, now jousting, now at the barriers, now with the often sending her messages, peradventure promising her great gifts whereby she might know his intent, and now with other like feats, he endeavored himself to purchase her love.

All which things the lady closely supported without giving sign or good answer unto the knight, saying to herself: "Whenas this knight shall discover that he can have neither answer nor yet good countenance of me, perhaps he will forbear any further either to love me or to give me these allurements."

Now for all this Tarolfo ceased not, following the precepts of Ovid, who says that a man must not through the hardness of a woman leave to persevere because with continuance the soft water pierces the hard stone. The lady, doubting lest these things should come to the ears of her husband, and that he should believe that the same happened through her good will, purposed to let him understand the same.

But yet after being persuaded through better advisement, she said: "I might, if I tell him, make such a brawl between them as I should never after live a merry life, and therefore he must be shaken off by some other means."

And so she imagined a trim guile. She sent to Tarolfo, saying that if he loved her so well as he made show of, she would require one thing at his hands; the which if she received she swore by her gods and by that loyalty that ought to be in a gentlewoman, that she would accomplish all his desire. And if he would not give her what she required, he should then content himself, no further to allure her hereafter but in what he would be willing she should reveal to her husband.

The gift she required was this: She said that she would have in that country in the month of January, a very fair garden and large, replenished with herbs, flowers and blossoming trees and fruits, as if it were in the month of May. She sent him this message, saying to herself that this is an impossible thing so that in this way I shall rid him from me.

Tarolfo, hearing this demand, although it seemed to him impossible to be done, and that he knew very well to what end she required the same, answered: that he would never rest, neither yet return into her presence, until such time as he might give her the demanded gift. And so forthwith departed his country with such a company as pleased him to take with him.

He sought all the west parts for counsel how to attain his desire, but not finding there what he looked for, sought the most hot regions, and so came into Thessaly, as he had been sent by a discreet man for that purpose. And having made his abode there many days, not yet finding what he sought for, it happened that now being almost desperate of his desire and rising one morning before the sun, prepared to enter the dawning day, he all alone began to wander the miserable plains that were now all imbued with Roman blood. And having traveled a long while upon the same, he suddenly espied before him at

185

the foot of a mountain, a man not young nor of too many years, bearded, small and very spare of person, whose attire showed him to be but poor, who roamed hither and thither gathering herbs and with a little knife digged up sundry roots whereof he had filled one of the skirts of his coat. Whom as Tarolfo saw, he marveled not a little, and doubted greatly lest it had been some other thing; but after his look did certainly show him to be a man, he drew near unto him, saluted him and asked him who he was and of whence and what he did there at so timely an hour.

To whom the old man answered: "I am of Thebes and Theban is my name, and I go up and down this place gathering of these herbs to the end that with the juice thereof I make divers necessary and profitable things for divers infirmities, whereby I may wherewithal to live. And to come at this hour it is need and not delight that constraineth me. But who are you, that in countenance resembles nobles and walk here all alone solitary?"

To whom Tarolfo answered: "I am of the extremes of the west, very rich and vanquished of conceits, pricked forwards to an enterprise, not being able hitherto to achieve the same and therefor to be the better able without impediment to bewail my lot, I go thus all alone wandering."

To whom Theban said: "Do you not know the quality of the place and what it is? Wherefore have you rather taken your way on the one side? You might easily here be rebuked with furious spirits."

Tarolfo answered: "God can do here as elsewhere. It is He that has my life and honor in His hands. Let Him do with me according to His pleasure, for assuredly death would be to me a rich pleasure."

Then said Theban: "What is that your enterprise, for the which (not being able to perform it) you abide thus sorrowful?"

To whom Tarolfo answered: "It is such as seems to me impossible to be able ever to attain, since hitherto I have here found no counsel."

Then said Theban: "Dare you utter it?"

Tarolfo answered: "Yea, but what profits it?"

"Peradventure nothing," said Theban, "but what does it hurt?"

Then said Tarolfo: "I seek counsel how may be had in the coldest month, a garden full of flowers, fruits and herbs, as fair as if it were in the month of May. Neither do I find who can therein either help me or give me encouragement that it is possible to be had."

Theban stayed a while in a muse without answer, and after said:

"You and many others do judge the skill and virtue of men according to their garments. If my goods were such as are yours, you would not have lingered so long in discovering your lack. Or if peradventure you had found me near unto some rich prince, as you have in gathering of herbs. But many times under the vilest vesture are hidden the greatest treasures of science, and therefor no one conceals his lack to whom is proffered counsel or help; and if therefor he opens the same it cannot prejudice him at all. But what would you give him that should bring to effect that which you go about thus seeking for?"

Tarolfo beheld him in the face as he uttered these words, and doubted lest he went about to deride him, for that it seemed to him incredible that he should be able to bring the same to pass unless he were a god. Notwithstanding he answered him thus:

"I have under my rule in my country many castles and therewithal great treasures, all the which I would divide with him evenly that would give me so great a pleasure."

"Truly," said Theban, "if you would do so much for me, I should no more need to go thus about in gathering of herbs."

"Assuredly," said Tarolfo, "if you be able to give true effect to what you promise and give it to me indeed, you shall never need to care nor yet to trouble yourself to become rich. But how and when can you bring me this to pass?"

Then said Theban: "The time when shall be at your choice, but for the manner how trouble not yourself. And I will go with you, trusting unto the word and promise you have made me, and when we shall be there where it pleases you to be, command what you would have done and I shall without fail perform the same."

Of this good fortune Tarolfo was so well contented in himsef as little more gladness could he have received if he had then held his lady embraced in his arms, and said: "Friend, unto me it seems long until you have performed what you have promised; wherefor let us depart without further tarrying and go thither where this is to be done."

Theban cast away his herbs and took his books and other things necessary unto his science, and with Tarolfo took his journey, and in short time they both came unto the desired city, very near unto the month in which the garden had been required to be made. Whereas all secret and close they did repose themselves until the wished time.

And now the month being entered, Tarolfo commanded the garden to be made to the end that he might give the same to his loved lady.

So soon as Theban had received this command he tarried the night ensuing, the which being once come he saw the horns of the moon gathered into a perfect roundness and to shine upon the frequented earth. Then he went him all alone forth of the city, leaving his apparel apart, barelegged, and his disheveled locks hanging upon his naked shoulders. The restless degrees of the night did pass. Birds, wild beasts and men without any noise did take their rest. The unfallen leaves without moving did hang upon the trees, and the moist air abode in mild peace. Only the stars did shine when as he oftentimes went about the grounds and came unto a place on a riverside, which it pleased him to choose for his garden.

There he stretched forth his arm three times toward the stars, and turning himself unto them he as often bathed his white locks in the running stream, crying as many times with a most high voice their help. And after setting his knees to the hard earth, began thus to say:

"O night, most faithful secreter of high things, and you, O ye stars, which together with the moon do succeed the splendid day, and thou, O singuler Hecates, become a helper to this my begun enterprise. And thou, O holy Ceres, the renewer of the ample face of the earth, also. And you whatsoever verses either arts or herbs, and thou whatsoever are bringing forth virtuous plants, and thou, O air, winds, mountains, rivers and lakes, and each god of the woods, and of the secret night, by whose help I have heretofore made the running streams to recoil, forcing them to return to their springs, and things running to become firm, and things firm to become running, and that has also given power to my verses to dry up the seas, that I at my pleasure might search the bottom thereof, and to make the cloudy times clear and (at my will) to fill the clear heavens with obscure clouds, to make the winds to cease and to turn as it seemed me best breaking therewith the hard jaws of the fearful dragon, making also the standing woods to move and the high mountains to tremble, and to return to their bodies out of the lake Styx those their shadows, and alive to come forth of their sepulchers, and sometimes thee, O moon, to draw to thy perfect roundness the attaining whereunto a ring of basons was wont to be a help, making also the clear face of the sun many times to become pale, be ye all present and aid me with your help. I have at this instant need of the sap and juice of herb, through which I may make in part the dry earth fastened through autumn and after through the withering cold winter, spoil of his flowers, fruits and herbs, to become flowering and to spring before the due time."

And having thus said, he said after many other things softly which he added unto his prayers. And these being ended and he a while silent, the stars gave not their light in vain. For more swifter than the flight of swiftest bird there appeared before him a chariot drawn by two dragons, whereupon he mounted, and taking the reins of the bridles of the two bridled dragons in his hand, was carried into the air.

He then leaving Spain and all Africa took his journey by other regions and first sought for the Isle of Crete. And from thence after with a short course he sought Pelion, Othrys and Ossa, Mount Nerium, Pachinus, Pelorus, and Appenine. Upon them all, plucking up and with a sharp sickle cutting such roots and herbs as best liked him, neither forgot he those which he had before gathered when he was found by Tarolfo in Thessaly. He took stones also upon the mount Caucasus and on the sands of Ganges; and out of Lybia he brought lungs of venomous serpents.

He searched the watery banks of Rodanus, of Seine at Paris and the great Po, of Arnus, of the imperial Tiber, of Niscus, of Tana and Danube; on those eke gathering such herbs as seemed to him most necessary for his purpose, putting these together with the others gathered on the tops of the savage mountains.

He also sought the islands of Lesbos and Patmos and every other wherein he perceived any profitable thing to be had for his attempt.

With all which things he came (the third day being not yet passed) to that place from whence he departed and the dragons that only had felt the odor of the gathered herbs did cast off their old hides of many years and were with new renewed and became young. There he dismounted from his chariot and on the green earth he made two altars, on his right hand that of Hecates and on the left that of the running goddess. That being done and devout fires kindled thereupon, with locks dispersed upon his old shoulders, he began with a murmuring noise to go about the same and with let blood oftentimes he bespread the blazing brands.

After he placed the same blood upon the altars sometimes softening therewithal appointed for his garden, and after that he softened again the selfsame three times, with fire, water and sulphur, setting

189

after a great vessel full of blood, milk and water upon the burning brands, which he caused to boil a good space, and put thereto the herbs and roots gathered in strange places, mingling therewith also divers seeds and flowers of unknown herbs, he added thereto stones, sought in the extreme parts of the east, and dew gathered the nights past, together with the flesh of infamous witches, the stones of a wolf, the hinder part of a fat Cyniphis and the skin of a Chilinder. And lastly a liver, with the lungs of an exceeding old hart and herewithal a thousand other things, both without name and so strange as my memory cannot again tell them.

After he took a dry bough of an olive tree and therewith began to mingle all these things together, in doing whereof the dry bough began to wax green and within a while after to bear leaves; and not long after the new appareling thereof, it was laden with black olives. As Theban saw this he took the boiling liquors and began therewithal to sprinkle and water in every place the chosen soil, whereon he had set slips of so many woods as he would have trees, and of as many sorts as could be found.

The which liquor the earth had no sooner tasted but that it began to spring, yielding flowers and new herbs, and the dry slips began to become all green and fruitful plants.

All this being done, Theban entering the city returned to Tarolfo, whom he found all in a muse, fearing to be scorned through his long abode. To whom he said: "Tarolfo, the thing you required is done to your liking."

This news pleased Tarolfo not a little, and happening the day following to be a great solemnity in the city, he went into the presence of his loved lady, who had not now seen him for a long time past. And thus he said to her:

"Madame, after a long and tedious travail I have performed that which you have commanded, and when as it shall please you to see it or to take it, it is ready at your pleasure."

She in seeing him marveled much, and the more hearing what he said and not believing the same to be true, made him this answer: "It pleaseth me right well. You shall let me see it tomorrow."

The second day was come and Tarolfo went again to his lady and said: "Madame, may it please you to walk to the garden, the which you required to have this cold month."

She then, accompanied by many others, was moved to see the

same; and they all being come to the garden entered therein by a fair portal, whereas they felt not the cold as abroad but the same to have a sweet temperate air. The lady went about the same and into every corner thereof, gathering both herbs and flowers, whereof she saw it very plentiful. And thus much more also had the virtue of the magical liquors wrought; the fruits which August was accustomed to bring forth, the trees there in this savage time did yield them very fair, whereof sundry did eat that accompanied the lady thither.

This garden seemed to the lady exceeding fair and admirable, neither did she think to have ever seen the like, and since she sundry ways knew it to be a true garden and the knight to have performed her request, she came toward him and said: "Without doubt, Sir Knight, you have deserved my love, and I am ready to stand to my promise. But I would pray of you this favor: that it would please you to tarry the time or ever you require me to your desire, that my knight be gone a-hunting or into some other place out of the city, to the end you may the more safely and without any suspicion take your delight of me."

This contended Tarolfo, who left her the garden and so departed. This garden was manifest to the whole country although never a one knew of a long time how it came to pass. And the lady that had now received it all sorrowful departed from the same. Returning to her chamber full of noisome care and grief, bethinking her in what way she might return back according to her promise; and as not finding any lawful excuse, so much the more increased her care. The which thing her husband espying began many times and often to marvel thereat, and to ask the cause of that her grief, to whom she answered: that she ailed nothing, being bashful to discover to him her given promise for her craved gift, doubting lest in so doing he should account her for lewd. Lastly she being unable to withstand the continual instigations of her husband that now still importunately desired to know the cause of her annoy, discoursed the same unto him from the beginning to the end, and that therefore she abode thus pensive.

The husband hearing this of long time suspected no less and thereby knowing in his conceit the purity of the lady, thus said unto her: "Go and covertly keep your oath and liberally perform to Tarolfo what you have promised. For he has with his great toil, of rights deserved the same."

And having thus said the lady began to weep and to say unto him:

"The gods keep me far from such a fault, in no wise will I do so. I will rather rid myself of life than do anything displeasing to you or dishonor to your person."

To whom the knight replied saying: "Wife for this matter that I will that you do no injury to yourself neither yet conceive any grief therefor. For in no wise shall it displease me. Go therefore and perform what you have promised. For you shall never be never a whit less dear to me but as you have performed this your promise to take you better heed hereafter of such like although a demanded gift may seem unto you impossible to be had."

As the lady perceived the will of her husband she decked and trimmed her and made herself very fair; took company with her and so went to Tarolfo's lodging and bepainted with bashfulness presented herself unto him. Tarolfo as soon as he saw her all marveling rose from Theban and encountered her with gladness and very honorable received her demanding the cause of her coming.

To whom she answered: "I am come to be wholly at your will. Do with me as it pleases you."

Then said Tarolfo: "You make me to muse above measure considering the time and the company wherewith you are come. This cannot be without some great alteration between you and your husband. Tell me therefore, I pray you, how the matter goes."

The lady then showed Tarolfo fully in order the whole matter and how it went, the which Tarolfo hearing he began then to enter into a far greater admiration than he had ever done before. And greatly to bethink him thereof and so in the end to conceive the great liberality of the husband that had sent his wife unto him. Whereupon he said to himself: whatsoever he be that should so much as but think villainy toward such a knight were surely worthy of great blame.

And so taking and talking with the lady he thus said unto her: "Madame, like a worthy lady you have performed what to me due is, for the which cause I account that received of your hands that I have of you desired. And therefore when it shall please you, you may return unto your husband, and thank him, I pray you, on my behalf. For this is so great a pleasure done unto me and excuse me of the folly I have heretofore committed toward him, assuring him that hereafter I shall never put the like in practice."

The lady, giving great thanks to Tarolfo for that his so great courtesy, merrily departed thence and returned to her husband, to whom she recited in order all that had been happened.

But Theban now coming to Tarolfo demanded how the case stood. Tarolfo declared unto him the whole discourse. To whom Theban then said: "And I, shall I then lose that which you have promised me?"

Tarolfo answered: "No, but when it pleases you take you half of all the castles and treasures I have in sort heretofore promised you. For I acknowlege that you have fully served my turn."

To whom Theban answered: "It may never please the gods since the knight was so liberal to you of his wife, and you again was not a villain to him and that his offer, that I become less than courteous. For above all things in the world that content me in that I have served your turn, and therefore I will that all that I ought to receive in payment of my travail remain all yours, in such sort as it has ever been heretofore."

Neither would he take of what was Tarolfo's anything at all.

It is now doubted, in which of these was the greatest liberality, either in the knight that had given liberty to his wife to go to Tarolfo, either in Tarolfo who sent the lady (whom he had always desired and for whose sake he had done so much to come to that pass, whereunto he was come, whenas she came unto him) back unto her husband free, or in Theban, who having abandoned his country, being now old for to gain the promised rewards, and being come thither, toiled himself to bring that to an end which he had promised, whereby he justly deserved the same, did now remit the whole to Tarolfo, and remained poor as he was at the first.

Giovanni Boccaccio: 14th century
Questioni d'Amore: Chapter 5
Trans. by H. C., 1566, modernized by
T. Bell. N. Y.: Hartsdale House,
1931

Country Life in England[1]

Margaret Paston to John Paston I (c. 1441)

To my ryth reverent and worscheful husbond Jon Paston.

Ryth reverent and worscheful husbond, I recommaunde me to yow, desyryng hertyly to here of yowre wylfare, thankyng yow for the tokyn that ye sent me be Edmunde Perys, preyng yow to wete[2] that my modyr sent to my fadyr to London for a goune cloth of mustyrddevyllers[3] to make of a goune for me; and he told my modyr and me, wanne he was comme hom, that he cargeyt[4] yow to bey it aftyr that he were come oute to London. I pre yow, yf it be not bowt, that ye wyl wechesaf to by it and send yt hom as sone as ye may; for I have no goune to werre this wyntyre but my blak and my grene a lyere[5], and that ys so comerus[6] that I ham wery to wer yt.

As for the gyrdyl that my fadyr behestyt[7] me, I spake to hym therof a lytyl before he yede[8] to London last, and he seyde to me that the faute was in yow, that ye wolde not thynke ther uppe to do mak yt; but I sopose that ys not so—he seyd yt but for a skeusacion.[9] I prey yow, yf ye dor tak yt uppe on yow, that ye wyle wechesafe to do mak yt ayens[10] ye come hom; for I hadde never more nede therof than I have now, for I ham waxse so fetys[11] that I may not be gyrte in no barre[12] of no gyrdyl that I have but of on.

1. These three letters are from the collection known as the Paston Letters. This collection of letters and papers of the family of John Paston (1421–1466), a country gentleman of Paston, in Norfolk, provides an excellent picture of social and domestic life in fifteen-century England.
2. to know
3. a gray woolen cloth
4. charged
5. ivy-green
6. cumbrous, cumbersome
7. promised
8. went
9. excuse
10. by the time that
11. dainty
12. band

Elysabeth Peverel hath leye seke xv or xvi wekys of the seyetyka, but sche sent my moder word be Kate that sche xuld come hedyr wanne God sent tyme, thoou sche xuld be crod[13] in a barwe.

Jon of Dam was here, and my modyr dyskevwyrd[14] me to hym; and he seyde be hys trouth that he was not gladder of no thyng that he harde thys towlmonyth than he was therof. I may no lenger leve be my crafte, I am dysscevwyrd of all able men that se me. Of alle odyr thyngs that ye deseyreyd that I xuld sende yow word of, I have sent yow word of in a letter that I did wryte on Ouwyr Ladyis Day laste was.

The Holy Trenyte have yow in hese kepyng. Wretyn at Oxnede in ryth gret hast on the Thrusday next before Seynt Tomas Day.

I prey yow that ye wyl were the reyng wyth the emage of Seynt Margrete that I sent yow for a rememraunce tyl ye com hom. Ye have lefte me sweche a rememraunce that maketh me to thynke uppe on yow both day and nyth wanne I wold sclepe.

Youre ys, M.P.

Margaret Paston to John Paston I (c. 1443)

To my rygth worschepful husbond Jhon Paston, dwellyng in the Innere Temple at London, in hast

Ryth worchipful hosbon, I recomande me to yow, desyryng hertely to here of your wilfare, thanckyng God of your amendyng of the grete dysese that ye have hade; and I thancke yow for the letter that ye sent me, for be my trowthe my moder and I were nowth in hertys es fro the tyme that we woste[15] of your sekenesse tyl we woste verely of your amendyng. My moder behestyd anodyr ymmage of wax of the weythe of yow to Our Lady of Walsyngham, and sche sent iiii nobelys[16] to the iiii orderys of frerys at Norweche to pray for yow; and I have behestyd to gon on pylgreymmays to Walsyngham and to Sent Levenardys for yow. Be my trowth I had never so hevy a sesyn as I had from the tyme that I woste of your sekenesse tyl I woste of your amendyng, and yyth myn hert is in no grete ese, ne nowth xal be tyl I woth that ye been very hol. . . .

13. wheeled
14. revealed
15. knew
16. noble: a gold coin worth about one dollar

I pray yow hertely that ye wol wochesaf to sende me a letter as hastely as ye may, yf wrytyn be non dysesse to you, and that ye wollen wochesaf to sende me quowe your sor dott. Yf I mythe have hade my wylle, I xulde a seyne yow er dys tyme. I wolde ye wern at hom, if it were your ese and your sor myth ben as wyl lokyth to here as it tys ther ye ben now, lever[17] dan a new gounne, thow it were of scarlette. I pray yow, yf your sor be hol and so that ye may indure to ryde, wan my fader com to London that ye wol askyn leve and com hom wan the hors xul be sentte hom ayeyn; for I hope ye xulde be kepte as tenderly herre as ye ben at London.

I may non leyser have to do wrytyn half a quarter so meche as I xulde seyn to yow if I myth speke wyth yow. I xal sende yow anothyr letter as hastely as I may. I thanke yow that ye wolde wochesaffe to remember my gyrdyl and that ye wolde wryte to me at this tyme, for I sopose the wrytyng was non esse to yow. Allmyth God have yow in hys kepyn and sende yow helth. Wretyn at Oxenede in ryte grete hast on Sent Mihyllys Evyn.

Yourrys, M. Paston

My moder gretit yow wel, and sendyt yow Goddys blyssyng and here; and sche prayeth yow, and I pray yow also, that ye be wel dyetyd of mete and dryngke, for that is the grettest helpe that ye may have now to your helthe ward. Your sone faryth wel, blyssyd be God.

Agnes Paston to Edmond Paston I (c. 1445)

To Edmond Paston, of Clyffordis Inne in London, be this lettre take

To myn welbelovid sone, I grete yow wel, and avyse yow to thynkke onis of the daie of youre fadris counseyle to lerne the lawe; for he seyde manie tymis that hosoever schuld dwelle at Paston shulde have nede to conne defende hym selfe.

The vikarie of Paston and youre fadre, in Lentyn laste was, where thorwe[18] and acordidde, and doolis[19] sette how broode the weye shuld ben; and nowe he hathe pullid uppe the doolis and setthe he wolle makyn a dyche from the cornere of his walle ryght overe the weye to the newe diche of the grete cloose.[20] And there is a man in Truntche

17. rather
18. concluded
19. boundary marks
20. enclosed field

hyghht Palmere to, that hadde of youre fadre certain bonde in Truntche over vii yere ore viii yere agoone for corn, and trwli hath paide all the yeris; and now he hathe suffrid the corne to ben withsette[21] for viii s.[22] of rentte to Gymmyngham, wich yowre fadre paide nevere. Geffreie axid Palmere why the rentte was notte axid in myn husbonddis tyme; and Palmere seyde, for he was a grete man, and a wyse man of the lawe, and that was the cawse men wolde not axe hym the rentte. . . .

I sende yow not this lettre to make yow wery of Paston, for I leve in hoope, and ye wolle lerne that they schulle be made werye of here werke; fore in good feyth I dare wel seyne it was yowre fadris laste wille to have do ryghht wel to that plase, and that can I schewe of good prcfc, thowe men wolde seye naye.

God make yow ryghht a good man, and send Goddis blesyng and myn. Wrettyn in haste at Norwich the Thorsdaie aftir Candelmasse Daie. By yowre modrc, Angneis Paston.

Paston Letters
Edited by N. Davis. Oxford: At the
Clarendon Press, 1958

21. taken in compensation
22. eight shillings

Part Five

PHILOSOPHY, RELIGION AND THE
RELIGIOUS LIFE

The selections offered here touch upon medieval philosophy and religious thought, but are more largely concerned with aspects of the religious life, including details of monastic life and some miracles recorded in the lives of the saints. Medieval philosophy meant largely the transmission of Platonic and Aristotelian traditions with additions, modifications and divergences occasioned by Christian theological concepts. Among the topics passionately expounded by medieval philosophers were Nominalism, Neo-Platonism and political theory. Religious thought dissected pagan and Christian principles, Church doctrine and metaphysics. It produced men such as Thomas Aquinas, Anselm, Roger Bacon, Alexander of Hales and Occam. The miraculous occurrences recorded in the vitae *of saints and ascetics, accepted devoutly by both reader and writer, were the phenomena that confirmed the sanctity of such lives.*

Miraculous Power of St. Martin

¶ LIKEWISE, in a certain village, St. Martin destroyed a very ancient temple and proceeded to cut down a pine tree that grew near the pagan shrine. The priest of the place began to object. Then, while at the Lord's bidding St. Martin overthrew the temple, the country folk fell silent; but would not allow him to cut down the tree. St. Martin patiently explained to them that there was nothing sacred in the stock. Let them rather follow the Lord, whom he himself served; the tree had to be cut down because it was dedicated to Satan. Then one of them, bolder than the rest, said: "If you have any faith in your God, whom you worship, as you declare, we ourselves will cut down this tree: you catch it as it falls. And if your Lord is with you, as you assert, you will escape unharmed."

Then St. Martin, courageously trusting in God, promised to do so. To this condition all the pagan throng agreed. They would readily sacrifice the tree, if only it crushed an enemy of their sacred traditions. And so, when the pine tree swayed in a direction that made it certain how it would fall when cut down, St. Martin was bound and placed on the spot where, as the pagans judged, there was no doubt about its fall.

Then they began to cut the pine amidst a joyful din. Nearby stood a crowd of wondering country folk. And now slowly the pine swayed, threatening to fall full length. The monks close by grew pale, and as danger became more imminent, they became terrified, losing all hope and faith, and awaiting the death of Martin. But St. Martin trusted in the Lord, and waited, undismayed. Now, as the tree fell crashing, he raised his hand against it, and as it fell and rushed on him, he made the sign of salvation. Then indeed—like a whirlwind driven back—it sprawled in the opposite direction, almost felling the people who had stood in a safe spot.

Then, raising a shout toward heaven, the pagans stood amazed at the miracle, the monks wept for joy, and the name of Christ was extolled by all in unison. And it was evident that this region had received salvation.

Sulpicius Severus: 5th century
Vita S. Martini: Corpus Scriptorum
Ecclesiasticorum, 13
Trans. by H. E. W.

A Royal Nun

¶ WHILE ALL THE NUNS were still sleeping, Queen Radegund cleaned and polished shoes and returned them to each nun. At all times, except on the days of Easter and high festivals or when sickness prevented her, she always led an austere life in sackcloth and ashes, rising for the singing before the congregation arose. In regard to the convent duties nothing pleased her except to be the first to serve and she chastised herself if she performed a good act later than another nun. So, sweeping in her turn the convent streets and the corners, cleaning whatever was foul, she did not shrink from taking away the loads whose sight makes others shudder. Carrying logs in her arms; looking after the hearth with bellows and tongs; falling down and recovering, unhurt; serving the sick beyond her seven-day assignment of labor; cooking the food herself; washing the faces of the ailing; offering hot drinks; she visited those she nursed, returning to her cell fasting.

Who will explain with what eagerness she would keep running to the kitchen, performing her *septimana*? Finally none of the nuns except herself brought in from the back door whatever wood was needed. She carried water from the well and distributed it in pitchers. Cleaning and washing the vegetables, poking up the fire with bellows, washing and bringing in the dishes. When meals were over, wiping the dishes herself, tidying up the kitchen until it shone, carrying to an assigned spot outside whatever was soiled. With the most sanctified humility bathing and kissing feet, and while still prostrated begging forgiveness from all for any negligence of which she was guilty.

Fortunatus: 6th century
Vita Radegundis
Trans. by H. E. W.

202

Advice to Monks

¶ THEREFORE let us seek, with all our striving, all our effort, all our desires, to deserve the attainment of such a great gift through the bountifulness of the Lord. For this is salutary for us, and helpful, glorious, everlasting, that no death, no insecurity, no oblivion can remove; but in that pleasant land it will make you rejoice with the Lord in eternal exultation. But if, as Virgil says, "chill blood obstructs the heart," of any one of the brothers, so that he can be trained neither in human nor sacred studies, still, equipped with moderate learning, let him certainly elect the following: "Let the country and the watering streams in the valleys please me." For it is not out of place for monks to cultivate gardens, till the fields, and to rejoice in the fruitfulness of the produce. For we read in Psalm cxxvii: "For thou shalt eat the labor of thine hands: happy thou shalt be, and it shall be well with thee."

If one asks for the authors of this kind of study, Gargilius Martialis wrote excellently on gardens, describing the nutritive values of vegetables and their properties in detail, so that from a perusal of that monograph, with God's help, everyone can be satisfied and healed. I have left this for you along with other books. Similarly, in agriculture, beekeeping, pigeon rearing, and fish breeding, among others Columella and Aemilianus are commendable authors. But Columella in sixteen books passes with fluent eloquence through the various branches of agriculture, suitable for scholars rather than the inexperienced, so that those who are interested in his work are furnished not only with the usual offering but with a rich banquet. Aemilianus too is a very eloquent expositor and in his twelve books on horticulture and cattle and other subjects he presents a full, clear discussion. Him also, together with the others to be read, I have left for you, with God's help.

Cassiodorus: 6th century
*Institutiones divinarum et humanarum
 litterarum*
Trans. by H. E. W.

Monks as Doctors

¶ I ADDRESS YOU TOO, worthy brethren who look after the health of the human body with diligent care and exercise the duties of blessed piety on those who seek refuge in the abodes of the saints. You are saddened by the sufferings of others, distressed for those in danger, stricken by the grief of patients, and always touched by sympathetic sorrow for the misfortunes of others. As it is proper for your skillful art to save the sick by your wholehearted zealousness, you will receive a reward from Him by whom what is temporal can be replaced by what is eternal. Learn therefore the nature of herbs and handle the compounding of species with scrupulous concern, but do not put your hope in herbs, nor health in human counsels. For though we read that medicine was established by the Lord, still He makes men sound who grants life without question; for it is written: "And whatsoever ye do in word or deed, do all in the name of the Lord Jesus, giving thanks to God and the Father by him."

But if you have no remarkable ability in Greek, you have to begin with the herbal book of Dioscorides, who discussed and described the herbs of the fields with amazing accuracy. Next, read Hippocrates and Galen in Latin translations, that is, Galen's *Therapeutica*, intended for Glauco the philosopher, and a certain anonymous book, compiled from various writers. Then the *De Medicina* of Aurelius Coelius and Hippocrates' *De Herbis et Curis* and various other books on the art of healing that I left for you, with God's help, on the shelves of our library.

Cassiodorus: 6th century
Institutiones
Trans. by H. E. W.

Duties of a Cellarer

¶ LET THE CELLARER of a monastery chosen from the congregation be intelligent, of mature character, sober, not greedy, not overweening, not boisterous, not insulting, not lazy, not prodigal, but God-fearing and like a father to the entire congregation. Let him take care of everyone, do nothing without the abbot's orders, and execute whatever he orders. Let him not offend the brothers. If any brother happens to ask him something unreasonable, let him not humiliate him contemptuously, but reasonably and with humility let him refuse the unseemly request. Let him guard his soul, always remembering the apostolic saying: "For they that have used the office of a deacon well purchase to themselves a good degree." Let him care with all solicitude for the sick, for children, guests and the poor, knowing without question that for all of them he will receive a reckoning on the Day of Judgment. Let him look after all the vessels of the monastery, and every article and any sacred altar vessels. Let him consider nothing negligible. Let him be neither miserly nor a lavish squanderer of the monastery's property, but let him do everything in moderation according to the abbot's bidding. Let him consider humility above everything, and for him who has no offering to make, let a soft answer be returned, as it is written: "To an answer given a soft answer is best." All that the abbot has enjoined, let him take under his care. What he has forbidden, let him not presume. Let him distribute to the brothers the assigned provisions without any disdain or delay, so that they may not be offended; remembering the divine saying about what he "who offends one of the little ones" deserves. If the congregation is very large, let solace be given to it, whereby it may be helped and may fulfill with equanimity the duty entrusted to it. At the proper time let the necessary things be given and let what requires seeking be sought, so that no one is disturbed or saddened in the House of God.

Benedict of Nursia: 6th century
Regula
Trans. by H. E. W.

Monastic Labors

¶ IDLENESS is the enemy of the soul and for that reason at certain times the brothers ought to be occupied in manual labor; at other times, again, in sacred study. So we believe that both times should be regulated by this arrangement: that is, from Easter until October 1st, going out in the morning from the first hour until almost the fourth, they should do what is necessary; from the fourth hour until about the sixth they should spend the time in study. Rising from table after the sixth hour they should rest on their couch in complete silence, or if one happens to want to read for himself without disturbing anyone else. Let the ninth period be a little earlier, the eighth hour being divided into two parts, and again let the necessary tasks be done until evening. If the place or poverty necessitates their being busy by themselves with harvesting the crops, let them not be disconsolate, because then they are really monks if they live by the labor of their hands like our father and the apostles. Let everything however be done reasonably on account of the weaklings.

From October 1st to the beginning of Lent, until the end of the second hour let them spend the time on study; from the third hour to the ninth let all work each at the task assigned to him. At the first signal of the ninth hour let each one leave his work and let them be ready until the second bell strikes. After their meal, let them study or chant the psalms. During the days of Lent from morning until the end of the third hour let them carry on their studies and until the end of the tenth hour let them work at assigned tasks. During these days of Lent let them have all the single books in the library that they are to read in entirety, in sequence; and these books are to be given at the beginning of Lent. Above all, let one or two elders be deputed to patrol the monastery at the hour when the brothers are studying and see whether by chance a lazy brother is found idling or telling stories and is not intent on his study and is not only useless to himself but also disturbs the others. If such a one is found—which God forbid—he should be rebuked once and a second time. If he does not improve, he should be subjected to correction according to the Rule, to inspire the others with fear. Brothers should not associate with each other at inconvenient hours. Likewise on Sunday all should be intent on study, except those who have been detailed for various duties. If anyone is so negligent and lazy as not to want either to meditate or to read, let him be given work to keep him occupied. For weak or sick brothers such tasks or skills should be assigned them as not only prevent them from being idle but also do not overwhelm them with the strenuousness of the work and make them avoid it; the weakness of such men must be taken into consideration by the abbot.

St. Benedict: 6th century
Regula
Trans. by H. E. W.

The Conflict of Good and Evil

¶ NO SOONER had Philosophy, who even in the gaiety of music preserved her wonted dignity of aspect and gravity of utterance, furnish'd her melodious strains, but I, who could not yet entirely forget my trouble, interrupted her as she was preparing to continue her discourse. Kind harbinger, said I, of true and perfect light! What you have hitherto said is as undeniably evident from its own divine testimony as it has been invincibly supported by your arguments; and I was formerly myself not altogether ignorant of what you have told me, though excess of grief had lately driven it from my remembrance. But the chief reason of my grief is this: that since the Governor of all is good, there should be any such thing as evil; or that it should escape with umpunity. And I think I may appeal to yourself, that this alone is a surprising paradox; but it is also a greater still, that wickedness should triumph as well as flourish, and that virtue should not only go unrewarded, but also be trampled on by reprobates and bear the punishment of their demerits. That these things should therefore be permitted under the government of God, who knows and can do all things and will do nothing but that which is good, is just reason not only of my wonder but complaint.

It would indeed be, said she, a most amazing and monstrous thing, if (as you imagine) in the family of so great a master and so finely regulated, the worthless vessels should be cleans'd and polish'd, and the more valuable be neglected. But it is not so; for if those conclusions, which I have made already, cannot be deny'd, I shall from thence convince you that God, of whose government we speak, has ordain'd that good men shall be always powerful, but the wicked contemptible and impotent; that vices never go unpunish'd, nor virtue unrewarded; that happiness shall always attend on innocence, and misery on offenses; with many other things of this kind, which will pacify your complaints and settle your mind on a firm and solid basis. So that having already shown you the form of true happiness, and where it dwells, I will (when all things necessary are premis'd) reconduct you to your native home. I will furnish your mind with wings, by the help of which she may soar aloft; and be assured that by observing my directions, following my track, and confiding in my convoy, you shall surmount all difficulties and return in safety.

> Strong are my wings to soar, and swift to fly,
> Up to the chrystal regions of the sky;
> The mind thus plum'd will higher worlds explore,
> And grovel on the humble dust no more;
> Now views high mounted on the verge of air,
> The fighting clouds below, nor dreads the war;
> The rolling air tho' warm, she yet aspires
> To warmer regions, and more hallow'd fires;
> Sees how the stars their various courses run,
> And contemplates the glories of the sun;
> Or slacks her sail to Saturn's solemn pace;
> Or stretches on with Mars a swifter race;
> With each revolving star pursues her way,
> And shines herself a star as bright as they:
> These regions known, she wings a loftier flight,
> And seeks beyond the spheres for native light,
> Than stars or sun more pure, more prevalently bright:
> Here reigns the mighty king, whom kings obey,
> And o'er the universe extends his sway,
> Unmov'd, he travels his creation o'er,
> And lights and rolls the orbs she visited before.
> This glorious height to climb, the wand'rer taught
> (Which now forgotten, must afresh be sought)

208

Hail to my native soil! all hail! she cries:
Thou well-known object of my longing eyes!
Receive an exile, exile now no more,
And I will ne'er again forsake thy shore
If downwards thence she looks, and seeks to find
The realms of night she 'scap'd and left behind;
She smiles to see the scepter'd tyrants frown,
And claims their terrors from the skies alone,
Yet barr'd forever thence, and to the skies unknown.

Oh! Madam, said I, what mighty things you teach me to expect! nor do I doubt but that you will enable me to obtain 'em; let me not therefore be delay'd a moment from pursuing that glorious object, to which you have rais'd my hopes. Come on, said she, and in the first place, you are to be inform'd, that good men are always powerful, and the wicked always impotent; propositions that are easily demonstrated by each other: for since good and evil are contraries, that which proves the power of the one, will likewise prove the impotency of the other; and if the weakness of the one appears, the strength of the other is by consequence apparent; but for your more abundant satisfaction, I shall proceed both ways and both ways confirm my propositions.

Boethius: 6th century
De Consolatione Philosophiae
Trans. by W. Causton, 1730

Portrait of a Saint

¶ A MAN of revered life, he was Benedict in grace and name, and from the time of his boyhood his heart was that of an old man. Living in righteousness, he gave his mind to no pleasure, but during the time he was still on this earth, the world he could have used freely in a secular way he despised as being barren with flowers. Of noble birth, in the province of Nursia, he had been sent to Rome to pursue the liberal arts. But when he perceived that many students were falling over the precipice of sin, the footsteps that he had set, as it were, on the brink of the world he retraced, for fear that, if he touched any of this knowledge, he too would afterward fall completely into the vast abyss. So, with contempt for the liberal studies, he left his home and his father's possessions, desiring to please God only, and sought the attire of the holy life. Knowingly unknowing, therefore, and wisely unlearned, he went into retreat. I have not discovered all that he accomplished but the few items I mention I found out from the report of four of his pupils, as follows: He surpassed Constantine, that most revered man who succeeded him in the administration of the monastery; also Valentinian, who for many years was at the head of the Lateran monastery; Simplicius, who, the third in succession, ruled that congregation after him; Honoratus too, who is the abbot of the monastery in which Benedict had previously dwelt.

Gregory the Great: 7th century
Dialogi
Trans. by H. E. W.

A Logical Explanation
of the Universe

MASTER: In my frequent speculation and my deeper inquiries, as far as in my power lies, I find that the basic and principal division of all things that can be perceived by the mind or transcend its objective is into the things that exist and those that are nonexistent. The general term for all these things is called *physics* in Greek and *nature* in Latin. Or have you a different view?

PUPIL: No, I agree with you. For pursuing the path of reason, I too find that this is so.

MASTER: Nature, then, is a general term, as we said, for all things that exist and are nonexistent.

PUPIL: That is so. For nothing in the universe, by our reasoning, can exist that cannot be included under such a term.

MASTER: Since then we both agree about this general name, I should like you to tell me the plan of such a division through differences into species; or, if you like, before I attempt such a division, it will be your turn to judge the things divided.

PUPIL: Pray proceed; for I am impatient and eager to learn from you the true scheme in these matters.

MASTER: It appears to me that the division of the universe falls into four species through four differences. The first is into the creator and the not-created. The second, the created and the creator. The third, the creator and the non-creating. The fourth, the non-creative and the non-created. Now of these four distinctions, two sets are contraries: the third is the contrary of the first, and the fourth of the second. But the fourth, whose difference is not being able to exist, is impossible. Does such a division seem right to you or not?

PUPIL: Right. But I should like you to repeat it, so that the contrariness of the forms may be clearer to me.

MASTER: You see, unless I am mistaken, the opposition of the third kind to the first. For the first creates and is not created; to this is opposed what is created and does not create. The second kind is contrary to the fourth; the second is created and creates, in universal contradiction to the fourth, that neither creates nor is created.

PUPIL: I see it clearly. But I am greatly worried about the fourth kind, that has been added by you. For I should not dare to hesitate at all about the other three, since the first, I think, is understood in the case of all things that exist and are nonexistent; the second, in primary causes; the third, in what is known in generation, time, and place. And for that reason, as I see it, it is necessary to discuss each item in greater detail.

MASTER: Your opinion is correct. But what should be the logical method of procedure, that is, what kind of universe should form the first step in the discussion, I leave to your judgment.

PUPIL: It seems to me proper to speak, before the other kinds, on whatever light the minds of men have shed on the first kind.

Iohannes Scotus Erigena: 9th century
De Divisione Naturae
Trans. by H. E. W.

Charlemagne as Educator

¶ CHARLES, by the grace of God King of the Franks and Lombards and Patrician[1] of the Romans. We send by our ambassadors loving greetings to you, Abbot Baugulf and all the congregation, and to the faithful entrusted to your care, in the name of Almighty God.

During recent years many monasteries submitted frequent memoranda to us. They contained information on the brethren who dwelt there and on their discussions, in our behalf, in their holy and devout talks. We know therefore that in many of their above-mentioned writings the sentiment was right but the expression crude. For what pious devotion faithfully dictated to their heart, the unlettered tongue could not faultlessly express in writing for lack of learning. Hence it was that we began to fear that perchance, since their skill in writing was small, their intelligence in understanding the Holy Scriptures would be still smaller than it should rightly be. And we fully realize that verbal mistakes are fraught with hazards, but that errors in judgment are much more dangerous. We therefore beseech you not only not to neglect the study of literature but, with a humble zest acceptable to God, to vie with each other in rivalry until you can more easily and more properly penetrate the mysteries of Holy Scripture. Now, since figures of speech, tropes, and other similar devices are found in the sacred writings, there is no question that everyone, on reading them, understands the spiritual significance all the more readily if he has been previously trained in the mastery of letters. For such a task men should be chosen who have the will and the capability of learning, and the desire to teach others. And this should be performed with the same zest as we earnestly show in laying down this command. For we hope that, as befits soldiers of the Church, you will be devoted in spirit, learned in expression, pure in life, schooled in eloquence. Thus, if anyone seeks you in the name of the Lord and on account of your reputation for holy converse, and recognizes you by sight, he may similarly acknowledge your wisdom that shines

---

1. A title conferred by Pope Hadrian in 774 A.D.

through your reading or chanting, and go away rejoicing, giving thanks to Almighty God.

Therefore do not neglect to have copies of this letter distributed to all assistants and to your fellow bishops in all the monasteries, if you wish to retain our good will.

Charlemagne: 742–814
De Litteris Colendis
Trans. by H. E. W.

Heathen and Christian

¶ Now, I BELIEVE, we have previously spoken sufficiently about the seven liberal arts of the philosophers, and for what purpose they should be studied by Catholics. We add what those who are termed philosophers themselves assert: If they have somehow chanced to pronounce truths that harmonize with our faith in their systems and writings, particularly the Platonists, not only should those truths not be feared, but they should be adapted to our use by these, so to speak, unlawful possessors. For just as the Egyptians had not only idols and lamentable misconceptions that the people of Israel abhorred and shunned, but also vases and ornaments of gold and silver and raiment that the Israelites, on their departure from Egypt, secretly appropriated for themselves, as though for a better purpose, not on their own authority but by precept and mandate, the Egyptians themselves unknowingly bestowing on them those goods that they used: so all the doctrines of the heathens have not only false and superstitious figments and pitiful burdens of fruitless labor that each of us, abandoning the society of the heathens under Christ's leadership, ought to abominate and shun, but also embrace the liberal arts, that we have summarily discussed before, more fitted for the use of the truth and certain very useful moral precepts; and many truths are found among them on the worship of the one God. Every Christian, on severing any wretched connection with them, ought, for the proper purpose of preaching the gospel, to take from them their gold and silver, as it were, that they themselves did not originate but mined

213

from certain metals of the all-pervasive Divine Providence and which they perversely and wrongly abuse in their worship of demons.

Their clothing too, that is, the customs of humanity adapted to human society, which we cannot dispense with in this life, it is permissible to take and keep, and convert to Christian use. For what else have many good men and faithful among us done? Do we not observe how Cyprian and the most eloquent scholar and the most saintly martyr left Egypt loaded with gold and silver and clothing? Or Lactantius? Or Victorinus, Optatius, and Hilarius? Or numberless teachers? Do we not see what, in earlier times, Moses, that faithful servant of God, did, of whom it is written: "He was learned in all the wisdom of the Egyptians"?

The superstitious nations, especially in those times, who, rejecting the yoke of Christ, persecuted the Christians, would never have adapted for all these men the studies that they thought useful if they had suspected that they would be used for the purpose of worshiping one God, who destroyed the vain cult of idols. But they gave gold and silver and their clothing to the people of God on their departure from Egypt, not knowing how the things they gave would be restored to the worship of Christ. For what occurred in Exodus is unquestionably a figurative account, betokening what I said without prejudice to an equal or greater intelligence. But the student, thus instructed in the Holy Scriptures, would never stop meditating, when he starts to examine these questions, on the apostolic dictum: "Knowledge expands a person, charity builds."

Hrabanus Maurus: 9th century
De Institutione Clericorum
Trans. by H. E. W.

St. Laurence's Martyrdom

¶ *August 10*. Rome, Via Tiburina. The natal day of St. Laurence, archdeacon and martyr in the reign of the Emperor Decius.

Saint Sixtus, on his way to the crown of martyrdom, left him all the resources and the treasures of the Church. This St. Laurence arranged, with generous liberality, for distribution to the sick and other poor and to widows and the needy. Learning of this, Decius Caesar summoned him into his presence and after hearing him handed him over to Valerian, Prefect of the City, who in his turn gave him into the custody of a certain Hippolytus; but Hippolytus released him along with many others. In the same place St. Laurence, after the healing of the widow Cyriaca and the restoration of sight to Crescentio, made the blind Lucullus also see, in the name of Jesus Christ. Hearing of this miracle, many blind men came to St. Laurence and were given sight. Observing this, Hippolytus believed, was instructed, and was baptized.

After three days, during which, with the permission of Hippolytus, now a Christian, St. Laurence distributed all the resources of the Church to the poor, he presented himself in the Palace of Sallust. Decius, in a rage, ordered him to be stripped and lashed with scorpions; afterward, bound in chains, St. Laurence was led to the Palace of Tiberius for a hearing. Blazing with anger, Decius ordered him to be scourged naked. As he was being beaten, he cried out to Caesar: "Behold, you wretch, realize that I do not feel your tortures."

Then Decius ordered the number of cudgels to be increased and plates of hot iron to be applied to his sides. St. Laurence said: "O Lord Jesus Christ, God through God, have pity on me, your servant, because though accused, I did not deny; questioned, I confessed you, Lord Jesus Christ."

After being lashed for a long time with whips loaded with lead, he said: "O Lord Jesus Christ, who deemed it worthy, for our salvation, to assume the form of a slave in order to free us from slavery to demons, receive my spirit."

And a voice was heard: "Many conflicts still await you."

Then he was stretched on a scaffold and lashed terribly with scorpions, but smiling and giving thanks, he said: "Blessed art thou, O Lord God, Father of our Lord Jesus Christ, who showed compassion for us that we did not deserve: but thou, O Lord, on account of thy piety, give us grace, that all who stand around may know that Thou consolest Thy servants."

Then one of the soldiers, named Romanus, believed in the Lord Jesus Christ and said to St. Laurence: "I see in front of you a very handsome man, standing with a linen cloth and wiping your wounds. I adjure you, by Christ, who sent His angel to you, do not abandon me."

Raised therefore from the scaffold and released, St. Laurence was returned to Hippolytus, in the palace. Coming over with a pitcher, Romanus cast himself at St. Laurence's feet to be baptized. Presently he was baptized and publicly professed himself a Christian; then he was taken outside the walls of the Salarian Gate and beheaded.

Now Decius Caesar hurried at night to the baths near the Palace of Sallust and on being shown St. Laurence, all kinds of tortures were applied: whips loaded with lead, cudgels, metal plates, nails, couches, staffs. Decius said to the blessed martyr: "Now lay aside your treacherous magic skill, and tell us your pedigree." St. Laurence replied: "As to birth, I am a Spaniard trained or brought up as a Roman, and a Christian from the cradle on, instructed in every sacred and holy law."

DECIUS: Sacrifice to the gods; for, if you do not, this night will be spent by you in torture.

ST. LAURENCE: My night has no darkness, but shines quite clear in the light.

When his face was cut by stones, he laughed and was comforted and said: "I give thanks to you, O Lord, for you are the Lord of all things."

Now a couch with three sides was brought in and St. Laurence, stripped of his garments, was stretched on an iron frame. When he was covered by the iron forks, he said to Decius: "I offered sacrifice to God in the odor of grace, because the afflicted spirit is a sacrifice to God."

The torturers, however, eagerly fed the coals, throwing them under the frame, and crushing the iron forks over him. Said St. Laurence: "Learn, wretch, the greatness of the Lord my God Jesus Christ's virtue, for your coals afford me coolness, but to you, eternal punishment. For the Lord Himself knows that, though accused, I did not deny; though questioned, I confessed a Christian; though roasted alive, I give thanks." And raising his eyes to the Lord, he called out to Decius: "Lo, you wretch, you have roasted one side, turn over the other side and eat it."

Giving thanks therefore to God and glorifying Him, he said: "I thank Thee, Lord Jesus Christ, that I have deserved to enter Thy doors," and he gave up his spirit.

In the morning, while it was still early dawn, Hippolytus took the body and embalmed it in linen cloths and spices, and entrusted this task to Justin the elder. Then Saint Justin and Hippolytus, weeping sadly, took the body of St. Laurence martyr and came to the Tiburina Road to the house of the widow named Cyriaca, in the Veranian field, where the blessed martyr had been at night to wash the feet of the saints with a linen towel. There at the evening hour they buried him on August 10th. They fasted, keeping night watch for three days with a crowd of Christians. Blessed Justin the elder offered a sacrifice of praise and all participated. Then Claudius, Severus, Crescentio and Romanus suffered the penalty on the same day as St. Laurence, the third day after St. Sixtus martyr. On the same day in Rome one hundred and forty-five soldiers were also martyred.

Notker Balbulus: 10th century
Martyrologium
Trans. by H. E. W.

Sketch of a Royal Monk

¶ THE YEAR 745 of the Lord's incarnation. Carolomannus confessed to his brother Pippin that he was mentally disposed to leave the world and for love of God to abandon the earthly kingdom, in order to gain in a future life a hundredfold possession. And in this year they made no expedition but each prepared himself, Carolomannus for the journey that he had decided on, and Pippin to follow his brother to the place, honorably with pomp and gifts and due lavishness.

The year 746 of the Lord's incarnation. Carolomannus proceeded to Rome and there he was tonsured and on Monte Soracte he built a monastery in honor of St. Sylvester and there he remained for some time. Then he arrived at St. Benedict's on Monte Cassino and there he was made a monk. Now a remarkable incident is told about this holy man. While he still resided in Rome in the monastery that he had built for himself and was venerated by all for his royal nobility and, what is more important, for his contempt of the earthly kingdom and the glory of the present world, and was extolled with praises, this man, filled with the Lord and fearing the popularity of human praise, who had given up so much for Christ, resolved to take flight rather than be a victim of vainglory.

Confessing this to one faithful companion only, whose loyalty in all respects he had tested from childhood, he fled that night without anyone knowing, and came to Monte Cassino. Carrying with him nothing of all the possessions that were materially necessary, naked he followed Christ. As was customary, he knocked at the monastery gate and sought an interview with the father. When he came into his presence, he immediately prostrated himself, protesting that he was a murderer, guilty of every crime, and begged for mercy, and sought an opportunity to repent. The father, recognizing that he was a foreigner, asked him his native country and his nation. He acknowledged that he was a Frank and had traveled from France on account of such a crime, gladly prepared to endure exile, provided only he would not lose the kingdom of heaven. The spiritual father, assenting to his pleas, ordered him to be received in the cell of the novices, along with his companion, and there to be tested according to the orders of the Rule, all the more strictly since he was a man of a foreign and unknown nation, thus fulfilling the apostolic injunction: "Try the spirits whether they are of God." So, after being tested in every ordeal, he was attached to the congregation along with his colleague, after promising, at the end of the year, steadfastness, improvement of character, and obedience, in accordance with St. Benedict's Rule. He began without rebuke to dwell among the brothers, being strong in all the virtues. Now it happened, as the custom is, that, being deputed as the weekly cook, a duty he performed willingly but, in his ignorance, giving offense to many, the cook, heated with wine, slapped him and said: "Is that the way to serve your brothers?"

Though deeply disturbed, he replied with a placid look: "May the Lord, brother, and Carolomannus forgive you!" For he had not revealed his name to anyone, to avoid being so recognized. Again, when he had made a mistake in supervising certain food supplies, he was struck once more by the cook; he made the same prayer as before. When he was cruelly beaten by the cook for the third time, indignantly the inseparable companion in his travels, unable any longer to endure that such a man should be treated so shamefully by such a worthless fellow, snatched up a pestle with which the bread was kneaded that was to be put into the brothers' vegetable plates, and struck him with all his might, with these words: "May neither God spare you, you worthless servant, nor Carolomannus forgive you." Hearing this, the brothers were greatly annoyed that a man of foreign birth, accepted in a spirit of mercy, should have presumed to do such things. At once therefore he was handed over to the guard so that such presumption would be punished more severely.

Next day, being released from custody, he was set in the midst of the monks. Asked why he had dared to lay a hand on a brother assistant, he answered: "Because I saw a servant who was worse than all others, and a man, the best and noblest of all that I know who dwell on earth, not only insulted by words but even struck by blows."

Aroused by a fit of excessive anger, that a man who had come as a foreigner should have preferred him to the others, they asked who this man was who excelled all in goodness and nobility, and why he had not excepted at least the father of the monastery. The other, driven by necessity, unable to hide what God wished to be manifest, said: "That is Carolomannus, once king of the Franks, who left his kingdom and the glory of the world for love of Christ and who, from such a lofty position, humbled himself to the extent of not only being insulted by the commonest persons but also lashed with whippings."

On hearing this, they rose trembling from their seats, prostrated themselves at his feet, begged for pardon for their contempt, and admitted their ignorance. He, on the other hand, cast himself upon the ground and tearfully started to deny it: it was not true, he was not Carolomannus, but a sinful man and a murderer; his colleague, terrified on account of the crime committed, had thought this out. There was nothing more to be said. He was recognized by all and treated with great respect.

We could not bear to pass over this episode; now let us return to our chronicle.

Regino of Prüm: 10th century
Chronicon
Trans. by H. E. W.

The Existence of God[1]

¶ THEREFORE, LORD, you who give mind to the faithful, give me to understand, as far as you can explain, that you exist as we believe, and that you are what we believe. And indeed we believe that you are the greatest thing imaginable. Or is there some other nature? *For the fool has said in his heart: there is no God.* But surely that very same fool, hearing what I say: "the greatest thing imaginable," understands what he hears, and what he understands is in his mind, even if he does not understand that it exists. For the existence of the thing in the mind, and understanding that the thing exists, are two different concepts. For when an artist plans what he is going to do, he has it in his mind, but he does not yet understand what he has not yet consummated. But when he has finished the painting, he has it in his mind and also understands that what he has done exists. Therefore even the fool is convinced that there is something in the mind, than which nothing greater is imaginable, because he understands this, when he hears it, and whatever is understood is in the mind. And surely the greatest thing imaginable cannot be in the mind only. For if it is in the mind only, it can be imagined to exist in reality also; because it is greater. If therefore the greatest thing imaginable is in the mind only, that very thing, than which a greater cannot be conceived, is a thing than which a greater can be conceived. But that is impossible. There exists therefore, without question, something than which a greater thing is inconceivable, both in the mind and in reality.

St. Anselm: 11th century
Proslogion. R. A. Browne, *British Latin Selections.* Oxford: Blackwell, 1954
Trans. by H. E. W.

1. Anselm's classic argument is that, if the concept of perfection exists in the human mind, the logical conclusion must follow that perfection exists in an objective sense. The argument, involving reality and idealistic existence, has been assailed by his critics. Anselm (1033–1109), a native of Aosta, became Archbishop of Canterbury. He is noted for his theological and philosophical treatises. His life, *Vita Anselmi,* was written by his friend Eadmer, a monk of Canterbury.

Abbot Suger of Saint-Denis[1]

¶ IN THE TWENTY-THIRD year of our administration, as we were sitting in the general chapter on a certain day, in conference with our brethren on men and private matters, the most deeply beloved brethren and sons began to beg me not to permit the fruit of our great labor to be relegated to silence; but rather to preserve for the memory of posterity, by pen and ink, the adornments that the abundant generosity of Almighty God had conferred on this church during the period of our incumbency, both in the acquisition of new additions and in the recovery of losses, in the multiplication too of improved possessions, in building construction, in storing up gold, silver, precious stones and excellent fabrics. For this one concession they promised us a double reward: by such renown we would deserve the perennial zest of all the brethren in future, when they prayed for the salvation of our soul; and by this example we would arouse their zealous concern for the reverence of the church of God. We therefore devoutly acceded to their equally devout and reasonable requests: not in order to acquire empty glory, or claiming any reward in the form of human praise or evanescent recompense; but to forestall, after our demise, a diminution in the church revenues through any or anyone's fraudulence, and to prevent the numerous additions conferred by the bountiful munificence of God during our administration from being furtively destroyed in the hands of evil successors. We have thought it honorable and useful, just as we considered it right to begin at the proper place, to describe the establishment of the buildings and the increase of the treasures, starting with the body of the church of the blessed martyrs Denis, Rusticus, and Eleutherius —a church that has most affectionately fostered us from our nursing days to old age. Likewise we have proposed to bring to the attention

1. Suger was the Richelieu of the twelfth century. He managed the affairs of France well, and also those of the royal Abbey of Saint-Denis, as can be imagined from reading this passage from his own account of his ministry and work.

of present and future readers the increase in revenues, beginning with his little township, that is, his first abode, and the surrounding area.

Latin text of A. Lecoy de la Marche: 1867
Trans. by H. E. W.

Ecclesiastical Administration[1]

¶ THIS MAN[2] then appears to have been divinely inspired to shed luster not only on one place over which he had jurisdiction, but on the entire realm of France. He advanced to this height, not for the purpose of elevating one class of monks, but every Order of the Church, by his own personal efforts. One may care to wonder, in the case of this man, that nature had endowed such a frail body with such a great and noble spirit. But possibly it wished, through this man, to demonstrate clearly that the noblest spirit may dwell in any skin whatever, and that virtue springs from any source; and also to inform us that the spirit is not impaired by a small body but that the body is graced by strength of mind. But since I realize that an erroneous opinion about this man has become deep-rooted in the hearts of certain men, it must be stated that while he was absent and far distant, he was called to the administration without any suspicion on his part, and that he accepted the invitation. Nor was it permitted him to refuse or to spend his life in obscurity,[3] not because of his active mind and his learning or the distinguished friendships of great men had now plunged him into the midst of affairs; but rather because beyond all this there is a divine dispensation that had prepared honor for this vessel of his Church. For he had acquired such great prestige that, even if he were dead and buried, his inherent virtue and those qualities in which he had been trained from boyhood would reveal his character. Such an effulgent halo shone around him for his first noble counsels that though he preferred obscurity, it was impossible to attain it. Everyone admired his modest, splendid spirit that trampled on every fear which beset the times, that laughed at every popu-

1. A passage from Suger's *Vita*, written by Brother William.
2. Abbot Suger.
3. At this time Suger was in Italy.

lar terror, every popular hope: a spirit, indeed, that was based on this earth, but that clung in its better essence to heavenly matters.

He was simultaneously administrator both of the monastery and of the palace; and he performed both functions without the court diverting him from his concern for the cloister or the monastery excluding him from the counsels of kings. For his righteous and remarkable counsels the king revered him as a father, respected him as a teacher. At his approach the prelates stood up, and he sat down first among them. For whenever passing affairs of state arose and the bishops were summoned to convene, the king would ask their advice, but they unanimously urged Suger alone to reply for all of them, such was his tried and tested sagacity. In his own words, as Job declared of himself: "After my words they spake not again; and my speech dropped upon them." Through his mediation the cry of the orphan and the widow's plight reached the king; and always he would intercede for them, and sometimes he would actually impose his commands. What man, oppressed and wronged, never received his protection, provided his cause was just? When he administered justice, he never, at any cost, swerved from the right, nor in his judgments did he dwell on a person's character, nor care for gifts or rewards. Who would not admire such a spirit, unmoved by greed, humble in the midst of happiness, tranquil in the secular storms that assailed him, undeterred by peril? His spirit was indeed too great to be credibly contained in such a small body.

His enemies reproach this illustrious man for his humble origin. But in their blind stupidity they do not realize that it is a greater reason for praise or glory to create nobility than to be of noble birth. Plato asserts that no king but must stem from humble folk; none but the humble can stem from kings. There have been many variations in all this, and fate has turned everything topsy-turvy. It is the spirit that creates nobility, and it is certain that his spirit was such that the following description is not undeservedly attributed to him: His spirit looked upon the truth, skilled in shunning what should be avoided, seeking what should be sought, evaluating things not by hearsay but according to their nature, interested in all worldly matters, meditating over all his actions; handsome, with grace, strong and sound and healthy, imperturbable, intrepid, capable of resisting every violence, of disregarding and disparaging all hazards.

That assuredly was the spirit of the man. Again and again this noble upright man attempted to give up the court and all administrative duties in order to devote himself to wider fields. But his fate, that had raised him on high, did not permit or allow him to grow old with the years; as he would have preferred, according to his own confession.

Although he might be absorbed in important state problems, neither public nor private business ever distracted him from divine worship. For whether he attended a gathering of brethren or celebrated divine service with his fellow Christians, he did not, as is the custom with some, listen in silence to the chanting of the psalms, but was always quite prepared to sing or read himself. There is another trait that I often admired in him. Whatever he had learned in his youth he retained in his memory, so that in every monastic duty no one could compare with him. One would have thought that he knew nothing apart from this duty, that he had learned nothing but that. He was so proficient in the liberal arts that he frequently discussed in the most analytical manner works on dialectics or rhetoric, not to speak of theological treatises with which he had grown up. He was so very knowledgeable in Holy Scripture that, on barely being questioned, he had a ready, adequate answer, without any hesitation. He could not, in the smallest degree, forget the pagan poets, for his memory was retentive; hence he would recite to us from memory anything from Horace that contained some useful point, as many as twenty verses, frequently even thirty. So whatever he had once grasped with his lucid mind and his felicitous memory could not be lost.

Why need I mention what is known to all, that he stood preeminent as the greatest orator of his time? For in truth, as Marcus Cato's dictum goes,[4] he was a good man, skilled in speaking. He had in fact such remarkable eloquence in both languages, that is, in the vernacular and in Latin, that whenever one heard words issuing from his lips, one could have believed not that he was speaking, but that his words were being read. He had a vast knowledge of history. If you mentioned any king or prince of the Franks, he would at once, with uninterrupted speed, run through all his exploits. He also narrated in eloquent style the deeds of King Louis[5] and likewise began an account of his son Louis. Prevented by death, however, he did

4. A reference to Cato's definition of an orator.
5. Suger (1081–1151) served Louis the Fat (1108–1137) and his son, Louis VII (1137–1180), the monkish king whom Eleanor of Aquitaine divorced to marry Henry II of England.

not complete his work. Who could have been more familiar with the subject, who could have written a more veracious account, than this man who was most intimate with both rulers, who was aware of every secret, without whom kings devised no schemes, and in whose abscence the court seemed empty? From the time when he was first admitted to the royal counsels until the end of his life, it is a fact that the realm was always in a prosperous condition, and that it expanded more widely and flourishingly by extending its frontiers and subjugating his enemies. When he was taken from our midst, instantly royalty felt the deep loss of his absence; for it is known that the Duchy of Aquitaine, no small territory, was lost on account of the lack of Suger's counsel.

Among his other virtues, this remarkable man had this outstanding quality: if any one of the meaner of his household was under an accusation, he did not give immediate credence, but as circumspectly as possible he called upon alert members to act as spies, for he thought it unseemly to punish anyone before a careful investigation had been made and the matter brought fully into the open. He punished the guilty, not so much for their sins, but as a means of prevention. Furthermore, in administering punishment he acted in such a manner that no sane person doubted his compassion and his unwillingness to inflict the penalty. As a cleric he would reprove; as a father he would be indulgent. He did not readily exclude his craftsmen[6] from his administrations, except for convincing and important reasons and for flagrant faults. For he declared that nothing was of less benefit to the state, while the excluded menials stole whatever they could and those who replaced them, fearing the same treatment, hurried on to accomplish their rapacities.

But many ignorant or envious men who did not know him well tried to distort his excellent character by evil misinterpretation. For, as Solomon says, his words were as goads, and as nails fastened above. Similarly, as in the case of blessed Job, the light of his countenance they cast not down. They considered him too harsh and rigid, and imputed to stubbornness what was really consistency. To those who were close to him and intimately associated with him, he appeared quite different. But though he was human enough and genial among friends, still he never broke out into hilarity and was never overwhelmed in sadness. His function was that of good parents, who are

6. Those engaged in construction work on the Abbey of Saint-Denis.

wont to rebuke children sometimes indulgently, on occasion threateningly, and at times even with a whipping. He disinherited nobody for a first offense, except when the crimes were of great enormity and he feared more offenses in the future than those he punished. Nor did he ever go to the length of inflicting torture, except when he had exhausted all remedies. This sage tranquilly and wholesomely dispensed the justice entrusted to him, with the result that today his name is renowned not only in Gallic territories but also among foreign nations.

What Christian monarch, hearing of his magnanimity, did not stand amazed or long to enjoy converse with him and to be guided by his counsel? Did not the most famous King Roger of Sicily[7] send him pleading letters of exhortation and designate gifts for him? Afterward, when his pious desire to go on pilgrimage was proclaimed, did Suger not prepare to meet him? Did not Henry, the powerful King of England, glory in his friendship and rejoice in his acquaintanceship? Did he not appoint him at the French court of Louis as an intercessor and bond of peace? Whenever he approached him regarding mutual peace between the two kingdoms, the king, contrary to his custom, met him outside the palace and hastened to embrace him; for he preferred converse with him to untold wealth. David too, pious King of Scotland, sent him, along with friendly letters, gifts consisting of a whale's teeth, of enormous size and of no little value. I have seen, as God is my witness, I have at times seen the King of France respectfully stand by as Suger was sitting on a low footstool, with a crowd of nobles around, and Suger dictating directions as though to inferiors, while they stood absorbed in concentrated attention on what was being said. When the conference was over, he wanted to lead the king aside, but the king did not allow him to move or rise from his seat. I mention this so that all his enemies and his detractors may know what prestige he enjoyed among kings, and in what reverence he was held by the nobility.

That devout Count Thibaut of Blois honored him in every possible way. He appointed him as the sole bailiff[8] to the kings of France. How often did Geoffrey Count of Anjou, Duke of Normandy, in a desire to flatter and also to beg favors, send envoys to him? How

7. Roger II of Sicily (1095–1154).
8. In Latin, this would be *advocatus;* a nobleman who protected ecclesiastical properties.

often did he write in his own hand humble letters to Suger in which, though he was of keen intelligence, spirited and powerful, he usually wrote, in the salutation, the other's name before his own?

Latin text of Lecoy de la Marche.
Paris, 1867
Translated by H. E. W.

Becket on Church and State[1]

¶ THOMAS, Archbishop of Canterbury, to William, Cardinal of Pavia.

The truth may be beclouded, but never extinguished, and the light after troubled darkness is received more gratefully. Would that you had known from the beginning what is now known to all through the testimony of our persecutor himself. Recently in the presence of the most Christian king, the archbishops, bishops, courtiers, nobles and all who were present, he publicly admitted that the sole reason for our exile and proscription was that we refused to observe for him the tithes that our elders were wont to observe for his predecessors. He also added repeatedly that the only request he made of us was for us to promise him simply and absolutely in the words of truth, without making any addition, by the integrity of our rank or by the honor of God, or by one of those statements that could preserve the security of honor and conscience, and because we refused to promise absolutely the tithes, some of which void the authority of the apostolic seat and destroy the freedom of the church, the king departed without consummating peace. We therefore beg your beloved self, weary as you are, to undertake the protection of Canterbury Cathedral; nay, of justice itself, and (as your kindness promised us on your departure) not resent it for the freedom of the church and our own person, who are ready to adhere to your allegiance, as befits your honor, but that you challenge those who are known to have been

---

1. A letter from Thomas à Becket, Primate of England, to Cardinal William of Pavia. The Cardinal had written to Pope Alexander III commending Becket's integrity, but the general tone of the letter was not very persuasive. It was during Alexander's pontificate that Becket was murdered by Henry II's knights.

227

opposed to truth and justice to this day, and that you unhesitantly trust our messengers in those matters that they have submitted to you from us.

Thomas Becket: 12th century
Materials for the History of Archbishop Becket: J. C. Robertson and J. B. Sheppard
R. A. Browne, *British Latin Selections*
Trans. by H. E. W.

King and State

¶ APULEIUS expresses this thought with elegance and brilliance, and I wish it would be listened to. For if every man works for his own cultural development and considers whatever is outside that as irrelevant, assuredly that will be the best attitude for one and all, and virtue will flourish and reason will prevail, with mutual charity all-pervasive, so that the flesh becomes subject to the spirit and the spirit serves the Lord with complete devotion. If these conditions continue, the limbs will not be burdened by a tumor in the head nor will the head be enfeebled by the deprivation of the limbs: such states of course arise from sinful weakness. For the misdeeds of the lower classes do not deserve a good ruler and the sins of the upper class are an opportunity and authorization for crime to the subjects. Hence this principle: Every head is feeble and every heart sorrowful; from the sole of the foot to the head there is no health therein.

So the ruler grows humane through the innocence of the people and the innocence of the ruler checks the movements of the people. For when God is tranquil, every creature is mild and serves man, and when God is indignant, every creature is armed for his revenge.

John of Salisbury: 12th century
Policraticus
Trans. by H. E. W.

Gluttony in the Church

¶ Who, when the monastic Order first began, would have believed that monks could fall into such idleness? How far we are from those monks who lived in the days of Anthony! If they came back again, from a feeling of love, as the occasion offered, they would so eagerly perceive the spiritual food that, utterly forgetful of bodily food, they would generally spend entire days with hungry stomachs but not hungry minds. And this was the right Order, when it first served the worthier organ. This was the greatest discrimination, when the greater part took more. This, in short, was true love, when the soul, by whose love Christ died, was refreshed with such solicitude.

"When ye come together therefore into one place," to use the words of the apostle, "this is not to eat the Lord's supper." There is no one in fact who seeks the heavenly bread, no one who offers it. There is no interest in the Scriptures, no interest in the salvation of souls; but nonsense and laughter and words are poured forth to the wind. In dining, the ears are fed on as many rumors as the mouth is on food. Completely absorbed in this, one knows no limit in eating.

Meanwhile dish after dish is set before one; and in place of meat, those who abstain are served double helpings of fish. When you have had enough of the first portion, if you get a second, you will think you have not yet tasted the first. Everything is prepared with such care and skill by the cooks that, after four or five platters are eaten, the first dishes do not impede the last ones, nor does satiety diminish the appetite. The palate, in fact, when enticed by new spices, gradually becomes unaccustomed to familiar foods and its desires are greedily renewed toward strange sauces, as if it were still starving. The belly is loaded without knowing it, but variety dispels disgust. For, as we disdain simple meals, just as nature fashioned, while menus are multiplied in numberless combinations, and as we spurn the natural flavors that God has placed in things and titillate the throat with adulterated flavors, the bounds of necessity are surely exceeded and yet the feeling of pleasure is still unsatisfied. For who can adequately describe in how many ways, not to mention other things, eggs alone are tossed and beaten, how eagerly they are turned over, and under, made soft, or hard, or smaller? And when there are fried foods, and roasted, stuffed, or mixed with other foods, served individually. What is the purpose of all these dishes, except to produce only disgust? Then the exterior appearance of these foods is so treated as to delight the eye as much as the taste. And when the stomach by frequent belchings announces repletion, still curiosity is not yet satisfied. But while the eyes are enticed by color, and the palate by flavor, the poor stomach, for which there are no glowing colors and soothing flavors, is forced to receive everything, and is more crushed and overwhelmed than refreshed.

Furthermore, what shall I say about the drinking of water, when not even under any circumstance is wine mixed with water permitted? Certainly all of us, from the moment we become monks, have weak stomachs, and warrantably we do not neglect the apostle's necessary advice about using wine; disregarding, however, for some reason or other, "moderate," that he placed at the beginning of the sentence. And would that we were satisfied with wine only even when it is unmixed! It is a shame to say it, but let it be a greater shame to practice it; and if it is shameful to hear, let it not be disgraceful to correct it. One may see at one meal a cup served half full, thrice and four times; so that, as different wines are more sniffed than drunk and not so much drained as sipped with intelligent relish and quick appraisal, the one that is stronger than the others is finally selected. What kind of practice is it that many monasteries are customarily said to observe, at important festivals, drinking in the monastery wine mixed with honey and sprinkled with spices? Shall we say that this is done for a weak stomach? I myself see that this has no other value except to increase drinking or to make it more pleasurable. But when the veins are gorged with wine, throbbing in the entire head, to a person thus rising from table what other pleasure is there except sleep?

Bernard of Clairvaux: 12th century
Apologia
Trans. by H. E. W.

Fathers and Sons on Careers

¶ DURING THE ENTIRE extent of his life my father bemoaned my entrance into the Order of the Franciscans and he was not consoled for not having a son to succeed him in the inheritance. He complained to the Emperor, who at that time had come to Parma, that the Franciscans had abducted his son from him. Then the Emperor wrote to Brother Elias, minister general of the Order of Franciscans, that, if he had any concern for his grace, he should listen to him and restore me to my father. Brother Elias had received me when he went to see the Emperor at Cremona as a legate of Pope Gregory the Ninth in the year 1238. Then my father went to Assisi, where Brother Elias was, and placed the Emperor's letter in the minister general's hands. The introductory part of the letter ran as follows: "To mitigate the regrets of Guido of Adam, my faithful servant," and so on. After perusing the Emperor's letter Brother Elias immediately wrote to the brothers of the convent of Fano, where I lived, that, if it was my wish, they should at once obediently return me to my father; otherwise, if I refused to go with my father, they should guard me dearly, like the pupil of their eye.

So a number of knights came with my father to the place of the brothers in the city of Fano, to see an end to my situation. To them I was made a spectacle and the cause of my own salvation. When the brothers had gathered with the ecclesiastics not of the Order in the chapter house and many words had been spoken back and forth, my father produced the minister general's letter and showed it to the brothers. After reading it, Brother Jeremiah, the guardian, in the presence of all, replied to my father: "Master Guido, we sympathize with your grief and are prepared to obey our father's letter. However, here is your son: 'He is of age; let him speak for himself.' Ask him whether he wants to go with you; let him go in the name of the Lord. But if not, we cannot use force to make him go with you."

So my father asked whether I should like to go with him or not. I replied: "No, for the Lord says, Luke ix: 'No man, having put his hand to the plough, and looking back, is fit for the kingdom of God.' "

And my father said to me: "You do not care about your father

231

and your mother who are afflicted with many sorrows on your account."

I answered: "Truly I do not care, for the Lord says: 'He that loveth father or mother more than me is not worthy of me.' Of you too he says: 'He that loveth son or daughter more than me is not worthy of me.' You ought therefore to care, Father, for Him who was crucified for us on the cross to give us eternal life. For it is He who says, Matt. x: 'For I am come to set a man at variance against his father, and the daughter against her mother, and the daughter-in-law against her mother-in-law. And a man's foes shall be they of his own household. Whosoever therefore shall confess me before men, him will I confess also before my Father which is in heaven. But whosoever shall deny me before men, him will I also deny before my Father which is in heaven.' "

And the brothers marveled and rejoiced that I said such things to my father. Then my father said to the brothers: "You have bewitched my son and ensnared him so that he disagrees with me. I shall complain again to the Emperor about you and also to the minister general. However, allow me to speak alone with my son without you and you will see that he will follow me instantly."

So the brothers allowed me to speak to my father without them because they were fairly confident about me on account of what I had already said. However, they listened behind the door to what we said. For they trembled like a reed in the water, afraid that my father would change my mind by his blandishments; and not only were they afraid for the salvation of my soul but also that my withdrawal would give others an opportunity for not entering the Order. My father therefore said to me: "My dear son, do not trust those pissintunic fellows, that is, those who urinate in their tunics, who have deceived you, but come with me and I shall give you all my possessions." In reply, I said to my father: "Go, Father, go. The wise man in Proverbs iii says: 'Withhold not good from them to whom it is due, when it is in the power of thine hand to do it.' "

And my father tearfully replied, and said: "What shall I tell your mother, son, who is ceaselessly troubled about you?" And I said to him: "You will tell her from me: This is what your sons says: 'When my father and my mother forsake me, then the Lord will take me up.' He also says Jeremiah iii: 'Thou shalt call me, My father; and shall not turn away from me.' For 'It is good for a man that he bear the yoke in his youth.' "

232

Hearing all this and despairing of my leaving, my father prostrated himself upon the ground before the brothers and others not of the Order who had come with him and he said: "I commend you to a thousand demons, accursed son, and your brother, who is here with you, and who has deceived you too. May my curse on you be unending, and commend you to the infernal spirits."

And he went away, disturbed beyond measure. But we remained, greatly comforted, giving thanks to our God and saying to ourselves: " 'Let them curse, but bless thou.' For 'he who blesseth himself in the earth shall bless himself in God. Amen.' "

So the ecclesiastics not of the Order departed, greatly edified by my constancy. But the brothers too rejoiced deeply because the Lord had acted manfully through me, their young novice, and they found that the words of the Lord are true, for he says Luke xxi: "Settle it therefore in your hearts, not to meditate before what ye shall answer. For I will give you a mouth and wisdom, which all your adversaries shall not be able to gainsay nor resist."

The following night the Blessed Virgin rewarded me. It seemed to me that I was lying prostrate in prayer before the altar, as the brothers are wont to do when they rise for matins. And I heard the voice of the Blessed Virgin calling me, and, raising my face, I saw the Blessed Virgin sitting on the altar in the place where the host and the chalice are set; and she had a little boy in her lap, whom she held out to me with these words: "Approach without fear and kiss my son whom you confessed yesterday in the presence of men." When I showed fear, I saw that the little boy opened his arms in eager expectation. So, trusting in the eagerness and innocence of the child and on the bountiful generosity of the mother herself, I approached and embraced and kissed him. And the gentle mother sent him over to stay with me for a long time. When I could not be sated with him, the holy Virgin blessed me and said: "Go, my beloved son, and rest, that the brothers who rise for matins may not find you here with us." I assented and the vision vanished. But in my heart such a sweetness lingered as could not be described. I confess truly that never in my worldly life did I experience such a sweetness.

Salimbene: 13th century
Cronica fratris Salimbene ordinis Minorum
Trans. by H. E. W.

Life in a Monastery

¶ As THERE WAS no abbot, the prior was determined above all to preserve peace in the monastery and to maintain the honor of the church in welcoming guests, wishing to disturb no one, to provoke no one to anger, in order to keep everyone and all conditions in a state of tranquillity. He disregarded, however, certain matters that needed correction in respect of our officials, and particularly of the sacristan, as though he was not interested in what he did about the sacristy. At the time when the office of abbot was vacant, he neither paid any debt nor erected any building; while offerings and revenues were foolishly dissipated. Hence the prior, who was the head of the monastery, appeared to many to be blameworthy and was considered negligent. This our brothers remembered among themselves when an assembly was held to elect an abbot.

Our cellarer welcomed all the guests of whatever rank at the expense of the monastery. William the sacristan himself gave and spent money; a kindly man, he gave what had to be given as well as what had not, blinding the eyes of all with his favors.

Samson the undersacristan, master over the workmen, left nothing broken, cracked, split, or unrepaired as far as lay in his power. Hence he brought into favorable notice the monastery and especially the monks in the cloisters. In those days our choir was built, with Samson in charge, prescribing the stories of the paintings and dictating elegiac verses. He collected a large supply of stones and sand for building the great tower of the church. Asked where he obtained the money for this, he replied that some burgesses had secretly given him money to build and finish the tower. Some of our brothers, however, said that Warinus, our monk, guardian of the shrine, and Samson the undersacristan planned together to steal furtively, as it were, some portion of the offerings of the shrine for the purpose of spending it on church necessities and nominally for building the tower: being driven to this decision because they observed that the offerings were being spent for irregular purposes by others who, to tell the truth, stole these monies. In order to divert from their person any suspicion of such a happy theft, the two previously mentioned men made a kind of chest, hollow and perforated in the center or on the top, and fastened with an iron lock. They had it set up in the great church near the door outside the choir where the people commonly passed, so that the men would put their alms in it for building the tower.

William the sacristan, however, suspected his associate Samson as did many others who had affection for this same William, both Christians and Jews. The Jews, I repeat, to whom the sacristan was said to be a father and a patron, were glad of his protection and had free entrance and exit and occasionally went through the monastery, wandering among the altars and around the shrine while mass was celebrated. Their donations of denarii were placed in the treasury in the care of the sacristan and, what is more absurd, their wives and little children were lodged in our quarters in time of war.

So a plan was made for his enemies or opponents to fall upon Samson. Going to Robert of Cokefield and his associate, who were guardians of the abbey, they induced them to the scheme that they had themselves forbidden in the name of the king: namely, that no one should carry on any work or building as long as the abbey had no abbot; rather, the coins should be collected from the offerings and kept to pay some debt. So Samson was caught and the strength went from him; and he could not do any other work as he wanted to. His opponents were able to postpone the matter but not to dismiss it; because, after his strength was renewed and the two columns had been upheaved, that is, after the two guardians of the abbey on whom the wickedness of the others depended had been removed, the Lord gave him in the course of time the opportunity to fulfill his vow to build the tower and finish it according to his desire. And it happened just as though a divine voice said: "Well done, thou good and faithful servant: thou hast been faithful over a few things; over many things, etc."

After the death of the Abbot Hugo, a year and three months later, the Lord King commanded in a letter that our prior and twelve men from the monastery, who represented the unanimous opinion of all, should appear before him on a set day to elect an abbot.

The day after receipt of the letter we met in the chapter house to discuss this important question. First, the Lord King's letter was read in the meeting; later, we asked and bound the prior, at the peril of his soul, to nominate twelve men, according to his conscience, to be considered along with himself, whose life and character were known to be firm against deviation from what was right. Granting the request at the prompting of the holy spirit, he named six on one side of the choir and six on the other, without objection. Then one man said: "What will happen if these thirteen men cannot agree in the King's presence in electing an abbot?" Another man answered: "That will be an everlasting disgrace for us and for our church." For this reason many wanted the election to be held at the house before the rest left, so that by this act of foresight no disagreement would arise in the King's presence. But that proposal seemed to us foolish and unsuitable without the King's assent, because we were not yet sure of being able to prevail on the Lord King to let us have a free election. Samson the undersacristan, speaking by the spirit, said: "Let us take a middle course, so that the danger either way may be avoided. Let four confessors from the monastery be chosen and two of the older priors of good reputation in the monastery, who, after seeing the holy relics and touching the gospels, will choose among themselves three men of the monastery, more suitable for this purpose according to St. Benedict's Rule, and let them put their names in writing and let them enclose the writing in a sealed envelope and thus enclosed let it be given to us on our way to court. When we come into the King's presence and we are assured of holding a free election, then only let the seal be broken, and thus we shall be sure who the three nominees will be, in the King's presence. And let us resolve, if the Lord King refuses to give us one of our own men, to take back the sealed envelope unopened and hand it over to the six sworn men so that their secret is concealed forever at the risk of their souls."

In this plan we all acquiesced, and four confessors were nominated and two other elders. This done, we went out singing *My Words*, and the six above-mentioned men remained, with the Rule of St. Benedict in their hands, and completed the matter as it had been outlined. While these six were dealing with this, we each thought, in our different ways, of different candidates; all of us, however, feeling certain that Samson was one of the three, and appraising his efforts and his risks of death on his way to Rome about the property of our church and how he had been treated and bound in chains and imprisoned by the Abbot Hugo when speaking in behalf of the common welfare, nor could he be induced to flatter, though he could be forced to silence. And the elders said that they had acted according to the orders given to them.

The next day therefore those thirteen men hurried on to court.

Last of all was Samson, controller of expenses because he was the undersacristan, bearing around his neck a case that contained the letters of the monastery, as though only an assistant to them all and without a squire carrying his frock on his arm. He went off to court following his companions at a distance. On the same day when the thirteen left, as we were sitting in the cloister, William of Hastings, one of our brothers, said: "I know that we shall have an abbot from among us," and, being asked how he knew this, he replied that he had seen in a dream the prophet clothed in white standing at the monastery gate, and he had asked in the name of the Lord whether we should have an abbot from among ourselves. And the prophet answered: "You will have one of yours but he will rage among you like a wolf." The interpretation of this dream coincided to some extent because the future abbot was eager to be feared more than loved, as many said. Another brother named Edmund sat down, declaring that Samson would be the abbot and describing the vision that he had had the night before. He said he had seen in his dream Roger the cellarer and Hugo the third prior standing before the altar and Samson between them, head and shoulders above them, wrapped in a long cloak and a cape fastened on his shoulders, and standing like a fighter ready for a duel. St. Edmund rose from the shrine (as it had seemed to him in his dream) and slowly as it were exposed his feet and his ankles, and as a man approached who wanted to cover the saint's feet, the holy man said: "Do not come near. Lo, he will cover my feet," extending his finger toward Samson. That is the interpretation of the dream. The appearance of the warrior signifies that the future abbot will always be involved in labor, when he disputes against the Archbishop of Canterbury in regard to the King's decrees; against St. Edmund's soldiers in rendering the scutages honestly; with the burgesses regarding encroachments in the market; with the sokemen for the suits of the hundreds: like a fighter wanting to defeat his opponents in a fight so that he can win back the rights and liberties of his church. He covered the holy martyr's feet when he satisfactorily completed the church towers that had been begun a hundred years before. Such dreams our brothers dreamed, that were at once made known first of all throughout the cloister, afterward at court, so that before night it was publicly said among the people that so and so and so were chosen, and one of them would be the abbot.

Now the prior and the twelve with him, after many efforts and delays, finally stood before the King at Waltham, a manor of the Bishop of Winton, on the second Sunday of Lent. The Lord King received them in a friendly way, and, declaring that he wished to act according to God and the honor of our church, he ordered the brothers through the intermediaries Richard of Winton and Galfrid the Chancellor, later Archbishop of York, to nominate three from our monastery. Now the prior and the brothers going aside as though to confer together, took out the seal and broke it and found these names listed in this order: Samson the undersacristan, Roger the cellarer, Hugo the third prior. Then the more dignified brothers blushed. They were also surprised that Hugo was both elector and nominated. However, unable to make any change, they agreed to change the order of the names, putting Hugo, because he was the third prior, first, Roger the cellarer second, Samson third; by changing the position of the words making the last first and the first last. The King, first asking whether they were born in his land and in whose dominion, said he did not know them, and ordered three others from the monastery to be nominated along with these three. When this was carried out, William the sacristan said: "Our prior ought to be nominated because he is our head." This was quickly granted. The prior said: "William the sacristan is a good man." The same opinion was expressed about Dionisius, and accepted.

When these men had been nominated without any delay in the King's presence, the King showed surprise and said: "They were quick about it; God is with them." Afterward the King commanded that for the honor of his kingdom they should nominate three persons from other monasteries. Hearing this, the brothers became afraid, suspecting some trick. Finally they made a plan to nominate three but on condition that they accept no one, except by the advice of the monastery to which they belonged. And they nominated three. Then the King thanked them and bade that the three names be removed from the nine and at once the names of the strangers were removed. Of his own accord William the sacristan made this concession; two names were removed from the five by the King's order and afterward one of the three, and then two were left, namely the prior and Samson.

Finally the previously mentioned intermediaries of the Lord King were called to a council of the brothers. Dionisius, speaking for all, began to commend the character of the prior and Samson, saying that they were both scholars, both good, both praiseworthy in their way of life, and of blameless reputation; but always he suggested in his talk a preference for Samson, profuse in his praise, saying he was a man scrupulous in his monastic ways, just in correcting excesses, adapted to work, wise in secular matters and tried and tested in various duties. The Bishop of Winton replied: "We understand quite well what you mean. From your words we deduce that your prior seems somewhat remiss and that you want to have the man called Samson."

Dionisius replied: "They are both good men but we should like to have the better one if God wills it."

The Bishop's answer was: "Of two good men the better man should be chosen. Speak frankly, do you want to have Samson?"

The reply, given decisively by several and by the majority, was: "We want Samson."

There was no dissent; some however remained deliberately silent, wishing to offend neither of the two. When Samson was nominated in the presence of the Lord King and a brief conference was held with his counselors, all were called and the King said: "You have presented Samson to me. I do not know him. If you presented your prior I would receive a man I have seen and know. But I shall do as you wish. Take care. By the true eyes of God, if you do harm, I shall exact the penalty from you." He questioned the prior whether he agreed and wished it so. The latter answered that he wished it so and that Samson was worthy of much greater honor. The nominee then prostrated himself at the King's feet and kissing them rose up quickly and quickly extended his hands to the altar, chanting: "Have mercy upon me, God," along with the brothers, head erect, his expression unchanged. Observing this, the King said to the bystanders: "By the eyes of God, this nominee of yours seems worthy of safe-guarding the abbey."

Jocelyn of Brakelond: 13th century
Chronica de rebus gestis Samsonis Abbatis
Trans. by H. E. W.

Monastic Supervision

¶ *January 16, 1248*: We visited the priests of the deanery of Buris, whom we had asked to appear at Meulers. We found that the priest of Pomerevalle is notorious and his bad reputation persists on account of his frequenting the taverns; he does not make confession to a penitential priest. Item, William, priest of Mesnières, is in evil odor for his business dealings, possessing farms that he visits so often that divine service is curtailed in his church. Item, the priest of Lortiey only rarely wears his cassock, does not confess to a penitential priest, is in very ill repute for incontinence, and drinks. Item, the priest of Aulayge is gravely branded for drunkenness and frequenting the taverns. They were admonished by us as the priests of the deanery of Longueville were. In regard to the cassocks and coming to the chapter house we ruled as before, and enjoined on the deacon to inflict punishment without mercy. Item, we found that a certain chaplain of Muliers said a mass for pay at a vigil of Christ's nativity.

January 19: We visited the priests of the deanery of Monte Fulcard, whom we summoned before St. Leodegar. We discovered that the priest of Nigelle had a bad reputation for business dealings and treating his father badly, who is patron of the church, and fighting in person with a certain knight with drawn sword, amid tumult and with the aid of relatives and friends. Item, the priest of Basinvalle, notorious in connection with a woman: although rebuked by the archdeacon, he persists, taking her to the marketplace and frequenting the taverns. Item, the priest of Vetus Nothomage goes about with girt sword, in disgraceful garb. Item, the priest of Boafle does not wear his cassock, branded for dealings with a woman; he sells his grain at a higher price on account of the term.

Item, the priest of Hamies, leprous, as it is thought, and infamous for incontinence.

Item, the priest of St. Rheims, notorious for drunkenness, does not wear a cassock, plays knucklebones, frequents taverns, and often fights there.

Item, the priest of Gilemerville does not reside in his church, as he ought, does not wear a cassock, and sometimes loses his clothes at gambling in the taverns.

Item, Robert, priest of Campenoiseville, has no cassock.

Item, priest of St. Martin in the Woods is fond of lawsuits, and is a wanderer.

Item, the priest of Petra Ponte drinks and plays knucklebones.

Item, Master Walter, priest of Grandis Curia, is notorious for excessive drinking. We admonished and also threatened them that if we find they acquire notoriety in these matters again, we shall punish them severely.

Item, in regard to cassocks and coming to the chapter house we ruled as before in the case of the other deaneries.

Item, we discovered that the priest of Mesnil, David, known for incontinence and several times rebuked by the archdeacon, relapsed and it is said that, although suspended, he celebrated mass; hence we told him to cleanse himself in these matters properly, or we should proceed to hold an investigation against him. To his answer that he had a reason for this, we assigned a day for his reply to the afore-mentioned items.

November 23, 1258: We visited the priory of Villacelle. The prioress was not there. The number of nuns was twenty-two. They say that there should be twenty, and the prioress had accepted two against the wish of certain nuns in the convent, and she increased the number by two against our own prohibition. They thought they had sufficient grain and oats until August. They had eight cows and four calves, six horses, and three fowls. They did not know how much they owed and were rather ignorant of the state of the nunnery. We afterward held a council on the question of the prioress' having taken in the two women as nuns, against our prohibition, and we gave the said prioress warning to send back the previously mentioned women, as indicated further on.

April 20, 1259: We received a letter from our royal master asking us to hasten to him, after reading the letter, as he was lying sick at Fontainebleau; no obstacle was to stand in our way. Disregarding our own serious illness, we hurriedly obeyed, spending the night at Geneville, and there we had another special messenger, who brought us a letter from our royal master, in which he sent word that we were not to go any farther, because he felt better, thank God, and was convalescing; and so we remained at Geneville.

August 27, 1262: At St. Laurence of Cornu Cervinum, and we visited there. There were five monks there; on account of the poverty of the abbey, they said, usually there were scarcely three. They had no chapter house nor did they maintain the rule of silence. They used pillows. We instructed the prior to look at the monks' boxes sometimes. They did not keep the fasts but said they had an indulgence, that those who stay outside their chapter houses may eat meat three times a week, and they asserted that they kept their fasts properly in this way. There was a house in ruins there that the prior said he would repair when he could.

Odo of Rouen: 13th century
Registrum Visitationum
Trans. by H. E. W.

The Universal Empire[1]

¶ IT VERY GREATLY CONCERNS all men on whom a higher nature has impressed the love of truth, that, as they have been enriched by the labor of those before them, so they also should labor for those that are to come after them, to the end that posterity may receive from them an addition to its wealth. For he is far astray from his duty—let him not doubt it—who, having been trained in the lessons of public business, cares not himself to contribute aught to the public good. He is no "tree planted by the waterside, that bringeth forth his fruit in due season." He is rather the devouring whirlpool, ever engulfing, but restoring nothing. Pondering, therefore, often on these things, lest some day I should have to answer the charge of the talent buried in the earth, I desire not only to show the budding promise, but also to bear fruit for the general good, and to set forth truths by others unattempted. For what fruit can he be said to bear who should go about to demonstrate again some theorem of Euclid? or when Aristotle has shown us what happiness is, should show it to us once more? or when Cicero has been the apologist of old age, should a second time under-

---

1. Dante's *De Monarchia* stands beside Plato's *Republic* as an exposition of political theory; like Plato, Dante postulates Right as the basis of society. References to "the Philosopher" are obviously to Aristotle, who was so called from the first half of the thirteenth century on.

take its defense? Such squandering of labor would only engender weariness and not profit.

But seeing that among other truths, ill-understood yet profitable, the knowledge touching temporal monarchy is at once most profitable and most obscure, and that because it has no immediate reference to worldly gain it is left unexplored by all, therefore it is my purpose to draw it forth from its hiding places, as well that I may spend my toil for the benefit of the world, as that I may be the first to win the prize of so great an achievement to my own glory. The work indeed is difficult, and I am attempting what is beyond my strength; but I trust not in my own powers, but in the light of that Bountiful Giver, "Who giveth to all men liberally, and upbraideth not."

Now, therefore, we must see what is the end of the whole civil order of men; and when we have found this, then, as the Philosopher says in his book to Nicomachus, the half of our labor will have been accomplished. And to render the question clearer, we must observe that as there is a certain end for which nature makes the thumb, and another, different from this, for which she makes the whole hand, and again another for which she makes the arm, and another different from all for which she makes the whole man; so there is one end for which she orders the individual man, and another for which she orders the family, and another end for the city, and another for the kingdom, and finally an ultimate one for which the Everlasting God, by His art which is nature, brings into being the whole human race. And this is what we seek as a first principle to guide our whole inquiry.

Let it then be understood that God and nature make nothing to be idle. Whatever comes into being, exists for some operation or working. For no created essence is an ultimate end in the Creator's purpose, so far as he is Creator, but rather the proper operation of that essence. Therefore it follows that the operation does not exist for the sake of the essence, but the essence for the sake of the operation.

There is therefore a certain proper operation of the whole body of human kind, for which this whole body of men in all its multitudes is ordered and constituted, but to which no one man, nor single family, nor single neighborhood, nor single city, nor particular kingdom can attain. What this is will be manifest, if we can find what is the final and characteristic capacity of humanity as a whole. I say then that no quality which is shared by different species of things is the distinguishing capacity of any one of them. For were it so, since this capacity is that which makes each species what it is, it would follow that one essence would be specifically distributed to many species, which is impossible. Therefore the ultimate quality of men is not existence, taken simply; for the elements share therein. Nor is it existence under certain conditions; for we find this in minerals too. Nor is it existence with life; plants too have life. Nor is it percipient existence; for brutes share in this power. It is to be percipient with the possibility of understanding. The distinguishing quality of humanity is the faculty or the power of understanding. And because this faculty cannot be realized in act in its entirety at one time by a single man, nor by any of the individual societies which we have marked, therefore there must be multitude in the human race, in order to realize it.

The proper work of the human race, taken as a whole, is to set in action the whole capacity of that understanding which is capable of development; first in the way of speculation, and then, by its extension, in the way of action. And seeing that what is true of a part is true also of the whole, and that it is by rest and quiet that the individual man becomes perfect in wisdom and prudence; so the human race, by living in the calm and tranquillity of peace, applies itself most freely and easily to its proper work; a work which, according to the saying: "Thou hast made him a little lower than the angels," is almost divine. Whence it is manifest that of all things that are ordered to secure blessings to men, peace is the best. And hence the word which sounded to the shepherds from above was not riches, nor pleasure, nor honor, nor length of life, nor health, nor strength, nor beauty; but peace. For the heavenly host said: "Glory to God in the highest, and on earth peace to men of good will." Therefore also, "Peace be with you," was the salutation of the Saviour of mankind. For it behoved Him, who was the greatest of saviours, to utter in His greeting the greatest of saving blessings. And this custom His disciples too chose to preserve; and Paul also did the same in his greetings, as may appear manifest to all.

Now that we have declared these matters, it is plain what is the better, nay the best, way in which mankind may attain to do its proper work. And consequently we have seen the readiest means by which to arrive at the point for which all our works are ordered, as their ultimate end; namely, the universal peace, which is to be assumed as the first principle for our deductions. As we said, this assumption was necessary, for it is as a signpost to us, that into it we may resolve all that has to be proved, as into a most manifest truth.

The first question is whether Temporal Monarchy [or the Empire] is necessary for the welfare of the world; and that it is necessary can, I think, be shown by the strongest and most manifest arguments; for nothing, either of reason or of authority, opposes me. Let us first take the authority of the Philosopher in his *Politics*. There, on his venerable authority, it is said that where a number of things are arranged to attain an end, it behoves one of them to regulate or govern the others, and the others to submit. And it is not only the authority of his illustrious name which makes this worthy of belief, but also reason, instancing particulars.

If we take the case of a single man, we shall see the same rule manifested in him; all his powers are ordered to gain happiness; but his understanding is what regulates and governs all the others; and otherwise he would never attain to happiness. Again, take a single household: its end is to fit the members thereof to live well; but there must be one to regulate and rule it, who is called the father of the family, or, it may be, one who holds his office. As the Philosopher says: "Every house is ruled by the oldest." And, as Homer says, it is his duty to make rules and laws for the rest. Hence the proverbial curse: "Mayst thou have an equal home." Take a single village: its end is suitable assistance as regards persons and goods, but one in it must be the ruler of the rest, either set over them by another, or with their consent, the head man amongst them. If it be not so, not only do its inhabitants fail of this mutual assistance, but the whole neighborhood is sometimes wholly ruined by the ambition of many, who each of them wish to rule. If, again, we take a single city: its end is to secure a good and sufficient life to the citizens; but one man must be ruler in imperfect as well as in good forms of the state. If it is otherwise, not only is the end of civil life lost, but the city too ceases to be what it was. Lastly, if we take any one kingdom, of which the end is the same as that of a city, only with greater security for its tranquillity, there must be one king to rule and govern. For if this is not so, not only do his subjects miss their end, but the kingdom itself falls to destruction, according to that word of the infallible truth: "Every kingdom divided against itself shall be brought to desolation." If then this holds good in these cases, and in each individual thing which is ordered to one certain end, what we have laid down is true.

Now it is plain that the whole human race is ordered to gain some end, as has been before shown. There must, therefore, be one to guide and govern, and the proper title for this office is Monarch or

Emperor. And so it is plain that Monarchy or the Empire is necessary for the welfare of the world.

Wherever there is controversy, there ought to be judgment, otherwise there would be imperfection without its proper remedy, which is impossible; for God and Nature, in things necessary, do not fail in their provisions. But it is manifest that there may be controversy between any two princes, where the one is not subject to the other, either from the fault of themselves, or even of their subjects. Therefore between them there should be means of judgment. And since, when one is not subject to the other, he cannot be judged by the other (for there is no rule of equals over equals), there must be a third prince of wider jurisdiction, within the circle of whose laws both may come.

The strongest opponent of Justice is Appetite, as Aristotle intimates in the fifth book to Nicomachus. Remove Appetite altogether, and there remains nothing adverse to Justice; and therefore it is the opinion of the Philosopher that nothing should be left to the judge, if it can be decided by law; and this ought to be done for fear of Appetite, which easily perverts men's minds. Where, then, there is nothing to be wished for, there can be no Appetite, for the passions cannot exist if their objects are destroyed. But the Monarch has nothing to desire, for his jurisdiction is bounded only by the ocean; and this is not the case with other princes, whose kingdoms are bounded by those of their neighbors; as, for instance, the kingdom of Castile is bounded by the kingdom of Aragon. From which it follows that the Monarch is able to be the purest embodiment of Justice among men.

Again, the human race is ordered best when it is most free. . . . This liberty, or this principle of all our liberty, is the greatest gift bestowed by God on mankind; by it alone we gain happiness as men; by it alone we gain happiness elsewhere as gods. But if this is so, who will say that human kind is not in its best state when it can most use this principle? But he who lives under a Monarchy is most free. Therefore let it be understood that he is free who exists not for another's sake but for his own, as the Philosopher, in his Treatise of simple Being, thought. For everything which exists for the sake of some other thing is necessitated by that other thing, as a road has to run to its ordained end. Men exist for themselves, and not at the pleasure of others, only if a Monarch rules; for then only are the perverted forms of government set right, while democracies, oli-

We are interested in the opinion of —

PROF D MERRIAM
GERMAN
WESTMINSTER COLL
FULTON MO 65251

concerning these books —

65420 2 PATTERNS OF MEDIEVAL SOC   C PE

R   1

M MARTIN

TOTAL BOOKS	C	D
2		

THANK YOU FOR CONSIDERING OUR BOOKS

garchies, and tyrannies drive mankind into slavery, as is obvious to any who goes about among them all; and public power is in the hands of kings and aristocracies, which they call the rule of the best, and champions of popular liberty. And because the Monarch loves his subjects much, as we have seen, he wishes all men to be good, which cannot be the case in perverted forms of government; therefore the Philosopher says, in his *Politics*: "In the bad state the good man is a bad citizen, but in a good state the two coincide." Good states in this way aim at liberty, that in them men may live for themselves. The citizens exist not for the good of consuls, nor the nation for the good of its king; but the consuls for the good of the citizens, and the king for the good of his nation. For as the laws are made to suit the state, and not the state to suit the laws, so those who live under the laws are not ordered for the legislator, but he for them as also the Philosopher holds, in what he has left us on the present subject. Hence, too, it is clear that although the king or the consul rule over the other citizens in respect of the means of government, yet in respect of the end of government they are the servants of the citizens, and especially the Monarch, who, without doubt, must be held the servant of all. Thus it becomes clear that the Monarch is bound by the end appointed to himself in making his laws.

But it must be carefully observed that when we say that mankind may be ruled by one supreme prince, we do not mean that the most trifling judgments for each particular town are to proceed immediately from him. For municipal laws sometimes fail, and need guidance, as the Philosopher shows in his fifth book to Nicomachus, when he praises equity. For nations and kingdoms and states have, each of them, certain peculiarities which must be regulated by different laws. For law is the rule which directs life. Thus the Scythians need one rule, for they live beyond the seventh climate, and suffer cold which is almost unbearable, from the great inequality of their days and nights. But the Garamantes need a different law, for their country is equinoctial, and they cannot wear many clothes, from the excessive heat of the air, because the day is as long as the darkness of the night. But our meaning is that it is in those matters which are common to all men, that men should be ruled by one Monarch, and be governed by a rule common to them all, with a view to their peace. And the individual princes must receive this rule of life or law from him, just as the practical intellect receives its major premise from the speculative intellect, under which it places its own particular premise, and then draws its particular conclusion, with a view to action. And it is not only possible for one man to act as we have described; it is necessary that it should proceed from one man only to avoid confusion in our first principles. Moses himself wrote in his law that he had acted thus. For he took the elders of the tribes of the children of Israel, and left to them the lesser judgments, reserving to himself such as were more important and wider in their scope; and the elders carried these wider ones to their tribes, according as they were applicable to each separate tribe.

Hence it is plain that whatever is good, is good for this reason, that it consists in unity. And because concord is a good thing in so far as it is concord, it is manifest that it consists in a certain unity, as its proper root, the nature of which will appear if we find the real nature of concord. Concord then is the uniform motion of many wills; and hence it appears that a unity of wills, by which is meant their uniform motion, is the root of concord, nay, concord itself. For as we should say that many clods of earth are concordant, because that they all gravitate together toward the center; and that many flames are concordant because that they all ascend together toward the circumference, if they did this of their own free will, so we say that many men are in concord because that they are all moved together, as regards their willing, to one thing, which one thing is formally in their wills just as there is one quality formally in the clods of earth, that is gravity, and one in the flame of fire, that is lightness. For the force of willing is a certain power; but the quality of good which it apprehends is its form; which form, like as others, being one is multiplied in itself, according to the multiplication of the matters which receive it, as the soul, and numbers, and other forms which belong to what is compound.

To explain our assumption as we proposed, let us argue thus: All concord depends on unity which is in wills; the human race, when it is at its best, is a kind of concord, for as one man at his best is a kind of concord, and as the like is true of the family, the city, and the kingdom, so is it of the whole human race. Therefore the human race at its best depends on the unity which is in will. But this cannot be unless there be one will to be the single mistress and regulating influence of all the rest. For the wills of men, on account of the blandishments of youth, require one to direct them, as Aristotle shows in the tenth book of his *Ethics*. And this cannot be unless there is one prince over all, whose will shall be the mistress and regulating influence of all the others. But if all these conclusions be true, as they are, it is necessary for the highest welfare of the human race that there should be a Monarch in the world; and therefore Monarchy is necessary for the good of the world.

Dante Alighieri: 1265–1321
De Monarchia
Old South Leaflets: No. 123. Boston, 1902

The Degeneracy of the Age

¶ OBSERVING ALL THE conditions of the world and carefully weighing them, everywhere we shall find corruption rampant, because it appears first in the head. For the Roman Curia that used and ought to be ruled by the wisdom of God is now ruined by the orders of the lay rulers, directed toward the guidance of the laity itself and embodied in the civil law. That holy seat is rent by the deceits and stratagems of the wicked. Justice is dying, every peace is violated, infinite scandals arise. The most perverse morality is the result. Pride is dominant, greed is aflame, envy corrodes every single one, lavishness shames that entire court, gluttony is in the ascendant. If then such things happen in the head, what happens in the limbs? Let us glance at the prelates, how they lust for money, neglect the cure of souls, promote nepotism and other carnal friends and wily lawyers who destroy everything with their counsels. They condemn students in philosophy and theology and prevent the two Orders that offer themselves voluntarily to the Lord from living freely and working for the salvation of souls.

Let us consider the Religious: I exclude no Order. Let us see how far they have severally fallen from their proper state and new Orders have frightfully collapsed from their former prestige. Every cleric is intent on pride, luxury, and avarice, and wherever clerics congregate, as at Paris and Oxford, they scandalize all the lay people by their dissensions and disturbances and other vices. Princes and vassals and soldiers oppress and rob each other in turn, and confound the enslaved people with wars and endless taxations, by means of which they strive to plunder the property of others, even duchies and kingdoms, as we see happening in these days. For the King of France most unjustly wrested these great lands from the King of England, as is well known. And Charles has now highhandedly subdued the heirs of Frederick. There is no concern for what is done, or how, whether rightly or wrongly, provided each one satisfies his own desire; yet they are slaves to the pleasures of gluttony and luxury and the other sinful evils.

The people, provoked by their rulers, hate them and have no feeling of loyalty to them, if they can evade it; and, corrupted by the evil examples of their superiors, they in turn oppress and deceive each other by fraud and guile, as we obviously see everywhere around us, and they are completely abandoned to luxury and gluttony and depraved beyond possible description. In respect of traders and craftsmen there is no question, for in all of them words and deeds are pervaded by fraud and trickery and falsity beyond measure.

Roger Bacon: 13th century
Compendium Studii Philosophiae
Trans. by H. E. W.

Human Frailties

¶ BEGINNING THEN, Barlaam started to spin a long story about the creation of the world and the sinfulness of man and the incarnation, passion, and resurrection of the son of God and also to speak at great length of the Day of Judgment and the retribution of good and evil, and to reproach those that served idols and to give the following example of their foolishness:

A certain archer caught a small bird called a nightingale, but when he was going to kill it, the nightingale was given a voice, and said: "What will it profit you, O man, if you kill me? You won't be able to fill your stomach with me, but if you would let me go, I would give you three counsels and if you followed them carefully, you would be able to derive great benefit from them." Astounded by its talk, the archer promised that he would release it if it gave him the three counsels. The nightingale replied: "Never try to understand what cannot be understood. Never grieve over a loss that is irreparable. Never believe an incredible remark. Guard these three counsels and it will be well with you."

The archer, according to his promise, released the nightingale. Flying through the air, it exclaimed: "Woe to you, O man, for you have had bad counsel and have this day lost a great treasure. For inside my stomach there is a pearl whose size exceeds an ostrich egg."

Hearing this, the archer was disconsolate for having freed it and he made an attempt to seize it, saying: "Come into my house and I shall show you every kindness and release you honorably."

To which the nightingale replied: "Now I know for certain that you are a fool, for from the things I told you, you have derived no benefit at all, because you are sorry about losing and not being able to recapture me and still you try to capture me, although you cannot use my way of flight, and in addition you believed that there is such a large pearl in my stomach, although my entire self cannot contain an ostrich egg."

Thus they are fools who put their faith in idols, for they worship things made by themselves and give the name of guardians to those that they themselves guard.

And he began to argue at length against the false delights and the vanity of the world and to adduce more examples in confirmation, saying:

"Those who desire corporeal pleasures and allow their souls to die of starvation are like the man who, while fleeing rapidly from a unicorn to escape being devoured by it, fell into a deep pit. As he fell, he clutched at a little shrub and caught his feet on a slippery, insecure pedestal. Looking around, he noticed two mice, one white and the other black, steadily gnawing at the root of the shrub that he had clutched, and just about to cut it off. Now at the bottom of the pit he beheld a terrible dragon, breathing out fire and ready to devour him with open jaws. On the pedestal where he had put his foot he saw four heads of vipers protruding. Raising his eyes, he caught sight of a thin stream of honey trickling from the branches of the shrub and, oblivious to the danger that surrounded him on every side, he immersed himself completely in the sweetness of a little honey.

"Now the unicorn represents the symbol of death, that always pursues and wants to catch man, while the pit is the world, filled with every evil. The shrub is the life of every man that, during the hours of the day and the night, is continuously consumed and on the point

251

of being cut in two, as it were, by the white mouse and the black one. The pedestal of the four vipers is the body composed of four elements and when these are disarranged the unity of the body is broken. The terrible dragon is the mouth of Hell, anxious to devour all. The sweetness of the bough is the false pleasure of the world, by which man is seduced to have not the slightest regard for his own peril."

He also added: "Again, those who love the world are like the man who had three friends, one of whom he loved more than himself; the second, as much as himself; the third, less than himself and almost not at all. Placed in a situation of great danger and summoned by the king, he hurried to his first friend to seek his aid, always saying how much he loved him. The other said: 'I do not know who you are, man. I have other friends, with whom I have to celebrate this very day, and whom I shall have as friends henceforth. However, I offer you two goat-hair capes to cover yourself with.'

"Disappointed, he then went to the second friend, and similarly asked for his help. The friend said: 'I have no time to enter a contest with you, for I am overwhelmed with many cares. I shall however accompany you a little way to the palace gate, and immediately return home to attend to my own affairs.' So, sadly, in despair, he proceeded to his third friend and with downcast mien said to him: 'I have no heart to speak to you since I did not love you as I should have, but, in the midst of tribulation and deserted by my friends, I ask you to help me and forgive me.' The other said cheerfully: 'I certainly admit that you are my dearest friend and, not forgetting your favors, though slight, I shall go ahead and intercede for you with the king not to hand you over to your enemies.'

"The first friend is the possession of wealth, for which man exposes himself to many perils and, when death finally comes, receives nothing from this wealth but rags for burial. The second friend is a wife, sons and parents who, going only as far as the tombstone, immediately return to attend to their own affairs. The third friend is faith, hope and charity and alms and other good works that, on our leaving the body, can precede us and intercede for us before God and free us from hostile demons."

Iacobus de Voragine: 13th century
Legenda Aurea
Trans. by H. E. W.

The Receptive Power Is of Divine Origin[1]

¶ THAT THE RECEPTIVE power stems from the divine power. First, the argument is as follows:

Since all nature is from God, as all Scripture asserts, the passive or receptive power is in the nature of the matter: therefore it is from God.

Likewise, whatever is matter and can assume a form is entirely from God: therefore the receptive power is from God.

OBJECTION: Whatever is from God has an image in Him: but the receptive power does not have an image in God, because nothing is receptive in Him: therefore the receptive power is not in God.

REPLY: It must be stated that the receptive power implies two characteristics, namely: capability and need. By reason of need it is not from God, nor does it have an image in Him. But by reason of capability, whereby it has one form or another, it is from God and has an image in Him, since it is the characteristic of God Himself to contain all things, as it is the characteristic of matter and power to have forms. However, God is said by different disputants to contain everything and matter contains form: for God contains and keeps everything and lacks nothing: matter contains form, receiving from it, as it were, complete being and perfection.

Alexander of Hales: 13th century
Summa Theologica
Trans. by H. E. W.

1. This passage illustrates the medieval scholastic method of argumentation, with its rigid syllogistic form and its objections and rebuttals. Alexander of Hales was a noted Franciscan who taught theology at the University of Paris. He postulates that divine knowledge is in man, but that the essence of divinity cannot be grasped by man.

Morality and the Arts

¶ IN THE OLD TESTAMENT we read that for the table of shewbread a golden crown was skillfully wrought. This signifies that we should cultivate eloquence, an active mind, chastity, fear of God, prudence, and virtues of every kind. The table of shewbread ornamented with gold stands for the man who is crowned king because he is eminent in word and deed. But today rusticity is mingled with learning in active and in contemplative life. The muses are silent, confounded, repelled, as if numbed by the sight of Medusa. But why, you ask? If you are a real scholar you are thrust out in the cold. Unless you are a money-maker, I say, you will be considered a fool, a pauper. The lucrative arts, such as law and medicine, are now in vogue, and only those things are pursued which have a cash value.

> John of Garland: 13th century
> *Morale Scolarium*
> Edited and trans. by L. J. Paetow, 1927

Obstacles to Truth

¶ THERE ARE FOUR great obstacles to the comprehension of truth that impede every philosopher and permit scarcely anyone to attain the true designation of philosopher; these are: the example of weak and unreliable authority, indurated custom, the intelligence of the ignorant populace, the concealment of ignorance itself under the guise of apparent wisdom. In these conditions every man is involved, every rank is associated with them. For everyone in the several pursuits of life and study and business employs the three worst arguments to deduce the same conclusion, namely: analogy with the past, custom, common belief; hence it must be accepted. But the opposite conclusion follows far better from the premises, as I shall demonstrate repeatedly by authority, experience, and reason.

If these three obstacles arc refuted by the marvelous power of reason, the fourth is always at hand and on everyone's lips, so that anyone may excuse his own ignorance; and though he may know nothing of value, yet in his ignorance he magnifies it, so that at least he may crush and destroy the truth by the miserable consolation of his stupidity. From such deadly plagues all evils fall upon mankind. For the most useful, the greatest and most beautiful evidences of wisdom are unknown, and the secrets of all the sciences and arts. But it is worse that men, blinded by the fog of these obstructions, do not perceive their own ignorance but conceal and defend them with every precaution in order not to find a remedy. And what is worst, although they dwell in the densest darkness of error, they think that they are in the full light of truth: because they believe that the greatest truths are in the last falsehoods, that the best is of no value, that the greatest ideas have neither weight nor price, and on the contrary they glorify the most false concepts, praise the worst, extol the most worthless, blindly declaring that all the brilliance of wisdom is something else, disdaining what they can obtain with great ease. And on account of their vast stupidity they expend the most strenuous efforts, spend much time, incur great expense in matters that are of no or of slight use or of no significance, in the judgment of the philosopher. For that reason the violence and the menace of these four causes of every evil must be discovered first of all and condemned and banished far from philosophical consideration. For when these three are dominant, no reason moves, no justice sits in judgment, no law is binding, right has no place, the law of nature perishes, the appearance of things changes, order is confounded, vice prevails, virtue is extinguished, falseness reigns, truth is blown away. For that reason, nothing is more necessary of consideration than the decided condemnation of these four obstacles through the worthy opinions of the philosophers, that cannot be gainsaid.

Roger Bacon: 13th century
Opus Maius
Trans. by H. E. W.

Papal Bull[1]

¶ THE HISTORY OF olden times teaches, and daily experience proves, that the laity have always felt hostile to the clergy and have constantly striven to overstep their bounds by wickedness and disobedience. They do not reflect that all power over the clergy, over the persons and property of the Church, is denied them. They lay heavy burdens on prelates, churchmen and both regular and secular clergy, crush them with taxes, taking sometimes half, at other times a tenth or a twentieth or some other portion of their revenues, trying to reduce them to slavery in a thousand ways. In the bitterness of our souls we must add that certain prelates and other ecclesiastical persons, fearful when there is nothing for them to fear, seek fugitive peace, and dread a temporal majesty more than the eternal. They may lend themselves to these abuses less through temerity than imprudence, but without obtaining due faculty and authorization from the Holy See. . . . To cut short these abuses we, in accord with the cardinals and by virtue of our apostolic authority, ordain the following: all prelates and in general all persons belonging to the Church, monks, or secular clergy who, without the consent of the Apostolic See, pay or promise to pay to laymen any imports, taxes, tithes or half tithes or even a one-hundredth part or any portion whatsoever of their revenues or of the goods of their church by way of a subvention, loan, gift, subsidy, etc., as also emperors, kings, princes, barons, rectors, etc., who levy the same, who exact such taxes or receive them or who even put their hand on valuables placed in the church or who co-operate in this sort of act, all these persons *ipso facto* incur excommunication. We interdict anyone who preaches in defense of these condemned acts. Under the penalty of deposition, we order prelates and all Christians not to permit these taxes to be collected without the express consent of the Holy See.

Pope Boniface VIII: 13th century
From J. H. Robinson: *Readings in European History*, 1904

1. Issued by Pope Boniface VIII (1294–1303) on February 25, 1296. This bull prohibiting taxation of the Church by lay powers arose from the practices of the French king Philip IV (1285-1314), who began to levy taxes on the clergy.

The Universals

¶ IT CAN BE manifestly proved that no universal has any real existence outside the mind. First: no universal is a single thing and one; for if this were asserted, it follows that Socrates is a universal, because one reason is not more cogent than another for one universal to be a single thing. Therefore no single thing is a universal, because every thing is one thing and not many. For if it is one thing and not many, it is one in number, for this is universally called one.

Now if a thing is many things, or many single things, or many universal things: if this first is granted, it follows that some thing will be many men; and then, although the universal is distinguished from a particular, it is not however distinguished from particulars. Now if a thing is many universals, I take one of these universals and ask: either it is many things, or one and not many. If the second hypothesis is admitted, it follows that it is one. If the first hypothesis is assumed, I ask: either it is many particular things, or many universals, and so on ad infinitum; or it will be conceded that no thing is universal, because it is not a single thing.

Similarly, if a universal is one thing existing in single things, distinct from them, it would follow that it could exist without them, because every thing can first exist naturally through the divine power without it; but this conclusion is therefore absurd.

Similarly, if that opinion were true, no individual thing could be created, if any individual thing pre-existed: because it would not draw its entire existence from nothing, if the universal that is in it were first in something else. For the same reason it follows that God could not destroy an individual thing simply, unless he destroyed the other individual things: because if he destroyed some individual thing, he would destroy the entire being of that individual thing; and consequently he would destroy that universal that is in it and in others; and consequently the others do not remain, since they cannot remain without part of their being, as the universal can.

William of Occam: 14th century
Summa Totius Logicae
Trans. by H. E. W.

Part Six

LITERARY, ACADEMIC
AND EPISTOLARY WRITINGS

This section is devoted to various aspects of the cultured and literate life in medieval times, ranging from student horseplay to mature philosophizing, and also to the medieval practice of letter writing. In the Middle Ages letter writing had to be taught, because literacy was rare. The epistolary art, therefore, was a formal literary genre with its own conventions, rhetorical devices, established idiom, tones and formulas. Models were set up for practical imitation. Professors, dictatores, *taught various types of letter writing, such as intimate, expository or supplicating, according to elaborate outlines that involved mode of address and of conclusion and insertion of aphorisms and quotations from Biblical or classical literature. Collections of model letters and manuals appeared frequently, and were often directed at various social categories such as students, courtiers or squires.*

Epistolary Advice

¶ GREGORY TO Candidus the Priest, on his going to his incumbency in Gaul.

As you enter, with the help of God our Lord Jesus Christ, into the patrimony that is to be governed among the Gauls, we wish that your esteemed person would buy, with the funds received, clothing for the poor and the English boys from seventeen or eighteen years of age, so that, dedicated to God, they may flourish in the monasteries; and so that the Gallic currency, that cannot be spent in our country, may be spent profitably in its own place of origin. If you get any of the monies of the incomes that are said to have been taken away, from these sums too we want you to buy clothing for the poor and, as we said before, for the boys who flourish in the service of Almighty God. But, since those who are to be found there are pagans, I wish a priest to be sent with them, in case any sickness occurs on the way, so that he can baptize anyone he sees on the point of death. Let your esteemed person act so that these matters may be quickly and diligently performed.

Gregory the Great: 7th century
Epistolae
Trans. by H. E. W.

Scholastic Dialogue[1]

PIPPIN: What is a letter?
ALCUIN: The guardian of history.
PIPPIN: What is a word?
ALCUIN: The expositor of the mind.
P.: What produces a word?
A.: The tongue.

1. The method of teaching by means of question and answer was prevalent in the medieval cathedral schools; this form of catechism was an outgrowth of the Socratic Method handed down through the writings of Plato.

P.: What is the tongue?

A.: The whip of the air.

P.: What is the air?

A.: The guardian of life.

P.: What is life?

A.: The joy of the blessed, the sorrow of the miserable, the expectation of death.

P.: What is death?

A.: The inevitable issue, an uncertain pilgrimage, the tears of the living, the thief of man.

P.: What is man?

A.: The possession of death, a transient wayfarer, a guest.

P.: How is man situated?

A.: Like a lantern in the wind.

P.: Where is he placed?

A.: Between six walls.

P.: Which?

A.: Above, below, in front, back, on the right and the left.

P.: How many companions has he?

A.: Four.

P.: Who are they?

A.: Heat, cold, dryness, moisture.

P.: In how many ways is he variable?

A.: In six.

P.: What are they?

A.: Hunger and satiety; rest and toil; wakefulness and sleep.

P.: What is sleep?

A.: The image of death.

P.: What is man's freedom?

A.: Innocence.

P.: What is the head?

A.: The summit of the body.

P.: What is the body?

A.: The abode of the soul.

P.: What is hair?

A.: The garment of the head.

P.: What is the beard?

A.: The distinction of sex, the honor of age.

P.: What is the brain?

A.: The guardian of memory.

P.: What are the eyes?

A.: The leaders of the body, the vessels of light, the witnesses of the mind.

P.: What are the nostrils?

A.: The attraction of odors.

P.: What are the ears?

A.: The bearers of sounds.

P.: What is the forehead?

A.: The image of the mind.

P.: What is the mouth?

A.: The nourisher of the body.

P.: What are the teeth?

A.: The cake of things bitten.

P.: What are the lips?

A.: The gateway of the mouth.

P.: What is the throat?

A.: The devourer of food.

P.: What are the hands?

A.: The workmen of the body.

P.: What are the fingers?

A.: The plectra of chords.

P.: What is the lung?

A.: The guardian of air.

P.: What is the heart?

A.: The receptacle of life.

P.: What is the liver?

A.: The guardian of heat.

P.: What are the bones?

A.: The strength of the body.

P.: What are the knees?

A.: The columns of the body.

P.: What are the feet?

A.: The mobile base.

P.: What is the blood?

A.: The moisture of the veins, the nourishment of life.

P.: What are the veins?

A.: The fountains of the flesh.

P.: What is heaven?

A.: A revolving sphere, a measureless summit.

P.: What is light?

A.: The appearance of all objects.

P.: What is the day?

A.: The inducement of toil.

P.: What is the sun?

A.: The splendor of the world, the beauty of heaven, the grace of nature, the glory of the day, the distributor of the hours.

P.: What is the moon?

A.: The eye of night, the herald of storms.

P.: What are the stars?

A.: The picture of the summit, the guides of sailors, the adornment of night.

P.: What is rain?

A.: The conception of the earth, the producer of crops.

P.: What is a cloud?

A.: The disturbance of the air, the mobility of water, the dryness of the land.

P.: What is the earth?

A.: The mother of growing things, the nurse of living things, the storeroom of life, the devourer of all things.

P.: What is the sea?

A.: The path of daring, the frontier of the land, the divider of regions, the home of rivers, the source of rain clouds.

P.: What is water?

A.: The support of life, the cleansing of sin.

P.: What is frost?

A.: The persecution of grass, the destroyer of leaves, the fetters of the land, the bridge of waters.

P.: What is snow?

A.: Dry water.

P.: What is winter?

A.: The exile of summer.

P.: What is spring?

A.: The painter of the earth.

P.: What is summer?

A.: The readornment of the land, the ripeness of the crops.

P.: What is autumn?

A.: The granary of the year.

P.: What is the year?

A.: The chariot of the world.

P.: Who drives it?

A.: Night and day, cold and heat.

P.: Who is the charioteer?

A.: The sun and the moon.

P.: How many palaces have they?

A.: Twelve

P.: Who are the officers of the palaces?

A.: The Ram, the Bull, the Twins, the Crab, the Lion, the Maiden, the Balance, the Scorpion, the Archer, Capricorn, the Water-carrier, the Fish.

P.: What is sand?

A.: The wall of the earth.

P.: What is grass?

A.: The garment of the earth.

P.: What are vegetables?

A.: Friends of physicians, the glory of cooks.

P.: What is it that makes bitter sweet?

A.: Hunger.

P.: What is wakeful sleep?

A.: Hope.

P.: What is hope?

A.: The consolation of toil, a dubious issue.

P.: What is friendship?

A.: Equality of minds.

P.: What is faith?

A.: The certainty of what is unknown and wonderful.

P.: I saw a woman flying, having a beak of iron and a wooden body and a feathered tail, bearing death.

A.: That is an arrow, the companion of soldiers.

P.: What is a soldier?

A.: The bulwark of empire, the dread of the enemy, a glorious slave.

P.: What is it that is and is not?

A.: Nothing.

P.: How can it be and not be?

A.: It is in name and not in fact.

Alcuin: 8th century
Disputatio Regalis et Nobilissimi Iuvenis Pippini cum Albino Scholastico
Alcuin (Albinus) was the tutor of Pippin, son of Charlemagne.
Trans. by H. E. W.

Alcuin as Teacher

¶ To MY MOST devout and most distinguished master David, most worthy of all power, Flaccus Alcuin sends eternal greetings of true salvation in Christ.

I, your Flaccus, am occupied, according to your exhortation and good wishes, in serving some monks in the monastery of St. Martin with the honey of the Holy Scriptures. I am eager to intoxicate some with the old wine of the ancient learning; and I shall begin to nourish others with the fruit of grammatical subtleties; certain others I long to enlighten with the movements of the stars, as a painter decorates the ceilings of some large mansion. "I am made many things to many men" so that I teach many to the profit of the holy church of God and to the honor of your imperial reign, so that the grace of Almighty God in me may not be in vain, nor the bestowal of your kindness. But to some extent your humble servant lacks the rarer books of scholastic learning which I had in my own country through the kind and very devoted diligence of my master and even through the sweat, such as it was, of my own effort. I am explaining these matters to your excellency if perhaps it may please your plan that longs so ardently for all knowledge, so that I may send some of our pupils to receive from you whatever is necessary for us and bring back to France the flowers of Britain; so that there may not be only in the area of York a "garden enclosed" but in Touraine blossomings of paradise with fruitful produce, so that as it came the South Wind would blow through the gardens of the River Loire and its aromas would flow and what follows in the Song of Songs, from which I have taken this metaphor, may happen finally: "Let my beloved come into his garden and eat the fruit, and let him say to his young friends: 'Eat, my friends, drink and be intoxicated, dearest ones. I sleep, and my heart is awake.' "

Or Isaiah the prophet's inspiring call to learn wisdom: "Ho, everyone that thirsteth, come ye to the waters, and he that hath no money; come ye, buy, and eat; yea, come, buy wine and milk without money and without price."

266

These are the things that your most noble devotion knows, how through all the pages of Holy Scripture we are exhorted to learn wisdom; that there is nothing more sublime in attaining a happy life, nothing pleasanter to practice, nothing more potent against vices, nothing more praiseworthy in every position of prestige, and even, according to the sayings of the philosophers, nothing more necessary for governing the people, nothing better for channeling life into good character, than the grace of wisdom and the glory of knowledge and the virtue of knowledge. Hence Solomon the wise exclaims about his glory: "For wisdom is better than rubies; and all the things that may be desired are not to be compared with it. It is this that exalts the humble, that honors the great. By it kings reign and the founders of the laws decree justice. By it princes rule, and the powerful decree justice. Happy are those that guard its ways, and happy are those who watch at its gates daily."

To learn this with all enthusiasm, and to possess it by daily practice, exhort, O Master King, all the young men in the palace school of your excellency, so that they may be proficient in it as their age develops, so that they may be deemed worthy to extend their hoary old age into honor and may be able through it to attain everlasting salvation. According to the extent of my humble talent, I shall not be slow to plant the seeds of wisdom among your subjects in these regions, being mindful of the proverb: "In the morning, sow thy seed, and in the evening withhold not thine hand: for thou knowest not whether shall prosper, either this or that, or whether they both shall be alike good."

In the morning, when my studies flourished with youth, I sowed in Britain. Now, with my blood growing cold, in the evening as it were I do not cease to sow in France, wishing each to prosper, by the gift of God's grace. To me, with my frail body, there is solace in the sentiment of St. Jerome, who declares in his letter to Nepotianus: "Almost all the physical virtues change in old age and, with the increase of wisdom alone, other characteristics decrease." And a little further on: "The old age of those who have equipped their youth with honorable skills and have meditated over the law of the Lord day and night, becomes more learned with age, more expert with experience, wiser in the course of time; and reaps the sweet fruits of the ancient studies." Into this letter in praise of wisdom and the studies of the ancients whoever likes can read more and understand how great was the passion of the ancients to flourish in the grace of wisdom.

Alcuin: 8th century
Epistolae
Trans. by H. E. W.

Strasburg Oath[1]

¶ PRO DEO AMUR et pro christian poblo et nostro commun salvament, d'ist di in avant in quant deus savoir et podir me dunat, si salvarai eo cist meon fradre Karlo et in auidha et in cadhuna cosa, si cum om per dreit son fradra salvar dist, in o quid il mi altresi fazet, et ab Ludher nul plaid numqua prindrai, qui meon vol cist meon fradre Karle in damno sit.

For the love of God, and for the common welfare of the Christian people and for our own, henceforth, in so far as God has given me knowledge and power, I shall defend my brother Charles in aid and in every thing, as a brother should be defended, on condition that he do likewise for me; and with Lothair I shall make no covenant which, through my will, may harm my brother Charles.

9th century
Trans. by H. E. W.

Hazards of the Road[2]

¶ TO HIS DEAREST Reg. Lupus sends greetings in the Lord.

We long for your arrival, as is fitting, for certain letters have already bespoken your coming. But we urge you to choose a route with the most vigilant caution, because in the reign of our king

1. The Strasburg Oath is of historical and literary significance as the first surviving specimen of French prose. An examination of the original text reveals how early French is just barely emerging from its Latin origins.
2. A letter indicating how hazardous travel was in the Dark and Middle Ages; burghers and peasants generally went armed, as protection against the brigandage, robbery and assault that were prevalent.

Charles, when disturbances arise, robberies are committed with impunity, and nothing happens more surely and more often than violent plundering. You must therefore seek such a group of fellow travelers whose number and courage will prevent the acts of the brigands or repulse them, if necessary. You would do us a kindness in bringing Sallust's *Catiline* and *Jugurtha* and the *Verrines Speeches* and whatever other texts, however defective, you know we have or don't have at all, so that by this favor of yours the defective texts may be corrected and those I do not possess, and never should, except through your help, may be secured all the more gratefully because unexpectedly. I wish you the best of health and good luck.

Lupus of Ferrières: 9th century
Epistolae
Trans. by H. E. W.

Classical Texts

¶ To my dear friend Ansbaldus, Lupus sends greetings.

I was sorry that, with such a great opportunity before you, to say the least, there was nothing you wanted to send or write me. However, although you so easily brushed off your interest in me, for which I reprimand you, I shall in no sense imitate you, but I shall embrace you with pious words although you spurn me. I shall have Cicero's letters, that you sent me, compared with my text, so that the truth, if possible, may be extracted from each. Now you, give this courier of ours Cicero's translation of Aratus, so that from it, which I believe I shall obtain, the parts that our Eigil indicated were missing may be supplied. Good-bye, and safeguard me always with your prayers.

Lupus of Ferrières: 9th century
Epistolae
Trans. by H. E. W.

A Nun Writes Comedies

¶ [CALLIMACHUS HAS A weighty secret to disclose. To his friends he cries: "Let's go into a hiding place, so that no one can come near and interrupt our talk."]

CALLIMACHUS: I'm in love.

FRIENDS: What?

CALLIMACHUS: I'm in love with something beautiful and charming.

FRIENDS: These two qualities are not always present in the same object, nor in everything. Hence an atom, that you're in love with, cannot be conceived as the object of your love.

CALLIMACHUS: It's a woman.

FRIENDS: When you say woman, you imply all women.

CALLIMACHUS: Not all equally, but one in particular.

* * * *

DRUSIANA (*the girl that Callimachus loves*): I wonder very much, Callimachus, what you want to discuss with me.

CALLIMACHUS: You wonder?

DRUSIANA: I do.

CALLIMACHUS: Now about this love.

DRUSIANA: What love?

CALLIMACHUS: Why, the love that I have for you more than for anyone.

DRUSIANA: What right of consanguinity or what established legal custom compels you to love me?

CALLIMACHUS: Your beauty.

DRUSIANA: My beauty?

CALLIMACHUS: Certainly.

DRUSIANA: What has my beauty got to do with you?

CALLIMACHUS: Nothing, unfortunately, to date; but I hope it will have something to do with me later on.

* * * *

[The Emperor Constantine and Gallicanus, who is off to fight the Scythians, are in conversation. The Emperor is ready to offer him high rewards.]

CONSTANTINE: If you want something else, say so.

GALLICANUS: I do want something else.

CONSTANTINE: What?

GALLICANUS: If I may presume to speak.

CONSTANTINE: Speak.

GALLICANUS: You will get angry.

CONSTANTINE: Not at all.

GALLICANUS: You will.

CONSTANTINE: I won't.

GALLICANUS: You will be indignant.

CONSTANTINE: Don't be afraid.

GALLICANUS: You asked me: I'll tell you. I love your daughter, Constantia.

* * * *

[Dulcitius is in love with Agapes, Hirena, and Chiona, who are in prison. Dulcitius approaches the prison, his soldiers saying that they will wait for him. The prison house is dark, and Dulcitius loses his bearings.]

AGAPES: What is that noise outside?

HIRENA: The wretch Dulcitius is coming in.

CHIONA: The Lord protect us!

AGAPES: Amen!

CHIONA: What is the meaning of this clashing together of jars and pots and pans?

HIRENA: I'll look. Come here, please look through the chinks.

AGAPES: What is it?

HIRENA: Look, that fool! He's mad. He thinks he is kissing us.

AGAPES: What is he doing?

HIRENA: One moment he is fondling the jars on his lap; then again he puts his arms around the pots and the pans, giving them sweet kisses.

CHIONA: What a foolish thing!

HIRENA: His face, his hands, and his clothes are so filthy, so soiled, that the blackness that clings to them makes him look like an Ethiopian.

AGAPES: That's how he ought to look, since he is in mind possessed of the devil.

HIRENA: There he is, getting ready to go away. Let us listen and see what the soldiers waiting at the door are going to do as he goes out.

* * * *

271

SOLDIERS: Who is this coming out? Someone possessed of the devil. Or rather the devil himself. Let us run.

DULCITIUS: Soldiers, where are you fleeing? Stop, wait. Take your lanterns and lead me to my bed.

SOLDIERS: It is our captain's voice, but the appearance is that of the devil. Let us not stop. Let us make haste and flee. The evil spirit will destroy us.

DULCITIUS: I shall go to the palace and tell the court what indignity I am suffering.

Hrotsvithae Opera: 10th century
Edited by Carl Strecker. Leipzig:
Teubner, 1906
Trans. by H. E. W.

Plea to Emperor Otto II[1]

¶ Gerbert to Otto.

To the most serene attention of my lord I should have preferred to report glad news rather than sad. But when I see my monks emaciated by hunger, crushed by stark want, how can I be silent? This evil might have been tolerable, if a greater hope had not at the same time been removed. By some papers or other documents called leases, the entire sanctuary of God is on sale, there is no collection of money to be found anywhere, the stores of drugs and the granaries are emptied, there is nothing in the exchequer. What then can I a sinner do? If it could be done with my lord's favor, it would be better for me alone to be in want among the Gauls rather than to go begging among the Italians with so many needy ones. Rainerius Francigena, a friend of ours, and desirous of your patronage, committed to my loyalty many items about the state of your empire, to be referred to you, and not to be intrusted to a legate, and not written down either, except by your order.

Gerbert: 11th century
Epistolae
Trans. by H. E. W.

1. A letter illustrating the candor of the relationship between an ecclesiastical prelate and a temporal ruler.

To a Friend

¶ Gerbert, formerly head of the episcopal school, to his friend Hugo. Greetings.

According to the amplitude of my mind my Lord has gifted me with the most ample honors. For what region of Italy does not contain the possessions of St. Columbanus? This indeed is due to the generosity and benevolence of our Caesar. But fate has decided otherwise. According to the amplitude of my mind it has burdened me with a host of enemies, For what district of Italy does not have enemies of mine? My strength is unequal to the strength of Italy. These are the terms of peace: If I am submissively despoiled, they will cease to strike. If I stand armed, with drawn blade, they will pursue me with swords. When they cannot strike with the sword, they will attack with a shower of words. The imperial majesty is held in contempt, both in my person and in itself in the dismemberment of God's sanctuary. Since I refuse to accept what is done according to the conditions of the leases, I am nicknamed traitor, monster, and tyrant. Caesar himself, the most excellent of all men, is compared by the thieves with a donkey. O most faithful of friends, do not deprive a friend of advice and aid. Remember what I told you, that I prefer to be a soldier in Caesar's camp than a king among strangers.

Gerbert: 11th century
Epistolae
Trans. by H. E. W.

Abelard to Héloïse

Abelard, having at last conquered the remains of his unhappy passion, had determined to put an end to so dangerous a correspondence as that between Héloïse and himself. The following letter, therefore, though written with no less concern than his former, is free from mixtures of a worldly passion, and is full of the warmest sentiments of piety, and the most moving exhortations.

273

¶ WRITE NO MORE to me, Héloïse, write no more to me; it is time to end a commerce which makes our mortifications of no advantage to us. We retired from the world to sanctify ourselves; and by a conduct directly contrary to Christian morality, we become odious to Jesus Christ. Let us no more deceive ourselves, by flattering ourselves with the remembrance of our past pleasures; we shall make our lives troublesome, and we shall be incapable of relishing the sweets of solitude. Let us make a good use of our austerities, and no longer preserve the ideas of our crimes amongst the severities of penitence. Let a mortification of body and mind, a strict fasting, continual solitude, profound and holy meditations, and a sincere love of God, succeed our former irregularities.

Let us try to carry religious perfection to a very difficult point. It is beautiful to find in Christianity minds so disengaged from the earth, from the creatures and themselves, that they seem to act independently of those bodies they are joined to, and to use them as their slaves. We can never raise ourselves to too great heights, when God is the object. Be our endeavors never so great, they will always come short of reaching that exalted Divinity which even our apprehensions cannot reach. Let us act for God's glory, independent of the creatures or ourselves, without any regard to our own desires, or the sentiments of others. Were we in this temper of mind, Héloïse, I would willingly make my abode at the Paraclete. My earnest care for a house I have founded would draw a thousand blessings on it. I would instruct it by my words, and animate it by my example. I would watch over the lives of my sisters, and would command nothing but what I myself would perform. I would direct you to pray, meditate, labor, and keep vows of silence; and I would myself pray, meditate, labor, and be silent.

However, when I spoke, it should be to lift you up when you should fall, to strengthen you in your weaknesses, to enlighten you in that darkness and obscurity which might at any time surprise you. I would comfort you under those severities used by persons of great virtue. I would moderate the vivacity of your zeal and piety, and give your virtue an even temperament. I would point out those duties which you ought to know, and satisfy you in those doubts which the weakness of your reason might occasion. I would be your master and father; and by a marvellous talent I would become lively, slow, soft, or severe, according to the different characters of those I should guide in the painful path of Christian perfection.

But whither does my vain imagination carry me? Ah, Héloïse, how far are we from such a happy temper! Your heart still burns with that fatal fire which you cannot extinguish, and mine is full of trouble and uneasiness. Think not, Héloïse, that I enjoy here a perfect peace; I will, for the last time, open my heart to you; I am not yet disengaged from you; I fight against my excessive tenderness for you; yet, in spite of all my endeavors, the remaining frailty makes me but too sensible of your sorrows, and gives me a share in them. Your letters have indeed moved me; I could not read with indifference characters wrote by that dear hand. I sigh, I weep, and all my reason is scarce sufficient to conceal my weakness from my pupils. This, unhappy Héloïse! is the miserable condition of Abelard. The world, which generally errs in its notions, thinks I am easy and, as if I had loved only in you the gratification of sense, imagines I have now forgot you. But what a mistake is this! People indeed did not mistake in thinking, when we separated, that shame and grief for having been so cruelly used made me abandon the world. It was not, as you know, a sincere repentance for having offended God which inspired me with a design of retiring; however, I considered the accident which happened to us as a secret design of Providence, to punish our crimes; and only looked upon Fulbert as the instrument of Divine vengeance. Grace drew me into an asylum, where I might yet have remained if the rage of my enemies would have permitted; I have endured all their persecutions, not doubting but God himself raised them up in order to purify me.

When he saw me perfectly obedient to His holy will, He permitted that I should justify my doctrine; I made its purity public, and showed in the end that my faith was not only orthodox, but also perfectly clear from even the suspicion of novelty.

I should be happy if I had none to fear but my enemies, and no other hinderance to my salvation but their calumny; but, Héloïse, you make me trouble; your letters declare to me that you are enslaved to a fatal passion; and yet if you cannot conquer it you cannot be saved; and what part would you have me take in this case? Would you have me stifle the inspirations of the Holy Ghost? Shall I, to sooth you, dry up those tears which the evil spirit makes you shed? Shall this be the fruit of my meditations? No: let us be more firm in our resolutions; we have not retired but in order to lament our sins, and to gain Heaven; let us then resign ourselves to God with all our hearts.

I know every thing in the beginning is difficult; but it is glorious to undertake the beginning of a great action; and that glory increases proportionably as the difficulties are more considerable. We ought, upon this account, to surmount bravely all obstacles which might hinder us in the practice of Christian virtue. In a monastery men are proved as gold in the furnace. No one can continue long there, unless he bear worthily the yoke of our Lord.

Attempt to break those shameful chains which bind you to the flesh; and if by the assistance of grace you are so happy as to accomplish this, I entreat you to think of me in your prayers. Endeavor with all your strength to be the pattern of a perfect Christian. It is difficult, I confess, but not impossible; and I expect this beautiful triumph from your teachable disposition. If your first endeavors prove weak, give not yourself up to despair; that would be cowardice. Besides, I would have you informed, that you must necessarily take great pains, because you strive to conquer a terrible enemy, to extinguish raging fire; and to reduce to subjection your dearest affections, you must fight against your own desires; be not therefore pressed down with the weight of your corrupt nature. You have to do with a cunning adversary, who will use all means to seduce you. Be always upon your guard. While we live, we are exposed to temptations. This made a great saint say, that "the whole life of man was a temptation." The Devil, who never sleeps, walks continually around us, in order to surprise us on some unguarded side, and enters into our soul to destroy it.

However perfect any one may be, yet he may fall into temptations, and perhaps into such as may be useful. Nor is it wonderful that man should never be exempt from them, because he hath always in himself their source, concupiscence; scarce are we delivered from one temptation, but another attacks us. Such is the lot of the posterity of Adam, that they should always have something to suffer, because they have forfeited their primitive happiness. We vainly flatter ourselves that we shall conquer temptations by flying; if we join not patience and humility, we shall torment ourselves to no purpose. We shall more certainly compass our end by imploring God's assistance, than by using any means drawn from ourselves.

Be constant, Héloïse; trust in God, and you will fall into few temptations. Whenever they shall come, stifle them in their birth! let them not take root in your heart. Apply remedies to a disease, said an ancient, in its beginning, for when it has gained strength, medicines will be unavailable. Temptations have their degrees: they are at first mere thoughts, and do not appear dangerous; the imagination receives them without any fears; a pleasure is formed out of them; we pause upon it, and at last we yield to it.

Do you now, Héloïse, applaud my design of making you walk in the steps of the saints? Do my words give you any relish for penitence? Have you not remorse for your wanderings, and do you not wish you could, like Magdalen, wash our Saviour's feet with tears? If you have not yet these ardent emotions, pray that He would inspire them. I shall never cease to recommend you in my prayers, and always beseech Him to assist you in your desire of dying holily. You have quitted the world; and what object was worthy to detain you there? Lift up your eyes always to Him to whom you have consecrated the rest of your days. Life upon this earth is misery. The very necessities to which our body is subject here are matter of affliction to a saint. "Lord," said the Royal Prophet, "deliver me from my necessities!" They are wretched who do not know themselves for such, and yet they are more wretched who know their misery, and do not hate the corruption of the age. What fools are men to engage themselves to earthly things! They will be undeceived one day, and will know but too late how much they have been to blame in loving such false good. Persons truly pious do not thus mistake; they are disengaged from all sensual pleasures, and raise their desires to heaven. Begin, Héloïse; put your design in execution without delay; you have yet time enough to work out your salvation. Love Christ, and despise yourself for His sake. He would possess your heart, and be the sole object of your sighs and tears; seek for no comfort but in Him. If you do not free yourself from me, you will fall with me; but if you quit me and give up yourself to Him, you will be steadfast and immovable. If you force the Lord to forsake you, you will fall into distress; but if you be ever faithful to Him, you will be always in joy. Magdalen wept, as thinking the Lord had forsaken her. But Martha said, "See, the Lord calls you." Be diligent in your duty, and obey faithfully the motions of His grace, and Jesus will remain always with you.

Attend, Héloïse, to some instructions I have to give you. You are at the head of a society, and you know there is this difference between those who lead a private life, and such as are charged with the conduct of others; that the first need only labor for their own sanctification, and in acquitting themselves of their duties are not obliged to practice all the virtues in such an apparent manner; whereas they who have the conduct of others entrusted to them, ought by their example to engage them to do all the good they are capable of in their condition. I beseech you to attend to this truth, and so to follow it, as that your whole life may be a perfect model of that of a religious recluse.

God, who heartily desires our salvation, hath made all the means of it easy to us. In the Old Testament He hath written in the Tables of the Law what He requires of us, that we might not be bewildered in seeking after His will. In the New Testament He hath written that law of grace in our hearts, to the intent that it might be always present with us; and, knowing the weakness and incapacity of our nature, He hath given us grace to perform His will; and as if this were not enough, He hath at all times, in all states of the church, raised up men, who by their exemplary life might excite others to their duty. To effect this, He hath chosen persons of every age, sex, and condition. Strive now to unite in yourself all those virtues which have been scattered in these different states. Have the purity of virgins, the austerity of anchorites, the zeal of pastors and bishops, and the constancy of martyrs. Be exact, in the course of your whole life, to fulfill the duties of a holy and enlightened superior, and then death, which is commonly considered as terrible, will appear agreeable to you.

"The death of the saints," says the prophet, "is precious in the sight of the Lord." Nor is it difficult to comprehend why their death should have this advantage over that of sinners. I have remarked three things which might have given the prophet an occasion of speaking thus. First, their resignation to the will of God. Secondly, the continuation of their good works. And lastly, the triumph they gain over the devil.

A saint who has accustomed himself to submit to the will of God, yields to death without reluctance. "He waits with joy," says St. Gregory, "for the Judge who is to reward him; he fears not to quit this miserable mortal life, in order to begin an immortal happy one." "It is not so with the sinner," says the same father; "he fears, and with reason; he trembles at the approach of the least sickness; death is terrible to him, because he cannot bear the presence of an offended Judge; and having so often abused the grace of God, he sees no way to avoid the punishment due to his sins."

The saints have besides this advantage over sinners: That having made works of piety familiar to them during their life, they exercise them without trouble; and having gained new strength against the devil every time they overcame him, they will find themselves in a condition at the hour of death to obtain that victory over him, on which depends all eternity, and the blessed union of their souls with their Creator.

I hope, Héloïse, that after having deplored the irregularities of your past life, you will die, as the prophet prayed, the "death of the righteous." Ah, how few are there who make their end after this manner! And why? It is because there are so few who love the cross of Christ. Every one would be saved, but few will use those means which religion prescribes. And yet as we can be saved by nothing but the cross, why then do we refuse to bear it? Hath not our Saviour borne it before us, and died for us, to the end that we might also bear it, and desire to die also? All the saints have been afflicted, and our Saviour Himself did not pass one hour of His life without some sorrow. Hope not therefore to be exempted from sufferings. The cross, Héloïse, is always at hand, but take care that you do not bear it with regret, for by so doing you will make it more heavy, and you will be oppressed by it unprofitably. On the contrary, if you bear it with affection and courage, all your sufferings will create in you a holy confidence, whereby you will find comfort in God. Hear our Saviour, who says, "My child, renounce yourself, take up your cross, and follow me." Oh, Héloïse! do you doubt! Is not your soul ravished at so saving a command? Are you deaf to His voice? are you insensible to words so full of kindness? Beware, Héloïse, of refusing a husband who demands you, and is more to be feared, if you slight his affection, than any profane lover. Provoked at your contempt and ingratitude he will turn his love into anger, and make you feel his vengeance. How will you sustain His presence, when you shall stand before His tribunal! He will reproach you for having despised His grace; He will represent to you His sufferings for you. What answer can you make? He will say to you, "Go, you proud creature, dwell in everlasting flames. I separated you from the world to purify you in solitude, and you did not second my design. I endeavored to save you, and you took pains to destroy yourself; go, wretch, and take the portion of the reprobates."

Oh, Héloïse, prevent these terrible words, and avoid by a holy course the punishment prepared for sinners. I dare not give you a description of those dreadful torments which are the consequences of a life of guilt. I am filled with horror, when they offer themselves to my imagination; and yet, Héloïse, I can conceive nothing which can reach the tortures of the damned. The fire which we see upon earth is but the shadow of that which burns them; and without enumerating their endless pains, the loss of God which they feel increases all their torments. Can anyone sin who is persuaded of this? My God! Can we dare to offend Thee? Though the riches of Thy mercy could not engage us to love Thee, the dread of being thrown into such an abyss of misery should restrain us from doing any thing which might displease Thee!

I question not, Héloïse, but you will hereafter apply yourself in good earnest to the business of your salvation; this ought to be your whole concern. Banish me therefore for ever from your heart; it is the best advice I can give you; for the remembrance of a person we have loved criminally cannot but be hurtful, whatever advances we have made in the ways of virtue. When you have extirpated your unhappy inclination toward me, the practice of every virtue will become easy; and when at last your life is conformable to that of Christ, death will be desirable to you. Your soul will joyfully leave this body, and direct its flight to heaven. Then you will appear with confidence before your Saviour; you will not read characters of your reprobation written in the Book of Life; but you will hear your Saviour say, "Come, partake of my glory, and enjoy the eternal reward I have appointed for those virtues you have practiced."

Farewell, Héloïse! This is the last advice of your dear Abelard! This last time, let me persuade you to follow the holy rules of the gospel. Heaven grant that your heart, once so sensible of my love, may now yield to be directed by my zeal! May the idea of your loving Abelard, always present to your mind, be now changed into the image of Abelard truly penitent; and may you shed as many tears for your salvation, as you have done during the course of our misfortunes!

Abelard: 12th century
Epistolae
Eighteenth-century translation

Héloïse to Abelard

¶ A CONSOLATORY LETTER of yours to a friend happened some days since to fall into my hands; my knowledge of the writing and my love of the hand gave me the curiosity to open it. In justification of the liberty I took, I flattered myself I might claim a sovereign privilege over everything which came from you. Nor was I scrupulous to break through the rules of good breeding when I was to hear news of Abelard. But how dear did my curiosity cost me! What disturbance did it occasion, and how surprised I was to find the whole letter filled with a particular and melancholy account of our misfortunes! I met with my name a hundred times; I never saw it without fear, some heavy calamity always followed it. I saw yours too, equally unhappy. These mournful but dear remembrances put my heart into such violent motion that I thought it was too much to offer comfort to a friend for a few slight disgraces, by such extraordinary means as the representation of our sufferings and revolutions. What reflections did I not make! I began to consider the whole afresh, and perceived myself pressed with the same weight of grief as when we first began to be miserable. Though length of time ought to have closed up my wounds, yet the seeing them described by your hand was sufficient to make them all open and bleed afresh. Nothing can ever blot from my memory what you have suffered in defense of your writings. I cannot help thinking of the rancorous malice of Alberce and Lotulf. A cruel uncle and an injured lover will always be present to my aching sight. I shall never forget what enemies your learning, and what envy your glory raised against you. I shall never forget your reputation, so justly acquired, torn to pieces and blasted by the inexorable cruelty of pseudo pretenders to science. Was not your treatise of Divinity condemned to be burnt? Were you not threatened with perpetual imprisonment? In vain you urged in your defense that your enemies imposed upon you opinions quite different from your meanings.

* * * *

O think of me—do not forget me—remember my love and fidelity and constancy: love me as your mistress, cherish me as your child, your sister, your wife! Remember I still love you, and yet strive to avoid loving you. What a terrible saying is this! I shake with horror, and my heart revolts against what I say. I shall blot all my paper with tears. I end my long letter wishing you, if you desire it (would to Heaven I could!) forever adieu!

Letter of Héloïse to Abelard: 12th century
Letters of Abelard and Héloïse: G. P. Putnam's Sons

A Martinet Schoolmaster[1]

¶ I HAD ONCE been whipped in school. The school was nothing more than a room in our house. For the master, on my account alone, had disregarded the interests of others whom he had at times accepted. My mother, increasing his fee and bestowing this honor, had wisely required him to do so. So, when my studies were over at a certain hour in the evening, I had gone over to my mother's lap, having been punished severely and undeservedly. When she started to ask me, as she invariably did, whether I had been whipped that day, I said definitely, "No!" in order not to inform on the master. Willy-nilly, she stripped off my tunic, that they call an undergarment or rather shirt, and observed the livid ribs on my back from the lashes of the osier twigs and also my bruised skin. With all her heart she bemoaned the punishment inflicted on my tender years cruelly and unreasonably, and in frenzied agitation, her eyes filled with sorrow, she said: "You will never henceforth become a cleric nor will you pay the penalty for another just to learn your letters."

To this I replied, regarding her with as much reproach as I could: "If I should happen to die, I would not stop learning and becoming a cleric." For she had promised that, if I wanted to become a knight, when I had reached the right age she would give me arms and military equipment.

Guibert: 12th century
De Vita Sua
Trans. by H. E. W.

1. This selection offers some insight into medieval teaching methods.

The Value of Literature[1]

¶ WHILE THE BENEFITS of literature are very pleasant in many respects, they are especially so in this regard, that, once the annoying element of intervals of time and place is removed, they offer the presence of friends one after the other and do not allow things worth knowing to fall into decay. For the arts would have died out, laws would have disappeared, every function of faith and of all religion would have collapsed, and the use itself of correct speech would have failed, had not the divine mercy procured for mortals the use of literature as a remedy for human infirmity. The examples of our ancestors that are inducements and stimuli toward virtue would arouse or serve no one at all, had not the devout solicitude of writers and the perseverance that triumphs over idleness transmitted them to posterity. The shortness of life, dull intelligence, sluggish indifference and useless occupation permit us to know very little, while forgetfulness, the defrauder of knowledge, the hostile and even faithless stepmother of memory, constantly shakes out this same knowledge from our minds and tears it away. For who would know about the Alexanders or the Caesars, who would admire the Stoics or the Peripatetics, if the memorials of writers did not make them known? Who would follow the revered footsteps of the apostles and the prophets had not literature consecrated them to divine posterity? Only then do triumphal arches benefit famous men in acquiring glory, when the inscription explains the reasons and the identity of the memorials. Only then does the onlooker recognize the liberator of his country or the founder of peace, when the inscription indicates Constantine, the conqueror, whom our Britain produced. No one was ever famous and perpetuated in glory except through his own or another's writing. The fame of a donkey and of any emperor, after a little time, is the same, unless the memory of either is extended, thanks to writers. How many great kings do you think there were of whom there is mention or thought anywhere?

1. An analysis of literature as an intellectual and spiritual stimulus by one of the most cultured and urbane of the Scholastics.

Nothing therefore is more advisable for those who seek glory than to merit the special favor of literary writers. For it is useless for great deeds to be achieved by them, that must be obscured in everlasting darkness, unless they shine in literary splendor. Whatever popularity or praises are acquired elsewhere are as though Echo, that you hear of in stories, received the applause of the theatre. It stops when it begins. Furthermore, literature faithfully offers comfort to grief, relaxation to toil, pleasantness to poverty, modesty in wealth and delights. For the spirit is redeemed from vices and is refreshed, even in adversity, by a kind of strange, gentle delight when it directs its mental shrewdness to reading or writing whatever is useful. You will find in human affairs no more pleasant or more useful occupation, unless by chance devotion, divinely inspired, participates through prayer in divine intercourse or, with heart expansive in love, mentally conceives God and ponders over His mighty deeds within itself as though with the hand of meditation. Believe one who has experienced this, for all the pleasures of the world grow bitter when compared with these practices; all the more so, indeed, as a man's intelligence becomes stronger and clearer and his unimpaired reason develops through the acumen of a saner judgment.

> John of Salisbury: 12th century
> *Policraticus*
> Trans. by H. E. W.

Scriptural Parody[1]

¶ THE BEGINNING of the Holy Gospel according to silver Marks. In those days the Pope said to the Romans: "When the son of man comes to the seat of our majesty, first say: 'Friend, for what have you come?' But if he comes knocking, giving nothing to you, cast him into the outer darkness."

Now it happened that a certain poor cleric came to the court of his Lord the Pope and cried, saying: "You at least, take pity on me, papal doorkeepers, for the hand of poverty has touched me. I am

---

1. Satires and parodies based on sacred literature and classical texts were not uncommon among medieval students, who thus gave ribald expression to their sophisticated and earthy attitudes.

needy and poor, and so I ask you to help me in my misfortune and my misery."

They however listened with deep indignation, and said: "Friend, the devil take you and your poverty; go back, Satan, for you do not understand what money understands. Amen, amen, I say to you: 'You shall not enter into the bliss of your Lord, until you have given the last penny.' "

The poor man went away and sold his cloak and his tunic and all that he possessed and gave it to the cardinals and the doorkeepers and the chamberlains. But they said: "What is this among so many?" And they cast him out of doors, and having gone out he wept that he loved the Lord and had no consolation.

Afterward a rich cleric came to the court, coarse, fat, and bulky, who had committed murder on account of a revolt. He gave first to the doorkeeper, secondly to the chamberlain, thirdly to the cardinals. But they thought that they would receive more. Now the Pope, hearing that the cardinals and the attendants had received a very large number of gifts from the priest, was sick unto death. The rich cleric sent him a gold and a silver electuary, and forthwith he was healed. Then the Lord Pope summoned to his presence the cardinals and the attendants and said to them:

"Brethren, see to it that no one leads you astray by empty words. For I give you an example so that you too may follow it as I follow it."

Carmina Burana: 13th century
Trans. by H. E. W.

Educational Travesty[1]

¶ THE CHIEF CAUSE of error in the study of wisdom is that for forty years there have been certain persons who made themselves masters and doctors of theology and philosophy, although they never learned anything worthwhile nor on account of their position do they wish or

---

1. It will be noted from this selection that attacks on educational methods and results are not restricted to our own times.

are they able to do so, as I shall take care to demonstrate in comprehensive detail in what follows, through the deductions that I make. Though I am sorry and, as far as I can, sympathize on these points, yet, since truth prevails, I shall explain to all some at least of the questions that are publicly discussed and are evident to all men, though few put their hearts to their consideration, just as they do not consider some useful matters on account of those causes of error that I examine here, by which almost all men are shamefully blinded. They are youths ignorant of themselves and the world and the learned tongues, Greek and Hebrew, that are necessary for study, as I shall show later on. They are unfamiliar with all branches and phases of knowledge of the philosophical world and of wisdom, when they make presumptions about the study of theology that demands all human wisdom, as the saints teach us; and all wise men know this. For if there is truth anywhere, it is to be found here. If falseness exists anywhere, here it is to be condemned, as Augustine explains in his book *On Christian Doctrine*. They are youths belonging to two Orders of students, as Albertus Magnus and Thomas Aquinas, and others who in many instances enter the Orders when they are twenty or younger. And this is particularly the case from the English Sea to the boundaries of Christendom and especially beyond the Kingdom of France, so that in Aquitaine, Provence, Spain, Italy, Germany and Hungary, Dacia and everywhere they are received into the Orders, in some places from their tenth year to the twentieth. They are capable of understanding nothing worthwhile on account of their youth. In addition, the causes of human error previously mentioned hold them in their grip, and for this reason when they enter the Orders they have no theological knowledge of any value. Hence many thousands enter without knowing how to read the psalter or Donatus; but immediately after taking the vow they are set to the study of theology. And from the beginning of the system of Orders, that is, from the time when study first flourished in the Orders, the first students were like the later ones, and they devoted themselves to the study of theology that demands all human wisdom. And for that reason it was destined for them not to be proficient in any sense, especially since they were not concerned to be taught philosophy by others after they entered. And chiefly because they presumed in the Orders to speculate on philosophy on their own account without a master, becoming masters in theology and philosophy before they were pupils. Hence infinite error prevails among them, though it does not appear to view for certain reasons; as the devil, with God's permission, takes care of it.

Roger Bacon: 13th century
Compendium Studii Philosophiae
Trans. by H. E. W.

On Translation

¶ I AM CONVINCED that it would have been better for the Romans if Aristotle's philosophy had not been translated, rather than to have been transmitted with such obscurity and carelessness; as can be seen from those who have studied his writings for thirty or forty years now. The more they labor, the less they know, as I have proved in the case of all who have adhered to Aristotle's works. Hence Master Robert, once Bishop of Lincoln of sacred memory, disregarded Aristotle's books and their systems entirely, and through his own experience and other authors and through other fields of knowledge he handled Aristotle's philosophy. And he knew one hundred thousand times better, and wrote on those matters of which Aristotle's books treat better than they can be comprehended in his own inaccurate translations. Witness the treatises of the Master Bishop *On Iris, On Comets,* and others that he wrote. So all those who have some knowledge ignore the inaccurate translations of Aristotle and seek such remedies as they can. This is the truth that men, absorbed in philosophy, refuse to consider but look for some solace for their ignorance, like brutes. If I had control over Aristotle's works I would have them all burned, because it is merely a waste of time to study in them and a cause of error and the multiplying of ignorance beyond the point of unraveling. And since Aristotle's labors are the basis of all philosophy, no one can estimate how great was the loss to the Romans through bad translations.

Roger Bacon: 13th century
Compendium Studii Philosophiae
Trans. by H. E. W.

Student Conduct

¶ REGARD AS MODELS of deportment the graven images of the churches, which you should carry in your mind as living and indelible pictures. Cherish again the violets of civility without blemish so that, when your blindness has vanished, the eyes of your soul may have no wasting disease.

Be not a fornicator, O student, a robber, a murderer, a deceitful merchant, a champion at dice. In the choir stalls a cleric should chant without noise and commotion. I advocate that the ordinary layman who does not sing be kept out of the choir. A student who is a churchman is expected to follow good custom, to be willing to serve, to fee the notary who has drawn up a charter for him, to gladden the giver. Do not constantly urge your horse on with the spur, which should be used only on rare occasions. Give your horse the reins when he wants to mount an incline. . . .

Avoid drunkards, those who indulge in secret sin, those who like to beat and strike, those who love lewdness, evil games, and quarrels. . . .

Have nothing to do with the prostitute, but love your wife. . . . When you walk after dinner keep on frequented streets, avoid insincere speeches. Unless you wish to be considered a fool learn to keep your mouth shut in season. Stand and sit upright, do not scratch yourself.

> John of Garland: 13th century
> *Morale Scolarium*
> Edited and trans. by L. J. Paetow,
> 1927

Student's Letter to Father

¶ MOST REVEREND FATHER AND MASTER:
I commend myself very humbly to you, with deep concern for your blessing and well-being, and I cannot express my gratitude for your dear fatherly care, since I am your son and your creature com-

pletely, next to God. So whatever I am, I am yours, and according to law what is mine cannot become more than mine; so that offering my person or any service that I could perform would be an equally useless and meaningless expression.

But what a child acquires by natural instinct I can retain more successfully. I ought to have spoken to my father always in the same terms, like a cuckoo, never varying: "Give! Give! Give!" and this song I am now forced to sing. For the money, whereby your generosity as a father lately released me for the study of letters, is quite spent, and I am living in debt to the extent of more than five *solidi*. I therefore crave your kindness, my respected father, devoutly, so that fatherly reverence may consider it worthy to give me some money with which I can now manage in school until the Feast of St. Michael. And may the Almighty Father keep you safe, in happiness and old age.

Thomas Sampson: 14th century
Oxford Formularies: Ed. by H. E.
Salter, W. A. Pantin, H. G. Richardson. Oxford: 1942
Trans. by H. E. W.

Letter to Posterity[1]

¶ GREETING. It is possible that some word of me may have come to you, though even this is doubtful, since an insignificant and obscure name will scarcely penetrate far in either time or space. If, however, you should have heard of me, you may desire to know what manner of man I was, or what was the outcome of my labors, especially those of which some description or, at any rate, the bare titles may have reached you.

To begin with myself, the utterances of men concerning me will differ widely, since in passing judgment almost everyone is influenced not so much by truth as by preference, and good and evil report alike know no bounds. I was, in truth, a poor mortal like yourself, neither

---

1. Petrarch, first and foremost of the Humanists, ranks second only to Dante among the great figures of Italian literature. This is his most famous letter, a kind of intellectual manifesto.

very exalted in my origin nor, on the other hand, of the most humble birth, but belonging, as Augustus Caesar says of himself, to an ancient family. As to my disposition, I was not naturally perverse or wanting in modesty, however the contagion of evil associations may have corrupted me. My youth was gone before I realized it; I was carried away by the strength of manhood; but a riper age brought me to my senses and taught me by experiences the truth I had long before read in books, that youth and pleasure are vanity—nay, that the Author of all ages and times permits us miserable mortals, puffed up with emptiness, thus to wander about, until finally, coming to a tardy consciousness of our sins, we shall learn to know ourselves. In my prime I was blessed with a quick and active body, although not exceptionally strong; and while I do not lay claim to remarkable personal beauty, I was comely enough in my best days. I was possessed of a clear complexion, between light and dark, lively eyes, and for long years a keen vision, which however deserted me, contrary to my hopes, and forced me, to my great annoyance, to resort to glasses. Although I had previously enjoyed perfect health, old age brought with it the usual array of discomforts.

My parents were honorable folk, Florentine in their origin, of medium fortune, or, I may as well admit it, in a condition verging on poverty. They had been expelled from their native city, and consequently I was born in exile, at Arezzo, in the year 1304 of this latter age, which begins with Christ's birth, July the twentieth, on a Monday, at dawn. I have always possessed an extreme contempt for wealth; not that riches are not desirable in themselves, but because I hate the anxiety and care which are invariably associated with them. I certainly do not long to be able to give gorgeous banquets. I have, on the contrary, led a happier existence with plain living and ordinary fare than all the followers of Apicius, with their elaborate dainties. So-called *convivia,* which are but vulgar bouts, sinning against sobriety and good manners, have always been repugnant to me. I have ever felt that it was irksome and profitless to invite others to such affairs, and not less so to be bidden to them myself. On the other hand, the pleasure of dining with one's friends is so great that nothing has ever given me more delight than their unexpected arrival, nor have I ever willingly sat down to table without a companion. Nothing displeases me more than display, for not only is it bad in itself, or opposed to humility, but it is troublesome and distracting.

I struggled in my younger days with a keen but constant and pure attachment, and would have struggled with it longer had not the sinking flame been extinguished by death—premature and bitter, but salutary. I should be glad to be able to say that I had always been entirely free from irregular desires, but I should lie if I did so. I can however conscientiously claim that, although I may have been carried away by the fire of youth or by my ardent temperament, I have always abhorred such sins from the depths of my soul. As I approached the age of forty, while my powers were unimpaired and my passions were still strong, I not only abruptly threw off my bad habits but even the very recollection of them, as if I had never looked upon a woman. This I mention as among the greatest of my blessings, and I render thanks to God, who freed me, while still sound and vigorous, from a disgusting slavery which had always been hateful to me. But let us turn to other matters.

I have taken pride in others, never in myself, and however insignificant I may have been, I have always been still less important in my own judgment. My anger has very often injured myself, but never others. I have always been most desirous of honoring friendships, and have faithfully cherished them. I make this boast without fear, since I am confident that I speak truly. While I am very prone to take offense, I am equally quick to forget injuries and have a memory tenacious of benefits. In my familiar associations with kings and princes, and in my friendship with noble personages, my good fortune has been such as to excite envy. But it is the cruel fate of those who are growing old that they can commonly only weep for friends who have passed away. The greatest kings of this age have loved and courted me. They may know why; I certainly do not. With some of them I was on such terms that they seemed in a certain sense my guests rather than I theirs; their lofty position in no way embarrassing me but, on the contrary, bringing with it many advantages. I fled, however, from many of those to whom I was greatly attached; and such was my innate longing for liberty that I studiously avoided those whose very names seemed incompatible with the freedom that I loved.

I possessed a well-balanced rather than a keen intellect, one prone to all kinds of good and wholesome study, but especially inclined to moral philosophy and the art of poetry. The latter, indeed, I neglected as time went on, and took delight in sacred literature. Finding in that a hidden sweetness which I had once esteemed but lightly, I came to regard the works of the poets as only amenities. Among the many subjects which interested me, I dwelt especially upon antiquity, for our own age has always repelled me, so that had it not been for the love of those dear to me, I should have preferred to have been born in any other period than our own. In order to forget my own time, I have constantly striven to place myself in spirit in other ages, and consequently I delight in history; not that the conflicting statements did not offend me, but when in doubt I accepted what appeared to me most probable, or yielded to the authority of the writer.

My style, as many claimed, was clear and forcible; but to me it seemed weak and obscure. In ordinary conversation with friends, or with those about me, I never gave any thought to my language, and I have always wondered that Augustus Caesar should have taken such pains in this respect. When, however, the subject itself, or the place or listener seemed to demand it, I gave some attention to style, with what success I cannot pretend to say; let them judge in whose presence I spoke. If only I have lived well, it matters little to me how I talked. Mere elegance of language can produce at best but an empty renown.

My life up to the present has, either through fate or my own choice, fallen into the following divisions. A part only of my first year was spent at Arezzo, where I first saw the light. The six following years were, owing to the recall of my mother from exile, spent upon my father's estate at Ancisa, about fourteen miles above Florence. I passed my eighth year at Pisa, the ninth and following years in Farther Gaul, at Avignon, on the left bank of the Rhone, where the Roman Pontiff holds and has long held the Church of Christ in shameful exile. It seemed a few years ago as if Urban V was on the point of restoring the Church to its ancient seat, but it is clear that nothing is coming of this effort, and, what is to me the worst of all, the Pope seems to have repented him of his good work, for failure came while he was still living. Had he lived but a little longer, he would certainly have learned how I regarded his retreat. My pen was in my hand when he abruptly surrendered at once his exalted office and his life. Unhappy man, who might have died before the altar of Saint Peter and in his own habitation! Had his successors remained in their capital he would have been looked upon as the cause of this benign change, while, had they left Rome, his virtue would have been all the more conspicuous in contrast with their fault.

But such laments are somewhat remote from my subject. On the windy banks of the River Rhone I spent my boyhood, guided by my parents, and then, guided by my own fancies, the whole of my youth.

Yet there were long intervals spent elsewhere, for I first passed four years at the little town of Carpentras, somewhat to the east of Avignon. In these two places I learned as much of grammar, logic, and rhetoric as my age permitted, or rather, as much as it is customary to teach in school: how little that is, dear reader, thou knowest. I then set out for Montpellier to study law, and spent four years there, then three at Bologna. I heard the whole body of the civil law, and would, as many thought, have distinguished myself later, had I but continued my studies. I gave up the subject altogether, however, as soon as it was no longer necessary to consult the wishes of my parents. My reason was that, although the dignity of the law, which is doubtless very great, and especially the numerous references it contains to Roman antiquity, did not fail to delight me, I feel it to be habitually degraded by those who practice it. It went against me painfully to acquire an art which I would not practice dishonestly and could hardly hope to exercise otherwise. Had I made the latter attempt, my scrupulousness would doubtless have been ascribed to simplicity.

So at the age of two and twenty I returned home. I call my place of exile home, Avignon, where I had been since childhood; for habit has almost the potency of nature itself. I had already begun to be known there, and my friendship was sought by prominent men; wherefore I cannot say. I confess that this is now a source of surprise to me, although it seemed natural enough at an age when we are used to regard ourselves as worthy of the highest respect. I was courted first and foremost by that very distinguished and noble family, the Colonnesi, who at that period adorned the Roman Curia with their presence. However it might be now, I was at that time certainly quite unworthy of the esteem in which I was held by them. I was especially honored by the incomparable Giacomo Colonna, then Bishop of Lombez, whose peer I know not whether I have ever seen or ever shall see, and was taken by him to Gascony; there I spent such a divine summer among the foothills of the Pyrenees, in happy intercourse with my master and the members of our company, that I can never recall the experience without a sigh of regret.

Returning thence, I passed many years in the house of Giacomo's brother, Cardinal Giovanni Colonna, not as if he were my lord and master, but rather my father, or better, a most affectionate brother— nay, it was as if I were in my own home. About this time, a youthful desire impelled me to visit France and Germany. While I invented

293

certain reasons to satisfy my elders of the propriety of the journey, the real explanation was a great inclination and longing to see new sights. I first visited Paris, as I was anxious to discover what was true and what fabulous in the accounts I had heard of that city. On my return from this journey, I went to Rome, which I had since my infancy ardently desired to visit. There I soon came to venerate Stephano, the noble head of the family of the Colonnesi, like some ancient hero, and was in turn treated by him in every respect like a son. The love and good will of this excellent man toward me remained constant to the end of his life, and lives in me still, nor will it cease until I myself pass away.

On my return, since I experienced a deep-seated and innate repugnance to town life, especially in that disgusting city of Avignon, which I heartily abhorred, I sought some means of escape. I fortunately discovered, about fifteen miles from Avignon, a delightful valley, narrow and secluded, called Vaucluse; there the Sorgue, the prince of streams, makes its rise. Captivated by the charms of the place, I transferred thither myself and my books. Were I to describe what I did there during many years, it would prove a long story. Indeed, almost every bit of writing which I have put forth was either accomplished or begun, or at least conceived there, and my undertakings have been so numerous that they still continue to vex and weary me. My mind, like my body, is characterized by a certain versatility and readiness, rather than by strength, so that many tasks that were easy of conception have been given up by reason of the difficulty of their execution. The character of my surroundings suggested the composition of a sylvan or bucolic song. I also dedicated a work in two books upon *The Life of Solitude* to Philip, now exalted to the Cardinal-bishopric of Sabina.

Although always a great man, he was, at the time of which I speak, only the humble Bishop of Cavaillon. He is the only one of my old friends who is still left to me, and he has always loved and treated me not as a bishop (as Ambrose did Augustine), but as a brother.

While I was wandering in those mountains upon a Friday in Holy Week, the strong desire seized me to write an epic in an heroic strain, taking as my theme Scipio Africanus the Great, who had, strange to say, been dear to me from my childhood. But although I began the execution of this project with enthusiasm, I straightway abandoned it, owing to a variety of distractions. The poem was, however, christened *Africa,* from the name of its hero, and, whether from his fortunes or mine, it did not fail to arouse the interest of many before they had seen it.

While leading a leisurely existence in this region, I received, remarkable as it may seem, upon one and the same day, letters both from the Senate at Rome and the Chancellor of the University of Paris, pressing me to appear in Rome and Paris, respectively, to receive the poet's crown of laurel. In my youthful elation I convinced myself that I was quite worthy of this honor; the recognition came from eminent judges, and I accepted their verdict rather than that of my own better judgment. I hesitated for a time which I should give ear to, and sent a letter to Cardinal Giovanni Colonna, of whom I have already spoken, asking his opinion. He was so near that, although I wrote late in the day, I received his reply before the third hour on the morrow. I followed his advice, and recognized the claims of Rome as superior to all others. My acceptance of his counsel is shown by my twofold letter to him on that occasion, which I still keep. I set off accordingly; but although, after the fashion of youth, I was a most indulgent judge of my own work, I still blushed to accept in my own case the verdict even of such men as those who summoned me, despite the fact that they would certainly not have honored me in this way, had they not believed me worthy.

So I decided, first to visit Naples, and that celebrated king and philosopher, Robert, who was not more distinguished as a ruler than as a man of culture. He was, indeed, the only monarch of our age who was the friend at once of learning and of virtue, and I trusted that he might correct such things as he found to criticize in my work. The way in which he received and welcomed me is a source of astonishment to me now, and, I doubt not, to the reader also, if he happens to know anything of the matter. Having learned the reason of my coming, the King seemed mightily pleased. He was gratified, doubtless, by my youthful faith in him, and felt, perhaps, that he shared in a way the glory of my coronation, since I had chosen him from all others as the only suitable critic. After talking over a great many things, I showed him my *Africa,* which so delighted him that he asked that it might be dedicated to him in consideration of a handsome reward. This was a request that I could not well refuse, nor, indeed, would I have wished to refuse it, had it been in my power. He then fixed a day upon which we could consider the object of my visit. This occupied us from noon until evening, and the time proving too short, on account of the many matters which arose for discussion, we passed the two following days in the same manner. Having thus tested my poor attainments for three days, the King at last pronounced me worthy of the laurel. He offered to bestow that honor upon me at Naples, and urged me to consent to receive it there, but my veneration for Rome prevailed over the insistence of even so great a monarch as Robert. At length, seeing that I was inflexible in my purpose, he sent me on my way accompanied by royal messengers and letters to the Roman Senate, in which he gave enthusiastic expression to his flattering opinion of me. This royal estimate was, indeed, quite in accord with that of many others, and especially with my own, but today I cannot approve either his or my own verdict. In his case, affection and the natural partiality to youth were stronger than his devotion to truth.

On arriving at Rome, I continued, in spite of my unworthiness, to rely upon the judgment of so eminent a critic, and, to the great delight of the Romans who were present, I who had been hitherto a simple student received the laurel crown. This occasion is described elsewhere in my letters, both in prose and verse. The laurel, however, in no way increased my wisdom, although it did arouse some jealousy —but this is too long a story to be told here.

On leaving Rome, I went to Parma, and spent some time with the members of the house of Correggio, who, while they were most kind and generous toward me, agreed but ill among themselves. They governed Parma, however, in a way unknown to that city within the memory of man, and the like of which it will hardly again enjoy in this present age.

I was conscious of the honor which I had but just received, and fearful lest it might seem to have been granted to one unworthy of the distinction; consequently, as I was walking one day in the mountains, and chanced to cross the River Enza to a place called Selva Piana, in the territory of Reggio, struck by the beauty of the spot, I began to write again upon the *Africa,* which I had laid aside. In my enthusiasm, which had seemed quite dead, I wrote some lines that very day, and some each day until I returned to Parma. Here I happened upon a quiet and retired house, which I afterwards bought, and which still belongs to me. I continued my task with such ardor, and completed the work in so short a space of time, that I cannot but marvel now at my dispatch. I had already passed my thirty-fourth year when I returned thence to the Fountain of the Sorgue, and to my Transalpine solitude. I had made a long stay both in Parma and

Verona, and everywhere I had, I am thankful to say, been treated with much greater esteem than I merited.

Some time after this, my growing reputation procured for me the good will of a most excellent man, Giacomo the Younger, of Carrara, whose equal I do not know among the rulers of his time. For years he wearied me with messengers and letters when I was beyond the Alps, and with his petitions whenever I happened to be in Italy, urging me to accept his friendship. At last, although I anticipated little satisfaction from the venture, I determined to go to him and see what this insistence on the part of a person so eminent, and at the same time a stranger to me, might really mean. I appeared, though tardily, at Padua, where I was received by him of illustrious memory, not as a mortal, but as the blessed are greeted in heaven—with such delight and such unspeakable affection and esteem, that I cannot adequately describe my welcome in words, and must, therefore, be silent. Among other things, learning that I had led a clerical life from boyhood, he had me made a canon of Padua, in order to bind me the closer to himself and his city. In fine, had his life been spared, I should have found there an end to all my wanderings. But alas! nothing mortal is enduring, and there is nothing sweet which does not presently end in bitterness. Scarcely two years was he spared to me, to his country, and to the world. God, who had given him to us, took him again. Without being blinded by my love for him, I feel that neither I, nor his country, nor the world was worthy of him. Although his son, who succeeded him, was in every way a prudent and distinguished man who, following his father's example, always loved and honored me, I could not remain after the death of him with whom, by reason especially of the similarity of our ages, I had been much more closely united.

I returned to Gaul, not so much from a desire to see again what I had already beheld a thousand times, as from the hope, common to the afflicted, of coming to terms with my misfortunes by a change of scene.

Francesco Petrarca: 1304–1374
A Selection from his Correspondence
Edited by J. H. Robinson. G. P. Putnam's Sons, 1898

That the Treasure of Wisdom Is Chiefly Contained in Books

¶ THE DESIRABLE TREASURE of wisdom and science, which all men desire by an instinct of nature, infinitely surpasses all the riches of the world; in respect of which precious stones are worthless; in comparison with which silver is as clay and pure gold is as a little sand; at whose splendor the sun and moon are dark to look upon; compared with whose marvelous sweetness honey and manna are bitter to the taste. O value of wisdom that fadeth not away with time, virtue ever flourishing, that cleanseth its possessor from all venom! O heavenly gift of the divine bounty, descending from the Father of lights, that thou mayest exalt the rational soul to the very heavens! Thou art the celestial nourishment of the intellect, which those who eat shall still hunger and those who drink shall still thirst, and the gladdening harmony of the languishing soul, which he that hears shall never be confounded. Thou art the moderator and rule of morals, which he who follows shall not sin. By thee kings reign and princes decree justice. By thee, rid of their native rudeness, their minds and tongues being polished, the thorns of vice being torn up by the roots, those men attain high places of honor and become fathers of their country and companions of princes, who without thee would have melted their spears into pruning hooks and plowshares, or would perhaps be feeding swine with the prodigal.

Where dost thou chiefly lie hidden, O most elect treasure! and where shall thirsting souls discover thee?

Certes, thou hast placed thy tabernacle in books, where the Most High, the Light of lights, the Book of Life, has established thee. There everyone who asks receiveth thee, and everyone who seeks finds thee, and to everyone that knocketh boldly it is speedily opened. Therein the cherubim spread out their wings, that the intellect of the students may ascend and look from pole to pole, from the east and west, from the north and from the south. Therein the mighty and incomprehensible God Himself is apprehensibly contained and worshipped; therein is revealed the nature of things celestial, terrestrial, and infernal; therein are discerned the laws by which every state is administered, the offices of the celestial hierarchy are distinguished and the tyrannies of demons described, such as neither the ideas of Plato transcend nor the chair of Crato contained. In books I find the dead as if they were alive; in books I foresee things to come; in books warlike affairs are set forth; from books come forth the laws of peace. All things are corrupted and decay in time; Saturn ceases not to devour the children that he generates; all the glory of the world would be buried in oblivion, unless God had provided mortals with the remedy of books. Alexander, the conqueror of the earth, who, the first in war and arts, assumed universal empire under his single rule, faithful Fabricius and stern Cato would now have been unknown to fame, if the aid of books had been wanting. Towers have been razed to the ground; cities have been overthrown; triumphal arches have perished from decay; nor can either pope or king find any means of more easily conferring the privilege of perpetuity than by books. The book that he has made renders its author this service in return, that so long as the book survives its author remains immortal and cannot die, as Ptolemy declares in the Prologue to his *Almagest*: He is not dead, he says, who has given life to science.

Who therefore will limit by anything of another king the price of the infinite treasure of books, from which the scribe who is instructed bringeth forth things new and old? Truth that triumphs over all things, which overcomes the king, wine, and women, which it is reckoned holy to honor before friendship, which is the way without turning and the life without end, which holy Boethius considers to be threefold in thought, speech, and writing, seems to remain more usefully and to fructify to greater profit in books. For the meaning of the voice perishes with the sound; truth latent in the mind is wisdom that is hid and treasure that is not seen; but truth which shines forth in books desires to manifest itself to every impressionable sense. It commends itself to the sight when it is read, to the hearing when it is heard, and moreover in a manner to the touch, when it suffers itself to be transcribed, bound, corrected, and preserved. The undisclosed truth of the mind, although it is the possession of the noble soul, yet because it lacks a companion is not certainly known to be delightful, while neither sight nor hearing takes account of it. Further, the truth of the voice is patent only to the ear and eludes the sight, which reveals to us more of the qualities of things, and linked with the subtlest of motions begins and perishes as it were in a breath. But the written truth of books, not transient but permanent, plainly offers itself to be observed, and by means of the pervious spherules of the eyes, passing through the vestibule of perception and the courts of imagination, enters the chamber of intellect, taking its place in the couch of memory, where it engenders the eternal truth of the mind.

Finally, we must consider what pleasantness of teaching there is in books, how easy, how secret! How safely we lay bare the poverty of human ignorance to books without feeling any shame! They are masters who instruct us without rod or ferule, without angry words, without clothes or money. If you come to them they are not asleep; if you ask and inquire of them, they do not withdraw themselves; they do not chide if you make mistakes; they do not laugh at you if you are ignorant. O books who alone are liberal and free, who give to all who ask of you and enfranchise all who serve you faithfully! By how many thousand types are ye commended to learned men in the scriptures given us by inspiration of God! For ye are the mines of profoundest wisdom, to which the wise man sends his son that he may dig out treasures: Prov. 2. Ye are the wells of living waters, which Father Abraham first digged, Isaac digged again, and which the Philistines strive to fill up: Gen. 26. Ye are indeed the most delightful ears of corn, full of grain, to be rubbed only by apostolic hands, that the sweetest food may be produced for hungry souls: Matt. 12. Ye are the golden pots in which manna is stored, and rocks flowing with honey, nay combs of honey, most plenteous udders of the milk of life, garners ever full; ye are the tree of life and the fourfold river of Paradise, by which the human mind is nourished and the thirsty intellect is watered and refreshed. Ye are the ark of Noah and the ladder of Jacob, and the troughs by which the young of those who look therein are colored; ye are the stones of testimony and the pitchers holding the lamps of Gideon, the scrips of David, from which the smoothest stones are taken for the slaying of Goliath. Ye are the golden vessels of the temple, the arms of the soldiers of the Church, with which to quench all the fiery darts of the wicked, fruitful olives, vines of Engadi, fig trees that are never barren, burning lamps always to be held in readiness—and all the noblest comparisons of scripture may be applied to books, if we choose to speak in figures.

Richard de Bury: 14th century
Philobiblion
Trans. by E. C. Thomas

Student Rivalries

¶ IN THESE DAYS there happened at Oxford a grave misfortune. For during two whole years was there great strife between the men of the south and the men of Wales on the one side and the northerners on the other. Whence arose broils, quarrels, and ofttimes loss of life. In the first year the northerners were driven clean away from the university. And they laid their expulsion chiefly to my charge. But in the second year, in an evil hour, coming back to Oxford, they gathered by night, and denying us passage from our quarters by force of arms, for two days they strove sorely against us, breaking and plundering some of the halls of our side, and slaying certain of our men. Howbeit, on the third day our party, bravely strengthened by the help of Merton Hall, forced our adversaries shamefully to fly from the public streets, which for the two days they had held as a camp, and to take refuge in their own quarters. In short, we could not be quieted before many of our number had been indicted for felonious riot; and amongst them I, who am now writing, was indicted as the chief leader and abettor of the Welsh, and perhaps not unrighteously. And so indicted we were hardly acquitted, being tried by jury before the king's judge. From that day forth I feared the king, hitherto unknown to me in his power, and his laws, and I put hooks into my jaws.

> Adam of Usk: 14th century
> *Chronicon*
> Trans. by F. M. Thompson

University Administration[1]

THE BOOK OF PROCTORS OF THE ENGLISH NATION[2]

1333. Term of the Proctor of the English Nation

In the year of our Lord 1333, at a convocation of all the masters actively functioning in the English Nation, there was co-opted as

1. This Register illustrates the international character of the university members as well as some of the procedures of academic government.
2. The term "English Nation" applied to the English students at the University of Paris. Each ethnic group had its own internal organization and interests.

proctor of that Nation Master John of Scenighen, German, at the Church of Saint Julian the Poor on the Tuesday after Epiphany, the time being computed by Master Robert called Free, of the Norman Nation, from the time of his rectorship.

1333. The term of the proctor John of Waltirstone, a Scot

In the year of our Lord 1332, at a convocation of all the masters actively functioning in the English Nation, there was co-opted as proctor of that Nation Master John of Waltirstone, a Scot, at the Church of Saint Julian the Poor on Friday next after the Feast of Purification of the Holy Virgin Mary, the time being computed by Master Peter Vieuxchamp, who during the preceding year was the sponsor of the said Nation and after everything had been accounted for was under obligation to the aforesaid Nation in the sum of 38 shillings, 8 pence, and a farthing—three silver farthings, however, to be deducted from that sum. . . .

Item: Under the said master John Waltirstone, Philip of Brechin, a Scot, who had no funds, took the baccalaureat.

Item: Under the same master, Master Andrew of Kalys, a German, who had no funds, took the baccalaureat.

Item: Under the same master John, Master William of Ramesland, English, who had three shillings, took the baccalaureat.

Item: Under the same master John, Master Andrew of Buyirgast, a Scot, whose funds were four shillings, took the baccalaureat.

Item: Under the same master, Master William of Edinburgh, whose funds were four shillings, took the baccalaureat.

Item: Under the aforementioned, Master Christian of Elst, whose funds were four shillings, took the baccalaureat.

Item: Under the same master, Master Walker of Coventry, whose funds were three shillings, took the baccalaureat.

Item: Under the same master, Master Rudolf of Cologne, who had no funds, took the baccalaureat.

Item: Under Master John of Scenighen, Master Reynard of Aix, whose funds were four shillings, took the baccalaureat.

Item: Under the same master, Master Herman of Gotland, whose funds were four shillings, took the baccalaureat.

Item: On St. Bartholomew's Day, at a convocation of all the masters of the English Nation at the Church of Saint Maturin, at the first hour, the question arose, in council, the aforementioned masters being present: Whether it was expedient for a certain sum of money, for which Master Conrad was obligated to the Nation, to be given from the funds of the Nation so that the appeal of Master Conrad of Montpellier should be submitted to the Court, on account of his poverty, the money having been assigned for candles for the Blessed Mary: that within five or six days a means should be devised for securing possession of another sum of money to replace the money granted or given in the appeal of the aforementioned before the Roman Court and candles for the Blessed Mary to be bought.

It was resolved that it was the Nation's pleasure and also expedient to do so, since the Nation had no other funds, and it was for the honor of the Nation. The following Masters were present: I, Master Ulrich of Augsburg, proctor: Master Hugh Scott, Conrad of Montpellier, Master Andrew of Poland, Master Jean de Gaspard, Master Theodore of Trèves, Master Werner Wolfram. . . .

In the same year of the Lord, on the eighth day of the month of March, all the masters actively functioning in the English Nation, a convocation was held at the Church of Saint Maturin, through the principal beadle of the said Nation, as is customary, for ordination. It was proposed and was so resolved for the supplicants by unanimous vote of all the masters, principally for the glory of God and the Blessed Virgin and consequently for the honor of the entire Nation, for them and their successors in perpetuity, that every year, through the sponsor of the said Nation at the time, there should be distributed a sum of money for twelve masters in the service of God at the Church of Saint Cosimo and Saint Damian, or elsewhere as the Nation arranges. . . . The masters also resolved that Bachelors and Licentiates, as elsewhere decided, should attend at the prescribed hours, and whoever was absent at vespers or compline should pay four pence, six pence for masses. If he does not pay when asked by the beadle in behalf of his Nation, for his insolence he shall pay one pound of wax for a candle to the Blessed Virgin.

H. Denifle
Chartularium Universitatis Parisensis,
Vol. I. Paris, 1889–1897
Trans. by H. E. W.

Judas Scene[1]

JUDAS: This penny is red.
CAIAPHAS: 'Tis good enough to buy meat and bread.
J.: This one is bad.
C.: Judas, hear what a good ring it has.
J.: This one is broken.
C.: Well, take another and stop grumbling.
J.: This one has a hole in it.
C.: Take another, then; here is a good one.
J.: This one has a false stamp.
C.: If you don't want it, I'll give you another.
J.: This one is black.
C.: Look at this one, and be done with it.
J.: This crack is altogether too large.
C.: Judas, if you'll hang yourself, here's a rope.
J.: This one is leaden.
C.: How long are you going to make fun of us?

Trierer Marienklage: 15th century
Trans. by Kuno Francke, 1903

Feudal Law[2]

¶ IN THE PREVIOUS BOOK, we discussed the origin of the feud and the progress of feudal law to the point where it reached such a magnitude that, leaving far behind both civil and pontifical law, it arrogated to itself juristic dominance. These matters we expounded,

1. Compare the subtlety of this scriptural parody with the somewhat coarse selection from the *Carmina Burana* included earlier. Out of context this scene may not be immediately meaningful, but careful rereading will bring out the subtle and powerful humor of the piece.
2. A later exposition, though not too far removed from the medieval feudal system to illuminate legal points concerning the possession of feuds, this selection shows the highly complicated procedures regarding feudal possession. Feuds (or fees or fiefs) were lands held from a lord in return for service given him.

as far as could be deduced from the writings of ancient authors and the commentaries of the most learned scholars. We further added a definition of feud and classified it, to clarify its character and significance. Then, though not with distinction, at least in so far as we could, we proceeded to reveal the causes, both efficient and material, that create a feud, grant and receive it, and that can be comprehended into a feud—all of which constitutes the subject of feuds.

It now remains for us to discuss the formal cause of the feud, and how a feud arises and becomes *in esse*, as the schoolmen are wont to say, so that it really is in being, and can be said to be so. For form gives existence to a thing and without it a thing cannot subsist. Of the categories of feuds previously postulated, there was one category that distinguished the new feud and the old. In respect of the old feud, it is acquired either by succession, or by a renewal of investiture—of which later. The new feud that is established from the beginning, in order to be so, consists of three parts: acquisition, constitution, and consummation. The form of the new feud consists of these elements: it is either acquired, or constituted, or consummated. These several factors have their own peculiar forms established by law: they cannot be disregarded. In respect of the acquisition of a new feud, as we suggested previously, in regard to the persons establishing a feud, everyone may grant or receive a feud who is permitted by law to give away property or to receive such property. And just as all things that have to do with the commerce of men can be given in feud, provided they are immobile, so too, it must here be added, in the same manner in which, by international or civil law, possession of things is acquired, feuds can, if the circumstances demand, similarly be constituted. Thus by donation, purchase, exchange and in the prescribed form, by prescription, stipulations, obligations, a feud is acquired. But here I take the term *feud* as a feudal contract. For I mentioned previously that the word *feud* is a homonym and sometimes signifies the contract itself and on occasion the hereditary right and the estate. Thus to be acquired by contract a feud is established by investiture without prescription.

But before we expound from the beginning the methods of acquiring a new feud, we must first explain through what persons a feud is acquired. In so far as feudal law is concerned, almost nothing is expressed on this matter except that we can acquire feuds either through those who are in our jurisdiction or through proctors or attorneys. But if the words of the texts are carefully weighed, we shall perceive that the reference extends beyond serfs or a proctor. The classes of persons are known from civil law, so that some have jurisdiction over themselves, while others are under the jurisdiction of others. Again, of those who are under the jurisdiction of others, some are serfs, others are under the authority of their parents. Serfs acquired everything for their masters, not only actual serfs who were completely under another's mastery, but even those who were merely employed, even if they served in good faith. What is still stranger, even another man's serfs, serving us in good faith, acquired possessions not for their own masters, but for those whom they served in good faith, because the act seemed to be performed for them and not for their real masters.

Sir Thomas Craig
Jus Feudale, Book 2
Trans. by H. E. W.

Part Seven

POETRY

Poetry was particularly plentiful throughout the Dark and Middle Ages and, obviously, popular. Sources of inspiration and imitation were sought in classical mythology, history, and Biblical and hagiographical literature. Gradually, and with increasing effect, secular motifs intruded, especially the love motif. Lyrical, devotional and patriotic themes also achieved popularity.

A Sixth-Century Epicure

REQUEST FOR FAVOR FROM A FEUDAL DUKE

The sheep comes running, shepherd,
And you provide its care.
So I come to you, my lord,
That you provide my fare.

CURSE ON THE CHEF!

Blackhearted wretch, all caked in smoke.
Face like a stewpot, smeared with soot.
Like your utensils, filthy black.
You three-legged pot, you slimy pan.
You don't deserve these verses mine.

I'll make a charcoal sketch instead,
Whose shameful likeness will recall
A pitch-blackhearted man withal.

TAKE IT EASY!

Drop business, lawsuits on the Palatine.
This festive table bids you dine and wine.
Let din of law and wrangling cases rest.
The day is joyous. To relax is best.

INVITATION TO DINE

'Twould be a pious deed, I vow
By Him who rules the stars above,
Or brother's care, a mother's love,
While I dine and eat enow,
Pray take you too a little food,
To make my pleasure doubly good.

Venantius Honorius Clementianus
Fortunatus: 6th century
Opera: Patrologia Latina, Vol. 88
Trans. by H. E. W.

Satan's Jealousy[1]

¶ WHEN HE beheld the new beings in their quiet abode, leading an undisturbed, happy life, accepting the law and obedient to the Lord of the Universe, and enjoying, amidst tranquil delights, the offerings placed before them, a spark of jealousy aroused his sudden vanity, and burning rancor grew into flaming bitterness.

It was then by chance near the time when he fell from on high and dragged his coiled length over the ground, and, crushing in his heart his recent downfall, he grieved the more that he had lost what another possessed.

Then his disgrace, steeped in resentment, thus poured forth its complaints from his heart, and released sighs with these words:

"Alas! That this creature should suddenly arise against me and that the hateful race should have grown by my downfall! Virtue kept me aloft; now, behold! abandoned I am driven forth and slime has taken the place of my angel prestige! The earth controls heaven; the soil, with the support of a foul fetter, reigns, and my power has been transferred and has gone from me!

"Yet it has not perished entirely. A large part retains its own force, and reputedly is most mighty in its power to harm. I am resolved not to defer aught; now, as the situation is, I shall enter the lists in cozening competition, while the first salvation, and candor untried and unaware of any wiles will be open to attack. And better will they alone be trapped by treachery, before they send their prolific progeny into the eternal ages. Naught immortal must be permitted to come forth upon the earth. Let the source of the race perish; sundering head from limbs will be the seed of death. Let the principle of life produce varieties of death; let them all be stricken as one. The root, once destroyed, shall not produce a live trunk. In my misery these consolations alone remain to me. If I cannot mount once more into the barriers of heaven, let heaven be closed to them as well. My fall must be considered lighter, if the new creature is destroyed by a like

---

1. This and the following selection, translated from the dactylic hexameters of Avitus, have been rendered in prose to illustrate better the interesting comparison with Milton's descriptions in *Paradise Lost*.

fate, if as a companion in destruction it experiences like punishments, and shares with me the fires that I foresee. But, that the reason for my deceit may not be thought puzzling, I must explain how of my own accord I once fell and rushed into headlong ruin: the expulsion that drove me from heaven, let it drive man too from the threshold of paradise."

Thus he spoke, and lamentations ended his doleful utterances.

Avitus: 6th century
Poematum de Mosaicae Historiae Gestis Libri V: Patrologia Latina, Vol. 59
Trans. by H. E. W.

Paradise

¶ So WHERE, beyond the Indies, the source of the universe begins, where it is said the earth joins its confines to heaven, a grove inaccessible to all mortals stands on a height, enclosed by an eternal barrier after he who committed the first crime fell and was driven forth; and in place of the guilty ones deservedly torn from their blissful abode, this sacred land now has heavenly ministrants. Here frost never comes in the alternating sequence of time, nor do the suns of summer return after the cold, when the cosmic course makes the year warm, nor do the fields turn white with frost under the thickening ice. Here the mildness of heaven maintains a perpetual springtime. The boisterous south wind is absent, and ever, in the limpid air, the mountains escape the clouds vanishing in the calm sky. Nor does the character of the region require rains that it does not experience, but the seeds are dowered, content with their own dew.

All the soil is verdant continuously, and the appearance of the steaming earth gleams pleasant. Always the grass stands upon the hills, and foliage on the trees. When they spread with frequent blossoming, they make their seeds firm with swift-flowing sap. For whatever comes forth for us during an entire year, a month's time ripens the fruit there. The lilies, never languid in the sun, glow. Nor does touch defile the violets, and comeliness, preserving the blush of the rose, pervades it with perpetual beauty. So, since there is no winter, and no burning summer's heat, autumn fills the year with produce, and spring with flowers. Here grows cinnamon that, as the false tale runs, is the gift of the Sabaeans. A living bird collects it when, at its birth, its end is nigh, and, burning its nest, it survives and is reborn, after seeking its own death; and not content to be born once only in its proper cycle, the prolonged age of its ancient body is renewed, and repeated rebirths freshen its consumed age.

There the branch exuding fragrant balsam urges on its perpetual flow from the rich stem. Then if haply a light breeze blows, the dense forest, stirred by faint zephyrs and gentle murmur, trembles in its leaves and health-giving flowers that, spreading afar, give forth sweet perfumes. Here a spring arises, aglow with clear gurgling water: the glowing beauty of silver is not such, nor do crystals draw such luminence from their glittering coldness. Here the verge of the river banks disdains the green-hued pebbles, and there rocks abound, gems that the arrogant world admires. The fields present varied hues, and adorn the plains with the diadem of Nature.

Avitus: 6th century
Poematum de Mosaicae Historiae Gestis Libri V: Patrologia Latina, Vol. 59
Trans. by H. E. W.

Processional

The banners of the King go forth,
Glistens the Cross's mystery
That flesh's Builder in the flesh
Was on a gibbet hung.

His vitals were transfixed with nails,
He stretched out His hands and feet:
For grace of our redemption
This Host was sacrificed.

Upon the cross He hung, wounded
By the point of a dire lance.
That He might wash us of our sins
He dripped water and blood.

Fulfilled is all that David sang
In his prophetic song of Faith,
Declaring to the nations,
"God from wood has reigned."

The tree is fit and glorious,
Adorned with purple of the King,
Chosen by honorable gift
To touch such sacred limbs.

Blessed it is upon whose arms
Has hung the ransom of an age;
It has become the body's scales
And taken spoil of hell.

You pour a sweet smell from your bark,
You outdo nectar in your taste.
Fertile with a joyous fruit,
In noble triumph you praise.

Hail altar, hail the Victim
For glory of the passion
By which life has accomplished death
And through death life restored.

Fortunatus; 6th century
Trans. by Albert Cook

Lament on Life

Lo! I sing cheerily
    In my bright days,
But now all wearily
    Chaunt I my lays;
Sorrowing tearfully,
    Saddest of men,
Can I sing cheerfully,
    As I could then?

Many a verity
  In those glad times
Of my prosperity
  Taught I in rhymes;
New from forgetfulness
  Wanders my tongue,
Wasting in fretfulness,
  Meters unsung.

Worldliness brought me here
  Foolishly blind,
Riches have wrought me here
  Sadness of mind;
When I rely on them,
  Lo! they depart—
Bitterly, fie on them!
  Rend they my heart.

Why did your songs to me,
  World-loving men,
Say joy belongs to me
  Ever as then?
Why did ye lyingly
  Think such a thing,
Seeing how flyingly
  Wealth may take wing?

Boethius: 6th century
De Consolatione Philosophiae
Translation attributed to King Alfred
the Great (and later modernized)

Love Rejected

HE:

To my God I'd like to turn,
And my wife I want to spurn.
Lord, naught else I crave but this,
In thy service gaining bliss.
Hence, my wife, from me.

314

SHE: God once joined us joyfully,
      Blessed my spirit happily.
      With my husband at my side
      I'd have known the Lord's own pride,
      With my husband dear.

HE: Ruination spares my lot,
      What you say means not one jot.
      If you crave to wed again,
      Go and seek 'mong other men.
      Hence, my wife, from me.

SHE: Day and night I grieve and moan,
      And bewail my dearest own.
      If the Lord keeps you away,
      By my side you cannot stay,
      O my husband dear.

Hisperica Famina: 6th–7th century
Trans. by H. E. W.

St. Eulalie

A good maiden was Eulalie,
beautiful was her body, more beautiful her soul.
The enemies of God wanted to subdue her,
wanted to make her serve Satan.
She would not have listened to the evil counselors
Without denying God who dwells above in heaven,
neither for gold, nor for silver, nor for raiment,
nor by royal threats, nor by prayer.
Nothing could ever make her yield,
The maid, without her always loving the service of God.
And so she was handed over before Maximian,
Who was, in those days, king of the heathens.
And he exhorted her to do what she had no care to do,
To renounce the name of Christian.
She preferred to give her life.

She would endure the tortures rather than lose her virginity.
For that she died in great honor.
They cast her into the fire, that she should burn in an instant.
She had no sin; that is why she did not burn.
The heathen king, despite that, would not convert.
He ordered her head to be cut off with a sword.
The maiden did not oppose this.
She is willing to leave the times, if Christ orders it.
In the form of a dove she flew away to heaven.
We all pray that she may deign to pray for us,
So that Christ may have mercy on us
after death, and let us come to Him
in His mercy.

Cantilena of St. Eulalie: 9th century
Trans. by H. E. W.

Lament for Charlemagne

From Eastern land to Western shore
Resounds the wailing evermore.
Alas! Alas for me!

Beyond the hosts across the mere
There's naught but piteous grief to hear.
Alas! Alas for me!

The Franks, the Romans, Christians true,
Heart-stricken, now have much to rue.
Alas! Alas for me!

Children, elders, nobles great
And mothers grieve the king's sad fate.
Alas! Alas for me!

The streaming tears shall never cease.
The world is mourning Charles' decease.
Alas! Alas for me!

Father he was to orphans poor,
To pilgrims, widows, maids demure.
Alas! Alas for me!

Lord Christ, who rule the host of heaven,
Send rest to Charles in Thy realm.
Alas! Alas for me!

This is the plea of Christians true,
Saints and widows, maidens too.
Alas! Alas for me!

An inscribed grave of earth lies o'er
The peace of Charles, now no more.
Alas! Alas for me!

Holy Spirit, that rules all thing,
Exalt his soul and comfort bring.
Alas! Alas for me!

Woe to Romans, woe to Rome.
Karolus rests in his last home.
Alas! Alas for me!

Woe to you, Italy fair.
Woe to every city there.
Alas! Alas for me!

France has suffered direful woes:
Grief no other nation knows.
Alas! Alas for me!

When earthy tomb in Aachen town
Covered that king of great renown.
Alas! Alas for me!

Dread dreams assailed me in the night.
The freshing day brought me no light.
Alas! Alas for me!

That carried to his death our king
Whose praises o'er the earth now ring.
Alas! Alas for me!

Columban, be done with weeping.
Pray for him in God's own keeping.
Alas! Alas for me!

Merciful Lord, Father of all,
Grant him a seat in Thy luminous hall.
Alas! Alas for me!

Embattled God, of heaven and hell,
In holy seat pray let him dwell.
Alas! Alas for me!

Among Thy own apostles let,
O Christ, this holy man be set.
Alas! Alas for me!

Anonymous: 9th century[1]
Poetae Latini Aevi Carolini 1
Trans. by H. E. W.

The Seafarer

Sooth the song that I of myself can sing,
Telling of my travels; how in troublous days,
Hours of hardship oft I've borne!
With a bitter breast-care I have been abiding:
Many seats of sorrow in my ship have known!
Frightful was the whirl of waves, when it was my part
Narrow watch at night to keep, on my Vessel's prow
When it rushed the rocks along. By the rigid cold
Fast my feet were pinched, fettered by the frost,
By the chains of cold. Care was sighing then
Hot my heart around; hunger rent to shreds
Courage in me, sea-wearied! This the man knows not,
He to whom it happens, happiest on earth,
How I, carked with care, in the ice-cold sea,
Overwent the winter on my wander-ways,

---

1. It has been suggested that the anonymous author may have been a monk attached to the Italian monastery of Bobbio.

All forlorn of happiness, all bereft of loving kinsmen,
Hung about with icicles; flew the hail in showers.
Nothing heard I here save the howling of the sea,
And the ice-chilled billow, 'whiles the crying of the swan.
All the glee I got me was the gannet's scream,
And the swoughing of the seal, 'stead of mirth of men;
'Stead of the mead-drinking, moaning of the sea-mew.
There the storms smote on the crags, there the swallow of the sea
Answered to them, icy-plumed; and that answer oft the earn—
Wet his wings were—barked aloud.
                              None of all my kinsmen
Could this sorrow-laden soul stir to any joy.
Little then docs he believe who life's pleasure owns,
While he tarries in the towns, and but trifling ills,
Proud and insolent with wine—how outwearied I
Often must outstay on the ocean path!
Somber grew the shade of night, and it snowed from northward,
Frost the field enchained, fell the hail on earth,
Coldest of all grains.
                              Wherefore now then crash together
Thoughts my soul within that I should myself adventure
The high streamings of the sea, and the sport of the salt waves!
For a passion of the mind every moment pricks me on
All my life to set a faring; so that far from hence,
I may seek the shore of the strange outlanders.
Yes, so haughty of his heart is no hero on the earth,
Nor so good in all his giving, nor so generous in youth,
Nor so daring in his deed, nor so dear unto his lord,
That he has not always yearning unto his seafaring,
To whatever work his Lord may have will to make for him.
For the harp he has no heart, nor for having of the rings,
Nor in woman is his weal, in the world he's no delight,
Nor in anything whatever save the tossing o'er the waves!
Oh, forever he has longing who is urged towards the sea.
Trees rebloom with blossoms, burghs are fair again,
Winsome are the wide plains, and the world is gay—
All doth only challenge the impassioned heart
Of his courage to the voyage, whosoever thus bethinks him,
O'er the ocean billows, far away to go.
Every cuckoo calls a warning, with his chant of sorrow!

Sings the summer's watchman, sorrow is he boding,
Bitter in the bosom's hoard. This the brave man wots not of,
Not the warrior rich in welfare—what the wanderer endures,
Who his paths of banishment, widest places on the sea.
For behold, my thought hovers now above my heart;
O'er the surging flood of sea now my spirit flies,
O'er the homeland of the whale—hovers then afar
O'er the foldings of the earth! Now again it flies to me
Full of yearning, greedy! Yells that lonely flier;
Whets upon the Whale-way irresistibly my heart,
O'er the storming of the seas!

Anglo-Saxon: 9th century
Trans. by Stopford Brooke

Watch-Song

O you who guard with arms this wall,
Sleep not, I warn, beyond recall.
While Hector watched in Troy of old
The wily Greeks could get no hold.
But Troy asleep at start of night,
Sly Sinon freed the Argive might.

By a rope the hidden Greeks slid down,
Invaded Troy and burned the town.
The wakeful geese with fearful call
Drove from Rome the assaulting Gaul.
Then were the geese, in silver gleam,
Revered by Rome as gods supreme.

Adore we Christ's divinity
And hail His praise in harmony.
Trusting in His watchful gaze
Watchfully let's hymn His praise.
Guard divine, Christ, King of all,
Watch and guard for us this wall.

To us be a wall impregnable,
To enemies be terrible.
No force can harm Thee vigilant,
Who rout all armies militant.
Gird these our walls, O Christ our Lord,
Defending them with Thy stout sword.

Holy Mary, Christ's own mother,
St. John too, secure this favor.
Your pledges here we venerate,
To you these walls are consecrate.
With him, men fight victorious.
Alone, spears fall inglorious.

Stout youth, courageous, bold in war,
Let your songs be heard afar.
And let each sentry armed stand,
To repulse every hostile band.
Let echo cry: "O soldier, watch!"
Let echo o'er the walls cry: "Watch!"

Anonymous: 9th century
Poetae Latini Aevi Carolini iii
Trans. by H. E. W.

Song of the Pilgrims[1]

Fair city of Rome, lording it over all
Cities on earth, and also most glorious,
Red and bedewed with the blood of the martyrs,
Shining and white with the lilies so virginal,
We greet you and bless you and hail through the ages.

Peter, knight puissant, O heavenly guardian,
Hearken in friendship to vows of the prayerful.
Sitting in judgment on all the tribes, twelve of them,
Judge us with mercy, mildly, indulgently.
Compassionate be when you make your decision
On earthly petitions that beg intercession.

---

1. This poem was intended to be sung by pilgrims bound for the tomb of
St. Peter in Rome.

Accept our entreaties, O Paulus, we beg you,
Whose persistence has conquered age-old philosophies.
Now in the royal mansion a chamberlain
Bring forth the dishes of all divine favors
So that through your teachings wisdom may come to us,
The wisdom that is in you now so abundantly.

Anonymous: 10th century
Text in J. Lindsay, *Medieval Latin
Poets:* London, 1934
Trans. by H. E. W.

Invitation to Love

Darling beloved,
Close to my heart,
Come into my chamber,
Gracious with art.

It has benches and hangings
And fairest of flowers.
There's sweet-scented grasses,
All clustered in bowers.

The tables are laden
With rarest of dishes.
The wine flows abundant,
There's all that one wishes.

Sweet harmonies echo,
And flutes play melodious.
A lad and a maiden
Sing songs that are glorious.

Her lyre is so lyric.
Softly his lute plays.
Filled goblets stand ready
To gladden the days.

322

Before sweet endearments
I care not for eating,
Nor so much abundance
As intimate meeting.

Come now, my dear sister,
Bright light of my eyes,
More loved than all others,
To your soul my soul cries.

All alone in the forest,
I sought sheltered places.
I shunned every tumult,
And avoided strange faces.

Dearest, don't tarry long,
Let's love while we both may.
Without you, life's fruitless.
Our love calls this day.

What boots it to tarry?
Delay, love, is wasted.
Do now what you shall do;
Ripe fruit must be tasted.

Anonymous: 10th century
Text in K. Breul, *The Cambridge
Songs;* Cambridge, 1915
Trans. by H. E. W.

The Good Old Days

Good was the age in the time of the ancients,
For faith was there, and justice and love;
Belief also, of which there is little now.
Everything is changed, it has lost its color.
Nevermore will it be as it was with the ancients.

St. Alexis: 11th century
Trans. by H. E. W.

Saint Alexis' Heavenly Love

St. Alexis is in heaven without any doubt.
He dwells with God in the company of the angels
With the maiden from whom he kept himself separated.
Now he has her near him,
Together are their souls,
I cannot tell you how great is their joy.

St. Alexis: 11th century
Trans. by H. E. W.

Come, Thou Holy Spirit

Come, Thou Holy Spirit, come,
And from Thy celestial home
Shed a ray of light divine.
Come, Thou Father of the poor,
Come, Thou Source of all our store,
Come, within our bosoms shine.

Comforter art Thou the best,
Thou the soul's most welcome guest,
Sweet refreshment here below.
In our labor rest most sweet,
Grateful coolness in the heat,
Solace in the midst of woe.

Heal our wounds, our strength renew,
On our dryness pour Thy dew,
Wash the stains of guilt away.
Bend the stubborn heart and will,
Melt the frozen, warm the chill,
Guide the steps that else would stray.

On the faithful, who adore
And confess Thee evermore,
In Thy sevenfold gifts descend.
Give them virtue's sure reward,
Give them Thy salvation, Lord,
Give them joys that never end.

Robert II, King of France: 11th century
Trans. by Edward Caswall

Woman Is Evil

Now with my tired pen,
I cease writing about the character of the evil woman,
because I have written less than is fitting.
If I were granted the tongue of Ovid, or of Cato,
and the mighty eloquence of exalted tongues, still
I could not explain in words and describe in writing
how cunning an evil woman is, how treacherous, how
shrewd, how destructive, or how wily.
Let all know my final word:
A good woman is a rarity; if there is a good woman,
she deserves a crown.

Petrus Pictor: 12th century
De Mala Muliere
Trans. by H. E. W.

The Battle of Life

Battlefields make up our life:
Enemies, and constant strife.
That's the way we live.

Not a day without a fight,
Not a night without its blight,
But a glimpse of peace.

Exposed I stand quite free from fear,
With din of battle coming near.
Wounds I scorn withal.

Wrath of foe shall pass me by.
Public wrath I shall defy,
War machines as well.

Lo! He comes from out of heaven,
By a cloud packed densely driven,
Ruler of the stars.

Against the ruthless foes that beat
Upon the mind, against defeat,
Battling I fight on.

Their bows and arrows he will break,
The foe's own weapons he will take
With his eternal fires.

So in fearless might I tower.
Nobly I shall overpower
Barbaric enemies.

Anonymous: 12 century
Trans. by H. E. W.

Advice to a Son

Astrolabe, my son, darling of your father,
I bequeath a few precepts
For your training.
Let your concern for learning
Be greater than for teaching.
By the latter you benefit others;
By the former, yourself.
When there is nothing more to learn,
Cease learning,
And say not you must stop before then.
Consider only what is said, not by whom.

Things well said bring glory to the author.
Pledge not allegiance to a favorite master,
Nor let the scholar hold you by his love.
Everyone is nourished by the fruit,
Not the leaves, of the tree.
And sense should be preferred to form.

Abelard: 12th century
Astrolabius, edited by H. Brinkman
Trans. by H. E. W.

Contempt of the World

O land without guilt, strong city, safe built in a marvellous place,
I cling to thee, ache for thee, sing to thee, wake for thee, watch for
    thy face:
Full of cursing and strife are the days of my life; with their sins they
    are fed,
Out of sin is the root, unto sin is the fruit, in their sins they are dead.
No deserving of mine can make answer to thine, neither I unto thee;
I a child of God's wrath, made subject to death, what good thing is
    in me?
Yet through faith I require thee, through hope I desire thee, in hope
    I hold fast,
Crying out day and night that my soul may have sight of thy joy at
    the last.
Me, even me hath the Father set free, and hath bidden come in:
In sin hath He found me, from sin hath unbound me, and purged me
    of sin.
In His strength am I glad, whom my weakness made sad; I that slept
    am awake;
With the eyes that wept, with the spirit that slept, I give thanks for
    His sake.
Things weak He makes sure, things unclean He makes pure, with His
    fresh watersprings;
Throughout all lands He goeth, for all things He floweth, and hallow-
    eth all things.

327

O home of salvation, a chosen nation, a royal race
Doth build and possess thee, increase thee and bless thee, engird and
    embrace;
Every heart boweth down to that grace which doth crown thee, O
    Sion, O peace!
Time is there none in thee, stars neither sun in thee rise not nor
    cease;
Of the saints art thou trod, and made glorious of God; thou art full
    of thy Lord;
And the sound of thee rings from the great ten strings of the deca-
    chord.
Thou hast lilies made sweet for their maiden feet who were clothed
    with lowliness;
And roses blood-red, as a saint's blood shed, in the beauty of holiness.
With His wings He shall cover thee, He that rules over thee even the
    Son,
The Mystic Lion, the Lamb out of Sion, the God which is One;
Purged of all reveling, clear of all travailing, pure of all strife,
Land of glad hours, made fair with new flowers, and sweet with new
    life.

> Bernard of Cluny: 12th century
> *De Contemptu Mundi*
> Trans. by Algernon Charles Swin-
> burne

Lament of
Richard the Lion-Hearted

Ah, certes will no prisoner tell his tale
    Fitly, unless as one whom woes befall,
Still, as a solace, songs may much avail:
    Friends I have many, yet the gifts are small—
Shame! that because to ransom me they fail,
    I've pined two years in thrall.

But all my liegemen in fair Normandy,
    In England, Poitou, Gascony, know well
That not my meanest follower would I
    Leave for gold's sake in prison-house to dwell;
Reproach I neither kinsman nor ally—
    Yet I am still in thrall.

Alas! I may as certain truth rehearse,
    Nor kin nor friends have captives and the dead:
'Tis bad for me, but for my people worse,
    If to desert me they through gold are led;
After my death, 'twill be to them a curse
    If they leave me in thrall.

No marvel, then, if I am sad at heart
    Each day my lord disturbs my country more;
Has he forgot that he too had a part
    In the deep oath which before God we swore?
But yet in truth I know, I shall not smart
    Much longer here in thrall.

                    Provençal: 12th century
                  Trans. early 19th century

A Song of Winter

Cold, cold!
Cold tonight is broad Moylurg,
Higher the snow than the mountain range,
The deer cannot get at their food.

Cold till Doom!
The storm has spread over all:
A river is each furrow upon the slope,
Each ford a full pool.

A great tidal sea is each loch,
A full loch is each pool:
Horses cannot get over the ford of Ross,
No more can two feet get there.

The fish of Ireland are a-roaming,
There is no strand which the wave does not pound,
Not a town there is in the land,
Not a bell is heard, no crane talks.

The wolves of Cuan-wood get
Neither rest nor sleep in their lair,
The little wren cannot find
Shelter in her nest on the slope of Lon.

Keen wind and cold ice
Has burst upon the little company of birds,
The blackbird cannot get a lee to her liking,
Shelter for its side in Cuan-wood.

Cozy our pot on its hook,
Crazy the hut on the slope of Lon:
The snow has crushed the wood here,
Toilsome to climb up Ben-bo.

Glenn Rye's ancient bird
From the bitter wind gets grief;
Great her misery and her pain,
The ice will get into her mouth.

From flock and from down to rise—
Take it to heart!—were folly for thee:
Ice in heaps on every ford—
That is why I say "cold"!

Irish Folk Song:? 13th century
Trans. by Kuno Meyer

A Reluctant Farewell

Innsprück, I must forsake thee,
My weary way betake me
    Unto a foreign shore,
And all my joy hath vanished,
And ne'er while I am banished
    Shall I behold it more.

I bear a load of sorrow,
And comfort can I borrow,
    Dear love, from thee alone,
Ah, let thy pity hover
About thy weary lover
    When he is far from home.

My one true love! Forever
Thine will I bide, and never
    Shall our dear vow be vain.
Now must our Lord God ward thee,
In peace and honor guard thee,
    Until I come again.

German Folk Song

Rondel

Is there a paradise, my dove?
What is paradise but love?
'Tis nothing really, my sweet love.
Where is paradise, my dove?
He who sleeps in love's embrace
Will enter paradise apace.
Where is paradise, my dove?
What is paradise but love?

Anonymous: 13th century
G. Raynaud, *Recueil de Motets Français des Douzième et Treizième Siècles* (Paris, 1883), Vol. 2
Trans. by H. E. W.

Life of Saint Millán

He walked those mountains wild, and lived within that nook
For forty years and more, nor ever comfort took
Of offer'd food or alms, or human speech a look;
No other saint in Spain did such a penance brook.

For many a painful year he pass'd the seasons there,
And many a night consumed in penitence and prayer—
In solitude and cold, with want and evil fare,
His thoughts to God resigned, and free from human care.

Oh! sacred is the place, the fountain and the hill,
The rocks where he reposed, in meditation still,
The solitary shades through which he roved at will:
His presence all that place with sanctity did fill.

Gonzalo de Berceo: 13th century
Trans. by Hookman Frere

A Wandering Student's Petition

I, a wandering scholar lad,
　Born for toil and sadness,
Oftentimes am driven by
　Poverty to madness.

Literature and knowledge I
　Fain would still be earning
Were it not that want of pelf
　Makes me cease from learning.

These torn clothes that cover me
　Are too thin and rotten;
Oft I have to suffer cold,
　By the warmth forgotten.

Scarce I can attend at church
    Sing God's praises duly;
Mass and vespers both I miss,
    Though I love them truly.

Oh, thou pride of N——,
    By thy worth I pray thee
Give the suppliant help in need,
    Heaven will sure repay thee.

Take a mind unto thee now
    Like unto St. Martin;
Clothe the pilgrim's nakedness,
    Wish him well at parting.

So may God translate your soul
    Into peace eternal,
And the bliss of saints be yours
    In His realm supernal.

> *Carmina Burana:* 13th century
> Trans. by J. A. Symonds, *Wine, Women, and Song*

Drinking Joys

Mistress drinks and master drinks.
Knights gets plastered, clerics clink.
This one drinks and that one too.
Servants can and maids oft do.
The swift, the slack,
The white, the black,
Of booze they never have a lack.

The steadfast man can take a nip,
The traveler always takes a sip.
The boor's a toper day and night.
The wizard too can get quite tight.

The sick and poor can drink their fill.
The exile and the stranger swill.
The youngster takes his liquor hard,
And so does every old dotard.
Bishops drink. You think they don't?
Deacons too, for that's their wont.

Beer for sister, beer for brother,
Beer for crone and beer for mother.
Men and maidens, drink it up!
Hundreds, thousands, love their cup.

Carmina Burana: 13th century
Trans. by H. E. W.

Gretchen

Up to this time, well-away!
I concealed the truth from day,
    Went on loving skillfully.

Now my fault at length is clear;
That the hour of need is near,
    From my shape all eyes can see.

So my mother gives me blows,
So my father curses throws;
    They both beat me savagely.

In the house alone I sit,
Dare not walk about the street,
    Nor at play in public be.

If I walk about the street,
Every one I chance to meet
    Scans me like a prodigy;

When they see the load I bear,
All the neighbors nudge and stare,
    Gaping while I hasten by;

With their elbows nudge, and so
With their finger point, as though
    I were some monstrosity;

Me with nods and winks they spurn,
Judge me fit in flames to burn
    For one lapse from honesty.

Why this tedious tale prolong?
Short, I am become a song,
    In all mouths a mockery.

By this am I done to death,
Sorrow kills me, chokes my breath,
    Ever weep I bitterly.

One thing makes me still more grieve,
That my friend his home must leave
    For the same cause instantly;

Therefore is my sadness so
Multiplied, weighed down with woe,
    For he too will part.

Carmina Burana: 13th century
Trans. by J. A. Symonds, *Wine, Women, and Song*

Cast Aside Study!

Cast aside dull books and thought;
    Sweet is folly, sweet is play;
Take the pleasure Spring hath brought
    In youth's opening holiday!
Right it is old age should ponder
    On grave matters fraught with care;
Tender youth is free to wander,
    Free to frolic light as air.
Like a dream our prime is flown,
    Prisoned in a study;
Sport and folly are youth's own,
    Tender youth and ruddy.

Lo, the Spring of life slips by,
　　Frozen Winter comes apace;
Strength is 'minished silently,
　　Care writes wrinkles on our face;
Blood dries up and courage fails us,
　　Pleasures dwindle, joys decrease,
Till old age at length assails us
　　With a troop of illnesses.
Like a dream our prime is flown,
　　Prisoned in a study;
Sport and folly are youth's own,
　　Tender youth and ruddy.

Live we like the gods above;
　　This is wisdom, this is truth;
Chase the joys of tender love
　　In the leisure of our youth!
Keep the vows we swore together,
　　Lads, obey that ordinance;
Seek the fields in sunny weather,
　　Where the laughing maidens dance.
Like a dream our prime is flown,
　　Prisoned in a study;
Sport and folly are youth's own,
　　Tender youth and ruddy.

There the lads who lists may see
　　Which among the maids is kind;
There young limbs deliciously
　　Flashing through the dances wind;
While the girls their arms are raising,
　　Moving, winding o'er the lea,
Still I stand and gaze, and gazing
　　They have stolen the soul of me!
Like a dream our prime is flown,
　　Prisoned in a study;
Sport and folly are youth's own,
　　Tender youth and ruddy.

Carmina Burana: 13th century
Trans. by J. A. Symonds, *Wine, Women, and Song*

Love's Plight

Tongue deceitful and mendacious,
Venomous and so loquacious,
Pull it out: it gets my ire.
Throw it in a blazing fire.

Calls me a deceiver ever,
Lover faithless but so clever—
Abandoning my former mistress,
Causing this one endless distress.

By the Muses nine I swear
And the god who for his fair
Victims changed himself to gold
And form of bull, to keep his hold.

By all the gods, by God divine,
I am not guilty of this crime.
By God divine and gods above,
I am not guilty, dear my love.

I swear by Mars, Apollo too,
Who know the art of those who woo,
I swear by you too, Cupid dear,
Whose wanton bow inspireth fear,

I swear by bow and arrows fierce
With which my heart you often pierce,
Sans guile, sans wile, sans each and both,
I vow to keep my sacred oath.

I vow to keep this holy oath:
To tell the reason nothing loth.
Among the hosts of damsels there,
There's ne'er a one I've seen more fair.

Among them you shine forth so bold
As pearl that nestles set in gold.
Shoulders, breast and thighs so shaped,
No goddess is more comely draped.

Brow and throat, your lips, your chin
Were made the gifts of love to win.
Your locks have held me in their sway,
Your golden locks in wild array.

Until, my love, the day turns night,
And toil becomes a peaceful sight,
Until the woods are bare of trees,
Until the fiery flame shall freeze,

Until the ocean knows no sail,
Until the Parthian weapons fail,
Mine, my dear, you'll always be
Nor e'er, I know, untrue to me.

Carmina Burana: 13th century
Trans. by H. E. W.

Earthly Vanity

All the world is just a madness.
Joys are false that offer gladness,
Passing, fading into air,
Like lilies of the field, I swear.

All is earthly, life is vain,
Offers nothing, shows no gain,
Drives the soul to deepest Hell,
Submerging us like watery well.

All I see upon this earth,
All I feel since primal birth,
I shall scorn or I shall be
Like the leaves on oaken tree.

338

All is carnal, laws shall die,
Vanishing like clouds on high,
Like shadows faint, funereal,
Like bodies not corporeal.

If we crush our fleshly lust
With the just and best we must
Enjoy the bliss of heaven in store
Through all the ages evermore.

Carmina Burana; 13th century
Trans. by H. E. W.

Love's Lament

O Love's own mate, O Love means sorrow,
Whose woes bode ill. Today, tomorrow
Gives no relief,
Brings only grief.

Alas, my sweet, a parting kiss
From you creates a heavenly bliss
For which the Trojan prince of old
Must have disdained fair Helen's hold.

Sing, O valley, joyfully,
Decked with roses gallantly,
Most resplendent of all vales
Queen of all the other dales,
Glory of the sun and moon,
Warbling notes of birds in tune,
Nightingale's delight and joy,
Solace for each love-sick boy.

Carmina Burana; 13th century
Trans. by H. E. W.

Bacchic Frenzy

Topers in and out of season!
'Tis not thirst but better reason
  Bids you tope on steadily!—
  Pass the wine-cup, let it be
  Filled and filled for bout on bout!
    Never sleep!
  Racy jest and song flash out!
    Spirits leap!

Those who cannot drink their rations,
Go, begone from these ovations!
  Here's no place for bashful boys;
  Like the plague, they spoil our joys—
  Bashful eyes bring rustic cheer
    When we're drunk,
  And a blush betrays a drear
    Want of spunk.

If there's here a fellow lurking
Who his proper share is shirking,
  Let the door to him be shown,
  From our crew we'll have him thrown—
  He's more desolate than death,
    Mixed with us;
  Let him go and end his breath!
    Better thus!

When your heart is set on drinking,
Drink on without stay or thinking,
  Till you cannot stand up straight,
  Nor one word articulate!—
  But herewith I pledge to you
    This fair health:
  May the glass no mischief do,
    Bring you wealth!

Wed not you the god and goddess,
For the god doth scorn the goddess;
   He whose name is Liber, he
   Glories in his liberty.
   All her virtue in the cup
     Runs to waste,
   And wine wedded yieldeth up
     Strength and taste.

Since she is the queen of ocean,
Goddess she may claim devotion;
   But she is no mate to kiss
   His superior holiness.
   Bacchus never deigned to be
     Watered, he!
   Liber never bore to be
     Christened, he!

Carmina Burana: 13th century
Trans. by J. A. Symonds, *Wine, Women, and Song*

Spring

Spring at last is come again,
Joyfully,
Decked with flowery blossomed train,
Glowingly.

Glades shine green the whole day long,
Sing the birds in tuneful song,
Melodiously.

Gather flowers, ye maidens fair,
Whose perfume must your swains ensnare
Wantonly.

Let us to the meadows hie
Mid dappled flowers and sunny sky
Sportingly.

Carmina Burana: 13th century
Trans. by H. E. W.

A Pastoral

There went out in the dawning light
   A little rustic maiden;
Her flock so white, her crook so slight,
   With fleecy new wool laden.

Small is the flock, and there you'll see
   The she-ass and the wether;
This goat's a he, and that's a she,
   The bull-calf and the heifer.

She looked upon the green sward, where
   A student lay at leisure:
"What do you there, young sir, so fair?
   Come, play with me, my treasure!"

Carmina Burana: 13th century
Trans. by J. A. Symonds,
Wine, Women, and Song

A Sequence in Praise of Wine

Wine the good and bland, thou blessing
Of the good, the bad's distressing,
Sweet of taste by all confessing,
   Hail, thou world's felicity!

Hail thy hue, life's gloom dispelling;
Hail thy taste, all tastes excelling;
By thy power, in this thy dwelling,
   Deign to make us drunk with thee!

342

Oh, how blest for bounteous uses
Is the birth of pure vine-juices!
Safe's the table which produces
   Wine in goodly quality.

Oh, in colour how auspicious!
Oh, in odour how delicious!
In the mouth how sweet, propitious
   To the tongue enthralled by thee!

Blest the man who first thee planted,
Called thee by thy name enchanted!
He whose cups have ne'er been scanted
   Dreads no danger that may be.

Blest the belly where thou bidest!
Blest the tongue where thou residest!
Blest the mouth through which thou glidest!
   And the lips thrice blest by thee!

Therefore let wine's praise be sounded,
Healths to topers all propounded;
We shall never be confounded,
   Toping for eternity!

Pray we: here be thou still flowing,
Plenty on our board bestowing,
While with jocund voice we're showing
   How we serve thee—Jubilee!

Poésies Populaires Latines du Moyen Âge, edited by E. Méril: 13th century

Trans. by J. A. Symonds, *Wine, Women, and Song*

Parzival Meets a Heathen[1]

Now many were sorely angered that I told not this tale afore,
Since it wearied them naught in the hearing—Now my words I with-
  hold no more,
But I give ye to wit full truly, as my mouth may the story tell,
The end of this wondrous venture for methinks it shall please ye well.
Ye shall know how the king, Anfortas, of his wound was made whole
  again—
Of the queen doth the venture tells us, who in far Pelrapär did reign;
How she kept a pure heart and loyal till the day of her great reward,
And earth's fairest crown was her guerdon at the hand of her faithful
  lord.
Ye shall hear the tale of its winning, if my skill fail me not alway;
Yet first must ye list the labor that Parzival wrought that day.

Now, tho' dauntless his hand had striven, but as children his foemen
  all,
And ne'er would I risk my hero might I rule that which shall befall.
I must sorrow sore for his peril, and fain would I speak him free,
But now must I trust that Good Fortune the shield of his heart may
  be.
For purity, and high courage, side by side in his heart they lay,
And ne'er had he cherished cowardice, nor shrunk from the knightly
  fray;
And I deem this shall surely give him such strength he his life may
  hold,
Since fierce strife draweth nigh unto him, and his foe is a hero bold.
For he meeteth a prince of battles who dauntless to strife doth ride,
And unbaptized was the foeman who rode here in his heathen pride.

Full soon had he come, our hero, to a mighty woodland shade,
And without, in the light of the dawning, his armor a knight displayed.

1. The theme of this medieval metrical romance is the Quest of the Holy
   Grail; the protagonist is the knight Parzival. In this passage, from Book 15,
   the Heathen turns out to be Parzival's own brother, Feirefis Angevin;
   together they ride off to King Arthur's court.

'Twere a marvel could I, a poor man, of the riches now speak to ye
That the heathen he bare as his decking, so costly their worth should
    be.
If more than enough I told ye, yet more would be left to tell;
Yet I would not his wealth were hidden—What of riches, I ween,
    shall dwell
In Bretagne alike and England, and be tribute to Arthur's might,
They had paid not the stones that, shining, glowed fair on his armor
    bright.
His blazoned coat was costly, and naught but the truth I say,
Ruby and Chalcedony, ye had held them not fair that day.
And bright as the sun was his vesture, on the mount of Agremontein,
In the glowing fires, Salamanders had welded that garment's shine.
There jewels rare and precious, with never a fault or flaw,
Glowed dark and light; of their nature, I ween, I can tell no more!

His desire was for love's rewarding, and the winning of high renown,
He had won from the hands of fair women the jewels that his pride
    did crown.
For the favor Frau Minne showed him with joy did his proud heart
    beat,
And it swelled high with manly courage, as is for a lover meet.
As reward for his deeds of knighthood on his helmet a beast he bare,
Ecidemon, all poisonous serpents they must of its power beware,
For of life and of strength doth it rob them, if they smell it but from
    afar—
Thopedissimonté, Assigarzionté, Thasmé, and Arabia,
They scarce of such silk might boast them as was covering for his
    steed—
He sought, that mighty heathen, in a woman's love his meed,
And therefore he bravely decked him, and fain would his courage
    prove,
And his manhood, it urged him onward to battle for sake of love.

Now the knight, so young and gallant, in a haven beside the wood,
But little known, on the water had anchored his ships so good.
And his armies were five-and-twenty, and they knew not each other's
    speech—
'Twas a token fair of his riches, and the lands that his power might
    reach,

As the armies, so were the kingdoms that did service unto his hand—
And Moors and Saracens were they, and unlike was each warlike
band,
And the hue of their skins was diverse—Thus gathered from lands
afar
Ye might see in his mighty army strange weapons of heathen war.

So thus, in search of adventure, from his army this man would ride,
In the woodland green he wandered, and waited what should betide.
And since thus it well doth please them, so let them ride, these kings,
Alone, in search of ventures, and the fair fame that combat brings.
Yet Parzival rode not lonely, methinks he had comrades twain,
Himself, and the lofty courage that lord o'er his soul did reign.
And that he so bravely fought here might win from a woman praise,
If falsehood should not mislead her, that injustice should rule her
ways.

So spurred they against each other, who were lambs in their purity,
Yet as lions were they bold and dauntless, 'twas a sight for a man to
see!
Ah! woe is me for their meeting, for the world and its ways are wide,
And they well might have spared each other, nor, guiltless, to battle
ride.
I should sorrow for him whom I brought here, save my heart did this
comfort hold,
That the Grail shall with strength endue him, and Love shelter the
hero bold,
Since he was of the twain the servant, nor his heart ever wavering
knew,
And ever his hand was ready to serve them with service true.

Wolfram von Eschenbach
Parzival
Trans. by J. L. Weston, 1894

Hymn

Sing, my tongue, the Saviour's
   glory,
Of His Flesh the mystery sing;
Of the Blood all price exceeding,
Shed by our immortal King,
Destined for the world's redemption,
From a noble womb to spring.

Of a pure and spotless Virgin,
Born for us on earth below.
He, as Man, with man conversing,
Stayed, the seeds of truth to
      sow;
Then He closed in solemn
   order
Wondrously His life of woe.

On the night of that Last
   Supper
Seated with His chosen band,
He, the Paschal victim eating,
First fulfills the Law's command;
Then as Food to all His brethren
Gives Himself with His own
   Hand.

Word made Flesh, the bread
   of nature
By His word to Flesh He
   turns;
Wine into His Blood He
   changes:
What though sense no change
   discerns?
Only be the heart in earnest,
Faith her lesson quickly learns.

Down in adoration falling,
Lo! the sacred Host we hail;
Lo! o'er ancient forms departing.
Newer rites of grace prevail;
Faith for all defects supplying,
Where the feeble senses fail.

To the everlasting Father,
And the Son who reigns on
    high,
With the Holy Ghost proceeding
Forth from Each eternally,
Be salvation, honor, blessing,
Might, and endless majesty.

St. Thomas Aquinas: 13th century
Trans. by Father Caswall

Song

When from the sod the flowerets spring,
    And smile to meet the sun's bright ray,
When birds their sweetest carols sing,
    In all the morning pride of May
What lovelier than the prospect there?
    Can earth boast anything more fair?
To me it seems an almost heaven,
So beauteous to my eyes that vision bright is given.

But when a lady chaste and fair,
    Noble, and clad in rich attire,
Walks through the throng with gracious air,
    As sun that bids the stars retire—
Then where are all thy boastings, May?
    What hast thou beautiful and gay
Compared with thy supreme delight?
We leave thy loveliest flowers, and watch that lady bright.

Would'st thou believe me—come and place
 Before thee all this pride of May,
Then look but on my lady's face,
 And which is best and brightest say.
For me, how soon (if choice were mine)
 This would I take, and that resign;
And say, "Though sweet thy beauties, May,
I'd rather forfeit all than lose my lady gay!"

Walther von der Vogelweide: 13th
        century
Trans. by Edgar Taylor, 1897

Knights on the March

But let us tell no further how there the work they plied.
Never to a king's country were known before to ride
Such well-appointed squadrons as thither were to speed.
They had whate'er they wanted, both weapons and eke weed.

The king of Rhine apparel gave to his liegemen bold,
To threescore and a thousand, as I have heard it told,
Besides nine thousand yeomen, on mirth and revel bent.
Those, whom they left behind them, soon rued that e'er they went.

In Worms, as their equipment was carrying through the court,
From Spire an aged bishop, of reverend report,
Thus bespake fair Uta: "Our worthy friends prepare
To yonder feast to travel; God watch and ward them there!"

Thereon the noble Uta bespake her children dear,
"Far better stay, good heroes, and tend your safety here.
I had last night, my children, a dream of ghastly dread,
How all the birds, that flutter throughout this land, were dead."

"Who cares for dreams," said Hagan, "and thinks by them to walk,
Ne'er in the path of honor with sturdy steps can stalk,
Or breathe the voice of reason, but wavers to and fro.
I rede, my noble master take leave and forward go.

"Yes, we shall ride full gladly hence into Etzel's land.
There ·kings need for their service many a good hero's hand,
And this fair feast of Kriemhild's awaits us there to view."
So Hagan urg'd the journey, which soon he came to rue.

He ne'er had giv'n such counsel but for what late had pass'd,
When scorn on him Sir Gernot had so unseemly cast,
Reminding him of Siegfried, and what had erst been done,
As though for that dislik'd him the journey to the Hun.

Then answer'd he of Trony, "Fear prompts not what I rede.
If so you'll have it, heroes, fall to the work and speed;
You'll find me not the hindmost to ride to Etzel's realm."
Soon shatter'd he thereafter many a shield and many a helm.

The boats were waiting ready, the band was muster'd there;
Thither his choice apparel each one made haste to bear.
Their toil was scarce well over ere eve fell on the lea;
So from their homes they parted as merry as might be.

Beyond the Rhine's fair current their hasty camp was seen;
Their tents and proud pavilions bespotted all the green.
The lovely queen her husband detain'd for that one night,
The last they spent together, dole mingling with delight.

At early dawn there sounded sweet flute and trumpet-clang;
'Twas the hour of parting; to work the warriors sprang.
With a hasty kiss fond lovers were then constrain'd to sever.
With woe and death fell Kriemhild soon sunder'd them forever.

The children of fair Uta a man had at their court,
Both alike and faithful, in all of best report.
The same, as they were going, drew the king aside.
"Woe's me," said he, "dear master, you to this feast will ride."

The good knight's name was Rumolt, a tall man of his hands.
Said he, "To whom commit you your people and your lands?
Would one could turn you warriors to do what best you should!
This message of your sister's it never seem'd me good."

"This is my will and pleasure; to thee my infant heir,
To thee I trust my country; of the women take good care;
Whomever thou see'st weeping, his woe with comfort charm.
Sure at the hands of Kriemhild we ne'er can come to harm."

For the kings and for their liegemen the steeds were ready ranged;
How many then, with kisses of true love interchanged,
Full flown with lively vigor, athirst for bold emprize,
Left each a stately lady to droop in tears and sighs!

When light into their saddles up sprang the warriors good,
Then might you see the women how sorrowful they stood.
All felt, they did forever, and to their doom, depart,
A dreary, dark foreboding, that shakes the firmest heart!

As the bold Burgundians rode forth in gallant show,
So see them all the country ran hurrying to and fro.
On either side the mountains both men and women wept.
Little reck'd they the weepers; their joyous course they kept.

In habergeons a thousand the knights of Nibelung's reign,
Who many a lovely lady, they ne'er should see again,
Had left at home in sorrow, rode gaily with the rest.
The wounds of Siegfried fester'd in Kriemhild's throbbing breast.

Nibelungen Lied: 13th century
Trans. by William N. Lettson

Sonnet of All He Would Do

If I were fire, I'd burn the world away;
If I were wind, I'd turn my storms thereon;
If I were water, I'd soon let it drown;
If I were God, I'd sink it from the day;
If I were Pope, I'd never feel quite gay
Until there was no peace beneath the sun;
If I were Emperor, what would I have done?—
I'd lop men's heads all round in my own way.
If I were Death, I'd look my father up;
If I were Life, I'd run away from him;
And treat my mother to like calls and runs.
If I were Cecco (and that's all my hope),
I'd pick the nicest girls to suit my whim,
And other folk should get the ugly ones.

Cecco Angiolieri: 13th century
Trans. by D. G. Rossetti

Ballata Concerning a Shepherd-Maid

Within a copse I met a shepherd-maid,
More fair, I said, than any star to see.

She came with waving tresses pale and bright,
   With rosy cheer, and loving eyes of flame,
Guiding the lambs beneath her wand aright.
   Her naked feet still had the dews on them,
   As, singing like a lover, so she came;
Joyful, and fashioned for all ecstasy.

I greeted her at once, and question made
   What escort had she through the woods in spring?
But with soft accents she replied and said
   That she was all alone there, wandering;
   Moreover: "Do you know, when the birds sing,
My heart's desire is for a mate," said she.

While she was telling me this wish of hers,
   The birds were all in song throughout the wood.
"Even now then," said my thought, "the time recurs,
   With mine own longing, to assuage her mood."
   And so, in her sweet favour's name, I sued
That she would kiss there and embrace with me.

She took my hand to her with amorous will,
   And answered that she gave me all her heart,
And drew me where the leaf is fresh and still,
   Where spring the wood-flowers in the shade apart.
   And on that day, by Joy's enchanted art,
There Love in very presence seemed to be.

Guido Cavalcanti: 13th century
Trans. by D. G. Rossetti

Notes on the Various Authors

Notes on the Various Authors

Abelard, Peter (1079–1142): A Breton who became a lecturer on Aristotelian philosophy and was appointed Canon of Notre Dame in 1115. He fell in love with Héloïse, the niece of Canon Fulbert, and married her. Disgrace and public ruin followed. Héloïse entered a nunnery. Abelard wrote on philosophical subjects; while his correspondence with Héloïse ranks high among spiritual confessions.

Adam of Bremen (died c. 1076): Master of a cathedral school. Author of a *History of Bremen* that extended to accounts of the Baltic countries and Scandinavia, and also included accounts of trade, peoples, and geographical ventures.

Adam of Usk (c. 1352–c. 1430): A Welshman, trained in law. Papal chaplain to Pope Boniface IX and Pope Innocent VII. He was compelled to flee from Rome on account of uprisings and finally returned to Wales. His *Chronicon*, which is a kind of personal memoir, is written with a pleasant sense of humor.

Adelard of Bath: Flourished in the twelfth century. Author of a scientific study, *Quaestiones Naturales*.

Adolphus: A fourteenth-century author of an anecdote that was the source of Chaucer's *The Merchant's Tale*.

Aeneas Silvius (1405–1454): The literary pseudonym of Enea Silvio de' Piccolomini, Pope Pius II. Author of an account of his own life in his *Commentaries*.

Alcuin (735–804): An English scholar who was invited by the Emperor Charlemagne to direct the palace school. He was also Abbot of Tours. Alcuin exerted great influence in his day in the First Renaissance, as it was called, that was stimulated by the Emperor. Alcuin produced poetry, theological disputations, and work of a more general nature.

Aldhelm (c. 639–709): Abbot of Malmesbury. Author of *On Virginity*, a composition in prose and verse.

Alexander of Hales (died 1245): A Franciscan who taught at the University of Paris. Philosopher and theologian. Author of *Summa Theologiae*.

Angiolieri, Cecco (c. 1250–1312): An Italian poet whose life was a sequence of wild escapades and passionate interludes.

Annals of Xanten: Records of the German town of Xanten, covering the period from 640 to 874.

Anselm (1033–1109): St. Anselm was Archbishop of Canterbury. Author of notable treatises on theology and philosophy.

Aquinas (1227–1274): St. Thomas Aquinas was one of the most outstanding personalities in the Middle Ages. An Aristotelian, he wrote abundantly on philosophy and theology. He also produced a number of famous hymns.

Asser (d. 910): Bishop of Sherborne. Author of a chronicle of English history covering the years 849–887.

Avitus, Alcimus Ecdicius (died c. 526): Archbishop of Vienne in 490. Author of poems dealing with Mosaic history.

Bacon, Roger (c. 1214–1294): Learned in Greek and Arabic, in science and mathematics, Roger Bacon was one of the most enlightened men of the thirteenth century. Exposed to persecution and confined to prison, he was frequently attacked by both scholastics and ecclesiastics. He finally joined the Franciscan Order. Bacon wrote voluminuously, on mathematics and astrology, philosophy and science. The *Opus Maius* is his greatest work, dealing largely with philosophy, theology, and experimental science.

Bede (c. 673–735): The Venerable Bede was associated from early boyhood until his death with the monastic school of Jarrow, in England. A cleric and scholar, he produced works on theology, science, and history. His most important achievement is the Ecclesiastical History of the English Nation.

Bernard of Clairvaux (1090–1153): Famous medieval churchman, who wrote on the Second Crusade.

Bernard of Cluny: A twelfth-century Breton monk. Author of a long poem *De Contemptu Mundi,* descriptive of the corruption of his times.

Boccaccio, Giovanni (1313–1375): Italian poet and humanist. Author of the *Decameron* and other tales of passion.

Boethius (475–524): Minister to the Gothic King Theodoric. Imprisoned on a charge of treason. Author of *De Consolatione Philosophiae* and other works.

Caesar of Heisterbach (c. 1180–c. 1240): A Cistercian monk, author of histories, homilies, and particularly of a collection of miracles.

Cambridge Songs: The earliest medieval treasury of songs and poems.

Cantilena of St. Eulalie: First extant specimen of French vernacular prose; ninth century.

Capellanus, Andreas: Flourished in the twelfth century. Author of *The Art of Courtly Love.*

Carmina Burana: A medieval songbook, associated with the Goliards or wandering students.

Cassiodorus (c. 487–583): Flavius Magnus Aurelius Cassiodorus Senator was one of the most important writers of the sixth century. He held high public office, and later founded a monastery at Vivarium, in southern Italy. Cassiodorus was an industrious collector and editor of ancient manuscripts. He is the author of an encyclopedic work entitled *Institutions of Divine and Secular Learning.*

Cavalcanti, Guido (c. 1255–1300): A Florentine poet, an intimate friend of Dante.

Charlemagne (742–814): King of the Franks. Active in propagating Christianity throughout Europe. Master of continental Europe included in Western Christendom. An able administrator, Charlemagne was also a patron of culture. He founded schools, sponsored scholars and teachers, stimulated literary productivity and architectural projects.

Dante Alighieri (1265–1321): One of the greatest universal poets. Author of the *Divine Comedy*. He also produced poems, political treatises, and pastorals.

Deeds of Hereward the Saxon: A twelfth-century account of the Saxon hero who fought against William the Conqueror.

Einhard (died 840): Einhard was a member of the Frankish nobility. Studied at Fulda; then was attached to the palace school of Charlemagne. Author of *Life of Charlemagne*.

Ekkehart IV (c. 980–c. 1051): A monk of St. Gall, in Switzerland. Author of an anecdotal history of the monastery of St. Gall.

Ekkehart of Aura: Abbot of Aura who flourished in the eleventh century. Author of a universal history.

Ennodius: Magnus Felix Ennodius was born in Gaul in 473, became Bishop of Pavia, and died there in 521. He was an orator, poet, and historian.

Étienne de Bourbon: A Dominican monk who died c. 1261. He compiled a collection of tales intended to convey a moral precept.

Eugippius: Belongs in the fifth century. He became Abbot of Naples. His biography of St. Severinus is at the same time an account of religious and civil life in his own age.

Fabliaux: Metrical tales, originally in French, belonging in the thirteenth and fourteenth centuries.

Fortunatus, Venantius Honorius Clementianus (530–609): An Italian who settled in Poitiers, France. Chaplain to a nunnery. Author of many hymns and occasional pieces.

Fredegarius: A seventh century historian, otherwise unknown, who continued the *History* of Gregory of Tours.

Froissart, Sir John (c. 1337–c. 1410): Born in France. At the age of about nineteen he started writing the history of contemporary wars. In 1360 he began travels: in England, Scotland, Italy, finally settling in Flanders. His *Chronicle* covers the period from 1326 to 1400, and describes events in France, England, Scotland, Flanders, Germany, Italy, Spain. Froissart also produced a considerable number of poems.

Fulbert of Chartres (c. 960–1028): Founder of a famous school at Chartres. Called by his pupils "Socrates." Author of hymns, discourses, and letters.

Fulcher of Chartres: Flourished in the twelfth century. As a priest he accompanied Robert of Normandy on the First Crusade. He personally witnessed many moving incidents, and wrote an account of the conflict.

Geoffrey Le Baker of Swynebroke: English chronicler. Author of a shorter *Chroniculum*, completed in 1347, and a more extensive *Chronicon*.

Geoffrey of Monmouth (c. 1100–1154): Bishop of St. Asaph. Author of a *History of the Kings of Britain*. It is notable for its romantic episodes dealing with King Arthur.

Gerbert (d. 1003): Pope Sylvester II. A distinguished humanist, author of a voluminous correspondence.

Gervais of Tilbury: A thirteenth-century author of a miscellany entitled *Imperial Leisurely Trifles*.

Gesta Romanorum: A collection of tales, mostly of historical dubiety, to which is usually attached a moral corollary. The authorship is unknown, but the tales were probably compiled in the thirteenth century.

Gildas (c. 493–570): British historian. Author of *The Fall of Britain,* beginning with the Roman invasion and continuing into Gildas' own days.

Giraldus Cambrensis (c. 1146–c. 1223): Of Welsh and Norman origin. Studied in Paris, lived in Ireland, made a journey through Wales. Author of a *Description of Wales,* a geographical treatise on Ireland, hagiographical and autobiographical memoirs.

Gonzalo de Berceo (c. 1180–c. 1246): A Spanish priest who wrote poetic versions of saints' lives, as well as a number of poems.

Gregory: St. Gregory (538–594), Bishop of Tours (Georgius Florentius), was one of the most dominant personalities in Central Gaul. Born of distinguished lineage, he was associated with kings, churchmen of high rank, as well as with the common people. He wrote on miracles, lives of the Fathers, and other ecclesiastical works. His chief claim to recognition, however, lies in his *History of the Franks,* in ten books, largely a revealing picture of his times.

Gregory the Great (c. 540–604): Pope from 590 until his death. Zealous in his ecclesiastical duties, he was also a voluminous writer of letters, dialogues, and homilies.

Guibert: Twelfth-century abbot of Nogent. Author of the *Gesta Dei per Francos,* a chronicle of the First Crusade.

Héloïse: Niece of Canon Fulbert; married to Abelard. Later, she entered a nunnery. See **Abelard.**

Higben, Ranulph (died 1364): A Benedictine monk who wrote a universal history extending to 1342, entitled *Polychronicon.*

Hisperica Famina: A collection of poems, many of them a macaronic composite of Greek, Latin, and Hebrew. Popular in the seventh and eighth centuries.

History of Apollonius, King of Tyre: This is a long narrative that was very popular in the Middle Ages and of which versions appeared in many languages. It is a composite of ancient legends, Greek mythology, and Christian elements.

History of the Seven Wise Men: A tale of which versions appear in Oriental literature. The putative author is Johannes of Alba Silva, who belongs to the early thirteenth century.

Hrabanus Maurus: A pupil of Alcuin. Archbishop of Mayence. Called Praeceptor Germaniae. Founded the library of Fulda. He is the author of *Clerical Principles.*

Hrothsvitha: A tenth-century nun of Gandersheim. Author of six religious dramas that were widely popular for centuries.

Ibn Hazm, Abu Mohammed Ali (994–1064): Arab who flourished in Andalusia, Spain. Author of *The Risala, The Dove's Neck-Ring.*

Ibn Khordadbeh: Arab official of the ninth century; of Persian origin. Chief of Posts of Djibal. Author of a geographical handbook entitled *The Book of the Roads and the Kingdoms.*

Isidore of Seville (c. 560–636): Notable as a churchman and a scholar. His most important work is *Etymologies* or *Origins,* an encyclopedic work that became a popular reference book during the Middle Ages.

Itinerarium Regis Ricardi: *The Itinerary of King Richard* is a twelfth-century historical document, presenting an absorbing picture of the Third Crusade.

Jacobus a Voragine (c. 1230–c. 1298): Archbishop of Genoa. His *Golden Legend* is a collection of tales of the saints, highly popular for centuries and translated into many languages.

Jacopone da Todi (1230?–1306): Franciscan monk. Reputedly, author of the Latin hymn *Stabat Mater Dolorosa.*

Jacques de Vitry: Cardinal Bishop of Tusculum. He died in 1240. Famous as a preacher, he also wrote several volumes of sermons that contain illustrative anecdotes intended to drive home some moral lesson.

Jocelin: A monk of St. Edmundsbury, in England. Author of a vivid account of monastic life ranging from 1173 to 1190.

Johannes Monachus: An Italian monk of the early eleventh century who collected a number of tales, some of them of Oriental origin, that contain both Scriptural and legendary elements.

Johannes of Alta Silva: Thirteenth-century writer. Author of *Dolopathos or The Kings and the Seven Sages,* a popular medieval legend.

Johannes Scotus Erigena (died c. 877): One of the most outstanding medieval scholars. Attached to the court of Charles the Bald. His greatest contribution is the *Division of Nature,* a philosophi-

cal dialogue whose purpose is a logical explanation of the universe.

John of Garland: Thirteenth-century author of a text of academic conduct, entitled *Morale Scholarium.*

John of Salisbury (c. 1115–1180): Educated in France, this scholar is considered among the most notable medieval personalities. He is the author of treatises on logic, politics, philosophy, and is particularly known for his abundant epistolary production.

John of Tynemouth or **John de Tinmouth:** Flourished in the fourteenth century. Putative author of *The Golden Legend.*

Jordanes: A sixth-century historian, and probably himself a Goth, who produced the *Getica,* an account of the Goths, abridged from an earlier work by Cassiodorus Senator, one of the most prominent literary men of his age.

Liudprand: Born in 922, Liudprand was a Lombard attached to the court of King Hugo of Italy; later, to that of Berengar; and finally to the Emperor Otto I. He became Bishop of Cremona. On several occasions he was sent as ambassador to the court at Constantinople. His *Antapodosis* is a survey of European history, while his *Report on the Embassy to Constantinople* is a fascinating, vivid account of court life.

Lupus (died 862): Abbot of Ferrières. An ardent humanist who dedicated himself to the collection and editing of ancient manuscripts. He was a prolific correspondent.

Luther, Martin (1483–1546): Augustinian monk. Proponent of reform of Catholicism.

Map, Walter (died c. 1210): Walter Map or Mapes was a Welshman attached to court circles. In 1179 he became Archdeacon of Oxford. Many satirical poems are attributed to him. He is also the author of a compilation entitled *Triflings of Courtiers,* consisting of anecdotes, legends, miraculous tales, personal memoirs, and contemporary sketches of historical value.

Nennius: A ninth-century historian. Author of *Historia Britonum.*

Nequam, Alexander (1157–1217): Englishman who became professor in Paris. Abbot of Circencester. Author of *The Nature of Things,* a scientific and theological exposition.

Niebelungenlied: Medieval German epic. It belongs in the corpus of Teutonic sages; thirteenth century.

Notker (c. 840–912): A Swiss monk, magister of St. Gall. Author of an anecdotal history of the Emperor Charlemagne and a *Martyrologium,* an account of the lives and experiences of martyred saints.

Odo: A thirteenth-century Archbishop of Rouen. Author of a *Register of Visitations.*

Odo of Cerinton: An English Cistercian monk, who compiled, early in the thirteenth century, a collection of fables based largely on medieval bestiaries.

Odo of Deuil: Fifteenth-century historian. Wrote an account of Louis VII's Crusade, *De Profectione Ludovici VII in Orientem·*

Ordericus Vitalis (died c. 1142): Author of an *Ecclesiastical History,* ranging from the creation to 1142.

Orosius, Paulus: A Spanish priest who fled from the Vandals to Africa, in 414. Author of *Historiae.*

Osbern of Canterbury: Flourished in the eleventh century. Author of a life of St. Alphege.

Otto (died 1158): Bishop of Freising. Author of a life of the Emperor Frederick I and a Chronicle.

Paris: Matthew Paris was a monk of St. Albans, in England, until his death in 1259. He is recognized as the greatest medieval historian. His works include the *Greater Chronicles,* biographies of abbots, and a *History of the Angles.*

Paulus Diaconus: A Lombard who flourished in the eighth century. He became a Benedictine monk and exercised great scholarly influence at the court of Charlemagne. Among his sermons, poems, letters and minor historical works, his *History of the Lombards* stands out prominently for its human interest and variety of content.

Peter of Blois (died c. 1200): A pupil of John of Salisbury, with whom he regularly corresponded.

Petrarch (1304–1374): Versed in law and letters, ecclesiastic and scholar, courtier and poet, Petrarch is often called "the first modern man." His poetry was inspired by his love for a certain Laura. He collected ancient manuscripts, was an industrious correspondent, and wrote a historical epic entitled *Africa.*

Petrus Alphonsus: A Christianized Jew of the twelfth century. He is the author of a collection of Arab fables that point a moral, particularly in the relationship of father and son.

Petrus Victor (died c. 570): Bishop of Tunis. Author of a *Chronicle*.

Philippe de Thaun: Anglo-Norman poet of the twelfth century. Author of a *Bestiary,* dedicated to Adelaide of Louvaine, Queen of Henry I of England. Also of *Liber de Creaturis,* or *Livre des Créatures,* an astronomical treatise.

Raymund of Agiles: Flourished in the twelfth century. He accompanied his master, Raymund of Toulouse, on the First Crusade. As an eyewitness, he wrote a vivid account of the campaign.

Regino of Prüm (died 915): Author of a Chronicle covering the period from the birth of Christ to the year 906.

Regula Reclusorum Angliae: This *Rule of the Monks of England* is putatively attributed to a thirteenth-century canon named Walter the Recluse.

Richard de Bury (1287–1345): Bishop of Durham and Lord Chancellor of England. His passion was book collecting. His *Philobiblion* is a glorification of the love of books.

Richer: Flourished in the tenth century. He was a student of medicine and a monk at Rheims. Author of an account of contemporary events.

Robert II (c. 970–1031): King of France; called the "Pious." Author of a number of well-known hymns.

St. Alexis: First extant specimen of French poetry; eleventh century.

St. Benedict: St. Benedict of Nursia founded a monastery at Monte Cassino, in Italy, in 529. He prepared a *Regula,* a kind of handbook, for the guidance of his monks. The *Regula* achieved wide recognition.

St. Martin of Tours: Born in Pannonia, he spent his early life in Gaul. He became a monk in Italy and, returning to Gaul, finally became Bishop of Tours. He died early in the fifth century. In addition to his life of Sulpicius Severus, St. Martin wrote historical works, particularly the *Chronicles.*

Salimbene: A thirteenth-century Franciscan. Author of *Chronicles of Brother Salimbene of the Franciscan Order.* This work deals with events and personalities in France and Italy from the year 1167 to 1287.

Sampson, Thomas: Fourteenth-century author of a series of model letters for students and others.

Saxo Grammaticus (1150–1206): Danish historian. Author of *Historia Danica.*

Seafarer: A ninth-century Anglo-Saxon poem.

Strasburg Oath: First extant specimen of French prose; ninth century.

Suger (1081–1151): Abbot of Saint-Denis. French prelate and statesman, Minister of Louis VII of France; called Père de la Patrie. Author of Life of Louis VI, letters, and works on the Abbey, particularly *De Rebus* in *Administratione Sua Gestis.* His life was written by Brother William.

Sulpicius Severus (365–425): Aquitanian priest. Author of *Chronicles,* and a life of St. Martin.

Thomas Becket, or **Thomas à Becket** (1118–1170): Chancellor to Henry II of England, Archbishop of Canterbury. A conflict with the king drove him to France, where he lived the monastic life. On his return to England, he was murdered, at the king's instigation, in the cathedral church.

Thomas de Celano (c. 1200–1255): A Franciscan monk, author of *Dies Irae,* the greatest among Latin hymns.

Thomas of Monmouth: A monk of Norwich who in the twelfth century composed a life of St. William of Norwich.

Trierer Marienklage: A fifteenth-century German Miracle play.

Vincent of Beauvais (died c. 1263): Author of the greatest medieval encyclopedia, *Speculum Maius.*

Walsingham, Thomas (1377–c. 1422): Prior of Wymondham, in England. He continued the historical sequence of Matthew Paris, known as the *Chronica Maiora.*

Walther von der Vogelweide: A thirteenth-century German lyric poet.

Widukind: A Benedictine monk who died c. 1004. Author of a *History of the Saxons.*

William of Malmesbury (c. 1080–c. 1143): An English monk who wrote a popular history of England, packed with appealing digressions and interesting anecdotes.

William of Newburgh (1136–c. 1198): Canon of Newburgh, in Yorkshire, England. Author of a *History of England.*

William of Ockham or **William Occam** (died c. 1350): An English Franciscan, educated at Oxford and Paris. Author of polemical and philosophical treatises, particularly a study of Aristotelian logic.

William of Tyre (c. 1130–1183): Born in Palestine, he trained in Europe, and finally returned to Palestine, where he became Archbishop of Tyre. A linguist and statesman, he was also familiar with political conditions in the East. His *History of the Crusades* became an authoritative source book.

Wolfram von Eschenbach (1170?–1220): German poet or minnesinger who was attached to the court of Count Hermann of Thuringia. Acquainted with the poet Walther von der Vogelweide. Author of the metrical romance *Parzival,* source of Wagner's opera *Parsifal.*